PUBLICATIONS OF THE CENTER
FOR JAPANESE AND KOREAN STUDIES

MINOBE TATSUKICHI

A Publication of the
CENTER FOR JAPANESE AND KOREAN STUDIES
University of California, Berkeley

MINOBE TATSUKICHI

Interpreter  of Constitutionalism in Japan

FRANK O. MILLER

University of California Press
Berkeley and Los Angeles   1965

University of California Press
Berkeley and Los Angeles, California

Cambridge University Press
London, England

The Center for Japanese and Korean Studies of the University of California is a unit of the Institute of International Studies. It is the unifying organization for faculty members and students interested in Japan and Korea, bringing together scholars from many disciplines. The Center's major aims are the development and support of research and language study. As part of this program the Center sponsors a publication series of books concerned with Japan and Korea. Manuscripts are considered from all campuses of the University of California as well as from any other individuals and institutions doing research in these areas.

Preface

Contrary to expectations, the reports issuing from the Official Constitution Investigation Commission in 1963 and 1964 have yet to precipitate a revision of the Japanese constitution. The government has not evinced serious intention of placing such a project on its agenda. Indeed, it appears that the electorate is not favorable to constitutional revision. One may hazard the judgment that existing uncertainty about the fate of the present constitution and its meaning for Japan's future is not now likely to be resolved by decisive electoral or parliamentary action.

If the general populace is not in a mood for constitutional changes, the same is not true of the social, political, and intellectual elite, among whom there has been a great stir, either of hope or of apprehension, in that direction. It is not too much to say that the past decade ranks after the days of the Liberty and Popular Rights Movement of the 1880's and the era of the Taisho Political Change as one of the periods of great agitation over questions of state structure and political order in Japan's modern history. A by-product of the intellectual and partisan struggle over constitutional revision during the past decade has been the proliferation of the literature of constitutional theory: a reconsideration of the history of Japanese constitutional theory since Meiji, and a reëvaluation of the political significance of theoretical and methodological traditions carried forward from the interwar period. The present study, proceeding under entirely different impulse, is concerned with a person whose name has been given new currency in that literature, and, in some of it at least, a new appreciation.

Minobe Tatsukichi's name is somewhat familiar to well-read students of western literature dealing with prewar Japan because of its regular inclusion in textbooks, general histories, scholarly monographs, and journalistic commentaries. Nevertheless it has been left to stand as a largely meaningless factor, devoid of personality, of intellectual content, and lacking, indeed, a significant place in the political history of Japan. References to Minobe, however numerous, tend to be brief and cryptic, seeming rather to obscure than to illuminate their subject. Writers have been for the most part content to echo one another in the terse identification of this scholar with the "liberal school" of constitutional interpretation, to which a certain unexplained importance attaches. They have almost invariably alluded to a celebrated cause of 1935, the Minobe Affair, or "the emperor-organ theory affair." They have differed only in their greater or lesser, but always inadequate, attention to theoretical analysis and historical development.

No less disconcerting than elusive general characterizations of Minobe are the frequent evocations of his name and authority in discussions of particular problems of Japanese public law. The narrowly selective and fragmentary nature of such notices makes them practically useless in themselves as keys to Minobe's general theory or method. Neither is there a general source to turn to for clarification or elaboration, for, without significant exception, none of Minobe's writing has been published in translation. Nor has anyone attempted a systematic exposition of his constitutional theory or of his interpretation of the Imperial Constitution.

In the most common and best remembered of Minobe's appearances in the literature, allusion to theoretical propositions has been secondary to attempts to explain the dramatic events which led to the assault upon him and upon his constitutional theory by the militarists and the civilian nationalists in 1935. The confrontation of Minobe and his enemies was an affair of high visibility at that time and accounts of the events in numerous commentaries and histories then and since have fixed Minobe's identity for us as a "liberal," an "antimilitarist" and a "defender of constitutionalism" in a way that no recitation of obscure points of theory could have done. And yet this identification remains hollow, for these accounts have failed to make fully understandable how this academic personage, purveyor of a "strange" notion of the emperor as "an organ of the state," could have drawn upon himself such a storm of vindictive abuse and upon his writings such a blanket of censorship. And they have left unmeasured the quality and depth of his "liberalism."

This firmly established image of Minobe the liberal suffered apparent betrayal when, for a brief time he came to life in the news reports of the Occupation, restored to the pinnacle of professional respectability and voicing personal and official opposition to revision of the Imperial Constitution. The sharp vignettes of Minobe's antirevisionist role have been left to stand alone in the literature, unexplained and altogether innocent of any reflection upon the meaning of the writing he did on the new constitution before his death early in 1948.

Explication of Minobe's constitutional theory and of his part as an exponent of an important and controversial school of constitutional interpretation in Japan will serve to make more complete our understanding of the constitutional politics of Japan in the modern imperial era. As Robert Ward has recently said, the roots of "the great and apparently sudden florescence of western-style democracy" in mid-century Japan lie deep in her post-1890 political experience.[1] To study Minobe's early career is to come to grips with some of the "erosive and catalytic agents" (to borrow from Professor Ward again) responsible for the breaking down of the authoritarian heritage and the slow development of democratic ways and institutions between the 1890's and the 1930's. Our study of Minobe will also help us to understand the constitutional strategy of the Japanese government in the early phase of the Occupation, still a subject of conjecture by scholars. It is with these two purposes in view that the present study has been compiled, and it is within these limits that it should be understood.

But there are problems other than those with which this study is directly concerned upon which it may nevertheless throw some light, however obliquely. If it seemed at one time that a view of Japan's constitutional development from Minobe's perspective had been rendered obsolete by the constitutional revolution of 1945–1947, there may now be reason to harbor reservation on that score. Doubts concerning the wisdom of the postwar constitutional legislation—the rupture of continuity, the substitution of major conceptual innovations, the libertarian emphasis, constitutional disarmament, and so on—easily thrust aside in 1946, have come to the fore with increasing insistence since 1952.

[1] Robert E. Ward, "Political Modernization and Political Culture in Japan," *World Politics*, 15 (July, 1963), 593.

These doubts have found expression in the professions of the conservative majority, which has run strongly toward constitutional revision since 1955. Whether or not this trend carries through to a formal change in the constitution, which seems unlikely at present, the process of constitutional change goes on from day to day in the subtler but no less real way of interpretation in practice. In the process the initiative and the preponderant influence has lain with the conservative and bureaucratic elements whose timid and unprogressive view of constitutional revision was rudely rejected by General MacArthur in 1946.

The constitutional issue in Japan today lies not in the balance between reform oriented toward democracy on the American model and a native authoritarian reaction, but in the balance between a revived conservative capitalist-bureaucratic order and the mass democracy of revolutionary socialism. Though neither of these camps has been capable of delivering the nation through the regular constitutional process, each regards itself as the legitimate successor to the prewar constitutional order. They have highly ambivalent attitudes toward the constitution of 1947 and they draw comfort from divergent lines of constitutional theory. It seems likely that an understanding of Minobe's work will give insight into the psychology and conceptual equipment of the conservative constitutional position in Japan today.

My interest in Minobe arose from cryptically enticing and, as it happens, quite misleading references encountered in the course of some research done under the direction of Professor Eric C. Belquist at the University of California, Berkeley. It ripened into a full-scale research effort under the tutelage of Professor Delmer M. Brown in his seminar in modern Japanese history, also at the University of California. In the later stages of the protracted and discontinuous course of my investigation and writing, the burden of advice, criticism, and encouragement fell chiefly upon Professor Robert A. Scalapino. Stepchild though the study was to him, he has nevertheless attended it with benevolence and has greatly enriched my view of the subject. Supplementing Dr. Scalapino's labors have been those of my colleague at the Ohio State University, the late Professor Kazuo Kawai, who never failed to respond generously and helpfully to my requests for advice.

Many others of my academic mentors and colleagues having no concern with the content of this work have contributed at one time or another indispensable doses of encouragement, admonition, or dissuasion as needed. Of these I can single out only a few to whom I feel particularly indebted: Professors Dwight Waldo, Harvey C. Mansfield, Harry V. Jaffa, and Louis Nemzer. My thanks are owing also to President Howard F. Lowry and Professor John W. Baker of The College of Wooster for their friendly concern for this work in its final stages.

At various stages in my research I have relied heavily upon the resources and upon the expert knowledge and good will of the staff of the East Asian Library at the University of California, Berkeley, and the Orientalia Division, Library of Congress, and I should like to acknowledge especially my debt to them. For the support of the Great Lakes Colleges Association and for the assistance and hospitality of Waseda University, under whose shelter the final editorial work was completed, I am most grateful.

Conventional phrases cannot begin to discharge my debt to my wife and daughters. Their good humor and understanding through it all deserve a nobler monument than this.

Frank O. Miller

The College of Wooster

Contents

The Political and Academic Background

Minobe Tatsukichi's middle school and undergraduate days in Tokyo coincided approximately with the third post-Restoration decade. The record leaves one to speculate on what may have been the immediate influence of the momentous events of those years on the young student. That some of them were portentous in relation to his later career there can be no doubt. We can recreate the *mise en scène* by reviewing the process which brought the Meiji constitutional system into existence, the sources of the political and juristic doctrine underlying that system, and the role of the state educational system in the generation and propagation of constitutional theory—all of which are related to various themes in this narrative.[1]

The Meiji Constitutional Reformation

The decade beginning in 1888, the year of Minobe's arrival in Tokyo, was in most respects a quieter, more stable period than the first score of years after the Meiji Restoration (1868). By 1886 the scandalous excitements of the "western craze" were on the wane. The promulgation of the Peace Preservation Ordinance the following December was symbolic of the failure of the last threat of violent opposition to the Meiji oligarchy. These years constituted the final phase in a process of consolidation from which the pattern of the modern Japanese state emerged roughly in the configurations it was to retain for the next half century.

The fruits of critical decisions made by government leaders in 1880–1881 were in this later period taking shape on every hand. The process of the transfer of government-capitalized industries to private hands had already resulted in the appearance of a new capitalist class, headed by an industrial-financial oligarchy closely wedded to the state and its purposes. Concurrently running its rapid course was the process of consolidation of landholdings at the expense of small peasants which resulted from a government policy of rationalizing the agrarian tax basis of its industrial program. Moreover, these reciprocal developments were from the beginning closely related to Japan's approach to her problems of foreign policy. Their consequences have been primary sources of Japanese political and social dynamics to the present time and have exercised momentous influence on the direction of constitutional development.

The major political achievement of the decade was the establishment of the Imperial Constitution. The creation of the privy council in 1888 was the last of a series of important modifications in government structure leading up to the promulgation of the constitution. New orders of nobility were established in 1884, and a western (German) type ministerial cabinet was created in 1885. The system of prefectural and local government crystallized in 1888. The constitution itself was published in February, 1889, together with the law under which the representatives to the new two-house parliament, or diet, were elected the following summer. This organic legislation was produced entirely within the inner councils of the government and under conditions of strictest secrecy. It was produced in the midst of and, to a large extent, as a result of a great ferment of ideas and political activity.

This political activity was carried on by diverse elements who had complaints against the nature, composition, and policies of a government dominated by bureaucrats of the erstwhile fiefs of Choshu and Satsuma (satchō), most prominently after 1880 Ito Hirobumi and Yamagata Aritomo. In substance, the underlying perturbation consisted of: (1) the bitter disappointment and belligerent resentment of the declassed and depressed ex-samurai who found fault with the slow and careful policy of the government in respect to the abolition of the unequal treaties and other foreign policy matters; (2) the quarrelsome discontent of the ambitious members of the minor fiefs who had been denied positions of importance in the councils of the government; and (3) the resentment and alarm of the landlords, peasants, and provincial businessmen who considered themselves victims of the government's fiscal and industrial policies.

These dissatisfactions manifested themselves after 1873 in local and national political associations propagandizing and agitating for the establishment of a parliament and other political innovations. The rhetorical basis of the agitation was derived for the most part from western political and economic literature. Such literature had increased from a thin stream through the latter years of the Shogunate to a yearly increasing flood of translations after 1860. The leading contributions to the early stages of this literary phenomenon were from England, France, and America; after 1875 the trend went sharply to ideas and works of German origin. During the period of agitation for the establishment of a parliament, English and French literature swayed the thinking of the antigovernment partisans. In general it can be said that the influence of French natural rights philosophy and republican doctrine was particularly prominent among those who spoke for the political associations led by Itagaki Taisuke and Goto Shojiro, known after 1881 as the Liberal Party (jiyutō). British constitutionalism and utilitarian economic ideas, strongly represented among the professors of Waseda and Keio universities, influenced Okuma Shigenobu and his followers, who in 1882 founded the Progressive Party (kaishintō). The activities of the antigovernment forces increased steadily, especially after 1877, reaching a peak in the period 1882–1885 in what is known as the Liberty and Popular Rights Movement (jiyu-minken undō). This movement, described by Takekoshi as "like that of a swarm of bees which might sting a horse but could not kill it," collapsed in 1885 as a result of internal conflicts of interest, police supression, and the defection of its prominent leaders.[2]

However important a role British and French ideas played in shaping the programs and inspiring the manifestoes of antigovernment forces, these ideas had little discernible effect on the shape of the constitutional structure that emerged between 1881 and 1890 save as such ideas had been assimilated into German constitutional experience.[3] British and French thought continued to find favor in some party, business, and private educational centers after 1890, but its prestige had already been greatly reduced under the tide of German intellectual influence when the government in 1881 made its decision to seek its institutional models and political rationalizations in Germany and Austria. The final rejection then of the policy advocated by Okuma within the government, calling for the early opening of a parliament, symbolized the official decision to "go Prussian."

In the years to follow, German influence showed itself in manifold ways. It was to Vienna and Berlin that the Satcho statesmen and their bureaucratic servants traveled for instruction on constitutional problems. German civil servants and academicians served prominently as advisors to the government in Tokyo and on the faculty of the Imperial University during the 1880's. During that and the following decade Germany was the Mecca for Japanese students on government scholarships. The law faculty of the Tokyo Imperial University became the citadel of an officially sanctioned line of political and legal theory closely bound to German thought. Thus not only government thinking but intellectual currents generally, and especially scholarship, fell under the sway of German schools and doctrines.[4]

The Imperial Rescript of October, 1881, announcing the emperor's intention to convene a parliament in 1890 signaled the settlement within the government of basic constitutional issues. The decision came as a direct result of the pressure of the antigovernment forces, to which the influence of Okuma and his followers were joined in 1880. It was a concession designed to appease and deflate the opposition. But it must also be seen as the culmination of the efforts of the government, especially since 1873, to establish a modern organic law for the state. Throughout the 1870's there was a division within the government between those who favored full parliamentary government and those standing for "gradualism." The latter group prevailed in 1878 in rejecting the "English type" constitutional project produced by the senate (genrō-in). The gradualists completed their triumph by forcing the withdrawal of Okuma from the government in 1881. The prevailing elements within the government wished to achieve an organization of the state which would facilitate the mobilization of the nation's social forces to bring about the objectives of the empire, as the government conceived them, and which would at the same time guarantee to the incumbent elements control of the government. After 1875 it was no longer possible for that organization to be exclusively bureaucratic; demands for parliamentary institutions and popular rights had become too strong.[5]

The essential character of the constitutional pattern then decided on was a strong assertion of the monarchical principle. It gave full scope to the autocratic pretension of the imperial tradition. It aimed at exploitation of the psychological potency of the paternalistic imperial institution in the generation and channeling of patriotic fervor and in the welding of a monolithic, conservative social ethic for the nation. The "constitutional" aspects of the new order—parliament, popular rights, the Rechtsstaat (hōchikoku)—were to be subordinated to the presumably overwhelming weight of monarchical paraphernalia. Moreover, any provisions for individual rights or popular participation in government were to be viewed not as concessions to popular demand but as reflections of imperial benevolence and as the means of better bringing the talents and labors of the nation to the service of the empire.

The decision of 1881 has been called a triumph of "Japanism" over western ideology. It bolstered those persistent elements in Japanese society who sought to conserve and promote the ethnocentric virtues of the "Imperial Way," the peculiar "national polity" of Japan, as the superior and more-or-less exclusive basis of ordering Japanese society and government.[6] Behind it, however, was not only the traditionalist position taken by such men as the court noble, Iwakura Tomomi, but also the strongly utilitarian attitude of the Satcho bureaucrats. It was the latter attitude which was the dominant factor in the constitution-making process. In the hands of these men the historical and ethical content of the imperial tradition was elaborated into an emperor system (tennōsei), the keystone of a modern bureaucratic state. Government leaders were ever ready to make the most of the presumption of sacrosanctity in the cry, "Preservation of national polity!" in order to stifle opposition and to secure for themselves exclusive control of the drafting of the constitution.

But the national polity issue tended to become secondary in the minds of the constitution makers as they set about the actual task of legislation. Once the fundamental choice had been made in favor of firm establishment of the monarchic principle, modified by a narrowly conceived constitutionalism, they became absorbed in the problems of arranging the structure and operation of government in terms of this principle, and in the modernization of the administrative system. In approaching these problems they became avid and purposeful students of German theory and experience. Although they selected most discreetly and sought diligently to cast their findings in terms congenial to Japanese experience, they borrowed more than they expected both of the substance and theory of western constitutional development as it was known in Germany.

The choice of Germany as model is not surprising. The vitality of monarchical institutions in the German states; the apparent success of the Prussian and the German imperial statesmen in accommodating post-revolutionary forces of liberalism so that the strength of the monarchy and its controlling bureaucracy was little impaired; the eminent achievements of Chancellor Bismarck's policy of national unification; the striking success of German arms and diplomacy; the prestige of German thinkers in the moral, social, and legal sciences—all these factors attracted and held the eager attention of Japanese statesmen, soldiers, and scholars in the three decades following 1880. German influence was not limited to constitutional matters. Under Yamagata's leadership, the Japanese took the Prussian army as its model after the German victory at Sedan, and, by successive steps in 1878 and 1882, instituted a command structure insulated from civilian control, modeled on that of the German Imperial General Staff system. German doctrines of protectionism to advance the development of industry were promoted through the Imperial University under Kato Hiroyuki. Under the administration of Mori Arinori, German pedagogical principles, with strong emphasis on nationalism and ethical training, were firmly established in the state educational system.

The task of preparing the constitution and its principal supplementary legislation fell to Ito Hirobumi and his chief assistants Inoue Ki (Kowashi), Ito Miyoji, and Kaneko Kentaro. Ito Hirobumi went to Europe where he consulted directly with Professor Lorenz von Stein at Vienna and with Professor Rudolph Gneist at Berlin. Ito Miyoji and Kaneko journeyed also to sit in the lecture halls of the two eminent jurists. Back in Tokyo the drafters relied frequently on the advice of Dr. Albert Mosse, whom they had first met in Germany and who had become a professor at the Tokyo Imperial University. They sought also the technical assistance of Dr. Hermann Roessler, a disciple of Gneist, who was employed as an advisor to the Japanese Ministry of Foreign Affairs. Inoue, to whom Ito assigned the principal responsibility for drafting the constitution, kept especially close contact with Roessler.[7]

Ito and his lieutenants were not primarily concerned in their German investigations with the basic constitutional pattern, for that had already been determined in principle. Instead, they absorbed themselves in problems of organization of the administration. Ito left Japan in March, 1882, with a commission charging him to "inquire into the origins, study the history, observe the operations, and study the virtues and faults of the constitutions of the European constitutional monarchies,"[8] which commission he carried out for the most part through the interpretations of German legal scholars. They confirmed his fears of parliamentarism and the necessity of limiting it in the interest of maintaining monarchical power and bureaucratic control of administration. Gneist was especially diligent in warning against the introduction of parliamentary institutions and practices incompatible with the traditions and psychology of the nation. Ito found in the south-German states excellent models of monarchical constitutions as yet relatively uncorrupted by revolutionary principles already at work in Prussia. In borrowing from them concepts and forms regarding imperial house law, regency, ordinance power, budgetary system, and constitutional amendment, he was able to retain for Japan a degree of autocracy beyond that known to the Prussian and Imperial German constitutions. Their congeniality was particularly happy, for in these areas of royal prerogative the Japanese found convenient European forms for clothing the indigenous Japanese substance.

In October, 1882, Ito wrote to Inoue Kaoru from Berlin, "although I think the matter of the constitution itself is already settled, at the same time the matter of administration will not be very easy. But I remain constantly eager to acquire an understanding of its principles." Thus, it was on the details of the organization of the parliament, on the constitution of the cabinet and the administrative structure subordinate to it, and on the perfection of the centrally controlled system of local government that the constitution makers concentrated between 1883 and 1889. Since they were of a less predetermined mind in respect to such matters, and since those matters related directly to their personal interest in the preservation of bureaucratic control of the government, Ito and his aides were receptive to foreign influence in regard to them. In this area, the constitutional structure and practice of the Prussian monarchy and the German Empire drew their admiring attention. And it was while in pursuit of further knowledge concerning these matters, particularly through study of the descriptive and analytic literature concerning them, that the bureaucratic scholars of Japan were led into the mainstreams of German constitutional theory and political science.

Constitutional and Legal Theory

The German authorities Ito consulted were men prominent in the development of constitutional theory in nineteenth-century Germany, where "the slow spread of constitutionalism . . . was a battle that was fought as vigorously in the classroom and in the technical works on political and juristic theory as it was in the antechambers of the diplomats and the barricaded streets of Vienna and Berlin."[9] Gneist and Stein were, for their day, moderate constitutional monarchists, who accepted with reservation the feeble parliamentary institutions that came to the Germanies in the course of the early nineteenth-century revolution.[10] But the constitutionalism which they promoted was conceived less a political movement than as an administrative reform by which the capricious tyranny of the *Polizeistaat* should give way to the rule of law—the *Rechtsstaat*—described by Stein as a state "in which every individual can establish his legal right against the administrative power through regular action in the courts. . . ."[11] The constitutions of the German kingdoms were interpreted not as steps toward democracy, and certainly not as assertions of popular sovereignty. They were taken rather to be patents of autolimitation on the part of the state (through the person of the monarch) by which the powers of government were brought under the rule of law. In constitutional terms this was manifested in elementary guaranties of individual rights and in a separation of powers, construed as a delimitation of the competence of the several organs of the state over which the monarch's prerogative remained complete and undivided.

Constitutionalism thus confined within the narrow scope of legalistic and bureaucratic *Rechtsstaatismus* was readily appreciated by Ito and his colleagues in the government. But in borrowing from it they reaped unanticipated problems arising out of the conceptual content and methodology of German legal science. Academic theories alone did not, of course, determine for Japan, any more than for Germany or any other country, the course of its constitutional development; they do seem, however, to have exercised substantial influence on critical areas of public opinion. In few countries besides Germany and Japan have constitutional issues become so tirelessly, voluminously, and heatedly fought by academic theorists, and by legal scholars in particular. Their constitutional literatures are strewn with the corpses of "battles of the monographs." Moreover, in both countries training in public law has played a large part in the education of all levels of the civil bureaucracy, and the doctrines dominant in centers of bureaucratic training tended to sift down through the education system to the population at large.

Of immediate relevance to the effect of German theory on Japanese constitutional ideas was the existence in the former of fundamental ideas initially hostile to monarchical absolutism and potentially reconcilable with parliamentary democracy. It is not that the legal theory anticipated and promoted parliamentarism; but, through stages of positivistic refinement, it became more and more unrelated to historical and political realities, and thus inapplicable to the issue of monarchy versus democracy. The implications of these ideas became more apparent in the works of various members of the generation following Stein and Gneist, notably in those of Georg Jellinek (1851–1911), Paul Laband (1838–1918), and Gerhard Anschütz (1867–1948). And it was these who were most influential in providing the methodology and suggesting the content of the theories of the "liberal school" of constitutional interpretation in Japan. Their fundamental ideas are summarized below.

The principle of constitutionalism, despite the restrictive definition attached to it, had the effect of reducing the monarch, along with other elements in the constitutional structure, to a status subordinate to a superior entity, the state. In the Hegelian tradition, high ethical and cultural value was ascribed to the state, which, in the form first of the Prussian state and later the empire, was viewed throughout the nineteenth century as the instrument of German national liberation and unification. The superiority of the monarch became a relative matter, not fundamental to the nature of the state, resting on social and political tradition and on sundry more-or-less utilitarian arguments which might vary from place to place and from time to time. This idea of the state had rich and far-ranging implications in conjunction with organic and corporate theories concerning its nature, and ethical, cultural, and racial theories regarding its purpose and destiny.

But the tendency in the dominant school of jurisprudence in imperial Germany was to purify the concept of the state personality of all historical and moral connotations. According to the *Rechtsstaat* concept, the state is a legal personality analogous to, but significantly different from, the legal personality (*juristische Person*) of private law. Its distinguishing characteristic is its possession of sovereignty, which, though subject to widely differing interpretations, implies at least the power to govern and the power to define its own competence and that of its organs. As a legal personality, the state is considered to be the subject—that is, possessor—of rights and duties (*Rechtssubjekt*), which are defined in the constitution and in other organic legislation by a process of autolimitation (*Selbstbeschrankung*). Through this notion of autolimitation, the absolute connotations of sovereignty, derived originally from the character of the absolute monarch and now imputed exclusively to the state, were reconciled with the practical limitations of constitutionalism and the rule of law.[12]

An essential corollary of the state-sovereignty theory was the concept of state organs, according to which the state acts in its manifold capacity through the acts of the person or persons constituting them. Supreme among the organs of the state is that office which is, by the terms of the constitution, the bearer of sovereignty (*Träger der Staatsgewalt* or *Regierungsgewalt*—in German law, the king), whose powers are exercised in conformance with the terms of the constitution.

Such a concept of the state and its organs and their relation to law is, *per se*, indifferent to the particular organic structure of the state; but it is not without political implications, some of which became evident in the role it assumed in Japan. The complex of ideas associated with the concept of the *Rechtsstaat* was in part a product of pre-French Revolution theories aimed at reconciling absolutism with the needs and demands of a rising middle class; at the same time it was a reaction against the threat of radical republicanism. As a matter of historical fact, it has existed as a vital proposition only in the presence of monarchy. Instrumental in the transition from absolute to constitutional monarchy, it also raised up in the state personality an obstacle to the assertion of popular sovereignty.[13]

The juristic concept of state personality was put forward as a universal principle of constitutional jurisprudence.[14] It worked in Japan to encourage those who rejected a parochial, tradition-bound view of the

Japanese constitutional system; its acceptance was conducive to the interpretation of the provisions of Japanese constitutional law by analogy to those of foreign constitutions. In this sense its effects were potentially liberalizing, for it brought Japanese constitutional theory into contact with the progressive tides then running in Europe.

Although certain German legal concepts played important roles in Japanese constitutional jurisprudence under the Meiji Constitution, it was perhaps of equal significance, in view of its long-run effects on Japanese constitutional theory, that German methodology in legal and political science greatly influenced Japanese scholars. This influence was responsible for the onesidedly legalistic aspect of Japanese constitutional theory, and for the domination of the field of political science by public-law methodology and by public-law theory concerning the nature of the state, law, society, and the relations among them.

German political thought in the nineteenth century was preoccupied with the state. Political science as a generic category was represented in that thought by state theory—*Staatslehre*. A science which had once pretended to responsibility for the general field of sociology, *Staatslehre* now comprised a field of sociological and philosophical investigation focused on the state. It was associated with two subordinate disciplines, the science of state law (*Staatsrechtslehre*) and political science (*Politik* or *Staatswissenschaft*). The first and greater of these subdisciplines, the science of state law, operated entirely within the pattern of the state as a concept delineated in the *Staatslehre*. The second and lesser of the two, political science, was thought of as dealing with the more ephemeral life processes of the state, an understanding of which was a matter of empirical observation and practical political intuition. Political science, thus conceived as statecraft, was put beyond the reach of systematic thought. The drive for the achievement of *Rechtsstaat*, the constant demand for authoritative interpretations of public law at each successive stage of national development, the endless legal disputation these evoked, and the close relationship which existed between the university faculties and the bureaucracy in Germany—all contributed to making state law the queen of the state sciences.

The period following the establishment of the Imperial German Constitution in 1871 was marked by the intensification of a movement in German public law towards positivism. The assertion by Georg Jellinek, in his *Allgemeine Staatslehre* (1900), of the necessity of a complete

methodological break between the study of the state in its social aspect
(historical and political) and the study of the state as a juristic phenomenon gave expression to this methodological development. The
school of conceptual jurisprudence which it represented flourished between 1890 and 1910.[15] This school assumed that the jurist was concerned with nothing but positive law and with the discovery of general
conceptual propositions under which each particular rule could be
ordered. As developed and applied by Paul Laband and Gerhard Anschütz, this methodology advanced toward an extreme conceptual idealism (*Begriffsrealismus*): a conceptual ordering of the valid public law
of a particular state from which all considerations of politics, political
theory, comparative or private-law concepts or methods were excluded.[16]
Laband's extreme legal positivism was by no means approved by Jellinek,
who denied the validity of a purely formal construction of law.

This legalistic atmosphere was, then, the one in which Japanese
theorists and teachers of public law became immersed following Ito's
pilgrimage to Vienna and Berlin. Of the German authorities mentioned
above, Jellinek shares with Johann Bluntschli the distinction of having
exercised more influence than perhaps any other foreign political thinker
on the development of political theory in Japan, particularly in respect to
methodology.[17] Minobe, who acknowledged his reliance on Jellinek, has
been described by one of his students as "the Jellinek of Japan." The
methodology of *Begriffsjurisprudenz* also left its mark, but the very terms
of the positivism under which men like Laband and Anschütz worked
denied the content of their work universal applicability and, in turn,
precluded enduring interest to the Japanese. In any case, their whole
body of constitutional commentary lost almost all relevance (sundry
abstract points such as the question of sovereignty and the nature of
German federalism were exceptions) when the German imperial regime
fell in 1918. The intellectual universality and tolerance of Jellinek seem
to have carried the greater and more enduring influence in Japan.[18]

Of even greater portent for the course of Japanese constitutional
theory than the influence of particular persons and systems of thought
was the imprint of the academic patterns of *Staatslehre* on the Japanese
universities. The spirit and mold of *kokkagaku* (*Staatslehre*) had been
well impressed on the law and political science faculty at Tokyo Imperial
University even before Minobe went to study in Heidelberg. At To-Dai[19]
the science of the state not only came to constitute the core of political

science (*seijigaku*) but, as in Berlin, developed chiefly along the lines of its subordinate discipline, the science of state law (*kokuhōgaku*, a direct translation of *Staatsrechtslehre*) and the principles and methods of jurisprudence (*hōritsugaku*, which means *Rechtslehre*).

Professor Royama finds the antecedents of Japanese state science in one of the two main currents of the period of "political enlightenment" early in the Meiji era.[20] The political enlightenment was displayed in the translation of foreign writings and the dissemination of new political ideas by the government and by the independent thinkers. Through this process of enlightenment ran two conflicting currents: (1) the interpretive tradition, which attempted to make western political ideas understood on a utilitarian basis, and (2) the critical tradition, which sought to generate independent participation in modern political thinking. Most bureaucratic scholarship was of the interpretive brand, and it was out of this tradition, especially after the publication by the ministry of education of Kato Hiroyuki's translation of Bluntschli's *Allgemeines Staatsrecht* in 1872, that the state-science school of political science emerged in Japan. At To-Dai, Kato zealously promoted German studies. Under his influence formal logic and systematic interpretation became the predominant methods, to the exclusion of empirical and critical investigation. The state-science school flourished during the 1880's, but it had vigorous competition from the writers and thinkers of the critical enlightenment, many of whom were partisans in the Liberty and Popular Rights Movement against the ruling oligarchy. The centers of this opposition were the intellectual leadership of the antigovernment parties, the faculties of the private universities, and journalistic circles. Great conceptual and methodological diversity prevailed among the partisans of the critical enlightenment, and this, combined with their inclination to expend their energies in destructive criticism of the government position, left them weak in relation to the tightly disciplined logicians of the state-science school.[21]

The influence of German thought on the making of the Meiji Constitution gave great stimulus to the advancement of state science at To-Dai. The promulgation of the constitution solidified the hold of that science and its methodology on the To-Dai law faculty and assured that its *Rechtsstaat* concept, with its underlying assumption of the organic or corporate nature of the state, would become the intellectual basis of bureaucratic thought.[22] It fell to the science of public law, with its emphasis on the interpretation of systematic theories of state sovereignty, to resolve the conflicts inherent in the new constitution—conflicts between bureaucratic monarchy and liberal parliamentarism. The bias of this public-law science was not in the direction of the discovery and illumination of the basic political principles of constitutionalism, but in the direction of the perfection of a bureaucratic *Rechtsstaat*.

The "bureaucratic constitutional thought" of Lorenz von Stein and Rudolph Gneist also made a deep imprint on the academic patterns at To-Dai during this period. The ideas of Stein, who thought of political science as a *Polizeiwissenschaft* (science of administration) and who defined state science as the study of the organs which constitute the state, were made known through the publication of translations of his writings on administration and constitutional law between 1887 and 1889.[23] Gneist's influence was felt through the presence on the law faculty of two of his disciples, Albert Mosse and Karl Rathgen. Rathgen, who lectured at To-Dai from 1882 to 1890, has been called the founder of Japanese political science. He equated political science with state science, the study of the character and processes of the state, whose substance he found in the relationships among such concepts as sovereignty, territory, and people. As subsequent discussion will show, Minobe Tatsukichi's constitutional views emerged from and in large part remained within the limits of the official political science of the Imperial University, a political science which in Royama's words, "neither saw with its own eyes, nor stood on its own feet. Rather it depended on *Staatslehre*. It was not an independent science but an auxiliary of the state bureaucracy in administration and legislation."[24]

The Academic Apparatus

Minobe's position in relation to constitutional thought in Japan cannot be appreciated in isolation from the circumstances of his career as a member of the state educational and civil-service system, at the peak of which he functioned for two decades as a teacher, publicist, and civil-service examiner. Nor can the impact of his ideas on the constitutional history of Japan be appreciated without an understanding of the political role of the civil bureaucracy of which the To-Dai law faculty was an important adjunct. The emergence, prosperity, and decline of

his constitutional position was, in a sense, a reflection of the vicissi-
tudes of the bureaucratic role.

The character of To-Dai as an integral part of the state administrative system is evident in the circumstances of its establishment and
in the language of the ordinance prescribing its organization and functions. The oft-quoted text of Article I of that ordinance expresses suc-
cinctly the state function of the university: "It shall be the purpose of
the Imperial University to teach the sciences and the arts and to probe
their mysteries in accordance with the needs of the state."[25] The establishment of the Imperial University at Tokyo followed by three months
the publication of Ito Hirobumi's statement of the principles of official discipline (*kanki go shō*), which called for election of officials by
examination. This declaration of principle was given substance in 1887
by the establishment of a civil-service examination and apprentice system patterned on that of Prussia.[26] The institution of a merit system,
based on competitive examinations, in the appointment of civil officials
was part of a general program of administrative rationalization carried
out by Ito, whose first major step had been the adoption of the ministerial cabinet system two years earlier. This program had considerable
political significance: it opened the way for a break in the Satcho monopoly of official positions, which had become a dangerous political
irritant and was depriving the government of access to the best talents.[27]

The institution which emerged in 1886 as the Imperial University
already had a twenty-year history. The period prior to 1886 had been
one of chaotic groping, full of false starts and reversals, during which
the university was the victim of internal feuds between the supporters
of classical Confucianist doctrine and traditional Japanese doctrine,
both of which were gradually submerged under the influx of western
learning and western instructors. The school had gone through repeated
reorganizations as government policies on education changed from year
to year. Two characteristics which appeared in this formative period
were to remain features throughout the subsequent history of the university until the reforms of 1946–1947. One, the close relationship between the university and the ministry of education initiated by the
ordinance of 1886, continued without substantial change thereafter.[28]
At the head of the university stood a president, appointed directly by
the minister of education, with full responsibility for preserving the
order of the university, superintending its affairs, and presiding over

the academic council. The minister of education's discretion was final, at least nominally, in all matters of curricula, standards, faculty structure, and the awarding of degrees; as a matter of practical effect, however, the university gradually gained autonomy in these matters. Administrative and instructional officers of the university held regular classified rank in the civil service.

The second major development of the early period was the fixing of the university's role as the center of bureaucratic training. Prior to 1878 this function was greatly subordinate to its role as the central administrative organ of the national school system. Kato Hiroyuki, who had promoted German studies at To-Dai and who was to become its president, was the leading figure in advancing the "training of bureaucratic talents" and the teaching of statism there.[29] In 1885, Kato, a vigorous spokesman for the antiparliamentary position of the government, won Ito's support in this goal. Their aim was not only to open the government service to talented youths throughout the empire but to ensure that the training of bureaucratic reserves conformed to the government's own view of service to the state.[30] In effect, they opened to those capable of meeting the academic tests, the road to social and economic advancement.

Official policy toward bureaucratic education evolved in the context of a more general middle Meiji development of which it was a part as both a cause and an effect. The close relations between imperial university law students and state officialdom with its official doctrines ran counter to the inclination prevailing widely in the intellectual world to shun the state as a subject for rational analysis or for philosophical consideration.[31] The bureaucratic mission was fixed on To-Dai just at the end of a period when "without question the subject that most interested the Japanese was . . . the theory and practice of political science."[32] It came just when this period of intellectual concern with the state, its high point usually dated as 1873–1887, gave way to one of mutual indifference between the state and intellectuals, a condition which persisted thereafter, with only slight interruption in the middle Taisho period. Kosaka Masaaki puts perhaps overmuch weight on this when he says "[the fact] that there was no adequate facing-up to the question of the state on the part of the intellectuals, led to the transformation of the state into a sacrosanct mystery . . . from something that could be dealt with theoretically and logically into something which had to be obeyed."[33] The problem of "how to think of the state," a focus of Japanese interest since before Meiji,[34] was left to constitutional theorists and public-law authorities. Appreciation of this relationship is doubtless of considerable value in illuminating the distinctive quality of Minobe's role as a constitutional theorist.

The government's policy of elevating To-Dai to a position of advantage relative to the private universities was designed also to break the dominance of the private university law schools. It was to this end that the government gave bureaucratic status to the To-Dai faculty, a special title to the To-Dai students, and liberal subsidies to qualified students in that institution, especially in the form of overseas education at government expense. The ordinance of 1887 specifically exempted from the examination system for civil officials, persons holding the doctorate of law or letters and graduates of specified government schools of law and letters. While a revision of the examination ordinance in 1893 abolished this general exemption of government-school graduates, To-Dai law graduates continued to enjoy an exemption from the qualifying examination for the higher civil-service examination for selection of judicial officers and foreign-service and consular officers.[35] Since private-school graduates seeking appointment were required to take the qualifying examinations, and since the examination board was dominated by To-Dai professors, private schools resorted to calling in To-Dai law faculty members to lecture, and private law teaching, like that of the Imperial University, became oriented toward the civil-service examinations. Graduates of private schools offering the most To-Dai lectures got the best results in the examinations.[36]

The consequence of the Kato-Ito policy was to liberate the civil service, to some degree, from the evils of *han* (fief) patronage. They did, in fact, in large measure succeed in an attempt to transform *han* bureaucracy into an academic bureaucracy. While the new regime broadened the field of talent recruitment, the influences of *han* connection and of "clan psychology" were by no means eliminated, and at the top the Satcho remained firmly in control, at least until the middle of the Taisho era. In 1899, under Premier Yamagata, steps were taken to insulate the civil bureaucracy from penetration by political appointees and to guarantee to it a high degree of internal cohesion based on firm tenure, strict observance of rank and subordination, and disciplinary autonomy. The examination principle applied only to the initial appointment; advancement thereafter depended on loyalty to superiors and conformance with the spirit of the service, in which inward exclusiveness and outward arrogance were prominent features.

Within this system the privileged position of the To-Dai alumni gave them an advantage in numbers and seniority that earned for them in academic circles and in the civil bureaucracy the title of *aka-mon batsu* (literally, the red gate clique) derived from *Aka-mon*, the name used casually to designate Tokyo Imperial University. To the government, To-Dai was the nursery of officials; to aspiring students, every one of whom, it has been said, hoped to become a *hakushi* (doctor) or a state minister, it was the path to an exclusive and exalted social distinction; to many critics it was known as the "den of the bureaucrats." To-Dai was frequently criticized for its share in the propagation of official narrowness and arrogance, for having fallen into the "deep-rooted abuses of Prussian official scholarship," to which genuinely academic objectives were sacrificed. The observance of bureaucratic mores by To-Dai faculty members accentuated a tendency toward academic aloofness and resulted in a highly formal relationship between teacher and student, with little intellectual and no social give-and-take. For the few favorite protégés at the graduate level, however, the relationship was rather more like the classical master-pupil relationship, which was quite personal.[37]

Whatever might be said of the civil bureaucracy as an administrative instrument, its political role was crucial in the constitutional history of the empire.[38] In establishing a civil bureaucracy well trained in the state sciences of law and administration and protected against the encroachments of parliamentary politics, the elder statesmen were motivated by a desire to create an efficient and responsive instrument by which the all-inclusive administrative prerogatives would be secured against parliamentary control. The system fostered throughout the political community acceptance of a bureaucratic *Weltanschauung* holding that the affairs of administration were naturally and exclusively the concern of the emperor's officials and could only suffer were they to be brought under the influence of public sentiment. The founders of the system succeeded to a substantial degree, and even during the brightest period of political party ascendancy the subservience of party politics to bureaucratic favor was notorious. For the most part parliamentary politics never escaped the pattern, early established, by which the major parties did not gain control of the civil service but, instead, became victims of collusive connections between their own leaders and ambitious members of that service. Bureaucratic influence in politics was manifested quite overtly in the more-or-less consistently antiparliamentary operations of the privy council and the house of peers. Through these bodies, to which leading civil servants were appointed in substantial numbers, the highest and most conservative elements of the bureaucracy gained a voice in both the administrative and legislative processes of government. In these positions they were able not only to preserve the bureaucratic system from attack but to exert an influence on the determination of public policy generally.[39]

An important determinant of the effects of the civil bureaucracy on the development of constitutional government in Japan was the state-law basis of its thinking. There was a strong emphasis in the training of civil servants on the methods and substance of legal science and on public law especially.[40] This concentration not only inhibited the development of administrative theory and practice; it served to fix the mold of state science and the science of state law on the intellects and attitudes of the bureaucracy as a whole. These attitudes and ideas were communicated to the public through both the ubiquitous operations of the civil service and an ideological feedback into the national educational system. Few official academicians managed to escape the bonds and weight of this intellectual millstone. They usually gained only a struggling foothold on the academic fringes, hampered by the pressures of professional bias and institutional inertia, weak and isolated in terms of their own rationale. State-law science remained dominant. The possibilities and limitations of an advance within that regime toward a liberal democratic constitutional theory are probably nowhere more clearly shown than in the work of Minobe Tatsukichi.

The ordinance of 1886 established the law faculty as one of five academic divisions of the Imperial University. The law faculty itself was divided into the law department, the political science department, and, for a time, departments of economics and commerce, which eventually became separate faculties. By 1893 official law studies in Japan, for which To-Dai had full responsibility after 1884,[41] had moved considerably toward complete domination by German jurisprudence. Under President Kato, the influence of German public-law theory had grown steadily following the introduction of the first courses in state law and constitu-

tional law in 1883.[42] The increasing strength in the public-law curricula
at To-Dai reflected the influence of German public-law theory on the
new constitutional system. Nevertheless, its significance in terms of
civil-service training might have been modified, if not eventually eliminated, had it not been for the growth of German influence in all
branches of the law. The adoption of German models for the civil and
procedural codes had the effect of nurturing most To-Dai law graduates
on the very meat and marrow of the *Rechtsstaat*. German legal theory
and methods became indispensable in the interpretation of every field
of Japanese law.[43] This development worked to break the isolation of
the German tradition in the public-law field and to remove the only
likely sources of challenge to the constitutional doctrines developed
there.[44] French and English legal traditions were submerged not only at
To-Dai; by 1900 the effects of the operations of the civil-service examination system had stifled the pursuit of such studies in the private law
schools as well.[45]

The basic pattern of the public-law and political-science program at
To-Dai continued without substantial change after 1893. At that time
there were chairs of constitutional law, state law, administrative law,
international law, legislative history (Japanese), comparative legislative
history (western), political science, and political history. A chair of
American constitutional history and foreign policy was added in 1918.
Courses in these fields constituted the core requirements for the degree
in political science, and were only relatively less prominent among the
requirements for the law degree.

The constitutional system to which Minobe devoted his scholarly
talents during all but the final years of his life was the product of a
counterrevolutionary *tour de force*, which achieved a contrived and unstable balance between the major currents running in the post-Restoration era. It was an attempt to fashion *de novo* and on unfamiliar alien
patterns a constitutional structure which, although it made begrudging
concessions to the principles of parliamentary government, was carefully
designed to favor the perpetuation of a narrow and authoritarian oligarchy of civil and military bureaucrats. The seat of instability in the
structure was in the admission, albeit under severe restrictions, of a
minimal institutional basis (a representative parliament and a bill of
rights) for a continuing drive toward liberalization and democratization.

The potential disequilibrium gained motion from the social and economic changes which were taking place in Meiji society even as the constitution was being drafted. During the second and third decades of the twentieth century the expansive and aggressive forces of the new capitalism, operating through the political parties and through the bureaucracy itself, supported by proletarian unrest and by a public opinion under the influence of the political slogans of the Allies in World War I, were to throw the balance strongly to the side of the liberal forces within the Meiji constitutional system.

The ascendancy of Minobe's constitutional theory during that period was the result not of its potency as political propaganda but of its compatibility with the prevailing spirit of Japanese politics. Its chief function was to give an interpretation, strictly within the official state-law tradition of Tokyo Imperial University, which sanctioned the pretensions of the parliamentary parties to a major role in the control of state policy. Minobe's chief contribution to the cause of liberal constitutional government was in imparting to the bureaucratic ranks passing through the university a legitimate intellectual basis for acceptance of the new balance in constitutional politics. This is not to suggest that Minobe's position on constitutional problems was opportunistic. He demonstrated great independence and conviction in developing his theories and expounded them at first against formidable academic and bureaucratic opposition. Later, in the failing days of "normal constitutional government," he displayed ample willingness to enter the lists of public controversy as well as notable courage in expressing the dictates of his theory in application to successive constitutional problems as they arose.

Minobe's work manifested both the virtues and faults discussed earlier as basic to the German influence. The positivistic, interpretive method, which he wielded so well in dispelling the authoritarian obscurantism of the traditionalist school, served nobly in combination with his liberal predilections for reaching a liberal, democratic construction of the Meiji Constitution. But it was clearly inadequate to cope with the hard facts of Japanese society, which never quite matched, and after 1925 increasingly belied, the social and political assumptions underlying his view of the constitution.

II

Minobe's Career to 1934

Minobe retired from the university in 1934. Although that event by no means closed his public career, it affords a convenient breaking point in the narration of his personal history. In 1934 Minobe was entering a period of official disfavor, as a result of which he wrote nothing on constitutional problems for nearly a decade. The events of his life for which he is perhaps best remembered today occurred after 1934, but they center around two distinct and disconnected episodes, and are best dealt with separately. His constitutional theory had matured before 1934, and relevant biographical data have been brought together in this chapter—data concerning his social connections, his education, his official career, and his writing—for the purpose of supplying personal context for analysis of that theory. His political orientation becomes evident in the course of discussion of the Uesugi-Minobe debate of 1912 and its relation to the constitutional politics of the Taisho era.

The biographical sources available do not provide an intimate account of Minobe's life. Nor is great detail necessary, for the ideas with which this study deals do not call for psychological explanations.[1] By and large, the data are sufficiently complete in respect to his official career to indicate the importance of the position he came to occupy in the interlocking academic-bureaucratic mechanism and to show to what extent his constitutional ideas became official doctrine.

Family Background and Early Years

On the record, Minobe Tatsukichi's family origins are obscure. His native place was in Hyogo Prefecture at Takasago, a minor city lying west of Kobe on the shores of the Inland Sea. He was born on May 7, 1873, the second of two sons of Minobe Sadakichi. Minobe Sadakichi was, as his father had been, a physician. He became, in 1870, master of a once vigorous but now moribund school established by the Himeji daimyo for the education of commoners of the merchant class. The school had behind it a tradition of Confucianist and, more recently, of imperial loyalist thought. According to Nakase, Sadakichi was known best to his contemporaries, however, not as a physician or teacher, but as a devotee of *go* and *sake*.[2] It may be inferred that the elder Minobe enjoyed little official favor or social prominence and, from the testimony of his son's interrupted education, that he was not affluent.

Minobe Sadakichi's first son, Shunkichi (born 1870), went from To-Dai to the ministry of agriculture and commerce, and then to the ministry of finance. He served as president of the Hokkaido Colonization Bank (1908–1916) and as governor of the Bank of Chosen (1916–1924). Subsequently he held managerial posts in various companies, including the managing directorship of the Manchurian Stock Exchange and the management of Harbin Beer, Limited. Minobe Shunkichi's second son, Yoji (born 1899), also gained prominence as a civil servant. He entered the secretariat of the ministry of commerce and industry in 1926 and rose to the position of chief of the general affairs section of the price bureau. In 1940 he was "loaned" to the staff of the planning board, the primary war mobilization and control agency of the state.[3] Yoji married a daughter of Tanaka Heihachi, manager of the Tanaka Mining Industries.

Minobe Tatsukichi married Tami, the third daughter of Kikuchi Dairoku (1855–1917), doctor of science, president of To-Dai from 1898 to 1901, and minister of education from 1901 to 1903. Kikuchi had been educated in England under government auspices. His work as an educator and his contribution to the conclusion of the Anglo-Japanese Alliance gained him the title of baron and appointment to the privy council (1908–1917). Minobe's only son, Ryokichi (born 1904), was educated in economics at To-Dai, where he taught before going to Hosei University as a professor of economics. Ryokichi was indicted in 1939 as a member of the so-called Labor-Farmer Faction Professor Group which was charged under the Peace Preservation Law with illegal political activities. Ryokichi married the daughter of Kosaka Junzo, a member of the house of peers (elected by the high taxpayers of Nagano Prefecture) and holder of proprietary interests in a number of electric power, brewing, and fertilizer enterprises. What Minobe Tatsukichi's relations were with these various connections of blood and marriage is not disclosed by the sources consulted in this study, but it appears that he may well be placed, on the basis of social class as well as of the doctrines he uttered, among what Suzuki Yasuzo calls the "bourgeois scholars."[4]

In 1888, after two years of English language study at Kobe, Minobe Tatsukichi followed his brother to Tokyo to enter the First District Higher Middle School, the officially established preparatory school for the imperial university. It seems likely that both he and his brother from the beginning aimed at entering the civil service. Of Minobe's experiences in middle school, little is recorded. He left after the first two years, possibly for financial reasons, but returned in 1893. Upon his graduation in 1894 he advanced directly to the To-Dai law faculty to work for a degree in political science. He graduated from To-Dai in July, 1897, at the age of twenty-four, and went to work in the municipal bureau in the prefectural government office of the home ministry. He remained there as a probationary appointee until the end of 1898, when he resumed his academic work.

Minobe was abroad from May, 1899, until November, 1902, on a commission from the ministry of education to pursue the study of comparative legal systems in England, France, and Germany. During his absence he was gazetted for appointment as an assistant professor of the To-Dai law faculty (June 14, 1899) and later as professor (October 25, 1902). He began lecturing on comparative legislative history (*hikaku-hōsei shi*) immediately upon his return to Japan. In August, 1903, he was awarded the degree *hōgaku hakushi* (roughly equivalent to doctor of law) on "recommendation of the president of the university," without a thesis. At the same time he was appointed to serve concurrently as professor of law at the Tokyo High School of Commerce and as provisional member of the higher civil service examination board. At the age of thirty he was solidly established in the academic bureaucracy.

The period from 1897 to 1899 was critical in the determination of Minobe's career. In the former year, "out of consideration of the poorness of my talents as a student and the difficulty of continuing the poverty-stricken life of a student,"[5] he abandoned his pre-graduation hopes of continuing at the university with further study and research.

In an effort to escape an embarrassing financial dependence upon his brother, and since there were at that time no fellowships or scholarships at the university, he applied for and received an appointment in the home ministry. His experience there was disillusioning: "I found the desk job quite stifling. I was spending my energy with anxiety without opportunity and I was overcome with a desire to return to academic life."[6] The opportunity to do so came through his contacts with Ichiki Kitokuro, who was then professor of law at To-Dai and special councilor to the home ministry. Ichiki suggested that Minobe return to the university and prepare for appointment to the professorship of comparative legislative history. Ichiki arranged the matter with other faculty members concerned and Minobe returned to To-Dai. His program, as was noted above, soon took him to Europe. Prior to his departure, he supported himself by part-time work at the home ministry and in this connection he produced his first published work, a translation of Albert Shaw's *Municipal Administration in Continental Europe,* which appeared under the imprint of the home ministry.

Minobe did not find the pursuit of historical studies congenial. In Europe he applied himself, not to the investigation of original sources, but to acquiring an acquaintance with the works of leading authorities.[7] While he acknowledged a sense of the importance of the historical method in legal studies, he did not find satisfaction in his position as lecturer in legislative history. When Ichiki gave up his chair of administrative law in 1908, Minobe replaced him. In 1910 he left the chair of legislative history and thereafter devoted himself exclusively to public-law studies, thus satisfying an inclination dating from his undergraduate days. Although it was not until 1920 that Minobe was given responsibility for teaching constitutional law at To-Dai, he was actively interested in that field from the first year of his professorship. He traced his predilection for public-law specialization to two causes: his "natural inclination for logical thought" and the influence of Dr. Ichiki.[8] Minobe had been a student in Ichiki's first class. He relates: "Naturally the lectures were unpolished and showed a number of faults, but we were bewitched by his erudite references and fine reasoning . . . In all the years since, I have never been so much influenced by any lectures as by those of this progressive young scholar. Truly my specialization in public law was determined at that point."[9]

In contrast to his very sympathetic reaction to Ichiki, Minobe's response to Dr. Hozumi Yatsuka was negative from the earliest contact.[10] Of Hozumi, Minobe said: "[He] spoke and wrote clearly and solemnly. But on almost every point he was antithetical to Ichiki, and he always spoke positively and with finality without the least regard for logic. . . . His lectures provided many examples of faulty reasoning, and though I sat under him for one year, unfortunately I could not find myself in harmony with him."[11] Hozumi had pioneered in the development of a systematic, theoretical interpretation of the Imperial Constitution. He felt himself particularly close to the thoughts and spirit of its drafters and sought to preserve their purpose by emphasizing the native ethical and historical traditions underlying their work. It has been said of him that he succeeded in reviving, in the guise of a German doctrine of state supremacy, the national-learning type of nationalist thought from the late Tokugawa, appealing to the state as the aegis of the socially downtrodden and seeking in the family system the proper analogue for ordering a secure national state.[12] His *Kempō Teiyō* (*Elements of the Constitution*) (1910) ranks with Ito Hirobumi's *Commentaries on the Constitution of the Empire of Japan* among the early constitutional commentaries.

The first substantial intramural challenge to Hozumi's "historical school" of interpretation came when Ichiki succeeded Sueoka Seiichi as professor of state law. Hozumi's lectures on constitutional law (*kempō*) dealt exclusively with the Japanese system. State law (*kokuhō*) was concerned with western constitutional systems, and as taught by Ichiki it was *Staatsrechtslehre*.[13] Professors Tanaka and Ukai, pointing up the significance of this disciplinary development in Japanese universities, state that "it may be safely said that this branch of study has had a particular reason for being in Japan, because it has served as a channel through which the theory of constitutionalism has constantly found its way from the rest of the world into [Japan]. . . . As a rule these chairs had a *raison d'être* as rival chairs against the orthodox school."[14] Not at first really disturbed by the institutionalization of this fundamental conflict, the historical school (which came to be known as the orthodox school) continued to prosper under a presumption of official favor. Hozumi himself retired in illness in 1910 and was succeeded by his protégé Uesugi Shinkichi, who was to become Minobe's arch academic antagonist.[15]

The Contest with Uesugi: Academic and Personal Aspects

Minobe began writing regularly on constitutional questions as early as 1903,[16] and in doing so he came immediately into conflict with Hozumi and Uesugi. In the second year of his professorship he set forth briefly and dogmatically elements of a theory which was to become the crux of a thirty-year academic and political struggle. In that article he said:

Among scholars who explain our state law there are those who frequently assert that the monarch is the subject of governmental power. This is an inadmissible error in juristic theory today. In present-day juristic thinking, the state alone is the subject of governmental power, and the monarch is an organ of the state. . . . [The contrary argument] is based on a childish outlook which, being unable to enter into abstract juristic concepts, seeks to build its juristic concepts directly on actual phenomena. . . . Japan's national polity in its historical basis is not like that of the states of Europe. There can be no argument that the nation's feeling of loyalty to the emperor and love of country is unequaled by that of the peoples of Europe. But historical bases are not adequate to explain the present state, nor can you base juristic concepts on political sentiment. In present day legal terms, Japan's national polity does not differ in pattern from the constitutional monarchies of Europe. . . . The texts of laws are not law textbooks, and juristic concepts are not determined directly by the text of laws. The purpose of a constitution is not to explain juristic concepts. Article I of our constitution means simply that our national polity is that of a monarchy, and that its monarchs are in succession from an eternally unbroken line of emperors. . . .[17]

These short passages reveal a bald statement of the emperor-organ theory and a defense of the conceptual method upon which it was based. They provide also an assertion of Minobe's belief that the constitutional law of Japan should be treated as belonging to the general category of constitutional monarchy as known in European constitutional theory, and that Article I of the Imperial Constitution was no bar to such a view.[18] Moreover, he demonstrated here the incisive style for which he was admired—and some of the dogmatism and intellectual arrogance which did not entirely disappear even from his mature writing. The subsequent twenty years were devoted to the refinement of his exposition of the state personality theory and its corollary, the organ theory, and to the interpretation of the Japanese constitution on the basis of that theory.

For several years Minobe and Uesugi managed to keep on civil terms. But in 1912 the rivalry assumed the proportions of a bitter feud marked by an unpleasant exchange of charges and countercharges in which theoretical arguments were obscured by bitter personal references and in which other extra-academic influences played an important part. The outcome of the debate was in a sense inconclusive, but it established Minobe's position in the constitutional field. The authorities of the university and in the ministry of education dealt with this situation by creating, in 1920, a second chair of constitutional law at To-Dai, to which Minobe was appointed. Thus the dual approach to constitutional-law instruction initiated with Hozumi and Ichiki was perpetuated under Uesugi and Minobe. But now the balance turned against the orthodox school. Uesugi's death in 1929 left Minobe in unchallenged possession of the field at To-Dai until the official interdiction of his constitutional theory the year following his retirement in 1934.

The rising and falling fortunes of these two academicians reflect their identification with contending influences in the nation's political history. But the clash of personalities in the contest was so sharp and explicit that it tended to overshadow the broader significance of their rivalry. Uesugi, a tall and very handsome man, quite Europeanized in habits and dress, gifted with a colorful and moving style of speaking and writing, was self-consciously patriotic; he identified this quality with unquestioning devotion to the uniquely virtuous property of the Japanese state, its divinely ordained monarchy.[19] An equal, if not greater, element in his character was his belligerent loyalty to his patron, Hozumi.[20] Uesugi clearly shared his preceptor's alarm and resentment at the intrusion of the Ichiki-Minobe line of interpretation,[21] and after he took over Hozumi's chair in 1910 was undoubtedly resentful in his own right about what he considered to be Minobe's interloping in the constitutional field. Uesugi had fallen heir to an isolated position among his colleagues, and the expressions of righteous indignation in his writings were frequently tinged with a defensive tone. His position became doubly painful when Minobe's position was officially sanctioned by the creation of the second chair of constitutional law and the extension of Minobe's civil-service examination responsibilities to that field.[22] Minobe and others of Uesugi's colleagues regularly accepted concurrent or visiting teaching assignments in various public and private schools, but Uesugi's teaching outside of To-Dai was usually limited to the imperial military and naval academies where his constitutional theory was favored and perpetuated.[23]

Minobe had few of the graces of which Uesugi could boast. He was a short, frail man of homely visage, who spoke with rhythmic, colorless monotony. It is related that students referred to him as *bora* (mullet). He preferred native dress and food, and his only regular recreational indulgence was attendance at *sumō* wrestling contests.[24] He was aloof and inaccessible except to a favored few of his pupils (Uesugi enjoyed rather intimate relations with his students).[25] Minobe's one apparent personal advantage as a teacher lay in the clear, incisive style and the tight logical development that characterized all his writing. His texts are devoid of color and literary embellishment, probably not a great defect in the eyes of students preparing for examinations in which rote learning was a valuable asset.[26] Minobe was wont to accuse his opponents of being intolerant, as indeed it appears they were; but Minobe himself was not entirely innocent of that quality. His intellectual arrogance was most pronounced in the imputation that the orthodox school suffered from a benighted provincialism deriving from a willful or inherent incapacity for right thinking.

If Minobe was sensitive to the unreasonableness of his critics and intolerant of their lapses, he maintained a strict intellectual straightforwardness himself. His arguments always appealed to reason, never, like those of his opponents, making recourse to public authority or obscurantism. Looking back on the 1912 debate he wrote:

The burden of Uesugi's attack was that in using the state-organ concept to explain the position of the emperor I had denied Japan's national polity and had made of Japan a democratic state. To this day I have been unable to understand that attack. Such an attack by a gang of ignorant street ruffians would have been comprehensible, but Uesugi himself was a professor of law at the university and as such was well acquainted with the significance of the use of the state-organ concept in jurisprudence. Moreover, Uesugi had himself until recently employed this concept. . . . Thus I was left speechless when on this occasion he charged me as a treacherous rebel. Had it been an academic difference I would have welcomed the challenge. We had often engaged in academic quarrels on various points of law. But this was no mere academic quarrel; he had raised the great sword of national polity from on high. . . . I began to hear from influential quarters that there was a growing movement in the ministry of education to force me to resign my position. . . .[27]

Minobe's clash with Uesugi is not to be explained simply on the basis of

Minobe's European experience. Hozumi had studied at Strasbourg under Laband, Uesugi at Heidelberg under Jellinek. It is ironic that Minobe, who gained a reputation as a Jellinekian, had not studied under Jellinek, whereas Uesugi had even lived in the Jellinek home and as late as 1924 dedicated the second edition of his *Teikoku Kempō* jointly to Hozumi and Jellinek.[28]

The issues between Uesugi and Minobe may be summarized as follows:[29] Uesugi initiated the debate by attacking Minobe's *Kempō Kōwa*.[30] He charged that in asserting that the state is the corporate body of the whole people, possessed of a juristic personality which is the subject of governmental power, which is exercised by the emperor not in his own right but as an organ of the state, Minobe had violated the principles of national polity. This theory, according to Uesugi, was the product of the European movement from absolute monarchy to popular sovereignty—a juristic expression of the incipient republicanism in the monarchies of the west. The corporate, state-personality theory was equivalent to an assertion of popular sovereignty. This fact, he asserted, was well understood by its European proponents: "their attitude toward democracy is one of admiration; they say, 'even though there is a monarch our state is democratic,' and this gives them a certain sense of pleasure."

To say that the emperor exercised the powers of government as an organ (albeit the supreme organ) of the state was, in Uesugi's view, the same as saying that he was a servant of the people, or a functionary of the state. In either case it was subversive of Japan's eternal and incomparable national polity as expressed in Articles I and IV of the constitution.[31] Minobe, he said, in spite of frequent protests of unqualified loyalty to the imperial institution, could not, if he honestly followed the logic of his argument, deny that he had said that Japan was a state in which the people were sovereign (*minshu koku*).[32] He had, however, attempted to evade this embarrassing issue by perversely and irreverently equating national polity (*kokutai*) with form of government (*seitai*). Ignoring the distinction between these terms makes it impossible, said Uesugi, to avoid the conclusion that national polity underwent a change in 1889. National polity has to do with the location of sovereignty; in Japan, it is expressed in an imperial monarchy in which the principle of personal imperial rule (*shinsei*) was established for all time at the founding of the state. What was changed in 1889 was the form of government, which has to do with the structure through which sovereign power is exercised.[33] Uesugi cited the authority of Hozumi in support of his criticism of Minobe, and declined to surrender to the popularity of the heresy among his colleagues: "I cannot sacrifice my firm belief to purchase the respect of young scholars."[34]

Minobe accused Uesugi of intolerance and intemperance in his attitude toward any theories other than his own. He noted that the sole test of validity applied by Uesugi to any theory was the unscientific one of conformance with the spiritual purport of the Imperial Constitution—that is, to the orthodox definition of national polity. Minobe protested that the corporate theory of the state together with the theory of the state as a juristic personality and the corollary organ theory were widely subscribed to by western scholars, including the monarchists. These theories were necessary to understanding the legal nature of the state and had nothing to do with the issue between monarchy and republic.[35] It is when the state is seen as a corporate body that the unity of monarch and people in a common purpose is clearly expressed. It can be seen, then, that the monarch exercises sovereign powers on behalf of the whole people rather than in his own interests. Uesugi erred, said Minobe, when he said that the emperor under the organ theory was analogous to a servant or functionary; the proper analogue was the brain in the human body.[36] Hozumi and Uesugi insisted on such a strict definition of monarchy as to deny this form of government to any other country in the world. Minobe ridiculed this as well as Uesugi's argument that because Japan had an incomparable national polity its constitution was incomparable also.

The Conflict with Uesugi: Political Aspects

It has been said that "the special character of this quarrel lay in the fact that it fortuitously brought into sharp focus before the eyes of the general public the close connection between legal thought and political thought lurking deep within juristic concepts."[37] It seems clear that had there been no more to it than the rather threadbare academic theories the whole affair would hardly merit attention. But the 1912 debate was precipitated out of extra-academic considerations which were plainly stated in its literature. It is because of its relationship to the political changes commonly alluded to as the Taisho Political Change (*Taishō seihen*). This refers to a series of episodes beginning symbolically with the death of Meiji Tenno in July, 1912 and extending to the accession of the party cabinet of Kato Takaaki in June, 1924. It was a period of transition from a *genro*-dominated oligarchic government to party government. It witnessed the decline in the power of the Satcho clique, signaled early in the period by the ruinous rivalry between its last two great representatives, Yamagata Aritomo and his ambitious fellow Choshuman Katsura Taro, and in 1922 by the death of Yamagata. It was highlighted by the establishment of the anti-Satcho administrations of Okuma Shigenobu (1914–1916) and Hara Kei (1918–1921), and it came finally to the emergence of "normal constitutional government" (*kensei jodo*) with the Kato Cabinet. In the opening phase of the Taisho Political Change occurred the succession in office of Saionji Kimmochi, Ito's protégé and successor as head of the Seiyukai, by Katsura. In December of 1912 Yamagata and Katsura were sufficiently united in interest to collaborate in the wrecking of Saionji's cabinet and in securing Saionji's removal from the political arena by having him named *genrō*. It was against the background of the succession from the second Saionji Cabinet to the second Katsura Cabinet that the Uesugi-Minobe quarrel had significance.

As Uesugi said: the whole thing began with Minobe's lectures to the conference of middle-school teachers. To conceive of such theories and to expound them in the university seminars was one thing; to recite them before teachers whose task is popular education and to extend the audience by publishing the lectures was quite another.

Uesugi found it especially reprehensible that the ministry of education should have given these teachers the impression that Minobe's heresy was officially approved. He felt obliged to warn the teachers and the public at large of the error in Minobe's doctrine, and to this end published his attack in the popular journal, *Taiyō*, and in the newspaper, *Kokumin Shimbun*, as well as in the academic journals.[38] But his complaint was even more serious: he charged that the ministry of education had attempted to promote through Minobe a construction of the constitution favorable to antibureaucratic forces. Uesugi accused Minobe of improper intervention in a current political controversy over the issue of ministerial responsibility. He asserted that Minobe was a partisan of Saionji against Katsura,[39] and alluded bitterly to the abuse he sustained in the press for his relation to Hozumi and to the bureaucratic opposition to the pretensions of the diet to command the responsibility of ministers of state. Before his death, Hozumi himself had joined Uesugi in damning the hidden purpose of Minobe's theory, to wit, to bring about the annexation of legislative and administrative powers by the diet under the control of political parties. In *Kempō Teiyō* he wrote: "Since the promulgation there have been among party politicians, and among scholars who uncritically echo their opinions, those who interpret the constitution in the sense of an English-type parliamentary party cabinet system, an interpretation which ignores the text and the spirit of the constitution. This is the origin of the troublesome constitutional issue of ministerial responsibility. . . ."[40]

Minobe did not deny his opposition to the despotic construction of the Imperial Constitution fostered and, as he implied, invented by the bureaucrats. He believed that in 1889 Japan had become a constitutional monarchy in the same sense as had the monarchies of Europe earlier in the nineteenth century.[41] He declared it to be a political rather than a constitutional question whether political parties were essential to constitutionalism, but he denied that a political-party system was incompatible with the indigenous national polity. He objected particularly to making support of the imperial prerogative a party "plank," as Katsura had done, since this implied that other parties were disloyal and gave the false impression of a complete absence of limits on the prerogatives of the throne. Minobe accused Uesugi of flouting the imperial will, as manifested in the establishment of the constitution, when he denied to the diet its full place in the processes of government.[42]

Minobe states bluntly the political motivations behind his constitutional theory in the preface to *Kempō Kōwa*:

It seems that although some twenty years have passed since constitutional government was put into effect in Japan, there has been hardly any general dissemination of knowledge concerning constitutional government. We frequently note that even among scholar specialists writing on constitutional matters there is a continuing reliance on national polity by those who would deprive the people of their rights and demand their absolute submission, and who promote despotic government under the guise of constitutional government. As a student of constitutional law I have for many years deplored this condition. . . . Above all it will be my earnest endeavor, by means of a clarification of the fundamental spirit of the constitution, to eradicate the advocacy of disguised despotism which is current in some quarters.[43]

The antithetical political orientation of the two men is well illustrated by comparing this quotation with the following excerpt from Uesugi's *Kempō Jutsugi:*

Recently again the strength of the Powers, one against the other, is waxing, national self-consciousness is growing. All the Powers are practicing imperialism, and the time has come when not to advance means to retreat. If the state does not develop it will be destroyed. . . . I believe that the development of the Japanese people in the Meiji era was chiefly the result of this strong self-consciousness. I believe that we can say that the victories in the wars with China and Russia were possible because of the rise of a firm national spirit. Since the strong self-consciousness which we as a nation developed in these two great wars has been paralleled by a gradual intensification of the struggle between the Powers, it has now become a question of who is to advance and who is to retreat, we or they. The times require that we strengthen this self-consciousness, and that we inculcate and train up a firm national spirit. It is in this sense that I believe it is now extremely important that I should give to the people my knowledge concerning the constitution.[44]

In these two statements are expressed Minobe's and Uesugi's respective affiliations with the two unreconciled forces at work under the Meiji constitutional system.

Uesugi devoted himself to the cause of authoritarianism, at the head of which stood the elder statesmen of the Satcho bureaucracy. The strength of this camp was based on the mobilization and exploitation of the social and intellectual traditions and sentiments of a people long accustomed to the acceptance of authority and newly revisited with an intense national self-consciousness. The fundamental rationale of its leaders was the idea that Japan's struggle to establish her position as a modern state, *vis-à-vis* the Powers, required that the leaders of the civil and military bureaucracies hold firm and unhindered control of all the processes of government, and that to this end the independence of the imperial prerogative must be maintained against all extra-bureaucratic pressures.

It was to the liberal and potentially democratic forces, at the head of which stood the political parties and the leaders of the new capitalism, that Minobe's sympathies were drawn. The strength of this camp lay in the social and political aspirations of the swelling urban and village middle classes, products of the post-Restoration economic and technological revolution, to which were joined at critical moments the mass restlessness of a depressed peasant and laboring population. These were the heirs of the preconstitutional *jiyuminken* movement; these were the eager consumers of the inflowing political and social ideas of the west. At the heart of the guiding philosophy of this camp was the idea that the free operation of a governmental system based on political liberty was prerequisite to the emergence of a healthy modern state in Japan, and that to this end the policies of the government and the execution of those policies should be made accountable to the representative organ of the people. Hasegawa Masayasu points out that Minobe's constitutional theory reflected the spirit of the change in late Meiji and early Taisho from a landlord parliament to a bourgeois parliament and that it was the emphasis it placed upon the role of the parliament that made his theory "liberal."[45]

Neither man acknowledged partisan connections; by and large, neither's writings disclose to what extent he sympathized with particular programs and actions in the political arena. Yet the political significance of the dispute was great, deriving from the close relationship of the Imperial University to the state bureaucratic and educational systems. Nor can there be any doubt that Minobe was on the side of the anti-Satcho constitutionalists. His often repeated "constitutional government is party government" was borrowed directly from the language of Okuma Shigenobu's memorial of 1881. The Katsura-Saionji-Yamagata clash of 1911 was preparatory to Okuma's becoming premier (1914–1916) with a cabinet that included Minobe's patron Ichiki, first as minister of education and then as home minister. It was said that Minobe escaped dismissal after 1912 through the intercession of Okuma and Ichiki.[46]

In spite of serious qualifications not so apparent then as now, it appeared by 1920 that the line of constitutional interpretation put forth by Minobe had triumphed over the position of the orthodox school, for it had achieved nearly universal academic acceptance and substantial official sanction. However much this triumph was deserved from a strictly academic point of view, the great prestige which Minobe's position achieved was initially dependent on (and ultimately was limited by) the fortunes of political liberalism in Japan and the world generally. The academic isolation in which Uesugi found himself in 1912 deepened as the ideological props of the conservative tradition shattered in the collapse of the power-oriented ethos of Imperial Germany. Minobe, in contrast, enjoyed the support of nearly all his colleagues. The number of those in and out of academic and official circles who were sympathetic with his "democratic aims" increased steadily.[47] Uesugi could only say, "It is beyond my power to prevail over Minobe's strong argumentation in the debates, but I have faith in the correctness of my views." He continued to expound the orthodox interpretation at To-Dai and at the military academies, both as a teacher and as a publicist.[48] He and his supporters succeeded in dulling the edge of the liberal victory. The ministry of education, under pressure of criticism in the diet, canceled a commission to Minobe to prepare middle-school textbooks on legislation.[49] Uesugi's attack, moreover, left with the public a lasting impression that the state-personality-organ theory was in some way subversive of national polity, a suspicion which Minobe's opponents never permitted to die.[50]

The favorable response to Minobe's constitutional theory reflected its accommodation of the goal of the opposition to the elder-statesmen regime: the bringing into operation of a parliamentary cabinet system. In the words of a declaration issued by one of the diet groups at the time: "That which is most estimable in constitutional government is the strict clarification of cabinet responsibility, and the performance of imperial government on a broad popular basis."[51] The specific objectives of their program were: (1) abolition of the influence of the elder statesmen in government, especially in making and breaking cabinets;[52] (2) abolition of the privileged position of the military oligarchy—the independence of the service ministers from cabinet control on certain matters, and the power of the army and navy staffs to control the appointment and withdrawal of the service ministers;[53] (3) reform of the civil-service appointment ordinances to enlarge the range of political appointments; and (4) recruitment of popular talents to government service in order to break the bureaucratic monopoly of position in the government and in the parties themselves.[54]

The first dramatic step toward the establishment of party government as a constitutional convention was the organization of the First Constitution Defense Movement in December, 1912. This movement was organized by the parties of the diet to protest the fall of the second Saionji Cabinet. As president of the Seiyukai, Saionji enjoyed the confidence of an absolute majority in the house of representatives. His cabinet was destroyed when the army withdrew its minister in opposition to the cabinet's fiscal policies. The indignation of the parties was exacerbated when the elder statesmen, who had connived in the army's recalcitrance, designated Katsura as new premier in spite of his having recently "withdrawn from politics" to take the office of imperial household minister. To make matters worse, Katsura manipulated the issuance of an imperial command to Saionji to call off the Seiyukai opposition, to sever his connections with the party, and to serve the throne as an elder statesman. Katsura, whom Ozaki Yukio accused of "hiding behind the throne and shooting down political enemies with imperial decrees as bullets," resigned under fire within ninety days.[55]

Two complementary factors contributed to the political revolution which ensued. In the first place, the vigor and resourcefulness of the elder statesmen and of the bureaucratic oligarchy generally had declined. Yamagata and Katsura in 1912–1913 were limited in dealing with the diet to the same tactics which they had used since 1890: corruption, electoral coercion, and imperial pressure. By 1912 Katsura had come around, too late, to Ito's strategy of establishing a parliamentary party under his own leadership. The Satcho leadership was riven by internal rivalries.[56] On the other hand, the parties in the diet had found in the patronage of private capital a substitute for official favor, and had come to regard themselves as at least the equals of the military and the bureaucracy in the determination of government policy, a sentiment in which they were encouraged by manifestations of widespread popular support. Indeed, the Constitution Defense Movement of 1912–1913 was possible only because the parties were willing, if only partially and temporarily, to renounce their long habit of coöperation with and reliance on bureaucratic leadership, and because many elements of the public were ready to follow the lead of the parties.[57] In the wake of Katsura's failure, important objectives of the parties were attained. Notably, in 1914 the Yamagata ordinances of 1899–1900 were amended so that the posts of minister and vice-minister of war and navy were opened to officers on the reserve lists, the scope of free political appointment was extended, and the privy council was reduced in size.[58] But it would be an exaggeration to say that the convention of party government had been firmly fixed then, or, for that matter, even after the Second Constitution Defense Movement had brought in the Kato Cabinet in 1924. Within less than a decade, party leaders had once more been excluded from the premiership.

The period of constitutional change beginning in 1912 was attended by an intense but uncoördinated journalistic campaign aimed at the infusion of western democratic and social democratic doctrine into the Japanese political scene. The goal of the writers in this movement was the popularization of the nation's political processes. Establishment of universal suffrage was a major objective, as were the rejection of militarism, the organization of labor, and reform of the rural tenancy system. Royama Masamichi refers to this movement as "the dawn of the democratic movement in Japan, when Japan was awakening to recollections of the Liberty and Popular Rights Movement."[59]

Miyazawa, writing in 1948, said that the appeal of Minobe's writings in the period of World War I lay in their reflection of his "strong democratic faith." But Minobe seldom strayed into the realm of popular politics. There is little in his writing, even in his occasional contributions to the popular press, akin to the reformist elan of his colleague Yoshino Sakuzo, who began developing in the pages of the magazine *Chūō Kōron*, in 1916, his democratic theory which he called *mimponshugi*.[60] Royama says of Yoshino that he sought to give democratic validity to the structure and operations of the coercive power of the state and in so doing brought the concept of the state back to the broad plain of social phenomena represented by objective governmental relationships.[61] While Yoshino and others were casting about uncertainly in an effort to put some political substance on the bare bones of legal constitutionalism, the main lines of constitutional theory, of which Minobe had become a leading representative, continued solidly within the methodological and conceptual traditions of the science of state law.[62]

Academic, Bureaucratic, and Publishing Activities

In October, 1920, the second chair of constitutional law was created at To-Dai and Minobe was appointed to it.[63] He continued to serve concurrently as professor of constitutional law at the Tokyo University of Commerce and occasionally as visiting lecturer at Chuo University. In 1924 he was appointed head of the law department at To-Dai,[64] which position he held until his retirement. In 1924 he took leave from To-Dai to serve as chairman of the commission to set up the department of law and literature at Kyushu Imperial University.

In addition to his duties as an instructor and administrator and as a higher civil-service examiner, Minobe performed variously in connection with several organs of the government. In 1911 he was appointed councilor to the cabinet legislative bureau, of which Ichiki was then chief; he was reappointed in 1920. Also in 1911 he was appointed to advise a commission established by the house of representatives to study the problem of revision of the electoral law. In 1917 and 1920 he served on cabinet commissions dealing with review of general legislation, and in connection with these appointments he was raised to the first rank of the higher civil service (*kōtōkan ittō*). In 1922 he visited Europe as an official representative to an international academic meeting at Brussels. To his academic honors and titles were added occasional marks of imperial approbation more or less concomitant with his academic status. He was nominated to the Imperial Academy in 1911.[65] In January, 1932, he was called upon to deliver one of the New Year lectures at the Imperial Palace, in discharge of which assignment of honor he addressed the emperor and other members of the court on "Trends in the Constitutional Systems of the Various States of Europe and America in the Twentieth Century."[66] He was appointed to the house of peers in May, 1932, with the court rank of senior third rank of the second order of merit.[67]

Minobe's manifold academic and bureaucratic activities were superimposed on a full career of writing. His life seems to have been an unbroken series of races against publishers' deadlines. His writing extended to virtually every aspect of public law, divided in roughly equal parts between administrative and constitutional law. In form, his publications fell into three groups. His most substantial contributions were authoritative textbooks intended primarily for the use of his own students but in fact enjoying wide usage throughout the state higher education system. Related to these publications were a few technical monographs and a large number of technical articles in the professional journals. His writing was not limited, however, to such formal works as these. He found frequent opportunity to render his individual and at times highly provocative comments on public issues from the point of view of his constitutional or general public-law theory. This occasional writing conformed with his positivistic principles, which called for the observation and criticism of the actual operation of the laws.[68] It was also quite clearly a response to pressure from editors and publishers. Interest in his writing was not limited to legal and academic circles. From 1925 on, his contributions were sought by the editors of *Chūō Kōron*, *Kaizō*, and

Nihon Hyōron, liberal literary-political journals with wide circulation among the intelligentsia. His occasional writings were of sufficient public interest to lead his publishers from time to time to publish collections of them.

While still a student in Germany, Minobe translated Otto Mayer's *Deutsches Verwaltungsrecht*. This was the beginning of his work in the field of administrative law, which some Japanese legal experts consider to be the more important and durable part of his contribution to Japanese public law jurisprudence. His writing in administrative law is for the most part of a technical and provincial character only remotely related to the subject of this study. His best-known *Nihon Gyōsei Hō* (*Japanese Administrative Law*), first published in 1909, went through many revised editions and was still one of the two or three leading textbooks of its type down to the end of the imperial era. Matching it was a casebook of judicial precedents in public law, the last revision of which was made in 1934.

Between 1929 and 1944 Minobe published a half score of monographs on various problems of administrative procedure, election administration, corrupt practices, and the law of economic regulation. Of these, only the essay *Kōhō to Shihō* (*Public Law and Private Law*), published in 1935, is of interest here. Although he was considered to be a "liberal" among administrative-law specialists, he has also been assigned a large share of responsibility for the narrow and excessive legal positivism of administrative science in Japan.[69] That his theory of administrative law was not effective as a tool of criticism of actual administration is indicated by his having been permitted to continue to publish in that field even after his constitutional theory was proscribed.[70]

Minobe's earliest writing on questions of constitutional law stemmed directly from his studies in comparative legal history in Germany and often took the form of translations from German public law literature. Best known of his works of this sort was his translation of Georg Jellinek's *Die Erklärung der Menschen und Burgerrechte* (1895).[71] Between 1904 and 1909 he published in the journals other paraphrase (*shōshaku*) translations from Jellinek and Julius Hatschek.[72] His *Kempō oyobi Kempō Shi Kenkyū* (*Studies on the Constitution and Constitutional History*) consisted of fifteen previously published articles dealing chiefly with problems in European constitutional theory and history and including translations from Jellinek and others. In 1918 Minobe published a small book entitled *Beikoku Kempō no Yurai oyobi Tokushitsu* (*The Origins and Special Characteristics of the American Constitution*).[73] This was followed in 1922 by a work consisting simply of translations of the texts of various postwar European constitutions: *Ōshū Shokoku Sengo no Shin Kempō;* and in 1930 by a volume entitled *Gikai Seido Ron* (*On the Parliamentary System*), which he described as an uncritical general account of the parliamentary systems currently in operation in representative states of the world. And, finally, in 1934 there appeared his *Kempō to Seitō* (*Constitutions and Political Parties*), consisting of essays on the Weimar and Austrian constitutions. Included among these were translations of essays from Heinrich Triepel and Richard Thoma.

The impact of Minobe's studies in European constitutional theory and history on his thinking about the Japanese constitutional system was strong. In his earliest major attempt to produce a comprehensive treatise on Japanese constitutional law he failed to get beyond the background of European theory. This work, published originally in 1906 as *Nihon Kokuhō Gaku* (*Japanese State Law*), was intended to be the first of four volumes on the constitutional and administrative law of Japan. The plan did not materialize, and in 1921 the original work was revised and republished as the first of two volumes on the constitution, under the title *Nihon Kempō* (*The Constitution of Japan*). In this work he developed in detail his view of the nature of law, the corporate theory of the state, the state-personality theory, the nature of constitutions and constitutionalism, and the purpose and method of constitutional-law study. This project also failed of completion; the second volume never appeared. His next major publication, however, may be taken as a supplement to *Nihon Kempō*. This was his *Kempō Satsuyō* (*Essentials of the Constitution*), a topically organized, analytic exposition of the Japanese constitutional system, prefaced by a one-chapter condensation of *Nihon Kempō*. In contrast to *Nihon Kempō*, which was fully documented with references to European sources and conflicting Japanese opinion, *Kempō Satsuyō* is almost entirely devoid of such references. *Kempō Satsuyō* and *Nihon Kempō* are mature products of Minobe's application of general western constitutional theory to the Japanese constitutional system; together with his *Chikujō Kempō Seigi* (*Commentary on the Constitution Article by Article*—short title, *Kempō Seigi*), they will provide the principal sources for the analysis of his theory in the following chapter. *Kempō Seigi,* published in 1927, was in effect, as Minobe indicated in its preface, the third edition of *Kempō Kōwa* (1911). It is a weighty and pontifical work, rich in exegetical references. Minobe intended that it should be the successor to Prince Ito's *Teikoku Kempō Gikai.*

The rather arid fare afforded by these admirable but ponderous works was leavened by the unending flow of Minobe's contributions to the constitutional *Tagesliteratur* of the interwar period. Fortunately, a substantial portion of this literature has been pulled together from scattered original publication forms into four volumes which fairly well cover the period from 1915 to 1935.[74] These articles are important for an appreciation of Minobe's position in Japanese constitutional history: they show the modification and adjustment of his attitudes toward various critical constitutional issues under the pressure of a changing political and social climate, and they display some of the chief causes of his troubles with the political right wing.

III

Minobe's Constitutional Theory: Methodology and General Theory of Law and the State

Minobe's constitutional theory is expounded chiefly in his mature writing of the interwar years in the major volumes *Nihon Kempō, Kempō Satsuyō,* and *Kempō Seigi,*[1] and in a number of monographs and articles which develop and elaborate specific points more fully. Our interest focuses in this chapter on his method and basic notions of the nature of law and the state, and on his idea of the spirit and substance of constitutionalism. In the next chapter it shifts to his application of these ideas in interpretation of the imperial constitutional system.

Methodology

Minobe belonged to the interpretive-analytic school of state-law science in Japan.[2] His speculations on legal theory and his critique of constitutionalism and of the Japanese constitutional system were consonant with the state-science tradition at To-Dai. His approach to constitutional problems was distinct from and, for the most part, uncomprehending of that taken by political positivists such as Onazuka Kiheiji and Yoshino Sakuzo. Within the pale of state-law science, Minobe's methodology was strongly colored by the influence of Georg Jellinek, an influence which made for a moderated legal positivism with a strong liberal bias. His adherence to the unsynthetized dualism in the Jellinekian method led him to take a distinctive position among Japanese public-law authorities, at once antagonistic to the obscure and unscientific *kaminagara* (god-imminent) spirit of the orthodox Japanese school and to the influence of German legal conceptualism and legal monism. It also gave to his work an ambivalent quality; while he could not quite escape from, he would not escape into the world of "national polity." It closed to him the pursuit of the arid comforts of conceptual idealism and led him to a positivist-*cum*-intuitive construction of the Meiji constitutional system.

Minobe's rejection of particularistic views of Japanese constitutionalism, especially strong in his early writing, probably owed much to the influence of Jellinek's cosmopolitanism, as well as to Minobe's own studies in European comparative legal history. He retained throughout his life a lively appreciation of historical change in human institutions, but his horizons were fairly well fixed by his early and sympathetic perception of that tide of the times, "the march of constitutionalism," in Europe at the turn of the century.[3] The salutary liberal and democratic bent which corrupted Minobe's positivism and permeated his public-law theory seems to have been the product of an intuitive evaluation of the lessons of his studies in comparative legal history. He was in his own person a paragon of individualism. He believed deeply in and generally succeeded in living up to the principle of intellectual toleration, which was for him not only an article of personal faith but an essential factor in the theoretic defense of civil liberty as an element in constitutionalism. Rarely does his writing manifest less than complete confidence in his own intellectual soundness and sincerity; nor did he scorn to play the censor; but he seldom made arguments *ad hominem* and he always shunned extra-rational authority or sanction.

Minobe's methodology is manifest in the organization as well as the content of his writing, especially in his earlier works. Specific discussions of the methodological problem include notably those in *Nihon Kempō*, in the introduction to *Kempō Seigi*, and in his criticism of Kelsen. The key lies in his interpretation and application of Jellinekian principles, as displayed in Minobe's definition of the problems of public-law jurisprudence, particularly with regard to the sources of law, his categories of that jurisprudence, and his interpretive construction of the Meiji Constitution.

Minobe was reticent in explaining his methodology and rather uncritical in his approach to the methodological problem, and yet he was in this respect ahead of his contemporaries in the general field of constitutional theory in prewar Japan. Faint praise, perhaps, for as has recently been asserted, in all the constitutional literature of the past century in Japan very few works have come seriously to grips with the problem of method and the few exceptions have moved along very narrow and rather obscure lines.[4] Kuroda Ryoichi, a writer who has explored this—by Marxian critical standards—methodological wasteland, has discussed the difficulty of clearly distinguishing schools of Japanese constitutional interpretation and of assigning scholars to them. He explains this problem as arising from political conditions which discouraged the development of constitutional interpretation as a branch of social science, leading scholars, instead, to develop highly individualistic positions which ignore methodology or fail to give it thorough and positive explication.[5]

PREMISES AND LIMITATIONS

Investigation of Minobe's views of the problem of methodology best begins in his *Nihon Kempō*. This work is virtually an *Allgemeine Staatslehre*; it consists of a full exposition of the general theory of law and the state upon which his interpretation of the constitution was based. In a note at the end of the opening section of Part II, Chapter I ("The Nature of the State"), he refers directly to Jellinek in support of the distinction between the sociological and the juristic view of the state:

It is clearly necessary to distinguish between two ways of conceiving the state. One has as its object of consideration the state as a social phenomenon. It observes the actual objective and subjective phenomena which constitute the concrete life of the state, seeking to make clear the existence and influence of the state, internally and externally. The other has as its object of consideration the juristic aspect of the state. It does not observe real phenomena, it seeks rather to clarify *the relationship between law and real state phenomena*.[6]

In explanation, he wrote further that:

theoretic concepts are constructed for the sake of theoretic explanations. Since the several disciplines differ in their conceptual aspects, it is natural that there should be concepts peculiar to each. Jurisprudence itself has its own peculiar concepts. *The determination of a view of the state consistent with these juristic concepts is* essential for the study of law, and for an understanding of the relationship between law and the state.[7]

For Minobe, as for Jellinek, the distinction between the juristic and the social or political aspect of the state was a matter of analytic technique rather than an absolute. The distinction between the sociological and juristic views of the state is valid, as Minobe said, only as discrimination in method of conceptualization. It does not mean that the state has a dual existence; it is merely a matter of distinguishing between a total observation of the state and one of several particular observations—political, economic, anthropological, or geographic, as well as juristic.[8] For both, methodological discrimination was necessary as a means of defending positive juristic science against the corrupting influences of conceptual patterns which might be valid for sociological, political, or philosophical thinking, but which conduced irresolvable contradictions and erratic departures in juristic thinking. It served specifically to insulate the corporate theory of the state and the theory of state personality, essential elements in their idea of the *Rechtsstaat*, from attacks based on sociological and philosophical justifications of political absolutism. Minobe shared in Jellinek's purpose of basing the positive interpretation of state law on a general theory of state law universally valid in time, place, and political circumstance. His methodological commitment was instrumental to the aim of limiting state power by law.[9]

His appreciation of Jellinek's position made Minobe wary of what he called the "erroneous methods of conceptual jurisprudence."[10] Jellinek was numbered among the German positivists who led the revolt against "the ambiguous and murky natural rights tradition," and his so-called *Zwei-Seiten* formula was generally taken for an expression of the trend towards the one-sided conceptual jurisprudence which reached its peak in Laband and Anschütz.[11] Nevertheless, the tenor of his *Allgemeine Staatslehre* is essentially hostile to a narrow refinement of juristic methodology. Minobe's statement of the purpose of the juristic method as clarification of the relationship between law and the objective and subjective phenomena constituting the concrete life of the state was true to the spirit of the *Allgemeine Staatslehre*. He insisted that "every juristic concept must have its basis in real phenomena, for concepts not based on reality are pure fancy or fiction."[12]

In compliance with this requirement Minobe devoted the first 174 pages of *Nihon Kempō* to a discussion of the real (i.e., the social and social psychological) nature of law and the state. His ideas of law and state, here and elsewhere, are tenuously anchored to "reality" in the form of "society." But this society comprised a shadowy substance imperfectly displayed in his recognition of the existence of society apart from the state, in his reliance on social psychology in the definition of law, and in his inclusion of the "rational conscience of society" among the sources of law. It can hardly be said that he came to grips with the problem of synthesis between sociological and juristic concepts. The sociology upon which he founded his jurisprudence was itself a purely conceptual system, unconcerned with empirical investigation. He seldom speculated in terms of social dynamics or social statistics. Neither the individual nor the social corporation seemed to have meaning for him except as integers in legal theorems. He could attack Kelsen for failure to recognize the nature of law as "social reality" and the nature of jurisprudence as a *social* science, but he himself failed to grasp the reality of the social phenomena underlying constitutional systems.[13]

THE ROLE OF HISTORICAL DATA

Minobe did not always observe the strictures of the analytic-interpretive methodology which governed his formal constitutional commentaries. In magazine and newspaper articles he argued often from an analysis and evaluation of political factors relating to constitutional problems. In doing so he pursued his constitutional philosophy beyond the horizons fixed by positive law, moving into the realm of current political controversy with characteristic individuality of view.

It was primarily through reference to the history of the evolution of various legal institutions of political society that Minobe sought to bring objective social validity to his interpretation of state law. He was not himself an historian, nor did he pretend to be one. As a student in Germany, however, he had gained an acquaintance with western legal and political historiography, concentrating on problems of constitutional and general public-law history. In Jellinek he found the rationale of his use of historical data in the interpretation of law. Thus, his attention to institutional history rather than to systems of thought has been traced to Jellinek's complaint that "the history of politics today is still too much the history of theories, and not enough the history of institutions themselves."[14]

Historical data had two distinct roles in Minobe's work. It appeared throughout his constitutional commentaries in the form of references to the legislative history of particular legal texts; in this use he was concerned chiefly, though not exclusively, with Japanese post-Restoration legal history. Historical study also oriented and limited Minobe's interpretation of the law. On the one hand, it imparted a conservative quality to his view of the Japanese Constitution. This was reflected in his acceptance of the carry-over of pre-Restoration customary law and political tradition in his interpretation of the nature of the monarchy and of the content of the imperial prerogative. It led him to ascribe to the constitution what Suzuki Yasuzo has called "a kind of immutability and supra-historicity."[15] On the other hand, the liberal convictions which weighted his interpretation of Japanese public law were molded by, and had their footing in, his understanding of western constitutional history—he was one of those who were denounced by Hozumi for having sought in the constitution, not Japan's unique national polity, but "the historical fruits of the west."[16]

The complex of ideas which Minobe embraced in his notion of constitutionalism can be traced back to his writing in the period 1903–1910, when he was engaged in serving up to his students and to the wider audience of the law journals a translation into Japanese of his lessons in western constitutional history. The crowded record of publication in this vein was capped by his *Kempō oyobi Kempō Shi Kenkyū* in 1910.[17] In the subsequent years his academic tasks centered immediately on problems of Japanese public law and there was no opportunity, and perhaps no inclination, to pursue the comparative historical approach farther.[18] These circumstances had important consequences for Minobe's constitutional theory. His view of European constitutional history and theory emerged from study of the conclusions of European legal and historical scholarship of the closing years of the nineteenth century and the early years of the twentieth. It derived, moreover, from a view of these matters conditioned by the attitudes of his German teachers. He did not seriously carry his comparative historical studies beyond this point. From what was, to begin with, a dated, rather provincial, and largely unassimilated construction of comparative legal and political history he arrived, by reduction and refinement, at a residue consisting of an essential definition of constitutional government.[19] *Nihon Kempō* spelled out the fruits of his European studies at length, with reference to specific historical developments concerning constitutions and constitutionalism; in *Kempō Satsuyō* his presentation of these views was scattered and in very generalized terms; and in *Kempō Seigi* they vanished save for a vestigial definition of constitutionalism in the introduction (pp. 15–22), containing the essence of his liberal faith and expressing the philosophy that guided his interpretation at every critical point of constitutional construction.

OPPOSITION TO NORMATIVE-LOGICAL APPROACH

Minobe's faithfulness to the moderate positivism of Jellinek brought him into conflict with the doctrines of Hans Kelsen as the latter's influence extended to Japanese academic legal circles after 1925.[20] His attack on Kelsen focused on the problem of method and thus provides insight concerning Minobe's own methodology. In his view the special character of the *reine Rechtslehre* of the New Vienna School lay in its assertion that jurisprudence is a purely normative science, in contrast to the causal sciences having to do with the physical world. As a consequence it was concerned exclusively with *sollen* and not at all with *sein*, and scorned all natural causal relationships known to psychology, sociology, and political science.

Minobe countered that "the nature of law is *sein*, and not *sollen*; it is *soziale Wirklichkeit*. Its method, consequently, is not logic but observation of social reality. Law, though constant in its nature, is a variable in content, containing elements other than commands. In law there is *Ermächtigung* as well as *Beschränkung*." Thus he asserted against Kelsen the Jellinekian thesis as he understood it. Like Jellinek, he would relegate the problem of *sollen* to political science, leaving jurisprudence to deal with *sein*, thus making of it a *Kausalwissenschaft*, a "lawyer science."[21] Minobe found Kelsen in grave error when, having defined the nature of law in Austinian terms as a *heteronome Soll-norm* produced by an act of legislation, he declared all questions concerning how law can arise from a legislative act to be outside the scope of jurisprudence. To say, as Kelsen does, that "why" is not a juristic question, to find that the source of law is not in psychology and sociology but in the axioms of normative thinking, in short, to put the question of the nature of law outside the province of jurisprudence is juristically self-destructive. "When we speak of the value of law, we mean its validity as law. *Geltung* is the heart of the question."[22] The content of law (*sollen* and *können*) is determined by "deliberate acts of human beings in society" but the validity of law depends on the recognition in the "general mind of society" (*shakai no ippanteki shinri*) that contrary action is not permissible.[23] All rules of society are valid because of their power over human minds; this social force is not a matter of *sollen* but *sein*. Since jurisprudence is a social science concerned with the observation of facts actually at work in society, it is wrong to treat it, as Kelsen does, as a *Methodenlehre* (that is, as a method by which value judgments concerning actual facts are made by reference to ideal rules). Jurisprudence is comparable to ethics and grammar rather than to logic and mathematics.[24]

THE INTERPRETIVE METHOD

Minobe's positivism was modified, if not compromised, by his insistence that interpretive construction of the law be kept in harmony with the "realities of social existence." His reliance on the idea of the conceptual autonomy of jurisprudence was clearest in his defense of the state personality-state sovereignty theory. The theoretical qualification of his positivism, arising from his steadfast adherence to the Jellinekian methodology, was transformed in his interpretive works on the Imperial Constitution into a substantial departure from the principles of legal positivism. This is true of *Kempō Satsuyō*, and even more so of *Kempō Seigi*, his *opus magnum* on the Meiji Constitution. The "positivistic discourse" of the latter work overlies an interpretation which consistently goes behind and between the established laws to refer to historical fact and constitutional theory. In its preface he said of his method that it "consists of an effort to make a critical analysis of the laws, especially to establish their true constitutional character, and, when the language of the law is very terse, to go beyond mere exposition of the text, supplementing the text with historical comment and theoretical principles, in the belief that the significance of the historical and theoretical bases of the law is equal to that of the language of the law."[25]

The interpretive method employed in *Kempō Seigi* was foreshadowed by the rules laid down in the section on "Methods in Constitutional Law" in the final chapter of *Nihon Kempō*, where he set forth as the objects of the science of constitutional law (1) to discover what is the actual constitutional law of the state, and (2) to explain that law systematically. The method appropriate to these purposes was the same as that for legal science generally. A method which seeks to determine what the law is by investigating the sources of law, including not only the expressions of the will recognized socially to be authoritative, but also social facts (convention and usage in all aspects of social life), the sense of social justice, and reason. It is only in explaining the law, not in discovering it, that juristic concepts and fictions are necessary and valid tools.[26]

But the juristic method commonly observed by Japanese public-law scholars, under the influence of Laband, was inadequate to the task:

There can be no doubt that the science of constitutional law differs from political science and its methods; nor that it is concerned with the established law of a particular state; but it greatly mistakes the nature of law and narrows the scope of the task of jurisprudence to make the logical construction of concepts the principal task of constitutional science. . . . Such methods are useful only for the explanation of law, and while it is no doubt one of the tasks of the science of constitutional law and of legal science generally to bring individual laws under such general concepts by logical processes, this is by no means the whole task . . . an even more important task is the discovery of what is the law. And the so-called juristic method of German constitutional law scholars (and of Japanese scholars even more so) has been quite inadequate for this task, and they have fallen far short of a true picture of the constitution. . . .[27]

There are textual gaps in constitutional law, and there is a wide gap between the general abstract rules of the constitution and the particular concrete rules which give them the force of law. Moreover, constitutional law is unstable in spite of its apparent rigidity. It tends to suffer essential change through legislative, administrative, and judicial construction. For

the existing constitution is the product of historical development. It is, moreover, ceaselessly changing through the effects of laws and ordinances apart from the actual constitutional text, as well as through the [actions of the] government and the parliament, the operations of which are greatly influenced by various political forces. Furthermore, since constitutional government has, to a degree, emerged as a modern universal system, its existence in any particular state is inevitably influenced by its existence in other states. Consequently, in order to discover the existing constitution, it is never enough merely to study the text of the constitution; it is essential to study the laws and ordinances which supplement and modify the constitution, to trace out the history, to investigate the precedents established by the government and the parliament, to consider the actual forces which effect the operation of the constitution, and finally to seek out the general principles of constitutional government by a comparison of the constitutions of other states.[28]

From the beginning, in departing from narrow legal positivism, Minobe was not merely satisfying the dictates of Jellinekian doctrine; consciously or not, he was building theoretical supports for a construction of the imperial constitutional system which a purely positive analysis of the law of the Japanese state would not permit. The methodological conflict between himself and those he accused of conceptual realism was the post-1920 successor of the earlier quarrel between his own positivism and the obscure doctrines of the *kaminagara* tradition. Like that earlier quarrel, it was essentially not a quarrel over method but between conflicting political values to be read into the laws, with the difference, however, that many of those who rejected Minobe's interpretation were not necessarily opposed to his political values. Thus Sasaki Soichi was at odds with Minobe not because he (Sasaki) was hostile to constitutionalism but because he could find little support for constitutional parliamentary democracy in a logical-positivistic reading of the Imperial Constitution. Sasaki and his followers, Tabata Shinobu and Oishi Yoshio, have insisted that subjectivity in interpretation sacrifices science to value, policy, and even theology. They point out that fascism could be read into the Meiji Constitution. Miyazawa has said that Minobe, Hozumi, and Uesugi all interpreted the constitution not as it was but as they wanted it to be. Whereas Sasaki claimed to interpret the constitution only as it was, Minobe took a positivistic approach modified by a frankly teleological method after the manner of the German, Heinrich Triepel.[29]

The clearest statement of Minobe's position on the methodological aspect of this conflict is to be found in the preface to the fifth (1931) edition of *Kempō Satsuyō*, where he puts his argument in terms sharpened by his recent engagement with the Kelsenians. There he stated that he was

opposed to attaching absolute value to the text of established laws, and to the idea that existing state law is identical with what is indicated by the texts of established laws. . . . Since the value of established laws as a source of law is relatively limited, the source of state law must be understood to consist also and equally of historical facts and the rational consciousness of society. . . . Since the value of logic in jurisprudence is limited, the principal task of legal scholars is rather to decide what is fitting in terms of social justice (*shakaiteki seigi*) and social advantage (*shakaiteki* ri-eki) . . . In deciding what is the law, it is extremely important that consideration be given to what is right and beneficial, and in this logic can be little more than an aid.[30]

So long as Minobe, in searching for the source of law, insisted on the necessity of looking to the history of particular laws and of comprehending the political factors influencing their origins and applications, as well as their various constructions in legislative and administrative action, the difference between himself and the strict positivists was largely a matter of degree. Indeed, adherence to a formula recognizing social causation as a condition of law, and giving due weight to all substantial factors, political and psychological, which determine the real content of law, would seem to be more faithful to positivistic principles than was the methodological narrowness or one-sidedness of the *Begriffsrealismus* or the *reine Rechtslehre*. Miyazawa says of his former teacher that he "belonged to the positivist school, properly speaking,"[31] and Ukai describes Minobe as "a positivist in the highest sense, combining a grasp of historical trends with real scientific analysis."[32] On the other hand, it would be difficult to reconcile with any definition of positivism Minobe's emphasis on "the rational consciousness of society," on "the sense of social justice" or "propriety," and on the sense of "social advantage" as sources of law. It has in fact been suggested that Minobe's reference to these factors is an admission of natural law principles. And Minobe himself acknowledged as much in the fifth edition of *Kempō Satsuyō*, saying:

it would be a very great error to say that facts have immediate force of law; for that would be to forget that, alongside facts, reason is an important element in the construction of positive law. Now this "reason" means that which is recognized to be legally necessary in accordance with the requirements of social justice and of social advantage in society at a certain time. It is not the eternally immutable truth asserted by the old natural law theorists; it is something that changes with the times—it is that which has, in the social consciousness, a natural force of law without the determination of the legislator, or without the force of facts. In this sense we can say that it is a kind of natural law.[33]

It is not surprising that Minobe should arrive at this position after starting from a definition of law as "a rule of will in social life which is

recognized in the social mind as being for human advantage and therefore inviolable."[34] He listed among the sources of law the law of reason
(*rihō;* that is, law based on the strength of reason), which he equated
with "the sense of social justice" or "right reason" (*jōri*). Reason as a
source of law has supplementary validity, he said, when judges, administrators, or scholars have recourse to it in cases in which established law
and customary law are silent. But it has also an original validity, for while
the state may make and enforce a law contrary to social justice, such law
is "bad law" (*akuhō*) and lacks a firm basis.[35] In dealing with this problem in *Kempō Satsuyō* he said:

Law of reason has of itself the force of law based on human rationality (*jinrui
no suirishin*) independently of the determinations of the legislator or of
custom. Just as existing facts have the power to sway the human mind, so
the human sentiment of justice, the consciousness of justice, reasoning from
the nature of things, the spirit upon which all modern law is based, the
necessary conditions of social life, in short, *all those things which are thought
to be necessary in modern law,* have the power to sway the human mind in
society, and consequently constitute a source of law independent of legislation
and customary law.[36]

Minobe believed human rationality to be an indirect source of law, that
it has a generative power manifested, under healthy social conditions, in
legislation's being based on reason. It is also a direct source of law, he
said, when it becomes the basis of legal disposition in the absence of
legislation or customary law, and when it supplies the standard for correct interpretation of legislation. This is true

especially in cases in which after enactment of legislation there are changes
in social conditions, or in the basic spirit of general state law, or when the
social sense of justice advances, even though there has been no corresponding
change in the language of the law, still it is proper that the interpretation
of the law should change, and it is then that law of reason acquires a validity
on a par with legislation. . . . Characteristically law of reason is even less
clear than is legislation and customary law, and its discovery is an important
duty of legal science. The chief means of its discovery are: analogy, calculations of social justice and social advantage, the history of Japan from ancient
times, comparison of foreign constitutions, and so on. *Especially indispensable
to an understanding of the authentic spirit of modern constitutionalism is a
comparison of foreign constitutions.*[37]

In terms of methodology, then, it was through the portals of "right reason" that Minobe's faith in the principles of constitutionalism, gained from his studies in European constitutional history and law, were brought into his interpretation of the Imperial Constitution. It would appear from his emphatic reassertion in 1931 of the role of the rational consciousness of society as a source of law that he had lost no confidence in the objective historical and social validity of his constitutional theory.

In the narrower, technical sense, Minobe's method impresses readers for its thorough and systematic comprehension of every legal aspect of whatever problem he confronted. This quality was manifested equally in his compendious works on the constitution and in his microscopic attacks on particular isolated problems. He took all public law as his province; there were very few aspects of it which he scorned to parse out to their ultimate components. His format was highly systematized, giving an appearance of close logic, accented by a terse, lucid style. This appearance was somewhat deceiving, for the blueprint to which he ordered the body of constitutional and administrative law reflected his own peculiar orientation, his will to find in that body of law a harmony with constitutional principles as he understood them. One of his eulogists has cut through the contradiction to make this somewhat atypical characterization:

Minobe's special quality was in his extremely sagacious intuition and his very salutary common sense, qualities which did not fail him to the end. He had this characteristic almost as a matter of natural disposition. . . . Before his faculties every complex rule and every law of insuperable legal technicality was appropriately and authoritatively analyzed and put in order without the least trace of difficulty. The word for Minobe is "intelligent." He did not care for philosophical thinking; he seemed rather to think that all could be comprehended by intuition without any necessity of a logical basis. . . .[38]

Theory of Law and the State

Because Minobe's interpretation of the Meiji Constitution depends so critically upon his general theory of law and the state and upon his theory of constitutionalism, a resumé of this general theory provides an illuminating introduction to his constitutional commentary. The significance of this general theory is heightened because professional and political criticism of Minobe's interpretive position was commonly aimed at these theoretical roots. His notion of constitutionalism derived logically from the idea of autolimitation applied to state sovereignty, which in turn rested upon the corporate theory of the state and ultimately on the nature of law as a social phenomenon. In tracing out the essential elements of his foundation work, this section will take up in order: the nature of law and the state, including the corporate theory of the state; the state as a juristic personality, including the nature of state sovereignty and the theory of state organs; constitutionalism and constitutions.[39]

THE NATURE OF LAW AND THE STATE

The purpose of Minobe's lengthy discussion of the nature of law and of the state (the first two hundred pages of *Nihon Kempō*) was to establish the definition of the state as a corporate entity, possessed of legal personality and thus of a capacity for rights and duties, and distinguished from other such legal personalities by its possession of governmental power or sovereignty. The state thus defined was the basis of his idea of the *Rechtsstaat* and of constitutional government. In the development of this definition he adhered to his methodological dictum of clarifying the relationship between law and real state phenomena. The zone of conjunction between law and state is the province of state law (*kokuhō*) or public law (*kōhō*), of which constitutional law (*kempō*) is one, and, in a sense, the superior part.[40]

Fundamentally, "laws are the inviolable rules pertaining to the relations between human wills in society." They are distinguished from other rules, such as moral admonitions, by virtue of their inviolability. Social life is a necessary condition of law, which has its basis in human psychology: awareness of the necessity of submission to fixed authority, inclination to conventional behavior, and sense of justice or righteousness. It is a characteristic of all law that its object is some human purpose, but the purpose of law is not necessarily social utility;[41] it may be, rather, the satisfaction of human emotions (*wertgefuhl*) of religious, aesthetic, or moral character. Thus Minobe arrived at his definition of law as "a rule of will in social life, which is recognized in the social mind as being for human advantage and therefore inviolable."[42]

In explaining or expounding the law the legal scientist finds it convenient to make use of legal concepts and legal fictions.[43] There are, in particular, six concepts basic to any exposition of the law: (1) Legal will (*hōritsu ishi, juristische Wille*): will evidenced in those external acts recognized by society as manifesting purpose involving a particular advantage (to the individual, corporation, or society) as its object, and to which a certain force is imputed by law. (2) Corporate or organic will (*dantai ishi* or *kikan ishi*): that will ascribed to an organized human collectivity (corporation) with respect to its own peculiar objectives. The will of the corporation is the will of its organs, and the will of the organs is the will of the persons who constitute the organs. Although the will of the corporation is the natural will of a natural person, the objectives of that natural will are the objectives, not of the natural person, but of the corporation: "This is by no means a legal fiction; it is a universal view of social existence. Nor is it peculiar to modern culture; it has always been so from ancient times."[44] (3) Representative and proxy relationship (*daihyō* and *dairi*): when the purposeful acts of a person are directed to the ends of another person (e.g., the corporation), then the former person stands in a relation of agent or proxy to a principal. Such a relation may exist not only between individuals, but between an organ and an organ, and between a corporation and its organs, and it may exist by law or by delegation.[45] (4) Advantage or benefit (*ri-eki*): all those things which fulfill human aspiration. Advantage (individual, corporate, or social) stands at the heart of all legal phenomena, as the complement of the concept of will. (5) Rights and duties (*kenri* and *gimu*): the power in an individual or corporation, recognized by law, to pursue by its own will its own objectives is a right. A limitation placed by law on one will for the sake of another's benefit is a duty. (6) Legal personality (*hōritsujō no jinkaku sha*, commonly contracted to *hōjin*): a volitional, acting entity which is recognized by law to be the subject of its own will and interests. Such an entity is said to have a capacity for rights, that is, to have the will to pursue its own ends; it may be a corporation as well as a natural person.[46]

Having defined law in social psychological terms, prescribed the task of legal science, and described the chief conceptual categories of that science, Minobe proceeded to a definition of the state. His discussion dwelt at first, and at considerable length, upon the "essential" character of the state, by which he meant the state as a social phenomenon. He was concerned with the state, not in its every aspect, but only to the extent necessary to provide the basis for its subsequent definition as a juristic phenomenon. On the authority of Jellinek, he disclaimed interest in the philosophical significance of the state. He likewise rejected the empirical approach to the problem: the state cannot be understood on a purely objective basis; it must, for his purposes, be defined as an intellectual phenomenon. He was concerned with the typical, not the exception; with the universal, not the particular phenomena of the state.[47]

Of the various theories concerning the state, Minobe believed that the corporate theory (*Gemeinwesen-oder Verbandstheorie*), which takes the state to be a governmental corporation (*tōchi dantai*),[48] most clearly explains the nature of the state as it must be viewed by a constitutional jurist. The power theory, the ethical theory, and the energy theory of the state he rejected outright. He acknowledged some validity in the organic theory but found that it resulted in semantic difficulties without serving any better purpose than did the corporate theory.[49] "This view of the state as a human corporation possessing governmental power is not only the common theory today, it is the only proper way to think of the state. . . ." Minobe's exposition of the corporate theory, and of various propositions that follow from it, may be summed up in the following way.

A corporation is an organized collectivity of persons having a common aim and possessing its own ends and its own vitality. To define the state as a corporation is to attribute to it a number of characteristics common to all corporations: (1) The state has its own ends, different from but not unrelated to ends of its constituents, and its own vitality or life. (2) The state has a will, for ends are understandable only as the ends of a will. Some authorities have denied that the state has a will of its own; others have recognized that the state has a will, but only as a legal fiction. "But the fact that the state has a will is not at all a mere legal concept; it is recognized as a social phenomenon. . . . All that the law determines is who, as an organ (*kikan*) of the state, occupies the position of making the will of the state, and also how that will is made." As Jellinek said, that the resulting will is the state's will is a matter of *Denknotwendigkeit*; it is not fiction. (3) The state is a unity. This unity transcends the superficial characteristics of temporal continuity and territorial integrity; it transcends the unity of will, which is, in any case, illusory. In order to discern the true basis of state unity one must look to the awareness of spiritual union (*seishinjō no renraku*) that exists among the people, for this is something that survives time and revolution. When the Japanese people boast of the excellence of their national polity, they only are emphasizing their pride in the superiority of their corporate self-consciousness.[50] (4) It follows from the corporate theory that, in the case of a monarchy, the monarch, as well as his subjects, is contained within the state. Hence Hozumi erred in saying that the emperor is the state,[51] for that would mean that the emperor is a corporation; he erred also in saying that the emperor is the external subject of the state.[52]

The state has, however, special characteristics that distinguish it from corporations generally. Unlike social corporations, it is a corporation not only of persons, but of territory. It has, moreover, a governmental organization (*tōchi soshiki*)—its most important distinguishing property—an organization possessing an unconditional power to bind the wills of its constituent members. The term by which this power is known is *tōchiken* (governmental power). It is not naked power, but legally recognized power resting on the general concurrence of society in its authority and in the necessity of submitting to it. Nor is it exclusively a property of the state, since political subdivisions possess it. But the state is the supreme governmental corporation. It is free from any control from above, and it is in this sense that the state is said to possess sovereignty (*shuken*, *Hoheitsgewalt*). The state, then, is "a supreme territorial, governmental corporation."[53]

According to Minobe the necessity of the state's existence arises from the fact that coöperative living (*kyōdō seikatsu*), a condition of all human life, spiritual and material, is possible only within the condition of order which prevails under the state. But the state does not exist merely as a manifestation of power applied to man's social nature. The element of "law consciousness" (*hōteki ishiki*) is a necessary condition of the state's existence. It is only when the actual controlling power is accepted in the social mind as legal power that the state can be said to exist. At the base of this social recognition of the legality of governmental power is "national psychology" (*kokumin shinri*), a product of the social nature of men, fostered and supported by racial self-consciousness, historical tradition, and religious faith.[54]

None of the theories concerning the purpose of the state can be taken to be universally valid. The purpose of the state changes with time and the level of culture. In European thought it has ranged from that of the severely restricted state of Smith and Locke to that of the total welfare state of Christian Wolff. On the basis of "concrete examples," Minobe concluded that the modern state has three primary purposes or duties: self-preservation, internal security, and the administration of justice. He spoke also of a fourth and supplementary purpose: the advancement of the cultural level of society. In matters of the mind and spirit, the state has only the negative function of maintaining the individual's opportunity to develop; in respect to material culture, the state may interfere with individual enterprise only when the interests of the whole society require it. In *Kempō Satsuyō* he added a fifth purpose: maintaining world peace and contributing to world culture.

Minobe's digression on the purposes of the state and the conditions of its existence did not contribute positively to the progression from his definition of the state as a corporation to his discussion of the juristic concept of the state. It did strike a relevant blow in favor of a pragmatic and relativistic view of the state's purpose. Most interestingly, it provided opportunity for noting his reservation concerning the *laissez-faire* connotations of the *Rechtsstaat*, the realization of the Kantian community of freedom under law. He suggested to his students that the socialist critique had produced a change, not a retreat to the *Polizeistaat*, but an advance to a new idea of the *Kulturstaat* (*bunka koku*) in which the state has the purpose of promoting the culture of the whole society.[55]

THE JURISTIC CONCEPT OF THE STATE

When Minobe had dogmatically defined the legal categories of rights and personality and had rendered his exposition on the character of the state as a sociological phenomenon, he proceeded to discuss the juristic implications of these propositions. In this discussion, his theoretical discourse moved farther into the arena of constitutional controversy.

Juristically speaking, persons are thought of as being the subjects of rights and duties. In jurisprudence, personality means nothing more than the capacity for rights. Most juristic authorities of the day, said Minobe, subscribed to the state-personality theory (*kokka hōjin setsu*), according to which the state is the subject of the right of government, and this, he asserted, was the only correct view of the state. Accordingly, he could see no merit in the position held by some authorities that the right of government (*tōchiken*) belongs to the ruler and that the state is the object of that right. Those who advanced this *Herrschertheorie* (*tōchisha setsu*) liked to quote Article I of the Imperial Constitution: "The emperor . . . rules the empire of Japan." But the object of the emperor's rule in that case was the Japanese state in its territorial sense, not that state as a vital corporation: "The constitution provides only that governmental authority issues from the emperor. Whether that authority, juristically conceived, belongs to the emperor as a right is not a constitutional question. To seek scientific concepts of the true nature of the state from the text of the constitution is to misunderstand the constitution." If the governmental power is the emperor's in his own right, then it is his to use to his personal advantage, and no one claims that the emperor rules to his personal advantage.[56]

The state-personality theory was not an entirely new idea, even in Japanese thought, but the body of doctrine concerning it came to Japan from Europe.[57] In its current form, it stemmed from the state-law studies of nineteenth-century Germany, where it had developed out of the recognition of the corporate nature of the state. As for Hozumi's denunciation of it as a "hateful deceit," Minobe pointed to Hozumi's own description of the state as an ethnic corporation (*minzoku dantai*).[58] Hozumi complained that "democratic revolutionary thought has tacitly and cunningly joined with [the state-personality] theory and under the false designation of state sovereignty is secretly attempting to undermine the basis of our national polity."[59] To this Minobe rejoined that "those who reject the state-personality theory are inevitably reduced to viewing the state as a governmental relationship with the ruler and the ruled confronting one another. This not only flies in the face of state unity, it admits the validity of the socialist and anarchist claims that the state is a coercive instrument of the strong over the weak."[60] Against the many criticisms of the state-personality theory on the ground that it lacked empirical validity, he reiterated his defense of the theory as the juristic expression of the fact that, as a matter of actual social phenomena, the state has its own ends and the will to pursue those ends.[61]

There remained several conceptual and terminological ambiguities which obstructed clear understanding of the state as a juristic personality and the peculiar rights that attach to it. Minobe devoted the third chapter of *Nihon Kempō* to the resolution of these problems.[62] That quality of the state by which it is said to have a capacity for rights he called *kokken* (*Staatsgewalt*). *Kokken* is the willpower (*ishiryoku*) of the state; it has no fixed content. It has three characteristics: (1) Supremacy—it is autonomous (*jishuteki, selbstherrlich*) within the circumstantial and legal conditions of its existence, it is independent (*dokuritsuteki, unabhängig*) in respect to other states, and it is paramount (*saikōteki, höchst*) internally. (2) Indivisibility—from which it follows that the state cannot at one time have two conflicting wills, and that the organs which determine its supreme will must be so constituted as to guarantee unity.[63] (3) Perpetuity—not absolute perpetuity, but a duration that is not teleologically or organically predetermined but continues until some sufficient cause of extinction (revolution, partition, and the like) arises.

The peculiar substantive right of the state is known as *tōchiken* (*Regierungsgewalt, Herrschergewalt*, governmental power or authority), the minimum content of which is the absolute right of self-organization and of territorial and personal supremacy, and the right to take all measures necessary to attain the ends of the state. Properly defined, it is the right to rule; thus it is distinct from other rights such as that of property. It is a multiplicity of specific rights, particular and positive in content, varying from state to state and from time to time. Those who have held it to be indivisible have confused it with *kokken*. The objects of *tōchiken* are people and territory, which are obviously divisible and transferable. *Tōchiken* is unconditional in the sense that its objects are bound by it regardless of individual volition. It is an original right based on the state's own will; it is valid in, and subject to the limitations imposed by, state law and international law. In short, *tōchiken* is that "monopolistic right of the state, within the limits of state and international law, to determine its own organization, and to control all persons and things within its territory and its own nationals abroad."[64]

An important corollary of the state-personality theory is the theory of state organs, and it was out of his discussion of state organs that Minobe came at last to the problem of state form and constitutionalism. The will and vitality of the state, like those of every other corporation, are expressed through the actions of the organs (*kikan*) with which it is equipped. The actions of state organs are attributed to the state both in the social mind and in state law. Every organ has its competence or jurisdiction (*kennō, kengen*) which within its proper sphere is comparable to a right, not of the individuals constituting the organ, but of the state. The organ's competence is exercised by the display of its will,

which is always a "legal will" and not a simple natural will. "The will of
that organ only, which is given by state law the competence to determine
the will of the state, and only when that will is displayed in the manner
prescribed by state law, has the effect of state will."[65]

At this point Minobe laid on his favorite whipping boy. Hozumi had
said: "Even though the state has no natural will, it has a legal will."
Minobe rejoined that there can be no subject of a legal will that is not
the subject of a natural will, and the state, since it has vitality, is necessarily the subject of such a natural will. Great mischief flowed from
Hozumi's talk about "the natural will that constitutes the will of the
state," Minobe felt, for in no case can a simple natural will have the
force of state will. Even in autocratic times, when the will of the monarch was law, not every expression of the monarch's will, but only those
expressed in a manner prescribed by law, had the effect of law. Under
constitutional government the monarch's natural will does not directly
constitute state will. Thus did Minobe set forth as a universal principle
of constitutional jurisprudence a proposition which, applied to the Imperial Constitution, served to negate the frequent assertion that direct,
personal imperial rule had been unimpaired by its promulgation.[66]

Among the organs of the state, Minobe distinguished between those
he called direct organs and those he designated as indirect organs.[67]
Direct organs have an immediate basis in the fundamental law of the
state; they constitute basic governmental organization. The addition or
subtraction of direct organs, or other substantial changes in the nature
of such organs or in the relations among them, constitute changes in the
form of government (seitai, Staatsform). Thus, when a parliament is
established as a direct organ, where formerly the monarch was the sole
direct organ of the state, the parliament is established by a change in the
organic law of the state, and not by delegation of competence by the
monarch or other organ of the state. This is another example of his
assertion of a general principle of constitutional jurisprudence which was
destructive of the claims of the orthodox school, for it certainly refuted
the contention that the diet existed solely on the basis of an imperial
commission (by delegation) and functioned in subordination to imperial
will.[68] He further classified direct organs functionally as ruling organs
(the emperor), participating organs (the diet), and electoral organs (the
electorate). The Imperial Diet was thus assigned a restricted and subordinate role in relation to the emperor; on the other hand, it enjoyed

a status superior to that of the privy council, the cabinet, the courts, or other "indirect organs" whose existence and competence derive from other organs by delegation.[69]

That there are various forms of state results from the fact that the arrangement of state organs does not conform to a natural pattern but is determined by human contrivance. And not all forms of state have significance for constitutional jurisprudence. Indeed, Minobe felt that he need concern himself with two only: the constitutional monarchy and the republic.[70] When the whole body of the people, or that portion which is politically competent, constitutes the sole primary organ of the state, then the state is a republic, a form of government identified in recent times with popular sovereignty and democracy (*minshusei*), that is to say, a form in which sovereignty is ascribed to the "whole people."[71] He insisted that monarchy (*kunshusei*) be defined in terms compatible with constitutional government (*rikken seitai*), by which he meant a form of government in which a popularly representative parliament constitutes one of the direct organs of the state.[72]

All attempts to define monarchy on the basis of the autocratic character of the subject of sovereignty, or of the source of state authority, or of the source of the supreme will of the state fail in application to modern states. The special nature of monarchy in modern public law does not lie in the autocratic monopoly of unlimited governmental authority, nor does it concede supreme governmental authority to the monarch. Such notions cannot be squared with the character of modern constitutional monarchy, which is joint government of monarch and people (*kunmin dōchi*):

It is a seldom used expression today, but formerly we used the phrase *kunmin dōchi* to express the idea of constitutional government. It states quite simply the flavor of constitutional government, that is, that we, the people, are not only the governed; we are at the same time members of the governing group. While we submit to the authority of the state, at the same time we participate in the government of the state indirectly through the parliament. When the monarch and the people jointly exercise state authority true constitutional monarchy exists.[73]

When the direct organs of the state include an autocratic organ (the emperor, for instance), then, no matter what limitations may be placed on the competence of that organ, the state is a monarchy. When the monarch is the sole direct organ of the state, then there is absolute monarchy. When there are other direct organs besides the monarch, then there is limited monarchy. The modern form of limited monarchy is constitutional monarchy.

Impatiently, Minobe chided those who balked at the designation of the Japanese monarch as an organ of the state:

In the modern idea of the state the monarch does not stand outside the state ruling the state; he himself constitutes one of the elements of the state. Nor does the monarch possess the state as though it were his personal property; the state itself is a corporation. The monarch does not rule in his own private interest but in the interest of the whole state. In fine, the monarch is an organ of the state and whether or not the term "organ" is used this idea is generally endorsed by all but those who insist on closing their eyes to the truth.

Those who object to calling the emperor an organ of the state do so by arguments based on "political sentiment worthless as legal theory."[74]

For Minobe, the differences between monarchy and republic and between constitutional government and despotism were equally merely matters of difference in the organization of the primary organs of the state—that is, of difference in state form (*seitai*), which he considered the same as "governmental organization" or "system of government" (*tōchi soshiki*).[75] He found little use in discussing either monarchy or republic in the contemporary context except as constitutional monarchy or constitutional republic. Practically, the issue could be narrowed further, for of the several types of constitutional government only two were applicable to Japan: the parliamentary cabinet type and the bureaucratic cabinet type. The basic differences between Minobe and his opponents all hinged upon the inclination of their respective constitutional interpretations toward one or the other of these alternatives.

Minobe was sensitive to criticism of his use in this context of the term *seitai* to the exclusion of the term *kokutai* (national polity). This difficulty was but a minor consequence of the logic of his state-personality theory. But its implications of iconoclasm afforded his critics one of their more effective weapons. He rebelled against the view held by many of his contemporaries that the term *seitai* is applicable only to the formal and changing manner in which governmental power is exercised —that is, to the differences between constitutional and despotic government—and that the establishment of the Imperial Constitution meant only that Japan's state form, in this limited sense, had changed. These men held that the distinction between monarchy and republic is a matter of substance rather than of form, a matter of the location of sovereignty, of whether it belongs to the autocrat or to the people. This distinction, they insisted, is one of national polity, which is, by definition, immutable. According to Japan's national polity, as they defined it, all governmental authority is vested in the emperor alone, and the promulgation of the constitution had not effected this eternal principle. It followed for them that the constitution must be construed so as to preserve this principle.[76] Minobe denied the validity of this position on the grounds that sovereignty belonged to the state and, therefore, that there could be no dispute whether it was vested in the monarch or the people. He felt that his opponents erred also in seemingly denying the character of monarchy to any but absolute monarchies.

Every discussion of the distinctions among monarchy, republic, democracy, constitutional government, dictatorship, and so on, has to do with the organization of the direct organs of the state, with state form (*seitai*): "If the organization of the direct organs of the state is changed, then there is a change in *seitai*." It is crucial to a thorough understanding of the problem to keep in mind that *seitai* has to do with law, with legal title, and not with actual power in the political sense. Bismarck, for example, had real power but not legal title. Ministers of state are the legally designated advisers of the emperor; in fact they may have less real power than the *genrō* on the one hand or their departmental bureaucrats on the other. Unfortunately, Minobe went on, some analysts insist on treating what is in fact a matter of state form as though it were a matter of national polity. This mischievous confusion of *seitai* and *kokutai* stems from the failure to take into account the distinction between juristic and political aspects of state phenomena. No harm is done if *kokutai* and *seitai* are used interchangeably to indicate government organization. But *kokutai* has a legitimate ethical and political meaning which should not be confused with the juridical definition of the form of government.

In its proper use, Minobe explained, *kokutai* refers to that unique and unbreakable faith of the Japanese people in the divinely sanctioned character of the Japanese monarchy as the unifying principle of the nation from the founding of the state.[77] The term *kokutai* had been brought into use in the late Tokugawa period, he noted, to give expression to the idea set forth in the *Jinnō Shōtōki*, a classical apologia of the imperial institution dating from the fourteenth century: "Japan is a divine country. It is only our land whose foundations were first laid by the divine ancestor. It alone has been transmitted by the Sun Goddess to a long line of her descendants. There is nothing of this kind in other countries. That is why it is said to be a divine country." Thus he identified *kokutai* with the literary history of Japan: to honor the record of Japan's history from ancient times is to honor *kokutai*. Later, in 1931, he attacked a proposal of the ministry of education to adopt a phonetic syllabary in part on the ground that it would alienate new generations from that historical literature, and would, ironically, weaken popular respect for national polity just when the government was seriously concerned with the problem of fostering such respect.[78]

In the sense of a valuable myth of the culture, then, *kokutai* might have great political and social significance. But it was not at all permissible, in Minobe's view, to make the national polity idea the vehicle for importing into legal thought the notion that even under constitutional government the whole of state authority belonged unconditionally to the monarch, or to use it as the basis for other despotic pretensions contrary to the great intention of the promulgation of the constitution, which was to establish constitutional government in Japan. It seems that efforts to find a rational accommodation for the concept of *kokutai* in the realm of public law were hopelessly burdened by what has been called the "amuletic" force of the term in the thought and expression of military, bureaucratic, and educational personalities.[79] Minobe was only relatively less burdened than were those whose views he disputed.

CONSTITUTIONS AND CONSTITUTIONALISM

Minobe discovered in the principles of constitutional government the outgrowth of two ideas at work in European political history: the idea of popular self-government (*kokumin jichi*) and the idea of liberty, relating respectively to the form and essence of constitutional government. "These two ideas run throughout the evolution of constitutional government from the beginning to the present, but there are great differences from country to country in the extent to which and the manner in which they have been realized. Moreover, great changes have come in these ideas since the end of the nineteenth century, and this revolution is still in progress."[80]

Popular self-government, Minobe observes, means not only government for the people but government by the people; it gives rise to the theory of popular sovereignty in the case of democracies and to the principle of popular participation in government in the case of constitutional monarchies. Its practical expression has been in the popularization of government through the spread of representative parliamentary institutions. But the theory of popular sovereignty suffers from the same error as that of monarchical sovereignty: both ignore the personality of the state as the real possessor of sovereignty. The notion of the collectivity of individual persons which underlies the idea of popular sovereignty should not be confused with the perpetual corporate entity which is the state. Moreover, "even if the popular sovereignty theory is construed to mean that the people are the source or brain from which the activities of the state issue, it is not a theory suitable for all states." Popular self-government requires that the exercise of authority, whether in the name of monarch or people, be determined according to the opinion (*i-ken*) or inclination (*i-kō*) of the people generally. And it is this rather than popular sovereignty that is fundamental to a constitutional system.[81]

In Minobe's view, if popular self-government through a representative system is to be realized, it is necessary first that the parliament be constituted in such a way as to represent popular opinion. It is in respect to this organizational problem that great diversity arises regarding bicameralism and the electoral system. Second, it is necessary that the parliament have real authority in the determination of state policy, and it is from this problem of competence that many systems and practices have arisen regarding legislative and budgetary powers and power to challenge and criticize government policies. He recognized that it is this latter power which has become in recent times the most important aspect of the role of parliament. Arrangements for making popular influence bear on the composition of the government (*seifu*, the government of the day), are, in his view, a *necessary* corollary of the representative system in the realization of popular self-government. Except where the presidential system operates, the common means of achieving popular government is some form of parliamentary cabinet system (*gi-in naikaku seido*).[82]

Minobe supplemented his description of the institutional pattern of popular government with a brief survey of the antiparliamentary criticism which had appeared concurrently with the spread of representative institutions since the mid-nineteenth century. Two lines of attack upon

parliamentarism were represented in Japan: that of the socialist-syndi-
calist opposition advocating the discarding of the capitalist system of
representation in favor of direct action as a means of achieving social
reform, and that of the former ruling groups who saw all the faults and
none of the virtues of popular government, who denied that parliamentarism was the necessary mode of constitutional government, who asserted its incompatibility with monarchy, and whose real objective was
bureaucratic government under the guise of monarchy. There is the
barest hint in the tone of his terse summation of the antiparliamentary
arguments of what is clear in the whole context of his writing—that it
was the second of these lines of attack which to his mind presented the
more palpable threat. He indicated his awareness that the appeal of the
philosophies on the right and left which flatly rejected parliamentarism
were strongly reinforced by the tide of reaction to the earlier great expectations of parliaments as promoters and defenders of rights and liberties. Out of the growing doubts concerning the efficacy of parliaments
in dealing with the complex problems of modern government and out of
the dissatisfaction with the evils of the party system, had come a decline
not only in the legal powers of parliaments but also in the real political
power and prestige of the parliamentary system relative to bureaucratic
and dictatorial alternatives.[83]

But Minobe saw no satisfactory substitution for parliamentarism.
Certainly a return to the old bureaucratic system was inconceivable; on
the other hand, to turn to methods of direct democracy would only
exaggerate the weaknesses of popular government. "The representative
system, for all its faults, is still relatively the most salutary way of constituting the organ of popular self-government," and efforts should be
directed not at its destruction but at its improvement. He envisioned
three urgent and promising lines of reform: (1) reform of the electoral
system to ensure fair representation of all forces in society; (2) reform
of the upper legislative chamber to counterbalance more effectively the
inadequacies of the popular chamber; and (3) subjection of party finances to public view in order to eliminate improper influence by capital
and other interests. Purged of its grosser defects, the parliamentary system would be more capable of satisfactorily performing services for
which it was essentially well conceived.[84]

Minobe's evaluation of parliamentary institutions in Japan will be
discussed at length below. At this point it may be noted, however, that

if Minobe seemed to grasp too readily at antiparliamentary or late parliamentary doctrines of the west, too easily assuming their appositeness to Japanese experience, that if he constantly and provocatively qualified his commitment to parliamentary democracy, he was nonetheless a tireless foe of all the aspects of the imperial constitutional system which were the immediate source of the frustration of parliamentary government in Japan. The quality of Minobe's attachment to constitutional democracy must be judged in the light of his treatment of what he called the essential character, as distinct from the formal aspect, of constitutional government. This character, he wrote, is to be found in the idea that the people should be emancipated from despotic authority and guaranteed in their liberties and equality: "It can be said that the most important ethical imperative of modern constitutional government is that each individual be respected for himself, and that each be permitted as far as possible to give expression to his own capacities. The history of modern cultural development is the history of the liberation of the individual."[85]

He traced the idea of liberty to its roots in natural law doctrine and in the ethical conflict between absolutism and the moral development of the individual. The idea gained its basic political formulation in the English Puritan Revolution, in the theories of Locke and Blackstone, and in their constitutional expression in the American and French declarations of rights. Minobe conceded "that this idea of individual liberty has merit up to a point." But the philosophy of extreme individualism upon which this notion of liberty was based had been sharply modified since the mid-nineteenth century. The reaction to the social irresponsibility and social injustices of *laissez faire* gave rise to a positive attitude toward the function of the state in the eradication of economic and social inequalities. The cultural (*bunka-teki*) duty of the state had come to stand alongside its duty to preserve order and administer justice.[86] Socialism rendered useful service in urging the necessity of qualifying individual liberty with social morality and in teaching that liberty means emancipation from all tyranny, economic as well as political—that the mission of the twentieth century is the extinction of all class oppression without denying any person his complete individual personality.[87]

The principle of individual liberty, Minobe explained, is constitutionally expressed through guarantees of legal equalities, freedom of life, inviolability of person, and freedom of corporate activity.[88] It is implemented through the operation of two constitutional rules: the rule of law and the separation of powers. Under the rule of law (*hōchi shugi*) "the freedom of the individual is limited by the governmental authority of the state, but it is reserved to the legislative power alone to determine the rights and duties of the individual, and the administrative and judicial powers can do so only in accordance with the provisions of law."[89] He emphasized the distinction to be made between declarations of future legislative principles, such as the French Declaration of the Rights of Man and Citizens, on the one hand, and guarantees of specific prescriptive rights, such as in the English Petition of Rights and Bill of Rights and the American bills of rights, on the other. Minobe was influenced by Jellinek's work in establishing the theory of subjective rights in German law. According to Jellinek the "personality" of the individual was shaped by the state, which recognized in the individual a certain state-free sphere which it defined by autolimitation of its own powers in the form of legislated guarantees. The real measure of individual rights was to be sought not in objectively existing propositions founded in natural law but in the positive law of the state (*subjektiven öffentliche Rechte*), a view which was supposed to account for the relative efficacy of the substantial pragmatic guarantees of Anglo-American law in contrast with the vacuous phrases of the French declaration. Jellinek did not deny natural law; he maintained only that it was of no concern to scientific jurisprudence. Rights conceived objectively become meaningful only when they are given subjective expression in the positive law of the state. The question of the individual's reliance on a "higher law" against the arbitrary will of the state lies, by this theory, outside the realm of jurisprudence. Minobe was conditioned to accept the form of the "guarantees" in Chapter II of the Imperial Constitution, which made it explicit that individual rights were determined by the legislative power of the state and which left the individual with the small comfort of the *Rechtsstaat* principle as his only protection, with no legal appeal to a higher law. On the other hand, Minobe recognized that legislation might make "bad law" if it ran counter to "reason" or "the sense of social justice," and he undoubtedly construed the idea of constitutionalism as dictating an expansive definition of the spheres of intellectual and political liberty.[90]

The separation of powers, conceived originally as a means of checking arbitrary action by state organs and later also as a defense of liberty, became in one form or another a universal feature of constitutional government. The rigid compartmentalization implied in early formulations has been modified, except in America, by the harmonization of executive and legislative powers under some form of the parliamentary cabinet system. He felt that this harmonization of powers had weakened but not completely voided the separation of powers as a constitutional principle. As for the assertion, made by Hozumi and others, that there was no separation of powers short of an absolute separation of powers, this was only an argument advanced to check parliamentary encroachment on administration.[91] Minobe supported the fusion of legislative and administrative powers through the parliamentary cabinet system because he considered it the best means of keeping administration accountable to popular will. That his conservative opponents concurred in this expectation is indicated by the fact that the bureaucratic centers in the Meiji state from an early date recognized in the drive for fusion of legislative and administrative powers a threat to their supremacy. Minobe continued, himself, to reserve a place for the idea of a separation of powers, at least to the extent that each branch of government be, as he insisted, free to judge what its own constitutional competence and responsibilities were. It was on the basis of his belief in the mutual independence of the diet and the executive organs in the matter of constitutional interpretation that he found both the necessity and practical possibility of formulating a construction of the constitution at odds with the traditional bureaucratic interpretation.

IV

Minobe's Constitutional Theory: Interpretation
of the Imperial Constitution

Interpretive analyses of the Japanese constitutional system tended to support one or the other of two opposing formulas contending within that system: strong imperial rule operating through a centralized despotic bureaucracy or constitutional government emphasizing the role of the diet. Minobe was conscious of his part as a state-law specialist in the resolution of this conflict.[1] As a willful partisan of parliamentary government, he undertook to formulate and propagate within the state-law tradition a reoriented interpretation of the dualism in the Imperial Constitution. His was an interpretation which responded to a new spirit in Japanese society by giving greater weight to the factors favoring the growth of constitutional (i.e., responsible, representative) government.

As Professor Ukai has pointed out, Minobe's emergence from the university coincided with the beginning of the period of expansion of Japanese capitalism. It was a time of growing strength for elements of Japanese society which were hostile to the authoritarian construction of the constitution that had been imposed by the bureaucratic ordinances and had found its doctrinal expression in the Ito-Hozumi line of constitutional interpretation.[2] It is clear, however, that, sharp as was his departure from the orthodox-historical interpretation, Minobe was no more able than were his opponents to escape the dualism of the Meiji constitutional system.[3] The hard fact of the diet was hardly more a problem for Hozumi than were the "peculiar strength of the monarchy" and the tradition of bureaucratic authority for Minobe. The distinctive position he took was the product of a highly eclectic approach; even so, his thinking was essentially restricted by the horizons and methodology of state law.

The critical problem for Minobe was: to elicit the form and substance of limited parliamentary government from the law of the Japanese state. The practical possibility of formulating and maintaining such a construction of the constitution existed in the actualities of Japanese politics in operation and in the availability of a body of juristic doctrine well conceived to serve that purpose. It was of prime importance that the necessary condition of latitude in constitutional interpretation existed in the lack of agreement on constitutional issues among the various elements in the political structure of the Meiji state. The daily operations of government gave rise to ceaseless contests within and between various quarters of the government and the diet. As Minobe noted, "The constitution is first of all the law of the organization and operation of the several organs of highest authority in the state. But since there is no authority to stand over these organs to supervise and correct them in respect to their proper organization and operation, this fact in itself is of the greatest moment" in determining what the law is.[4]

The tendency for divergent constructions to arise was abetted by the simplicity of the constitutional text itself, which was laconic to the point of obscurity on critical points. The result was the generation of endless, conflicting probings of the interstices of the text. Minobe frequently cited this problem as the excuse for his systematic analysis, as in the preface to *Kempō Seigi:*

With the exception of Prince Ito's *Kempō Gikai* there has as yet been no authoritative exposition of the text of the constitution. This is a most serious defect of our legal scholarship. Since the constitution is superior to general law and, moreover, since it is very simple in form, there is need for exposition and room for explanation. Ito's commentary itself is so simple that it leaves many things in doubt. The purpose of this writer is to correct this situation.

The daily conflicts in interpretation arose regarding particular problems of governmental powers and relationships turning chiefly on the question of the political responsibility of the government. But the contending views were always traceable to divergent conceptions of the fundamental intent and spirit of the constitution. In this debate, the views of Ito carried much weight; his interpretation was, in effect, "official." At the same time, the fact that the authors of the constitution were known made it possible to criticize and debate the constitution and the official interpretations of it with little risk of lese majesty.

The second condition of the emergence of new interpretation was the existence of a body of solid juristic doctrine which could support the development of limited, representative, responsible government within a strong monarchical framework. This theoretical foundation was the *Staatsrechtslehre* of the late period of Imperial Germany, to which the public-law authorities of the Japanese imperial universities were thoroughly exposed. Minobe went farther than any of his academic contemporaries in seizing on the liberal constitutional possibilities in that doctrine, and in advancing from them to a thoroughly liberal construction of the Meiji system. In the state-personality theory he had discovered an academically respectable and bureaucratically tolerable formula upon which to build a public-law theory in harmony with new *jiyu-minken* spirit in Japanese politics.[5] While his approach by way of state-law precepts and methods gave his work a quality of arid formalism, this approach no doubt enhanced the chances of acceptance of his liberal constitutional interpretation in legally oriented bureaucratic and academic circles, even though the construction he imposed was perhaps even less sensitive to native values than were formulations advanced by such an academic "radical" as Yoshino Sakuzo.[6]

The distinguishing characteristics of Minobe's interpretation of the Imperial Constitution were traceable to his methodological bent. They derived, in a general sense, from his faith in the principles of political and intellectual liberalism. This faith, coupled with a sense of temporal and cultural relativity, supported his confident expectation that parliamentary government would be realized in Japan and justified his efforts to promote its development. In the narrower sense, his theory of legal interpretation permitted his thought to transcend the bonds of the discouraging language of the constitution itself or of the Satcho ordinances by which its general provisions had been given concrete application.[7]

Of equal importance with the language of the laws was the actual organization and operation of the several elements of the government structure. But these facts were to be given weight as sources of law only to the extent that they were in accord with relevent social values.[8] There was no doubt in Minobe's mind that the overriding social imperative of modern civilization was the achievement of the freedom of the individual personality and that constitutional government was the "universal trend of the times" because it satisfied, in the sphere of state law, this prevailing sense of social justice and social advantage. He took it as a duty incumbent on all those engaged in practical as well as theoretical interpretation of the law to be guided by this aspiration of society.[9]

Minobe admitted a great latitude in defining the content of ideas such as liberty and the form of their institutional expression. He adopted a tolerant, relativistic attitude toward such things as the concepts of private property and political equalitarianism: he rejected *laissez faire* but was barely tolerant of socialism; he accepted universal suffrage but was a strong supporter of bicameralism. He was by no means an advocate of direct institutional translation, recognizing that the form constitutionalism took in Japan must be conditioned by other fundamental principles and institutions deeply rooted in Japan's history and social conditions. But, that a liberal constitutional order, centered around the representative parliament, should come to prevail in some form, he seemed to have no doubts, his expectation being supported, presumably, by a simplistic view of the nineteenth-century transformation of the British monarchy and by Jellinek's lessons on *Verfassungswandlung* under Bismarck's constitutional system.[10]

Significance of the Promulgation of the Imperial Constitution

A key to Minobe's solution of the problem of blending monarchy and constitutionalism in Japan is given in his brief discourse on the promulgation of the Imperial Constitution and the events leading up to it. As might be expected, he viewed those matters in a light which accorded well with his own interpretation of the meaning and purpose of the constitution.

The bias of his constitutional theory was founded (logically at least) on premises manifested in his explanation of the coming of the constitution to Japan. He accepted without critical inquiry an interpretation of early Meiji political history which put Japan in the full tide of western constitutional development. At the same time, he recognized (albeit in a restricted sense) the bondage of the new legal-political order to pre-Meiji institutions and ideas. Without such concessions he must have put himself in opposition to the imperial constitutional system. With them he achieved a somewhat uneasy and critical harmony with that system, maximizing always those aspects of Meiji history and those terms of the law of the Meiji state which supported his "advanced" interpretation of the constitution.

His treatment of the making of the Meiji Constitution was as thin and formalized as were his discourses on European constitutional history.[11] Whether his evaluation of those events was valid is a problem for the political historian. To some among his critics the error in his constitutional interpretation was traceable to his failure to appreciate the true legal and historical significance of the making of the constitution. In this matter, as in others, Minobe pursued an independent and somewhat ambivalent course between the orthodox-historical position and that of radical political criticism.

Hozumi Yatsuka laid down the orthodox position that the constitution was the basic law of the governance of the state, the law proclaimed by the emperor for the guidance of all, establishing the norms of national polity and the form of government of the Japanese state. Although it prescribed the rules of power relationships, these rules did not originate in the written constitution but were based on the preëxisting social fact of authority and obedience. Hozumi argued that definitions of the constitution which acknowledged the participation of the governed in the constituent process were neither valid for Japan nor at all harmonious with the true meaning of the term "constitution." "What must be sought in Japan's constitution is Japan's special national polity and not the historical fruits of the west."[12] The constitution, Hozumi asserted, did not limit the imperial prerogative; it did not define the relation of the emperor and the people; it merely brought government officials as well as ordinary subjects under the rules of public law. In this view, the constitution was, then, but a proclamation by the emperor of already existing power relations. Hozumi's successor Uesugi Shinkichi and, later, Sato Ushijiro carried on in this perspective. For them the constitution established and fixed the essential elements of the political organization of the state as they existed at the time. They insisted that the language and spirit of the constitution be construed at every turn to conform to the historical tradition of autocratic imperial rule which it had been the supreme mission of the Restoration to bring back to full vigor.[13]

Other views were also strongly advanced, however. From the eve of the promulgation some writers were insisting that to adopt a constitution meant to define the proper use of the powers of government, to guard against their abuse, and to define the rights of subjects against the sovereign.[14] In 1918 Sasaki Soichi[15] set forth such a "radical" view thus:

They are needlessly concerned who feel that it debases our country to say that constitutionalism began for us with the promulgation of the constitution and that before that we had autocracy. If the term constitution is applied to the prepromulgation history of Japan there is still nothing peculiar about us in that respect since the same loose extension of the term can be made for every country. Certainly the principle of the participation of the people in the process of government of the empire dates from the Restoration and not earlier, and the first legal expression of this principle is in the Imperial Constitution. In spite of the position of many scholars to the contrary the current usage of the term constitution is not equivalent to the basic law of the state. It has specific historical content: participation of the people in the process of government through the medium of a representative organ.

Sasaki went on to point out that the origin of the constitution was to be found not so much in its textual precedents as in the thought advanced by the people themselves.[16] Accordingly the constitution was to be understood against the background of the Liberty and Popular Rights Movement of early Meiji. Suzuki Yasuzo, a later student of the problem, concluded that constitutional history starts with the origins of the parliamentary institution and that in the case of Japan he would date that event from the 1874 petition for the establishment of a popularly elected parliament.[17]

Minobe could neither fully embrace nor totally reject either of these contrasting views of the significance and consequences of the adoption of the Imperial Constitution. His appreciation of various western constitutional ideas and his sympathetic alignment with new political and social trends in Japan alienated him from the historical school. On the other hand, he was too much committed to his role as expositor of the law of the Meiji state and too thoroughly conditioned to the juristic regimen to wander far onto the free but hazardous and uncharted paths of political criticism. A smooth and systematically consistent transition led from his general theory of law and the state to his theory of the Japanese Constitution. His discussion of the adoption of the constitution and of the consequences of that action provided the connective link. From that discussion emerged various important technical propositions relating to the law of the constitution and a clear view of the color of his interpretive bias.

In *Kempō Satsuyō* he defined "constitution" in its essential meaning as the basic law of the organization and processes of the state. In this sense (as contrasted to the modern tendency to apply the term to the basic law of "constitutional" states only) the constitution is coëval with the state and is a condition of the state's existence.[18] Constitutional government in Japan dates from 1890, but the historical "constitution of Japan" dates from the founding of the empire. From this acceptance of the historical constitution, Minobe proceeded to conclusions distinctly different from those at which Hozumi arrived. In the first place, Minobe did not see in this historical constitution the expression of imperial will, for "it was not established and modified by an autocratic legislator; it was rather self-established and self-modified as a matter of historical phenomena."[19] Prior to the Restoration the government of the empire was a feudal monarchy which in its perfected form manifested four outstanding characteristics: (1) proxy or figurehead monarchy in which the *de facto* rulers purported to govern by commission of and in the name of the emperor; (2) a compound state in which the authority of the central government extended no farther than to the heads of the clans; (3) feudalism, that is, the linking of property and authority, and the prevalence of lord-vassal relations; and (4) government organization based on class privilege.[20]

The introduction of a written constitution in 1889 wrought a notable change: No longer was the constitution simply a matter of historical data; it was now revealed in authoritative legal texts and could be changed thenceforth only in accordance with the prescribed procedure. For the first time it became possible and necessary to distinguish between the constitution in its essential sense and in its formal sense, between the basic laws of the state, whether laid down in the text of the constitution or not, and the constitution as set forth in the 76 articles of the Imperial Constitution.[21]

The Constitution of the Empire of Japan, as the name implied, was intended to establish the fundamental law of the Japanese state. But it did not in fact entirely accomplish that purpose. For the Imperial Constitution did not embrace all of the basic law of the Japanese state. As Minobe saw it, interpretation of the constitution had to give due weight to every element of the essential constitution regardless of inclusion in or exclusion from the formal text. The only important reason for distinguishing essential and formal is that matters fixed in the text of the written constitution can be changed only by the formal method of amendment, while matters not incorporated in the document can be altered without reference to the formal amendment procedure. From this elementary distinction came two important consequences for Minobe's interpretation. First, it provided the basis for his frequent reference to preconstitutional law and custom in explaining the monarchical institution and the imperial prerogative. Second, it provided a margin of flexibility in his view of the constitution, for, unlike the orthodox school, he did not impute to the historical constitution a quality of immutability.

The somewhat conservative effects of Minobe's recognition of the historical constitution and the technical problems of interpretation arising under his theory of its incomplete translation into the written form were overshadowed by his emphasis on the revolutionary implications of the promulgation:

The great project of the Meiji Restoration was to overturn this state of affairs [the feudal monarchy] and to restore the bureaucratic monarchy opening up the path to constitutional government. . . . The period from the Restoration to the twenty-third year of Meiji [1890] was indeed the period of constitutional preparation in which the great enterprise . . . was achieved. Western ideas of constitutional government were widely disseminated in Japan from the Opening to the end of the *bakufu*, and the statesmen of the Restoration believed that its great purpose could be consummated only by the establishment of constitutional government. . . .[22]

In his sketchy outline of the developments of this period of preparation Minobe dwelt first very briefly on the steps toward the reëstablishment of the unitary state and the elimination of the legal institutions of feudalism. He then concentrated on the moves leading to the establishment of the diet: the rapid succession of experiments in separation of legislative and administrative functions within the government, the interaction between the policy of gradualism within the government and the mounting pressure for immediate action from outside the government, the drafting of the constitution, and, finally, the opening of the Imperial Diet in November, 1890.[23]

Minobe said that where his orthodox contemporaries went wrong in their interpretation of the constitution was primarily in their failure to comprehend the idea of constitutional government and their refusal to accept the necessary consequences of its adoption in Japan. Their error, he noted, was but a perpetuation of the thinking of the constitution drafters themselves. They did not recognize that the constitutional change brought about by the inauguration of the Imperial Constitution was equally as sharp as that wrought by the Restoration: the promulgation signified a change from bureaucratic despotism to "the completely different and new principle of constitutionalism as the basic rule of political organization." Their blindness engendered the further error of reading the idea of autocratic monarchical authority into the constitution by reference to national polity and the admittedly strong monarchical factor in the Imperial Constitution. He protested that national polity "does not explain our present constitutional system," and that to assert theories of omnipotent monarchical powers "is to go against the whole spirit of the constitution." Giving undue weight to the monarchical factor caused the constitutional factor to be overlooked and resulted in the extinction of the fundamental spirit of the constitution.

In view of the actual character of government in Japan, advocacy of direct autocratic imperial rule was tantamount, Minobe reasoned, to advocacy of bureaucratic despotism: "It is regrettable that even today there are those who say that these [concepts] carried over from our past are special virtues of Japanese society and that the idea of seeking constitutional principles is contrary to national polity. . . ." The national polity argument was hostile to constitutional government and was advanced "solely for the purpose of preventing the dissemination of constitutional ideas. . . ." So also was the perverted concept, gained from several German theorists, which identified constitutional government with a rigid separation of powers and thus denied that constitutional government was primarily representative government.[24]

Because the men who established the Meiji constitutional system were ignorant or careless of the principles of constitutionalism, because they innocently or willfully misconstrued the idea of constitutional government, and because there was unavoidably a pronounced lag in the response of actual political phenomena and political thinking to the newly adopted principles of government, it was possible to overemphasize the mere words in which the constitution and its supplementary ordinances were drafted. "Generally the text of a law represents the thinking of its drafters and it is inescapable that their lack of understanding, and their carelessness, mistakes, and ineptitude in writing should be perpetuated," Minobe explained. "It becomes necessary then to recognize that a law may be defective or in error. The aim of the person who analyzes the law is to correct the error and overcome the defect. . . ."[25] Minobe accepted the obligation to identify and abandon the errors of the founding fathers and of existing constitutional commentaries, errors stemming from a mistaken notion of the significance of the promulgation of the constitution.

Principles of the Imperial Constitution: Monarchy

The Imperial Constitution compounded characteristics of monarchy based on Japan's peculiar national polity as it emerged from her own ancient history and of constitutionalism imported from the west in recent times.[26] The unusual strength of monarchy in Japan was demonstrated by the emperor's retaining exclusive initiative in the matter of constitutional amendment, the isolation of the Imperial House Law beyond the competence of the diet (except as it might be affected by constitutional amendment), and the preservation of the emperor's broad, independent ordinance power. Moreover, the conduct of foreign relations was reserved exclusively to the emperor. In the privy council he had an advisory organ independent of the diet, and in the house of peers (based in part on orders of nobility) a potent check on the popular chamber of the diet.[27] This historically rooted monarchism was merged with an alien, and seemingly incongruous, constitutionalism and its underlying principles: popular participation (*yokusan*) in government, responsible government, and the rule of law. The external forms of constitutionalism, to the extent that they were compatible with the Japanese concept of monarchy, were taken into the Imperial Constitution. The extent to which the spirit of constitutionalism was realized depended, however, on the application of the constitution rather than on its specific language, for the textual bases for a parliament-centered interpretation of the constitution were obscure, scattered, equivocal, and negative.[28] It was inevitable, Minobe felt, that the form of constitutional government in Japan should be molded around, and in important respects qualified by, the monarchical institution. He sought to discover in that institution the basis for its adaptation to constitutional government and to construct for parliament a role equal with, if not superior to, that of the bureaucratic adjuncts of the monarchy.

Minobe did not deny that monarchical sovereignty (*kunshu shuken*) was central to the Japanese scheme of government. But he believed that serious error could be avoided in the analysis of its juristic meaning only if it were viewed in the context of state-personality theory. The prime error to be avoided was that which equated personal autocratic imperial rule with an immutable national polity. This mistaken notion perpetuated into the constitutional era autocratic theories inimical to constitutional government and created a presumption against all interpretations inclining toward limitation of imperial autocracy, holding that such interpretations implied acceptance of alien notions of popular sovereignty and were therefore abhorrent. Minobe held that the way to combat this error was to establish, as a matter of juristic theory, that the state, rather than the emperor or the people, was the subject of governmental authority, and that the emperor exercised the powers of government as an organ of the state. Then, when it was further established that the arrangement of state organs determines form of government and not national polity, it would be clear that the creation of a new and "constitutional" disposition of state organs and even the creation of new state organs need in no way conflict with national polity.

The theory of state sovereignty and its corollary theory of the monarch as an organ of the state, developed fully but in the abstract in *Nihon Kempō*, was first applied directly and explicitly to the Japanese Constitution in *Kempō Kōwa*, where the emperor-organ theory was stated thus: "There can be no doubt that the emperor as monarch of the Japanese Empire . . . occupies the position of supreme organ of the Japanese Empire. . . . To call the emperor an organ of the state follows naturally from the fact that the state is a corporate body. . . . Historically, and especially recently, we have believed that governmental authority exists for the common purpose of the entire nation and this is all that is implied when we say that the emperor is the supreme organ of the state."[29]

Minobe protested as basically meaningless the theoretical dispute opposing popular sovereignty and monarchical sovereignty, for neither side really got to the point. Whether the authority to exercise governmental power came from the monarch or the people was, he held, a matter of form variable with time, place, and historical conditions; in no case was it an inherent quality of states generically:

The monarchical principle and the principle of popular sovereignty are really only constitutional principles, merely differences in form. Regardless of either, governmental power is vested always as a right in the state, which is the subject of that power. Under popular sovereignty the people govern as an organ of the state, and even under monarchy it is as an organ of the state that the monarch is the highest source of governmental authority. . . . The term "sovereign" means strictly speaking "the highest organ.". . . In our constitution the monarchical principle must be construed in the above manner with the meaning that the monarch occupies the position of the highest source of governmental authority as chief of state and its supreme organ.[30]

From this position Minobe proceeded to attack what he considered to be common misunderstandings concerning the Japanese monarchy, errors deriving from the application of a fallacious concept of sovereignty. He argued, for instance, that to insist that the emperor has unlimited powers denies the character of the state as a corporation endowed with governmental powers. Such governmental power is always limited, and especially so under constitutional government; the constitution is, in a sense, a statement of the terms of limitation. As for the frequent assertion that because sovereignty is indivisible the entire governmental power belonged to the emperor, he countered that it is only state will or personality that is indivisible. There is no reason why it cannot be expressed through a multiplicity of organs. In this respect Minobe felt that the monarchical principle in Japan was really no different from what English constitutional scholars call "parliamentary sovereignty," that is, the sovereignty of the king in parliament. The sovereignty of the emperor means only that he is supreme within the organization of governmental power; it says nothing of the substance or extent of his powers. With the promulgation of the Imperial Constitution, the historically confirmed position of the emperor had not changed, but "everyone knows that there has been a very great change in his legally guaranteed powers . . . that whatever powers he has come from the constitution only and from no other source," that he holds his prerogative as his own constitutional competence and not as an agent or representative of some other organ, and that the constitutional limits of his power are autolimitations, limitations to which he has given his own sanction.[31]

It was specifically in relation to Articles I and IV of the Imperial Constitution, the so-called national polity articles, that Minobe's state-sovereignty theory entered his constitutional commentary. The purpose of Article I ("The Empire of Japan shall be reigned over and governed by a line of Emperors unbroken for ages eternal") was, he said, to fix monarchy as the perpetual form of government of Japan in positive law as it had always been in historical fact. In other words, it declared that among the organs of the Japanese state the autocratic organ was supreme. It in no way defined the powers of the emperor, nor did it imply that the emperor had a monopoly of all governmental power. As a description of the form of the state rather than a definition of the emperor's powers, the statement might better have been set forth in a separate initial chapter of the constitution, he noted.[32]

Article IV ("The Emperor is the head of the Empire, combining in Himself the rights of sovereignty, and exercises them, according to the provisions of the present Constitution"), on the other hand, did define the position of the emperor "as an organ of the state." Its meaning was essentially the same as that of the second paragraph of the Preamble: "The rights of sovereignty of the State, We have inherited from our Ancestors, and We shall bequeath them to Our descendents. Neither We nor they shall in the future fail to wield them, in accordance with the provisions of the Constitution hereby granted." The term "head of the Empire" (*kuni no genshu*) was the equivalent of the German *Oberhaupt des Staats* (Bavarian Constitution of 1818) and of the French *Chef d'État* (Charter of 1814). "Rights of sovereignty" (*tōchiken*) meant *alle Rechte der Staatsegalt* (also Bavarian), "the totality of rights possessed by the state."[33] Conceived as a right (*kenri*), it was limited not only in the method of its exercise but in its substance and objects, as are all rights by definition. The phrase "combining in himself" (*sōran*, literally "superintending" or "bringing together") corresponded to *Träger* in the phrase *Träger der Staatsgewalt* in German monarchical theory. Accordingly, the emperor was in all respects in his own person the embodiment of the state, and all rights of the state were exercised by him in person or by others made competent by his commission. The only exception to this was the legislative power, which the emperor exercised jointly with the diet, which owed its competence to the constitution directly and not to imperial commission.[34]

Minobe's rejection of the national polity theory of the Japanese monarchy did not lead him to minimize the place of monarchy in the Imperial Constitution. He recognized that within the conceptual confines of the state sovereignty theory and hedged about by the specific restraints of constitutionalism, the monarchy continued to occupy the central position in the positive law of the Meiji state and in the sentiments of the Japanese nation, enjoying vigor and power unparalleled among the contemporary monarchies of the world. Still, he saw in the strong monarchical coloration of the Meiji Constitution something other than a legitimate response to an historical national sentiment: "It is no doubt true that the makers of the constitution believed . . . that it would be dangerous to give great power to the diet and especially to the house of representatives," and it was for that reason in part that so much weight was given to the monarchical principle.[35] Minobe, in consideration of exactly opposite dangers, subjected many of the autocratic features of the constitution to severely restrictive interpretation.

THE IMPERIAL PREROGATIVE

The broad scope of the autocratic prerogative was an outstanding characteristic of the Imperial Constitution. Minobe referred to this distinction as the principle of the central position of the prerogative (*taiken chūshin shugi*): "The competence of the diet is clearly subordinate to the prerogative. . . . The government could not function for a day without the prerogative, but the functions of the diet are not at all necessary to the continued operation of the government."[36] Despite this and other acknowledgments of the importance of the prerogative, the striking thing about Minobe's position, compared with that of any other contemporary Japanese legal authority, is the limitations he placed upon its exercise, and especially his acceptance of the idea of legislative absorption of the prerogative.

As Minobe understood it, the imperial prerogative in its broadest sense was coëxtensive with the whole of the governmental power of the state, embracing all legislative, judicial, and administrative powers. This was the meaning of Article IV, according to which the emperor, in his capacity as head of the state, exercised the state prerogative (*kokumu-jō no taiken*) autocratically, albeit with the assistance of ministers of state (Article LV). In so far as the emperor acting on the advice of his ministers was taken to mean the government, the state prerogative was the prerogative of the government as distinct from the diet, the courts, the military, and so on. Some aspects of the total imperial prerogative, however, were distinguishable from the general governmental power of the state—for instance, the emperor's prerogative of military command, which he exercised as supreme commander with the assistance not of ministers of state but of autonomous military command organs.[37] The legislative prerogative (Article V) the emperor exercised with the consent of the Imperial Diet. The judicial prerogative properly speaking (i.e., excluding administrative adjudication) was exercised through an independent court system in the name of the emperor (Articles LVII, LVIII, and LXI). The balance of the imperial prerogative was commonly called the autocratic prerogative (*dokusai taiken*) since it was not, by the terms of the constitution, exercised necessarily through or with the consent of other organs. This autocratic prerogative extended to matters usually deemed to be executive or administrative.[38]

A restrictive definition of the imperial prerogative advanced by Hozumi and some later writers[39] held that the entire imperial prerogative was embodied in the enumeration of the autocratic powers of the emperor under Articles VI to XVI, the so-called prerogative items (*taiken jikō*).[40] The purpose of this definition was, apparently, to exclude from the prerogative all acts of state for which the constitution provided participation by other organs (for example, the diet or the courts), so that the absolute autocracy of the powers under Articles VI to XVI could be maintained.[41] Such an interpretation was in Minobe's view an intolerable manifestation of autocratic thinking, altogether at odds with the principles of responsible representative government.[42] By treating the whole of state power, including legislative and judicial powers, as being within the scope of the imperial prerogative, he would establish a presumption adverse to claims that the prerogative was necessarily insulated against parliamentary influence or control.[43]

The propositions Minobe laid down concerning the enumerated prerogative items are summarized below.[44]

(1) The commonly asserted theory of a mutually exclusive relationship between the prerogative items and the legislative power was erroneous. It misconstrued the basic principle of the constitution, assuming incorrectly that the constitution was based on strict separation between the legislative and administrative powers, whereas in fact the legislative as well as the administrative powers were united in the emperor. "In the strict sense the emperor's prerogative is the emperor's autocratic prerogative, which means that the consent of the diet is not necessary for its exercise. But to say that it does not require the consent

of the diet does not mean that it cannot be submitted to the consent of the diet. If it is enacted with the consent of the diet it is enacted also by the emperor and there is no conflict with the constitution." Since this seems to indicate that legislative regulation of the prerogative could come about only with the emperor's consent, it should be kept in mind that Minobe assumed the operation of a parliamentary cabinet system. Accordingly, the imperial sanction would be granted on the advice of a cabinet which held its position politically by virtue of its claim on the confidence of the diet majority. It is "an undoubted fact in political practice if not in theory" that except for matters of Imperial Household Law the competence of the diet extended to any matters of state for which ministers of state were responsible.[45] Indeed, since what is determined with the diet's consent can be altered only with the consent of the diet, the legislative power is protected from the autocratic prerogative, is in fact superior to the autocratic prerogative. For example, once the imperial prerogative of prorogation had been submitted to regulation by the Diet Law, it could not be restored to the emperor's autocratic discretion without the consent of the diet.[46]

(2) The imperial prerogative was not unlimited—it could be exercised only in conformance with the terms of the constitution or of laws and treaties. To say that it could not be limited by any other organ did not mean that it could not be limited by law or treaty. Since no law or treaty could be made without imperial sanction, any law or treaty limiting the prerogative constituted a case of autolimitation (*jiritsuteki seigen*), which in no way violated the character of the prerogative.[47]

(3) Although Article IX alone among the prerogative articles specifically authorized delegation of the prerogative, there could be no doubt that the whole prerogative could be delegated—otherwise the constitution required the impossible in the form of personal performance by the emperor.[48]

(4) In accordance with the requirement of constitutional government that all exercise of the prerogative be made on the responsibility of ministers of state, it was properly within the liberty of subjects to discuss and criticize the exercise of the prerogative, even though the particular action be published in the form of an imperial command. In lectures at Kyushu Imperial University, Minobe plainly expressed his thoughts on this score:

There is an idea current that the imperial prerogative is sacred and inviolable —that because it is executed by imperial will there can be no discussion of it nor can anyone debate its merits in any particular instance of its exercise. This idea is asserted with special vigor and breadth against academic theory, so that anything may be construed as "discussion of the imperial prerogative" or "interference with the imperial prerogative" and thus as lese majesty . . . this is a gross error contrary to the spirit of the constitution. Constitutional government is responsible government. All exercise of the prerogative is made on the responsibility of state ministers and their responsibility can be debated. . . . The principle of sacred inviolability extends only to the person of the emperor.[49]

THE INDEPENDENT ORDINANCE POWER

Two intertwined facets of the autocratic prerogative were of such moment in relation to Minobe's problem of constitutional interpretation as to warrant special identification and examination here—those relating to the troublesome problems of the independent ordinance power and civil-military dualism.

The constitution failed to define the scope of that part of the legislative power which was shared by the emperor and the diet under Article V. On the other hand, it provided a fairly precise catalogue of prerogative items, in Articles VI to XVI. This encouraged those concerned to treat the former as a residual category extending only to those matters not included within the latter, that is to say, within the ordinance power of the emperor. In other words there was a tendency to exclude from the former those matters within the power of the government, by ordinances issued independently of the diet and under penal sanction, to dispose of such matters as the organization and competence of governmental offices and agencies, and even of the rights and duties of subjects. Hence the importance of the commentator's interpretation of the independent ordinance power.[50]

Minobe, as has already been indicated, held that the autocratic character of the imperial prerogative did not bar its submission to regulation by diet-approved laws. Apart from this idea of possible parliamentary absorption of the prerogative, he imposed a rather restrictive construction upon some specific aspects of the prerogative, including the scope of the related ordinance power. Even so, the ordinance power of the

Japanese monarch remained, in Minobe's view, a formidable limitation on the "constitutional" character of the fundamental law of the Meiji state. "There is no positive limit," he maintained, "to the area that can be regulated by law (*hōritsu*); it is a fundamental rule that any regulation whatsoever can be made by law. Contrariwise, that regulations can be made independently by imperial ordinance stands as an exception to the principle that every exercise of the legislative [lawmaking] power requires diet concurrence, and this exception is limited to those matters only which are permitted by the constitution. . . ."[51] This statement clearly acknowledges the existence of the independent ordinance power as a limitation on the potential maximum legislative competence of the diet; and Minobe insists that the exception be narrowly interpreted: "Law is the rule; ordinance the exception; and generally exceptions are narrowly construed."

Minobe defined "independent ordinance" as "an ordinance issued independently on the emperor's prerogative [and] being neither for the purpose of executing a law nor by legislative delegation."[52] In this section the term is extended to cover emergency ordinances and treaties, both of which significantly subtracted from the diet's role in the determination of law. Under Article VIII of the Imperial Constitution the government had the power to legislate by imperial ordinance in the place of diet-approved law "in case of urgent necessity to maintain public safety or to avert public calamity" when the diet was not in session. Such ordinances were called emergency ordinances (*kinkyū meirei: Notverordnung*). Emergency ordinances were equivalent to laws (*hōritsu*) in content and effect, could extend to any matters to which laws were applicable, and could amend or repeal existing laws.[53] They required privy council deliberation before issuing and had to be submitted to the next session of the diet for approval or rejection. The emergency ordinance power was employed extensively after the first instance of its use (Imperial Ordinance No. 134 of 1894 on press censorship), perhaps most memorably in the drastic revision of the Peace Preservation Law in 1928 and in the implementation of the early Occupation directives in 1945.

Minobe interpreted the emergency ordinance power narrowly with respect both to the conditions and the consequences of its exercise; at the same time he acknowledged that the limits of this power as he described them had been frequently transgressed in practice. He argued that such an ordinance power could be used properly only for preventative or protective purposes and not for positively advancing public welfare. It was not properly used as an expedient for circumventing diet opposition to government legislative projects. The constitution assigned to the diet *post facto* supervision of all such ordinances. Disregarding certain contrary precedents, Minobe reasoned that every emergency ordinance should be submitted at the beginning of the session (regular or extraordinary) of the diet following its issuance. This requirement held, in his view, even for emergency ordinances which had been revoked by the government before the diet reconvened and for those about which by their very nature there was no question of continuing validity. The function of the diet in respect to emergency ordinances was, however, merely a matter of "consent," which did not include initiative or amendment, and thus differed from its function of "concurrence" in respect to the making of *hōritsu*: the expression of a positive intention and a request for imperial sanction.[54] The effect of consent was to discharge the government of its responsibility and to convert the ordinance in effect, although not in form, to a statute. Failure of either house of the diet to consent immediately destroyed the validity of the ordinance. A vote of non-consent by either house constituted an attack on the responsibility of the cabinet.

Article IX gave to the emperor the power to issue or cause to be issued "the ordinances necessary for carrying out the laws, or for maintaining public peace and order, and for the promotion of the welfare of subjects," but also provided that no such ordinance should "in any way alter any of the existing laws." Some authorities, consequently, interpreted this as a broad grant of administrative ordinance power applicable to all matters except those which the constitution reserved for diet laws. Viewing such construction as a departure from constitutional principles almost without parallel in western constitutional systems, Minobe imposed as narrow an interpretation as possible. The purpose of Article IX was, he said, not to lay out the area of administrative action, but "to define the limits of the exercise of the police power as an exception to the ordinary legislative power"; it was merely the formal constitutional expression of the universal practice of delegating discretion to the administration in the exercise of the police power. Taken as a grant of general administrative ordinance power, how could it be reconciled with the cardinal principle of constitutional government requiring diet participation in the making of law? Thus taken, it served, indeed, only "to justify despotism in the government of Japan."[55] Properly understood, the article sanctioned restriction of the freedom of subjects by ordinance only "within the limits of police necessity," which was a matter of administrative discretion in the enforcement of law, the preservation of public order, and the advancement of public welfare. Since ordinances issued under this article could not infringe upon laws, extending the scope of laws would correspondingly diminish the scope of this ordinance power. Unfortunately, the penalties attached to such ordinances were sufficiently severe to encourage the government to rely on them rather than to seek diet enactment of appropriate laws.[56]

In support of his contention, Minobe pointed to the separate provision for particular matters which, if Article IX had been intended as a general and unrestricted grant of administrative ordinance power, would have been covered by it. As an example of this, he pointed to the provision of Article X according to which the organization of the administrative structure and the entire civil-service system fell under the authority of imperial ordinance, subject only to the limited capacity of the diet to obstruct through its budgetary powers, and, more significantly, subject to privy council review. Ordinances issued under Article X, like those under Article IX, could not transgress or replace established laws. During the era of party government the chief obstacle to cabinet control of the prerogative under Article X was the privy council and, to a lesser extent, the house of peers.[57]

A major exception to the principle of diet participation in the legislative process existed in the emperor's power to make treaties under the foreign relations prerogative (*gaikō taiken*) set forth in Article XIII. The emperor's power to represent Japan in all relations with foreign countries was exercised on the responsibility of ministers of state, but was, by the terms of the privy council ordinance, subject to review by that body, although failure to comply with this latter requirement could, in Minobe's opinion, reflect only on the responsibility of the ministers of state and not on the validity of a treaty. Since treaties were often of such a character as to affect domestic law, the question arose whether diet consent was necessary to give the provisions of a treaty the force of law internally. In contrast to his narrow interpretation of the ordinance power, Minobe's reading of Article XIII gave the widest latitude to autocratic discretion in the making of treaties: "There can be no doubt that under our constitution the emperor's power to conclude treaties is plenary, unconditional, and exclusive, except as the terms of a particular treaty may call for legislative implementation."

The law of Japan differed, he contended, from that of states in which the effect of treaties as domestic law depended on supplementary legislative action. To assert, as did a resolution of the Sixth Diet (1894), that diet enactment was necessary to give internal force to treaty provisions was to imply that the constitution sanctioned the possible violation of a treaty. That resolution rested also on the equally untenable assumption that state will was divided into two possibly conflicting parts, one dealing with international law, the other with internal state law. Moreover, since an imperial edict promulgating a treaty was a complete expression of state will, a treaty (jōyaku) thus promulgated was as valid as state law as were expressions of state will in the form of laws (hōritsu) or ordinances (meirei). But it was equally true, according to Minobe, that the diet's legislative discretion could not be foreclosed by the stipulation in a treaty calling for enactment of appropriate laws. In such cases the diet was free to refuse to act or to act contrary to the intention of the treaty. In such cases the option of the diet, expressed or implied, constituted an understood condition of ratification.[58]

Finally, there was reserved to the emperor an exclusive and autocratic military prerogative, usually designated as the supreme command prerogative.[59] It consisted of two elements, matters of military command (gunreiken) being established in Article XI ("The emperor has the supreme command of the army and navy") and matters of military administration (gunseiken) in Article XII ("The emperor determines the organization and peace standing of the army and navy"). The command authority included the direction, discipline, training, and disposition of all armed forces; administration authority covered external organization of military forces (e.g., the number of army divisions or fleet units), supply of munitions, and determination of the military obligations of subjects. As items of the autocratic prerogative, both powers were subject to disposition by ordinance without reference to the diet except for budgetary requirements. Under Minobe's interpretation, however, both were subject to parliamentary absorption and to diet influence through the convention of cabinet responsibility to the diet.[60]

The manifold difficulties that arose in respect to the military prerogative were not, Minobe held, the result of the form of their expression in the text of the constitution, for they were no more or less baldly autocratic than were most others of the prerogative items. The difficulty, he explained, sprang rather from the status of presumptive autonomy which the military advisory organs had achieved in the preconstitutional period. This special status was carried over into the constitutional period, confirmed, elaborated, and extended through a series of imperial rescripts and ordinances by virtue of which the military command organs not only maintained their independence but gained a stranglehold on the principal civil organ of government, the cabinet. Indeed, the constitutional debates concerning the military prerogatives came to center about the consequent conflict between the civil and military organs of the government.

THE CABINET AND OTHER ORGANS RESPONSIBLE
FOR THE EXERCISE OF THE PREROGATIVE

Minobe's interpretation of the monarchical aspects of the Imperial Constitution leans heavily on his definition of the roles of the several agencies through which the imperial prerogative was exercised. Chief among these, in his view, were the ministers of state—collectively, the cabinet.

Ministerial Advice and Execution.—Ministerial responsibility under the Meiji Constitution displayed two distinct aspects. On the one hand there was the relation of responsibility to the monarch—the only responsibility recognized by the constitution or in the orthodox commentaries—and the relation of responsibility to the popular political organs of the state, the diet and the electorate, which existed, if at all, only by unwritten constitutional convention. Only the former relationship is of concern at this point.

Minobe asserted that it was a corollary of the concept of the "sacred inviolability" of the emperor (Article III) that his exercise of the prerogative be always on the advice of a minister. Since the emperor was not personally responsible, legally or politically, for his acts—criticism thereof constituting felonious lese majesty—it followed naturally, then, that ministers of state must be responsible. They alone were liable to criticism regarding the legality or wisdom of all imperial acts, and it was therefore incumbent that the emperor act only on their advice. This constitutional principle had its counterpart in the west but was not of western origin. It had been a constant feature of Japanese constitutional theory and practice for centuries and was "the basis upon which the dignity of our national polity has been maintained."[61] But when translated into the text of the constitution, this venerable tradition took on a new meaning, Minobe explained: the acts of the emperor now had no legal effect unless made on the advice of ministers of state. Minobe pursued this point unequivocally, declaring—the point merits reëmphasis—that the constitutional provision that the emperor exercise his prerogative on the advice of state ministers meant that he could exercise governmental power *only* on their advice, that the principle of inviolability applied only to the person of the emperor and not to imperial commands relative to matters of state, all of which were subject to criticism as to the legality or prudence of the advice of the countersigning ministers.[62]

This interpretation of imperial inviolability was but the first proposition in a formula by which Minobe sought to demonstrate the constitutional necessity and propriety of the political accountability of ministers of state to the diet. It was a forced construction of Article III, deriving from his interpretation of the ambiguous terms of Article LV: "The respective Ministers of State shall give their advice to the Emperor, and be responsible for it. All laws, Imperial Ordinances, Imperial Rescripts of whatever kind, which relate to affairs of State, require the countersignature of a Minister of State." To the text of this latter article he supplied a gloss wholly consistent with the imperatives of responsible parliamentary government.

He did not deny that the imperial prerogative embraced the total authority of the state, nor that the organs through which the prerogative was exercised, save only the diet, owed their competence to the imperial commission alone, nor that legally, regardless of what conventions limiting the imperial discretion might prevail, the emperor alone determined the appointment and dismissal of ministers—in short that the government was the emperor's government discharging his prerogative. Nevertheless, Minobe discarded as "unreasonable" the contention that the emperor in fact exercised the prerogative personally and autocratically (*shinsei*) and that the ministers of state assumed responsibility for his exercise of discretion only because "the emperor cannot bear responsibility" or because "the monarch can do no wrong":

The simple and correct basis of ministerial responsibility is this, that ministers of state are the emperor's assistants and they are responsible for their assistance. . . . This is what distinguishes them from lesser officials who must obey commands of their superiors regardless of the legality or good judgment of those commands, and who have no responsibility for the errors of the superior command. . . . Ministers of state cannot plead a superior order of the emperor, indeed it is their duty to admonish the emperor not to sanction illegal proposals or acts against the interest of the state, and to resign if their advice is not accepted. . . .[63]

On this point Prince Ito had written: "The Ministers of State are charged with the duty of giving advice to the Emperor; they are to serve as the media through which the Imperial commands are conveyed. . . . [They] have the duty of encouraging all that is proper and discountenancing all that is improper; and when they fail to discharge this duty, they will not be able to release themselves from responsibility by pleading an Order of the Sovereign. . . ."[64] Although Ito categorically denied that the diet had the power to command the responsibility of ministers of state, his words were more favorable to Minobe's position than were those of Hozumi, who had expressed the view that the "requirement of countersignature of laws and ordinances is only the external expression of the rule that the operation of the prerogative must be through the government. The minister of state has the duty to present his opinion, but he has no authority to resist the emperor's exercise of the prerogative."[65] Somewhat differently, Minobe took "shall give their advice" in Article LV (from *hohitsushi*, literally, "to assist") to mean: "to give their opinions to the end that there be no error in the exercise of the prerogative."[66] Accordingly, the ministerial countersignature represented an assumption of responsibility for such advice and no expression of imperial will has legal effect without such countersignature.[67]

What conservative writers had in mind operationally when they spoke of "personal rule" by the emperor is ambiguous. To Minobe's mind it was a euphemism for bureaucratic despotism, a slogan used as a counter to the idea of cabinet responsibility to the diet. We may note on the basis of some recent studies based on the testimony of high officials of the imperial government that Minobe's own view of the nature of ministerial responsibility in relation to the emperor seems to have been borne out in actual practice during the prewar decades.[68]

Division of Executive Responsibility.—Whatever may have been the proper relationship between the emperor and the agencies which exercised the prerogative, a matter of even greater consequence was the undeniable and dismaying diffusion of responsibility and authority among them. Even if it were conceded that the emperor could act only on the advice of ministers, there remained the troublesome fact that there were several sources of such advice, none of which could claim a general responsibility for the whole of the imperial prerogative.

This diffiusion of authority was of the greatest significance in the maintenance of administrative integrity and in implementing even the most rudimentary notion of the cabinet's responsibility to the diet. The cabinet was the government, but only in a very imperfect sense could be said that it governed. Minobe's approach to this embarrassment was to construe the controlling law so as to support the broadest possible definition of the cabinet's control over the prerogative. He reminded his students that the cabinet's responsibility could be made inclusive of the whole prerogative, and this without the least conflict with the text of the constitution—indeed, in perfect harmony with the concept of constitutional government to which the Japanese monarchy had been committed by the promulgation of the Imperial Constitution. Standing against this view was the uncongenial fact that organs other than the cabinet held responsibility for particular portions of the prerogative, that various consultative organs had the capacity to obstruct the agencies responsible for advising the throne, and that the principle of ministerial solidarity was hardly recognized at all in the constitution and was only imperfectly implemented by the ordinance establishing the cabinet.

By sanction of constitutional practice, the responsibility of the cabinet extended only to the state prerogative (*kokumu taiken*). As Minobe put it, it was as though Article LV had read: "shall give their advice on matters of state prerogative."[69] While this state prerogative was a general authority, not necessarily limited by the enumeration of prerogative items in Chapter I of the constitution, two aspects of the prerogative were excluded from it and thus put beyond the competence of the cabinet. One of these, the imperial household prerogative, was concerned with such things as succession, regency, imperial household finances, etc. Such matters were handled under the Imperial Household Law. This law, enacted by imperial decree, gave legal expression to the rule of imperial family autonomy, one of the prominent indices of the strength of the monarchy in Japan.[70] Outside and independent of the cabinet, the Imperial Household Ministry was charged with responsibility for advising the throne on all matters coming under the Imperial Household Law. The Imperial Household Ministry was said to be "above politics" and divorced from state administration. The office of imperial household minister (*kunai daijin*) was one of great honor, surpassed in that respect only by the office of lord keeper of the privy seal (*naidaijin*), whose closeness to the throne made him a key figure in the delicate, obscure, and frequently important consultations between the *genrō* and other "important persons" and the emperor on critical occasions of state.

The autonomy of the Imperial Household Ministry did not, as a matter of practical effect, greatly embarrass the cabinet, although the imperial household minister was numbered among those persons close to the throne whose good will or hostility could ease or obstruct the course of cabinet operations. Although apparently not counting it a matter of great moment, Minobe nevertheless was probably on the whole opposed to the political influence of the palace officials. In 1924 he wrote in *Kaizō* deprecating the choice of Baron Kiyoura as premier, but conceding that the role of the lord keeper and the *genrō* in making the selection had been constitutionally correct. In 1932, however, he was sharply critical of inner court circles for the generous confidence they accorded the transcendental administration of Admiral Saitō.[71] In 1945, when a conflict arose between the cabinet and the inner court circles over abortive efforts in the office of the lord keeper at drafting a revision of the constitution, Minobe, who was then associated with the cabinet, shared cabinet resentment at the "irresponsible" power wielded by officials in the palace.

Discomfited as it was by the autonomy of the imperial household ministry, the cabinet was troubled even more by the frustrating complexity, elusiveness, and ambiguity of its relations with the independent organs of military command. Few provisions of the constitution were so productive of dramatic conflicts and disruptive consequences as were those setting forth the imperial military prerogative, nor did any other single aspect so draw the attention and arouse the apprehensions of foreign observers as did the condition of "dual government" (*nijū-seifu*), stemming from the separation of the military and the government (*heisei bunri shugi*), which resulted from those provisions. The direction and intensity of Minobe's constitutional liberalism is clearly indicated in his interpretation of the military prerogative; it was above all his application of that interpretation to the problems of government in

Japan, especially in the period after 1928, that provoked attack from his adversaries on the right.

In accordance with the idea that matters of military command should be insulated against political interference, the military prerogative of the emperor was distinguished from the state prerogative items. Separate organs, the army general staff (*sambō hombu*) and the navy staff (*kaigun shireibu*), were created to assist him in the exercise of that prerogative. The ordinances governing the military command organs left them in no way responsible to the cabinet, the prime minister, or any other minister of state. By these ordinances, they had direct access to the emperor (*i-aku jōsō*)—that is, the authority to report directly to the throne through the emperor's chief military aides, seeking by their advice imperial sanction of military command decisions.[72]

Moreover, the command responsibility the army general staff and the navy staff extended to many matters which in other countries were regarded as administrative and left as a rule to the responsibility of the military ministries. And, as if to assure ministerial nonintervention, only general officers and admirals were eligible for appointment as war minister and navy minister respectively.[73] Beyond protecting military independence, reservation of these posts to senior military officers meant that cabinets could be formed and maintained only on terms which would induce or permit such officers to participate. The navy's opposition within the cabinet had been instrumental in the destruction of Saionji's first cabinet in 1906, and the withdrawal and withholding of support by the army in 1912 caused the fall of his second cabinet. Thereafter the sensitivities of the two services were a considerable factor in determining the composition and policy of each successive government, and became a major factor in the rise and fall of cabinets after 1935.

The anomaly of these circumstances was heightened by the Cabinet Ordinance exemption of both ministers from the internal discipline of the cabinet. Although Article VII of the Cabinet Ordinance provided: "Except for matters of military plans and military command which have been reported directly to the Throne . . . the Minister of War and the Minister of Navy shall report to the Prime Minister," the value of this reporting was, at best, dubious. The service ministers, naturally bound by professional interest, loyalty, and responsibility not to their colleagues within the cabinet but to leaders of the military bureaucracy, were free to define "matters of military" discretion, and thus were in effect free of the supervisory control of the prime minister. Moreover, having direct access to the throne, although presumably only for those military command matters, they were at times in a position to extort from the cabinet satisfaction of the political objectives of the military leaders, or at least to thwart the extension of civil control over military policy.

The resulting dualism in Japanese government and the consequent conflicts over important matters of policy between the military and the cabinet (with the upper echelons of the civil bureaucracy often holding the balance of power) have comprised a frequently if still incompletely told tale.[74] The institutionalization of the principle of civil-military separation had been conceived and brought about by the military statesmen of the Meiji era deliberately and with full knowledge that it departed from the norm prevailing under western constitutional regimes. The parallel between the steps taken between 1885 and 1890 insulating the Japanese military command from parliamentary interference and those which accomplished the same thing in Prussia and Germany between 1861 and 1883 is too plain to suppose a coincidence. There can be little doubt that Yamagata and his colleagues took a lesson from the "political generals" of Prussia with whom they shared an abhorrence not only of the idea of military accountability to the parliament but of all the political and social consequences flowing from the establishment of a representative parliament.[75]

However much various commentators may have deplored it, there was no serious challenge to the legality, if not the propriety, of the distinction between civil and military prerogatives. The autonomy of the military command organs was all but unanimously accepted as a firmly, some would say immutably, fixed principle of Japanese constitutional law and practice.[76] Minobe joined in the acknowledgment and indicated an appreciation of the arguments in favor of isolating matters of military security and command from political interference. But he did not concur in the opinion of some of his contemporaries that the independence of the military command organs was a necessary consequence of the constitution itself. It was, he felt, based on preconstitutional practice carried over and implemented by ordinances but for which "ministers of state might logically be taken to be competent advisors" in matters of the military prerogative.[77] Not only did the civil-military dualism lack expressed or implied constitutional sanction; it represented, he declared, a serious abuse of the principle of responsible government. Suitable didactic material was available in the unhappy experiences of the German Empire. Minobe pointed to the autonomous general staff system as "the main reason why Germany was criticized as a militarist country" and as a contributing cause to popular defection from the monarchy. His references to the too-late attempt to discard that system by imperial decree in October, 1918, were clearly suggestive of what he would have deemed a salutary course of action for Japan.[78]

Minobe's criticism centered on the failure to hold the autonomous powers of the military command organs within a strict definition of military command and on the violation of cabinet integrity by the military service ministers. To be sure, the constitution reserved to the emperor, as generalissimo, an autocratic authority over all matters of military command (Article XI); parliamentary interference could occur only through the budgetary powers of the diet. Nor was there any doubt that the emperor exercised the military command prerogative not through ministers of state (the cabinet) but through the autonomous organs of military command. Thus, the military prerogative was free, not only of parliamentary influence (in this it was not different from the treaty-making prerogative, for instance), but even of civil control or interference within the executive sphere.

But there remained much uncertainty as to the scope of the military command prerogative and the limits of the competence of the military command organs, especially whether the autonomous responsibility of those organs extended to matters of military administration (Article XII) as well as military command. Minobe likened the distinction between these two elements to that between adjudication and judicial administration, according to which adjudication was made by judges independently of the executive but the administration of the judicial establishment was, through the ministry of justice, a matter of cabinet responsibility. His insistence on preservation of the distinction aimed patently at limiting the competence of the military command organs: "Since the exercise of military command is placed beyond the responsibility of state ministers and thus constitutes an important exception to the general rule that ministers of state are responsible for all matters of state, it is necessary that its scope be properly defined. If it is given an unduly extended latitude the government of the state will be controlled by military power and the evils of militarism will arise." He included within the proper scope of military command: (1) the power to direct the activities of the armed forces once they had been put into action by decision of the government; (2) determination of the internal organization of the armed forces; (3) military training and education; and (4) military discipline.

Several matters involving the military were outside the competence of military command, however: all military expenditures were subject to the diet's budgetary powers and were properly a subject of cabinet responsibility; military command could not, except under conditions and within the limits of extraordinary crisis, determine the rights and duties of subjects; and the external organization of the armed forces, since it was so important in respect to foreign policy and fiscal policy, was properly a matter of cabinet responsibility.[79] But, Minobe noted, these limitations had not been observed in practice: "hitherto there has been no firm provision in law concerning the boundary between military command and military administration. This boundary had been established rather by custom, and in actual practice military command has not infrequently encroached upon the sphere of military administration so that matters of pure military administration have been treated as matters of military command, with the result that the integrity of state administration has been damaged."

The transgressions Minobe charged to the military command organs were not entirely of recent occurrence. Indeed, he was challenging the constitutionality of the position attained by the military in relation to the government from the earliest days under the constitution. His indictment consisted of four counts: (1) While the province of the superior organs of military command was to submit defense plans for imperial decision, to be made on the advice of ministers of state, the military had in fact virtually monopolized the process of defense planning to the exclusion of the cabinet. (2) Although the war and navy ministers were, as members of the cabinet, organs of military administration and not of military command, they had repeatedly reported directly to the throne without reference to the cabinet and without leave of the prime minister—and not only on military command matters but on questions of military organization and other aspects of military administration. We note here that the minister of war (and navy) continued as members (ex officio) of the military command organs. Thus they occupied an anomalous position, being in some matters independent of their civil colleagues and yet sharing in the collective responsibility of the cabinet on all matters of state.[80] (3) By sending military forces abroad on imperial sanction obtained by direct petition to the throne, the organs of military command had invaded the area of foreign relations, properly the responsibility of the cabinet. Similarly, the appointment and dismissal of military officers, properly a matter of state prerogative under Article X and thus to be determined on the responsible advice of ministers of state, had been in practice determined exclusively by military command organs. (4) The service ministers had employed military ordinances to dispose not only of military command matters but also of matters of military administration; they had indeed used them to amend or to abolish imperial ordinances.[81]

The long-standing conflict between the cabinet and the military command erupted spectacularly in a much-publicized dispute arising out of Japan's adherence to the London Naval Treaty in 1930. In April, 1930, the cabinet, under Prime Minister Hamaguchi, whose Minseito was the minority party in the house of representatives, and Foreign Minister Shidehara, accepted a compromise on the heavy cruiser ratio and voted to sign the London Naval Treaty. The cabinet sought and received imperial approval of its decision. The Japanese plenipotentiary at London had urged the government to accept the compromise even though it had been made at the expense of one of the three minimum conditions stated by Japan at the opening of the conference. The navy staff, which had dictated the original position, made known its opposition to the compromise from the first. Immediately after the cabinet decision, Chief of the Navy Staff Kato Kanji, with the support of the supreme war council, reported directly to the emperor in opposition to the treaty. Partisans of the navy's position and members of the opposition (*Seiyukai*) attacked the government in the diet, charging that the cabinet's failure to harmonize its diplomacy with the military command's decision on defense requirements was an unconstitutional interference with the imperial military prerogative. The prime minister successfully defended the treaty before a hostile privy council without entering into the constitutional question (his party having meanwhile gained a clear victory in a general election). The treaty was ratified in October. There were a number of collateral issues in the dispute, notably in respect to the role of

Navy Minister Takarabe, who attended the London Conference as principal technical advisor to the Japanese delegation and who more or less supported the government against the navy staff.[82]

In the course of this policy crisis, Minobe entered the lists with a spate of journal articles in defense of the cabinet, resolving in its favor the two immediate constitutional questions arising from the dispute: (1) whether it was constitutionally possible and proper for the government to reach a decision on national defense contrary to that of the navy staff and of the supreme war council, and, having done so, to report it to the throne and have it confirmed; and (2) whether it was constitutionally proper for the navy staff and the supreme war council to report to the throne in opposition to an international treaty which had already been signed.[83]

The second of these questions was at the time, and is for us, of relatively minor consequence. Minobe's answer to it was, in brief, that signature of the treaty constituted an expression of state will contingent only on subsequent ratification, and that ratification was entirely a matter to be settled between the cabinet and the privy council, the military command organs having absolutely no constitutional basis for intervention.[84]

It followed inevitably from his view of the supreme command prerogative that he responded affirmatively to the first question, holding that it was not the autonomous status of the military advisory and consultative organs that was at issue. As noted earlier, he accepted their autonomy as firmly established in practice and constitutionally permissible, although not mandatory. The dispute had to do rather with the scope of the independent supreme command. The matter over which the navy staff and the cabinet had come into disagreement on this occasion concerned not military command but military administration, a subject properly within the competence of the cabinet. The navy, after all, was but a creature of the state; it was not self-constituted. The determination of its size and strength was a matter relating directly to foreign policy and the economy of the state and was thus a matter of state for which the cabinet bore full and exclusive responsibility.

To be sure, Minobe explained, it did not follow from this that the organs of military command were excluded entirely from the determination of national defense policy. The navy staff and the supreme war council were indeed obliged by the ordinances under which they functioned to plan and to advise the emperor on national defense problems. In any case, it was quite proper that the cabinet rely in military matters as in all others on the best technical and professional advice available. It was, perhaps, understandable that the military command organs should pretend to vest all their functions and decisions with that special sanctity which covered their exclusive relation to the monarch in matters of military command. But, to the cabinet, the conclusions of the military organs on such matters as the strength of the military establishment were advisory only. The cabinet had to reach its decision within the broader scope of other concerns of state.[85]

Minobe's part in the London Treaty affair was not limited to his published articles. Important officials and other influential persons consulted him directly. Although this fact was generally known and has been often alluded to in the chronicles of those times, the only firsthand report we have is Harada Kumao's narrative of his activities in the service of the *genrō* Saionji. Harada relates that the great confusion of opinion concerning the government's claim to responsibility for national defense led him to seek out Minobe for clarification. The interview occurred in June at the university over lunch, with the chief of the secretariat of the lord keeper of the privy seal and two senior career officials of the foreign ministry present. Harada says only that "when several points of constitutional theory had been clarified we took our leave." Harada consulted Minobe again in August concerning the role of the privy council in respect to the cabinet's responsibility for the treaty. After both interviews he reported their substance to Saionji and to others.[86]

The happy augury of the cabinet's victory on this occasion was not to be fulfilled. Indeed the results were clouded, even as they were recorded, as a consequence of the government's policy of avoiding the constitutional issue in the hope of salvaging the treaty. In the diet the cabinet met all questions simply with an assertion of its authority under Article LV. Before the privy council the premier pretended that there was no conflict between the cabinet and the navy, and he induced the council to accept the navy minister as spokesman for the navy. Minobe, although a critic of official secretiveness in relations between government and diet,[87] found some excuse for the government's reticence before the diet on this occasion: "If the government clearly announces its opinion, immediately there is a clash between the military and the government and the result of such a clash inevitably threatens the life of the cabinet.

. . . This is probably why the present cabinet has avoided as much as possible answering the pertinacious questions of members of the diet. . . . Even though it seems to us weak and a violation of the principle of open government, it must be admitted that from the cabinet's point of view it is unavoidable."[88] But the cabinet's equivocation before the privy council was, apparently, another thing; Minobe could only deplore it. The government's case, he asserted, was constitutionally strong, but the cabinet had squandered the advantage enjoyed in public opinion vis-à-vis the military and the privy council—betraying the very constitutional justification for its action, a price too great even for the ransom of a cabinet.[89]

Baron Harada's diary notes that in general the government was inclined to accept Minobe's theory, that Premier Hamaguchi himself approved of it. Why then did the cabinet not take its stand on Minobe's assertion that "the navy general staff advises the throne in the exercise of the imperial prerogative of supreme command, but the views of the navy general staff are only advisory to the government; they have no conclusive authority"? The cabinet, Harada suggests, sought to prevent a stiffening of the atmosphere; therefore it preferred rather to pretend that there was no constitutional issue than to adopt an unappealingly bold, even dogmatic professorial stance in addressing its opponents.[90]

Far from marking a recession of military influence in Japanese government, the naval treaty controversy seems rather to have been the high-water mark of party government, after which the tide of "normal constitutional government" ebbed rapidly. This defeat may have served more than any other single event to crystallize military opposition to party government.[91] If the Minseito had been guilty of trepidation, the leaders of the Seiyukai were by no means guiltless, for they had pursued a short-sighted and viciously opportunistic policy of heckling the government, playing the game of the military politicians, and nourishing the spreading fires of violent opposition.[92] It may not be too farfetched to suppose that participation in this momentarily successful combination against the military was the most immediate of the causes that brought the wrath of the extremists down on Hamaguchi, Saionji, Makino, Ichiki, and others during the succeeding five years. Certainly there was little Minobe could have done more likely to have ensured him the precedence which he enjoyed as a target of the antiparliamentary, militarist movement.[93]

Minobe's attack on the problem of the military in government did not deal only with the conflict of competence between the cabinet and the organs of military command. He was concerned also about the participation of military men in the cabinet (*bukan daijin seido*). To this end he turned the principle of civil-military separation against the military, pointing out that strict adherence to its purport prohibited the participation of active-duty military men in the government of the country. "No one," he declared, "pretends that active-duty military men can be forbidden to have opinions about and knowledge of government; the question is whether it can be permitted for them to become active in current political affairs." Since military interference in civilian affairs was no less dangerous than civilian interference in military affairs, it was difficult indeed "to reconcile the role of military men with that of cabinet officers, especially with that of the prime minister."[94] Doubtless he had shared with liberal political elements the hope that the fall of the government of Admiral Kato Tomosaburo in 1924 marked the end of the military prime ministers. Even when he conceded that the choice of prime minister might properly fall on men other than party leaders in the house of representatives, he did not include military men among those he considered eligible.[95] When a civilian was named acting minister of war in 1930 during an illness of the minister, General Ugaki, Minobe was critical of the circumstances relating to the appointment, but he concluded that "in view of the fact the reasons for prohibiting the appointment of civilians . . . are very weak, this event may be a portentous step in the direction of making civilian posts of the service ministries."[96]

Military intrusion on the cabinet was assured, however, by the presence there of senior military officers as minister of war and minister of navy. This unhealthy condition was aggravated, Minobe noted, by the failure of the service ministers to keep within the strict limits of their competence. Because they had not adhered faithfully to their cabinet roles as ministers of military administration but had presumed to function as though they were advisors to the throne on matters of military command, "a very strange character" had been imposed on Japan's cabinet system. Vitiation of the principles of cabinet solidarity and administrative integrity destroyed one of the necessary conditions of effective cabinet responsibility. True, this perverted position of the war and navy ministers "astride the separation of military and government" was sanctioned by law and custom;[97] on the other hand, it had no positive constitutional sanction and there was no need for those who shunned an attempt at constitutional amendment to despair of a remedy for the malady. Since the principle of separation of military and civil affairs had been established not by the provisions of the constitution but by convention and by imperial ordinances, Minobe held that "if it should in the future be desirable to amend it, making military command also a matter of cabinet responsibility, and thus to bring the armed forces under cabinet supervision, no constitutional amendment would be needed; rather it could be accomplished by amending the ordinances" governing the cabinet and the military command organs.[98]

The responsibility of the cabinet extended, then, to all matters of state, to all of the imperial prerogative except portions falling within the inexactly defined provinces of the imperial household and the supreme command. Within the area of the state prerogative itself the responsibilities of the cabinet were qualified by the operation of the separation of powers in accordance with which an independent judiciary exercised the emperor's judicial prerogative,[99] and the Imperial Diet participated with the government in the performance of the legislative prerogative. In spite of these limitations and the difficulties it experienced in relation to other executive agencies of the monarchy, the cabinet wielded formidable power; it enjoyed an especially great advantage of authority and prestige in comparison with the diet. If there existed seats of power outside the cabinet at times capable of determining the course of government, the cabinet nonetheless was the government, its offices the focus of all politics, its minister president, the prime minister, the chief political officer of the empire.

Cabinet Solidarity.—It is only as it relates to the major problem of responsible government that the cabinet concerns us here, and for that reason the only problem requiring further comment is that of cabinet solidarity, an essential component of the interpretive structure upon which Minobe founded his case for responsible government in Japan.[100]

Minobe argued for the necessity of cabinet solidarity and for removing all obstacles to its achievement. Since the Imperial Constitution (Article LV) spoke only of individual ministers (namely, "the respective ministers of state" and "a minister of state"), their collective identity rested primarily on the Cabinet Ordinance of 1889.[101] The Cabinet Ordinance itself made no explicit reference to cabinet solidarity; consequently the convention of solidarity rested on little more than the implications of the prime minister's supervisory powers and on the weight of practical necessity. Neither of these was sufficient to overcome all obstacles to solidarity; indeed, the whole position was discounted by some commentators who, as part of their defense of the bureaucratic cabinet idea, emphasized the individual responsibility of ministers to the emperor. Minobe saw in the cabinet the agency for unifying and harmonizing the separate and particular responsibilities of the several ministers. He described the cabinet as "the collegiate organ existing for the purpose of permitting joint deliberation concerning the duties of ministers of state."[102] In effect, the ministers bore collective as well as individual responsibility for their advice and administrative performance, and that responsibility extended to all matters of state, and even to imperial household and supreme command matters when they impinged upon any of the legitimate subjects of ministerial responsibility. If the cabinet failed to achieve and preserve unanimity its only recourse was resignation. The function of cabinet deliberations was the attainment of the indispensable unanimity through discussion and compromise, hence the convention that cabinet meetings be secret and that the emperor never attend them.

The burden of maintaining cabinet solidarity rested upon the prime minister. But the powers he enjoyed under the Cabinet Ordinance to control the individual and collective affairs of the ministers of state, while rather broad, did not suffice to overcome the lack of real political solidarity among his civilian colleagues. Even the important role he played in the formation and retirement of the cabinet was seriously complicated by his lack of freedom of choice in filling the posts of minister of war and minister of navy. Since these ministers were not subject to party pressures, and since their positions as military officers were entirely independent of the cabinet's pleasure, the premier had no means short of resignation to compel their adherence to the cabinet line once they were appointed. In devious ways and in direct ways, the special status of the military members was a solid obstacle to cabinet solidarity.

Cabinet-Privy Council Relations.—Prominent among the bureaucratic adjuncts of the monarchy and notable for its proportions as an obstacle to responsible government in Japan was the privy council.[103] Created by Ito in 1888 to formalize the final stages of deliberation on the draft of the Imperial Constitution, the privy council continued as a consultative organ of the monarchy under the terms of the constitution itself.[104]

The distinctive characteristics of this institution were its consultative function, its close relation to the monarch, and its bureaucratic composition. The privy council had no administrative functions; its duty was not to "advise" (*hohitsu*), but to give "counsel" (*komon*) to the emperor in response to imperial inquiry about matters of state and imperial household affairs.[105] The privy councilors were responsible to the monarch only, their function of counseling bearing none of the connotations of political responsibility implied in the function "advising" or "assisting." The privy council had absolutely no legal relationship to the diet, but there tended to be a rapport between the council and the bureaucratic elements of the house of peers. The cabinet alone bore full responsibility for its action in following or rejecting the opinion of the councilors and for any failure to bring matters before the council.[106]

The "privy council problem" under the Meiji Constitution arose not only from its irresponsibility and power but also from the character of its personnel. It was conceived as, and continued to the end to be, the preserve of the highest echelons of the bureaucracy—in the early period the Satcho oligarchs and their minions.[107] Although members of the cabinet were members *ex officio* of the privy council, its size was adjusted to keep them in the minority. It is not surprising that occasions for conflict between the two bodies increased rapidly as the cabinet fell under the influence of the parliamentary parties. The council tended to assume a supervisory attitude toward the cabinet, especially in matters of foreign, military, educational, and civil-service policy. The prestige of the council among the bureaucrats and the quasi-sanctity of its relation to the throne made it very difficult for the cabinet to recommend a course of action to which the council had raised objections. That there were so few open clashes was due very likely to the cabinet's clearing proposed action with members of the council before committing itself publicly.

Minobe harbored fundamental doubts as to the validity of such an irresponsible center of power under constitutional government; he criticized its excesses of power and sought to interpret its role narrowly, aiming to clear the way for full cabinet responsibility.[108] His criticism of the privy council began with the fact that it was absolutely divorced from official contact with the diet or the people[109] and was protected from the cabinet's encroachment by the council president's veto over nominations to the council and by the effect of Article VI of the Privy Council Ordinance, which gave the council itself a veto over any proposed changes in that ordinance. Thus, he noted, the privy council was irresponsible. Councilors, most of them being retired officials, lacked the restraint and understanding that might have been imposed by active administrative responsibility. In view of these circumstances, it was improper and "dangerous" that the privy council have the power to advise against the granting of imperial sanction to important constitutional laws or constitutional amendments approved by the diet.

It might be argued, Minobe observed, that there was relatively more justification for the operation of the privy council as a check on the government regarding policies made and executed unilaterally by the latter, as in the case of treaties, emergency ordinances, proclamations of martial law, and imperial ordinances bearing penal sanctions. But this function, he held, were far better entrusted, as in some other countries, to a committee of the diet. To be sure, the privy council had been described and equipped by its basic ordinances to function as a constitutional court, as "the guardian of the constitution"; but there was no constitutional authority for such a role. Constitutional interpretations made by the council upon imperial inquiry had no legally binding effect on the cabinet or any other organ of government. The Privy Council Ordinance bound the cabinet to advise solicitation of the council's opinion regarding matters enumerated in Article IV of the ordinance, but the cabinet was nevertheless completely on its own responsibility in advising the throne, whether its advice was in harmony or at odds with the opinion of the privy council. Particularly objectionable in Minobe's opinion was the council's evil and reckless abuse of its powers in its covert opposition to the government's efforts to make changes in the civil-service and educational systems.

Regardless of the theoretical freedom of the cabinet to advise the emperor in a manner contrary to the opinion of the privy council, it was in practice hardly able to do so. To force imperial choice between conflicting recommendations would, in effect, direct the throne to the advice of the lord privy seal and the genrō. The cabinet, participating in the privy council, would find itself in the awkward position of asserting a minority view. In view of the great prestige of the privy council as "the emperor's highest resort of counsel," the cabinet typically had little practical alternative other than submission or resignation.

The council's obstructive role was more acutely exposed in April, 1927, when it counseled the emperor not to sanction an emergency financial ordinance proposed by the Wakatsuki Cabinet. The cabinet was forced to resign, even though it had a substantial majority in the house of representatives. Minobe dubbed the succeeding Tanaka Cabinet, "cabinet by grace of the privy council."[110] Clearly such a situation was out of keeping with basic constitutional principles, for, aside from the loss of the monarch's confidence, the only proper reason for the resignation of a cabinet was internal disunity or loss of public confidence as reflected in the diet. When in 1928 the privy council approved an emergency ordinance amending the Peace Preservation Law, Minobe found the council's action to be correct despite his strong objections to the content of the measure and to the method of its adoption: "That the ordinance should be issued is an evil, but for the privy council to bring down the cabinet would be an even greater evil." It was not the proper function of the privy council to substitute its judgment on matters of fact, nor to supervise the cabinet, nor to make demands on it or question its responsibility. The privy council did not in any sense represent the public.[111]

Minobe regarded the political weight of the council as "the result of the system and not of personality, for it does not appear that privy councilors have been superior to cabinet ministers." If the system had merit, it was "in its capacity to counterbalance certain evils inherent in party government, but in this respect it merely duplicated the role of the house of peers." Minobe could hardly have foreseen his own role as a privy councilor, in the days of the council's expiration, when he concluded with the judgment that "the privy council system is probably fated for abolition in the future development of our constitutional system."[112]

Monarchy was the first of the two major components in Minobe's construction of the imperial constitutional system. He recognized in its "peculiar strength" the prime distinguishing characteristic of that system. His interpretation was one which duly credited the vast legal powers and the complex bureaucratic paraphernalia which vested and supported the monarchy. It fully appreciated the hold which that institution had on the passions and sentiments of the Japanese. At the same time, his interpretation insisted on finding in the elements of Japanese monarchy under the Meiji Constitution an essential compatibility with constitutionalism. This he achieved by construing narrowly every autocratic factor, by discounting the gap between constitutional practice and his constitutional theory on the basis of his expressed faith in the continuing development of the Japanese state in the spirit and form of constitutional democracy, and by striking on every opportunity at the institutional obstacles to this development. Three key propositions emerged as indices of his constitutional liberalism: that the imperial prerogative was limited in scope and in the mediacy of its exercise, that the cabinet's responsibilty could and should be extended as nearly as possible to cover the entire prerogative, and that there was no constitutional obstacle to the subjection of the prerogative, in part or in whole, to parliamentary influence or control.

V

Minobe's Constitutional Theory: An Interpretation of Meiji Constitutionalism

Minobe said in the introduction to *Kempō Seigi* that "the principles that have ruled the governments of western states since the French Revolution, insofar as they are compatible with the principles of monarchy derived from our own peculiar history, have been taken into our constitution." The Meiji constitutional system, as he would have us see it, was the product of an equation in which western constitutionalism and Japanese monarchy were bound in a kind of mathematical relationship. It was a relationship too complex, indeed, to be represented by any simple conventional symbols, a relationship of mutual reaction and accommodation. The implication of unilateral adjustment in the passage cited above is somewhat misleading, for the accommodation as he elaborated it was definitely reciprocal. That passage would have conveyed the sense of his interpretation more adequately had it gone on to say that the native idea of monarchy was carried forward under the Imperial Constitution only insofar as it was compatible with the essentials of the western theory of constitutional government. And these he equated with limited, responsible, representative democracy.

Throughout his discussion of the monarchical aspects of the constitution, Minobe curbed and tailored the content and form of Japanese monarchy to accord with the irreducible requirements of the abstract idea of constitutional government. But constitutionalism itself had to be defined, not merely as theory, but concretely as legal and political phenomena; it had to be brought to earth, given reality in terms of law, made a positive operating premise in the thinking of the governing class.

In his efforts with this problem, Minobe had not only to advance the novel and alien against the traditional and native; he had also to defend and promote his position in competition with various other doctrines and philosophies relating to constitutional government in the west.

Minobe believed three basic propositions of modern constitutional theory were immanent, however imperfectly manifested, in the Meiji constitutional system: they were representative government, responsible government, and the rule of law. How he demonstrated the juristic basis of their existence in the law of the Imperial Constitution, how he projected his faith in their fulfillment in constitutional practice, and what he conceived to be the adaptations and qualifications necessary to conform with the realities of Japanese politics and with his own critical reservations concerning the course of modern constitutional development— these are the major themes upon which we now focus.

The Diet

Constitutional government, according to Minobe, is representative government, government with popular approval. Its first and minimum condition is the existence of a popularly representative parliament with power to participate in legislation and to oversee the conduct of administration. This prime requisite had been formally satisfied in Japan with the opening of the Imperial Diet in 1890.

Historically, in the west, representative government had been a response to the idea of popular self-government. But there was a direct conflict between Japanese principles of monarchy and the notion of government by the people or their representatives; consequently, the Japanese constitution limited the meaning of representative government to the proposition that government by the monarch and his agents be in harmony with the inclinations (i-kō) of the people, as indicated in the expression "government by the monarch and the people jointly" (kumin dōchi). The popularly elected house of representatives brought the inclinations of the people to bear on the processes of government. This characterization of the role of the diet was doubtless an unavoidable affirmation of the formal incompatibility between the Japanese principle of monarchical sovereignty and the idea of popular sovereignty. It did not prevent Minobe from projecting for the diet, and for the cabinet based on the diet (at least in his writing prior to 1932), a role which, if it failed fully to provide for supremacy of popular will in government, did not fail to do so because of formal denial of popular sovereignty.

Among modern constitutional states, Japan was unique in the weakness of its parliamentary institutions. It was not merely a deficiency arising from inexperience and a hostile social environment, but one built into the constitution as specific limitations on the powers and functions of the diet. With their attachment to the imperial tradition and their appreciation of the merits of monarchy, the bureaucratic authors of the constitution regarded with fear and abhorrence the prospect of a growing popular influence in public affairs inherent in a representative parliament. They sought to ensure the continued subordination of the diet to a monarchical-bureaucratic scheme by reserving broad independent powers to the emperor, by holding the cabinet responsible to the emperor, by making the privy council independent of the diet, by circumscribing the budgetary powers of the diet, by including in the imperial prerogative the power to prorogue the diet and to dissolve the house of representatives, and by granting to the very narrowly representative upper house full legislative powers.

Throughout the period concerned here, Minobe was dedicated to the advancement of the diet to what he considered its proper position as the representative organ of a constitutional monarchy. He believed that the inner logic of the adoption of constitutional government in 1889 led inevitably to a magnification of the role of the diet. He was not, however, a revisionist in the strict sense of the word; with the exception of his forecast of the eventual abolition of the privy council and his criticism of the constitutional position of the house of peers, he suggested no changes in the Imperial Constitution itself. His goal, he felt, was obtainable by a "correct reading" of that constitution, by changes in various supplementary laws and ordinances, by the gradual evolution of appropriate customs and conventions, and by instilling in the people "not only as a matter of knowledge but as a matter of deepest sentiment, a respect for and faith in the diet, its members, and the most important organs of the diet, the political parties, and making them aware that as citizens it is their great duty to function as electors."[1]

The scope of his labors in behalf of the diet and the breadth and persistence of his attacks upon all antiparliamentary forces invites the judgment that he favored parliamentary supremacy. His emphasis on the diet indeed bespoke his faith in the efficacy of representative government and his distrust of the alternatives.[2] It may be surmised that Minobe was not altogether disinterested in his defense of the Minseito when that party was attacked for having affronted national polity with its slogan *gikai chūshin seiji* (government centered on the diet). The idea, Minobe said, was not intended as a contradiction of the legal position of the emperor at the center of government; its purpose was to indicate that of all the political forces that might seek to dominate the ministerial advisors of the throne, that represented by the majority in the house of representatives should prevail, rather than that of the clans, the peers, the bureaucrats, or the military.[3]

It must be noted in qualification of this view that Minobe understood that the cabinet, not the diet, was the heart of government as a matter of political fact as well as of legal theory, and he entertained some misgivings about various aspects of the doctrine and practice of representative government. For instance, he expounded the merits of strict proportional representation, and at the same time he endorsed the virtues of bicameralism and the prerogative power of dissolution as checks against the rise of representative despotism (*shūgi-in sensei*). He defended the idea of majority party government but he also conceded that it was legal fiction to equate the acts of the house of representatives with popular will, and he regarded sheer majoritarianism as a dangerous working principle. The ambivalence between reserve and enthusiasm in his attitude toward parliamentarism was roughly paralleled in the dichotomy between his formal legal commentaries and his occasional political tracts. In the latter, he pursued his political inclinations freely in a way impossible in works of legal interpretation, often giving expression to ideas which only with great difficulty could be read into the hard lines of his formal constitutional interpretation.[4]

Minobe defined the diet juristically as "an independent state organ which participates in the governmental power of the state representing the people."[5] In terms of the state-personality theory, the diet was a representative direct organ, as such enjoying status superior to that of all other state organs except the emperor, for it owed its competence directly to the constitution and was subject to no supervision in the exercise of that competence. "The Imperial Diet," Minobe noted, "takes part in the government of the state as representative of the people; it does not derive its competence from the emperor. Consequently as a fundamental rule the diet occupies a position of complete independence in relation to the emperor (except in the matter of opening and closing its session and in the selection of members of the house of peers)."[6] This independence distinguished the diet from those organs, such as the cabinet, the privy council, or the courts, which gained their competence by imperial delegation. Accordingly, Minobe refuted classification of the diet as an organ of imperial rule. If the diet were but an agent of the emperor, its competence originating from the imperial prerogative, then it was no different from the preconstitutional *genrō-in*, and the Imperial Constitution lost one of the essential qualities of constitutional government.[7]

It was necessary to the constitutional role of the diet that it be popularly representative, Minobe held, for constitutional government meant government conducted with popular assistance. The diet existed for the purpose of representing the people; indeed, it was as representative of the people (*kokumin ni kawarite*, or *kokumin daihyō toshite*) that the diet participated in the exercise of governmental power. Its decisions were legally the will of the people, and only the fiction of the representative relationship made the popular influence feasible. It could not be denied, Minobe observed, that the constitution said neither that the diet represented the people nor that the people had the power to participate in government. On the other hand, he believed it was universally accepted "in the public mind" that the main purpose of parliaments was to give representation to the people, and law is exactly that which is recognized in social consciousness to be law. Popular participation was, moreover, clearly contemplated in the preamble: "hoping to maintain the prosperity of the state in concert with Our people and with their support. . . ." The very *raison d'être* of the diet was to enable subjects of the emperor to assist in the affairs of state.[8]

But the idea of popular representation was clouded by doctrinal conflicts and ambiguities quite apart from any supposed antagonism between it and traditional Japanese political values. Some commentators asserted that a parliament was representative only as a matter of political convention. They insisted that even though the political purpose of parliaments was to reflect popular opinion, parliament legally exercised its own discretion completely uncontrolled by external commissions or commands. They denied that "the people" constituted such a legal personality as is necessary to a representative relationship. But Minobe insisted that a representative relationship did indeed exist legally.

Granted that the diet does not achieve its competence by delegation (elections merely determine which persons shall be members of the diet); still, he said, there is a representative relationship. To say that the diet represents the people means only that legally the acts of the diet are viewed as expressions of popular will, albeit this constitutes representation by legal construction (*hōtei*) rather than by deputization (*juken*). Granted that "the people" do not constitute a willing personality; this is not to the point, for the diet does not represent an already existing will. It is only when the diet has already acted that the people can be said, legally speaking, to have a will.[9] The constructive representative relationship assumed in constitutional law is, moreover, independent of the special character of the house of representatives in its pretended political representation of the people. Indeed, the practical impossibility of achieving and maintaining through known electoral techniques an accurate concordance between parliamentary will and popular will warrants the establishment of precautionary restraints such as that afforded by bicameralism. According to the juristic formula, it was the diet, not the house of representatives alone, which represented popular will.[10]

In offering such an "undemocratic" definition of the representative relationship between the diet and the people he was, of course, paying his due to the *law* of the Meiji Constitution. It will be evident in what follows that he was not indifferent to the difficulties placed in the way of responsible parliamentary government by the house of peers, and that he was greatly interested in the *political* role of the house of representatives. Far from forgetting that the function of parliament, in constitutional theory, is to reflect popular opinion, to give the inclinations of the people an expression in government, Minobe protested that the existing constitutional system not merely failed to implement that principle but in fact obstructed its realization. His approach to this problem is exemplified in his critiques of the house of peers and of the electoral system.

REFORM OF THE HOUSE OF PEERS

In his endorsement of the bicameral principle Minobe paraded the conventional arguments (citing Esmein and Bryce): as a check on excess of legislative power and on the natural tendency of parliaments to attempt to become the focus of political power, as a check against deadlock between government and parliament, and as a check against legislative error.[11] His commitment to the idea of democratic participation in government did not lead him to espouse majoritarianism: "I concur in J. S. Mill's statement that the value of bicameralism lies in its restraint upon arbitrary action by a majority party. Opponents have a plausible argument when they say that bicameralism runs counter to the unity of electoral will. But such arguments erroneously assume that the house of representatives correctly represents electoral will. No electoral system known can achieve such a true reflection of electoral will as they assume."[12] The house of peers was needed, then, but only for the purpose of "correcting" the evils that arise from a union of the government and a majority of the house of representatives, not for the purpose of preventing such a union.

Both the composition and the powers of the Japanese house of peers failed to measure up to the criteria of a properly constituted upper house, Minobe felt. It was desirable that the upper house be constituted on a basis different from that of the lower house, and in such a way as to avoid parallel partisan divisions in the two houses. Appropriate standards for selection of its members were such qualities as knowledge, experience, and representation of various social groups. Minobe doubted, however, that the orders of nobility qualified on any of these counts for their heavy representation (195 seats) in the house of peers.[13] Apart from the special representation accorded to the Imperial Academy (4 seats) and to the higher taxpayers (66 seats), there were 125 lifetime imperial appointees. The cabinet controlled the selection of these appointees and in practice based its choice of nominees on partisan considerations, with the result that party strife was projected into the house of peers.[14]

More serious than these defects of composition were the excessive power and privileged status of the house of peers. A proper ordering of bicameral parliaments required, in Minobe's view, that the upper-house power should not deprive the lower house of its legislative primacy. The Japanese house of peers, however, was given complete legislative equality with the house of representatives. That condition, coupled with the fact that the upper house could not be dissolved, gave it an absolute veto over the house of representatives and over the government.[15] Moreover, the house of peers was unembarrassed by that Achilles' heel of its famous namesake, vulnerability to "packing." The constitution placed determination of the composition of the upper house in the House of Peers Ordinance (which, by its own terms, could be amended only with the consent of that chamber), and thus beyond the reach of the house of representatives and the government. This arrangement in Minobe's opinion was "perhaps the most unreasonable feature" of the Japanese constitution.[16] He recommended a number of changes in the ordinance: reduction of the number of seats by one half; abolition of pay for representatives of the orders of nobility; substitution of "a suitable electoral organ" to replace the cabinet in making imperial nominations; establishment of fixed terms for representatives of the nobility and for imperial appointees, renewable by thirds; and abolition of representation of high taxpayers.[17]

Minobe concluded, however, that effective reform of the house of peers was impossible "unless on the occasion of some future amendment of the constitution," for modification of the membership provisions would not accomplish much unless accompanied by reduction in constitutional powers. He proposed that should such an occasion arise the house of peers be reduced from its status of legislative equality to that of a control organ with power to delay or to force reconsideration, but not to veto.[18]

ELECTORAL REFORM

That achievement of a perfect representative relationship between the people and parliament was impossible was no reason, in Minobe's view, for neglecting to remedy obvious defects in that relationship. It was especially important that there be a close and satisfactory relationship between the electorate and the house of representatives, which was politically the real agency of popular participation in government. An important key to that relationship was the law governing the election of members of the house of representatives.[19] Though he had been a sympathetic observer of the drive for universal suffrage in Japan,[20] Minobe's great concern was for the eradication of those aspects of the system which negated or perverted the meaning and value of the ballot. He demonstrated this concern by his contributions to the electoral reform debate which engaged the attention of publicists, politicians, and, presumably, the public in the period 1929–1934.[21]

The credit and viability of democratic parliamentary government was at issue in Minobe's attack on the problem of electoral reform. Constitutional government is parliamentary government and parliamentary government is party government, but is party government popular government? The hostility of the genrō toward political parties had been incompatible with constitutional government and was inevitably abandoned. The surrender had not been complete, however, for there persisted an inclination to reserve the benefits of the new dispensation to the two major political factions with which the old bureaucratic forces had merged. The continuation of the two-party system in Japan, Minobe said, resulted from the imperatives of party finance: "It is not because Japan, under present political and social conditions, has no need of parties other than its two major parties." To make matters worse, the extension of the suffrage had been coupled with a tightening of restrictive police measures aimed at checking the development of "proletarian parties" (musan seito).[22] Moreover, the result of the victory of party government (1924) had not been entirely gratifying to the Japanese people, for the parties were highly culpable on the score of venal subservience to special interests and of manifold forms of corruption and malpractice. The result of the introduction of universal suffrage had been to inflate the incidence of electoral corruption. Public opinion was susceptible to antiparliamentary preaching from the left and from the right. The abandonment of parliamentary government was, to Minobe, a thoroughly repugnant idea, yet the threat of its popular rejection seemed to him clearly present so long as the party system remained unregenerate.[23]

As Minobe saw it, however, the practical choice was not one between perfection and damnation. No system could entirely escape the weakness of "human nature." The inequities of majority rule and a high incidence of ignorant and venal electoral behavior were inherent in universal suffrage. Quite apart from the party system, important factors contributing to the decline of parliamentary government were to be found in the drastic economic changes following the war.[24] Nevertheless, it was urgently necessary to look to the faults of the party system itself. Since the electoral law was a major determinant in this system, it was understandable that people should hope to advance the health of party government by effecting appropriate changes in the electoral law. The main objects of public indignation and of professional concern were corrupt practices and the unscrupulous struggle for power, phenomena by no means limited to the electoral process itself.

Minobe conceded the seriousness of the corrupt motives and behavior of the parties. Election bribery, subservience of diet members to special interests, partisan abuse of police power in electoral campaigns —all of these were indeed damaging to parliamentary government and it was only "natural that the government should respond to the growing public clamor against these iniquities." But in Minobe's view they were but symptomatic of a defect running straight to the heart of the electoral system, and he disparaged most of the officially sponsored reform proposals because they aimed at specific abuses rather than at underlying causes. They failed on grounds of inadequacy, impracticality, or misdirection.[25]

Minobe proposed to overcome two basic defects of the existing electoral system. The first of these was the multi-member, single-vote district system, which failed to give fair minority representation in the diet. It distorted the relative popular strength of the two major parties; it necessitated excessive campaign costs by multiplying the number of separate contests; and it scarred the representative character of the parties and the diet with sectional conflicts. The second, more general defect arose from the "individualism" (kojin shugi) rationale of the electoral system. The idea that the electoral process consisted in the exercise of individual voter's free choice among a number of candidates on the basis of their qualifications was quite illusory; it put upon the individual elector a duty of which he was incapable, however well intentioned, well trained, and experienced he might be. It debased and obscured the significance of the individual ballot, leaving the voter vulnerable to improper influences, and it encouraged non-voting and thus added to the difficulty of campaign finance by generating a furious scramble for stray ballots. By ignoring the role of political parties, the election law presumed a condition altogether at variance with the fact that elections are contests between parties, that the primary function of the elector is to choose between parties rather than to select qualified individuals, and that, ultimately, the house of representatives is really concerned not so much with legislating as with supplying the basis for the formation of a cabinet. In combination, these two defects produced an inaccurate reflection of public sentiment regarding the major parties and virtually squeezed out the minor parties. They weakened internal party control and tended to remove parliamentary parties from effective popular surveillance.[26]

Minobe decided that the electoral scheme offering greatest promise of overcoming the basic defects he had identified was the strictly limited list system of proportional representation (*genkaku kōsoku no mei-boshiki hirei daihyō*).[27] Used in a single national constituency, this system would maximize minority representation, would reconstrue the elector's function as one of making a choice between parties, would stabilize party leadership, and would enhance internal party discipline. To be beneficial, the reform he proposed required what many would strongly object to, namely that the internal control of party leadership be scrupulously maintained, that the entire membership of the party submit uniformly and willingly to the authority of the party leaders.[28]

The sources of the idea of the strict list system of proportional representation lay in the doctrinal baggage of the promoters of *parliamentarisme integrale* in postwar Europe. Minobe urged that reference be made "not to the systems of England and America which have by long tradition influenced our legislators, but to the systems of continental Europe, particularly to those of Germany."[29] He doubtless realized that there was no hope of the adoption of so radical a model for it was quite without significant political support in Japan. His espousal of it represented an "off-beat" venture into the realm of rationalized democratic theory which seems especially strange in view of his rather sophisticated critique of the existing system, his generally limited commitment to the dogmas of parliamentary democracy, and in view of the by then considerable evidence of trouble in the Weimar party system. There can be little doubt that what attracted him to the list system was, first of all, that it offered solutions, in theory, to the problem of fair representation and to the problem of simplifying and purifying the electoral process. Furthermore, the concept of political parties inherent in the list system was congenial to his interpretation of the legal and political powers and functions of the diet. However that may be, the tone of his essays on electoral reform shifted from urgency and hopefulness to skepticism and resignation; we hear no more from him of proportional representation after 1934.

POWERS OF THE DIET

Definition of the constitutional role of the Imperial Diet was one of the most contentious problems before the interpreters of the Meiji Constitution. It involved legalistic disputes of vexing obscurity and complexity turning not so much on the laconic text of the constitution as on the application of general theoretical concepts of legislative power, the separation of powers, and the like. Each interpreter's underlying constitutional philosophy played a large part in his resolution of the problems. Few other constitutional questions elicited so clearly the contrast between the liberal and the orthodox positions.

The same theoretical premises which led him to give a narrow construction to the prerogative ordinance power induced Minobe to view the powers of the diet broadly. The provisions of the constitution did not define those powers; they merely indicated some of the important ways in which the diet exercised its competence and some of the ways in which the powers of the diet were limited.[30] Even as elaborated by various supplementary laws,[31] the terms of the constitution were inadequate. Real understanding of the diet's function was possible only when the language of the law was read in the light of the logic of constitutional government.[32]

Minobe proceeded on this basis to find for the diet a competence coëxtensive with the totality of the legislative and administrative matters (excluding imperial household affairs) for which ministers of state were responsible. This perspective, taken together with his denial of an exclusively autocratic character in the imperial prerogative, was the basis for his belief in the possibility that under the Meiji Constitution the whole of the state prerogative of the emperor could be submitted to regulation by statute law (horitsu) and thus brought under the control of the diet.[33] Tomio Nakano called this view "the theory of the parliamentary absorption of the ordinance power." While these are not Minobe's words, they fairly well express the sense of his theory which can be summarized thus: Properly interpreted and implemented, the constitution gave the cabinet complete and exclusive competence to advise the emperor on all matters of state. Properly interpreted and implemented, the constitution provided for a cabinet of men commanding the confidence of the majority in the house of representatives, with all extracabinet or supracabinet obstacles to cabinet accountability to that majority removed or abated.[34]

Minobe did not argue that diet participation in all such matters was constitutionally required, only that there was no constitutional obstacle to it; nor did he envisage the diet as the prime mover in the legislative process. As a matter of constitutional prescription, the diet's consent was required only in respect to approval of constitutional amendments, enactment of statutes, confirmation of emergency ordinances, and approval of the budget. The diet had no right of consent regarding administrative matters other than the budget unless such matters were submitted to it by the government. In respect to statutes, the diet's power of consent included the power to initiate bills and to amend government-sponsored bills. It had no such initiative regarding constitutional amendments and emergency ordinances; it could reduce but not increase items in the budget. The diet enjoyed several formal powers, such as receiving petitions, addressing the throne, the interpellation of ministers, and so on, some of which were important as means by which the diet extended its influence over administration, and as a means by which it might influence the exercise of the imperial prerogative.[35]

The submission of any particular part of the prerogative to regulation by diet-enacted law served only to give the diet a veto over future changes in the exercise of that prerogative. It gave the diet no unilateral control over the matter, for the diet could not by its own will bring such matters under the terms of a law, nor unilaterally make any changes in the provisions of such a law once enacted. It is clear that the real test of the diet's control of the prerogative lay in the operation of the conventions governing the relations between diet and cabinet.

Much may be made of the formal limitations on the powers of the diet under the Imperial Constitution and its supplementary ordinances and laws. Minobe was certainly aware of the fact that among modern parliaments the Imperial Diet was exceptionally weak. One might suggest, however, that those formal limitations were not in themselves a bar to effective parliamentary government. For example, one of the most serious and most frequently cited weaknesses of the diet lay in the provision of the constitution allowing the government unilaterally to continue the budget. As a matter of fact, this power was not used after 1900. Every cabinet came before the diet with new demands for more or less urgent revision of some aspect or another of the budget. The diet's failure to exploit this and other levers to assert the supremacy of its will would seem, then, to have been due to other causes: the extra-parliamentary and mostly extraconstitutional bureaucratic barriers to effective parliamentary cabinet government, the weakness and corruption of the parliamentary parties, and the continuation of an authoritarian psychology in Japanese politics. Minobe recognized these limitations and was a resolute, if frequently unrealistic, foe of them all. If, under the actual circumstances of Japanese constitutional practice, his assertions concerning the legislative powers of the diet were of little practical importance, they nevertheless constituted a vigorous assault on the bureaucratic concept of the legislative process advanced by conservative constitutional authorities.

Typically, Minobe stood in the forefront of Japanese liberal constitutional theorists in subscribing to the dual doctrines of the fusion or harmonization of legislative and administrative powers and the superiority of statutes over ordinances (*hōritsu jō-i*).[36] The constitution established a formal separation of powers (Articles V and LVII), but there was no provision for harmonizing the various state processes with the three-fold pattern of state organs. Consequently it was necessary to take note of the difference between the reality and the form of the separation of powers, and the reality consisted not so much in a separation as in a fusion of legislative and administrative processes of the state. This view of the three-power constitution was important as an antidote to the narrowly formal view upon which orthodox authorities based a view of the legislative power quite inimical to the pretensions of the diet.

Minobe believed that in a constitutional state, parliamentary consent was required in the exercise of legislative power—in the exercise by the state of the governmental power whereby it establishes in written form new legal rules as between government and people. Such was the meaning of Article V: that all legislation (*hōki*), except as specifically provided otherwise, required the consent of the diet. The diet was intended to be the legislative organ.[37] Consequently it was wrong to construe the legislative power (*rippōken*) in Article V in its formal sense, taking it as a definition of only that type of legislation known as statute (*hōritsu*) and which by the terms of Article XXXVII required diet approval. Such an interpretation was not only false, Minobe thought; it generated a further absurd proposition: that the scope of the legislative power was strictly defined by those articles of the constitution which expressly provided for regulation by statute, the so-called "legislative items" (*rippō jiko*), all other matters being left to the absolutely autocratic discretion of the government. He observed that the provisions of the constitution which required the enactment of statutes usually had to do with the rights and duties of subjects. Their purpose, he believed, was not to give a catalog of "legislative items" but to guarantee those matters expressly against manipulation by the prerogative ordinance power without the consent of the diet.[38]

The legislative power was, as a general rule, coëxtensive with the authority of the state, and the proper means of its exercise was the enactment of statutes by the diet. Since statutes could be enacted only with imperial sanction, it could not be counted a violation of the imperial prerogative if prerogative matters were determined by statute. Legislation by ordinance, on the other hand, was a departure from the rule, and while any proper subject of legislation might be determined by statute, only certain specifically enumerated matters (e.g., Imperial Household Law, emergency ordinances, treaties, etc.) could be determined by ordinance. In principle, there was no positive limit to the contents of a statute, but there were strict constitutional limits to the contents of an ordinance.[39] As a matter of fact, there were a number of specific and implied limitations on what could be regulated by statute. For instance, statutes could not touch upon imperial household matters, the constitution of the house of peers, or the competence of the judiciary. Statutes were theoretically limited by international law. But as a result of the formal separation of powers, there was no review of the constitutionality of any statute which met the formal requirement for enactment.[40]

The conflict over the legislative power was important as it related to the overshadowing problem of responsible government. The diet's power of legislative consent was important chiefly because it was one of the weapons in the arsenal of obstruction by which acceptance of the convention of cabinet accountability to the diet was extorted from the bureaucratic oligarchs. Minobe recognized that the formal powers of the diet were of less significance than the political role realized through three functions of the diet: constant exposure of official operations to public view; provision of a political basis for the formation of cabinets; and the recruitment and training of statesmen from outside the bureaucratic ranks.[41] It was the political role of the diet which was the bone of contention in the constitutional debates concerning the parliamentary cabinet system and party government.

Responsible Government

"Constitutional government is responsible government": for Minobe this was the second great rule of constitutionalism, a close corollary of the principle of popular government. The idea of the accountability of government to public inquiry and criticism was the antithesis of the habit of official secrecy which characterized despotic regimes. With the inauguration of the constitution, that venerable maxim of Japanese officialdom which said of the people, "let them be made to depend on government; let them be kept in ignorance," had been replaced by the proposition that the affairs of government should, within the limits of reason, be kept exposed to public view, the better to ensure that government be conducted in harmony with the inclinations of the people. Fulfillment of that proposition required at very least that the people be free to inquire into and to criticize the actions of those responsible for the exercise of governmental power. This requirement was usually implemented through some form of ministerial accountability to parliament— under appropriate conditions, some form of the parliamentary cabinet system.[42]

Ministerial responsibility in the sense of accountability to the people through the diet was quite a different thing from the exclusive individual responsibility to the emperor in the orthodox interpretation of Article LV.[43] Minobe's treatment of the relationship between the ministers of state and the emperor and the problem of the division of responsibility among the administrative organs makes it clear that his primary concern was to clear the way for the assertion of ministerial responsibility to the diet. When he linked Article LV with Article III (sacred inviolability of the emperor) and introduced analogies from modern western monarchical theory, he was striking at the bureaucratic inclination to conceal the processes of administration behind the sacred aura of the monarch. His criticism of the irresponsibility of the privy council, the organs of military command, and the house of peers was aimed chiefly at the capacity of those bodies to obstruct or nullify the tendency of the cabinet to come under the influence of the house of representatives.

To make a persuasive case that the parliamentary cabinet system and, ultimately, party government were in harmony with the letter and spirit of the constitution required no little ingenuity. By the terms of the constitution, the confidence of the diet was not in the least a condition of a minister's tenure. It was beyond dispute that the makers of the constitution had repelled any suggestion of ministerial responsibility to the people beyond the vague obligation that due consideration be given to the "susceptibilities of the public" in the selection of ministers.[44] That ministers might be deemed in any sense the tools or agents of the diet was no part of the bureaucratic notion of the cabinet which they borrowed from Germany, where the distinguishing characteristic of the Bismarckian constitutional system was the absolutely exclusive dependence of the ministers on the confidence of the monarch.[45] Yet within a decade after the First Diet opened, the Satcho leaders had been compelled to find a *modus operandi* with the diet, and the relations between the two moved steadily in the direction of a party cabinet system.[46]

Certainly a form of such a system existed in practice by 1920. But the conventions of its operation were not even by then firmly established and its future was clouded by the persistence of bureaucratic opposition, which remained entrenched at crucial points of power within the governmental structure and was ever ready for a reversion to transcendental government.[47] The task confronting those, like Minobe, who sought by reasoned arguments from the law and from constitutional theory to advance the course of parliamentary government was to demonstrate the constitutional legitimacy of the parliamentary cabinet system, to negate the allegation that party government was hostile to national polity, to lay the constitutional groundwork for the elimination of bureaucratic obstruction, and to argue in defense of that system against the new authoritarian attack upon it.

THE PARLIAMENTARY CABINET SYSTEM

In Japan, as in most other parliamentary countries, the nature of the relations between the cabinet and the diet was determined more by convention than by law. But this did not mean that there was no legal basis for cabinet responsibility to the diet—or so Minobe argued. It was true, he observed, that, under Japanese law, ministers of state were under no special legal responsibility. They were subject to the civil and penal codes, as were other subjects, but they were not subject to the disciplinary regulations that applied to other government officials, nor did the constitution provide for impeachment.[48] There were, however, various constitutionally assigned legal powers of the diet as well as the laws of the respective houses, and from these ministerial responsibility to the diet flowed as a political consequence:

If the right of the diet to question a minister does not imply that minister's responsibility before the diet, then it has no meaning. The fact that the diet can question no one else arises from the fact that no one else is responsible to it . . .[49]

Legally the right of the diet to criticize the cabinet takes the form of the right to question, the right to address impeachment memorials to the throne, the right to pass resolutions of non-confidence, and the right to withhold approval of government-sponsored legislative bills and budget estimates. The consequences of such action (e.g., resignation, prorogation, dissolution, compromise, etc.) are a matter of practical politics and not of law; but the right to take those steps is the diet's as a matter of law. There can be no doubt that our state law recognizes the responsibility of ministers of state to the diet. The diet is not only an organ which participates in making law, it is also an organ which superintends administration.[50]

The responsibility of ministers in this broad sense was total; no part of their actions as ministers was exempt from parliamentary inquiry. As a consequence, ministers of state had, in addition to their function of advising the throne and supervising their respective departments, the function of attending sessions of the diet in order to represent the government's views and to respond to interpellations. Under the system of strict bicameralism ministers were accountable legally and in practice to either house of the diet.[51]

That the political consequences of the legal power of the diet to challenge and criticize the actions of state ministers came to take the form they did was not a result of legal necessity. It was the result of the practical necessity of maintaining a coöperative relationship between the diet and the cabinet. It was only after a decade of unhappy experience with various tactics of intransigence and subornation on the part of the bureaucratic cabinets, and of willful obstruction on the part of the diet, that the convention was set that when the government lost the confidence of the diet it must dissolve the house of representatives or resign. Minobe believed that the emergence of that convention from the operational exigencies of the Meiji state provided the fundamental condition of the existence of a parliamentary cabinet system. It satisfied one of the requisites of constitutional government:

constitutional government is the antithesis of oligarchic government; it is government carried on with the assistance of the people. Therefore it is a basic principle of constitutional government that the cabinet, which bears responsibility for government of the state, must have the confidence of the people. Thus, even though the selection of the prime minister naturally belongs to the free choice of the sovereign, politically it is not based on the sovereign's individual discretion, for he must make the confidence of the people the standard of his selection. Since, under constitutional government, the organ which represents the popular view is the parliament, and especially the house of representatives, the political basis of the cabinet's status lies in the confidence of the diet and particularly of the house of representatives.[52]

The establishment of such a relationship between the government and the diet was neither fortuitous nor inevitable. It was promoted in the interpretive scholarship of the liberal school, for whom such a relationship was foreordained in the experience of parliamentary monarchies universally; it was promoted by the creed and actions of the political parties, for whom responsible government was the ultimate shibboleth. Indeed, the problem of responsible government was for all but the most abstractly inclined of the constitutional theorists, as well as for political practitioners, the problem of party government.

PARTY GOVERNMENT

There can be little doubt that Minobe believed in the constitutional propriety and political efficacy of party government. He was at the same time fully aware of the weakness of Japanese political parties and of governments based upon them, and he was greatly concerned with discovering and eradicating the sources of those defects. Minobe's treatment of parties and their constitutional role was duly sensitive to the extralegal character of parties as well as to the high mutability of the customs governing their relation to the operations of government and the resulting dependence of the fortunes of the parties in Japan on their effectiveness as practical instruments of government. The keynote of his approach to the party system prior to 1920 was the demonstration of its constitutional legitimacy; throughout the period of "normal constitutional government" he emphasized the rationalization of party government and the electoral process; entering the period of crisis after 1930, he focused on the salvage of a chastened and restricted constitutional role for the parties, whose imputed sins were seriously discrediting constitutional government.

As was intimated earlier, the phenomenon of the political party was an embarrassment to Minobe. To be sure, as a jurisprudent scholar in Jellinek's tradition he was obliged to concern himself with the social realities underlying the state and the law. He could not escape the fact that "parliamentary government is, whether we like it or not, party government." Neither could he ignore the fact that it was around the role of political parties in the processes of government that the great constitutional issues of his time swirled. Indeed, he did not scorn to argue the political consequences of his constitutional theory, and despite the rather mechanistic level of his thinking about the parties he was not lacking in insight concerning the conditions and results of their existence under the Meiji state.

In his formal constitutional commentaries Minobe had little to say directly on the subject of party government. He did observe that it was a common, if not inevitable, corollary of parliamentary government and he asserted that while the organization of the imperial government created serious obstacles to the full realization of party government, there was no fundamental conflict between party government and the letter and spirit of the Imperial Constitution. This deliberately restricted handling of the political question is epitomized in a brief passage in *Kempō Kōwa*:

It is really impossible long to maintain under constitutional government a cabinet aloof from the parties. There is an unavoidable natural tendency to approach the parliamentary cabinet and the party cabinet. But a pure parliamentary cabinet has not yet appeared in Japan and the chief reasons for this are that the strength of the political parties is largely confined to the house of representatives and does not extend to the house of peers; and there is absent in the house of peers any sense of deference to the decisions of the house of representatives as evidence of public sentiment. Furthermore . . . the war and navy ministers . . . have never been selected with a view to the parties, and this is one of the circumstances which stands as an obstacle to the establishment of a pure parliamentary cabinet government. This is not the place to argue the relative merits and shortcomings of parliamentary party cabinets, but their development is a natural tendency along with the operations of constitutional government. There are some who argue that the constitution does not permit party cabinets or parliamentary cabinets. But this seems to me to be a narrowminded, thoughtless, and completely unreasonable position. . . .[53]

The experience of the Taisho Political Reform imparted a "self-evident" quality to the easy equation of parliamentary government and party government.[54] On the other hand, a few years of "normal constitutional government" brought fuller awareness of the tenacity of the forces resisting the realization of that "new era in Japanese constitutional government" which began with the abortive party government of Okuma and Itagaki in 1898.[55]

Full appreciation of the significance of Minobe's interpretation of the constitution in relation to the question of party government might begin with his direct attack on the problem of responsibility; but it could not end there. On the legal justification of the responsibility of the government to the diet he was firm, and beyond that he could point to the apparently well-established custom in accordance with which a government losing the diet's confidence had no recourse but resignation or dissolution. He could note the tendency for such a practice to result in party government. He could argue that party government was the normal means by which the diet could perform two of the principal political functions assigned in constitutional theory to the representative organ: motivating the formation of cabinets and cultivating extrabureaucratic administrative talent. But when all was said and done, he could not find in the constitution itself a preference as between the political alternatives of the transcendental and party types of government.

It would be a mistake, however, to take at its face value his apparent neutrality on the issue of party government. A theory of constitutional indifference under the circumstances, served the cause of party government by denying any requirement for an autocratic type of cabinet. Moreover, his view of the constitution, taken as a whole, implicitly favored party government. Narrow construction of the prerogative ordinance power, maximal view of the legislative power and of the diet's role in its exercise, criticism of bureaucratic obstacles to cabinet control of state administration—cumulatively these interpretations provided a constitutional jurisprudence notably congenial to the free play of political forces inclining to produce party government.

Minobe's commitment to party government was undissembled in his occasional writing. His critical essays on the issues of the period show that he understood that the movement toward responsible government in late Meiji and early Taisho was aimed at putting parliamentary party leaders in command of administration and that he was sympathetic with that movement.[56] In late Taisho and early Showa, with the parties at the center of the stage and performing none too felicitously, his emphasis shifted to the perfection of parliamentary party government and the abatement of the abuses associated with it. This was the period of his interest in the operations of the German republican constitution, especially in its constitutionally prescribed parliamentary cabinet system and in the constitutional role assigned to parties.[57] His criticisms of the privy council and the military command were made chiefly with the idea of emancipating the cabinet from bureaucratic extortion. Whatever other result might be expected to flow from making the cabinet solely responsible for all phases of state administration, to advocate such a monopoly of control in conjunction with the proposition that the cabinet was legally and politically responsible to the house of representatives meant under the circumstances an endorsement of full-fledged party government.

Such a development had it materialized, would have been revolutionary indeed. For the cabinet in Japan, even when of a purely bureaucratic stripe, had always been the victim of conflicting pressures from the genrō, the military command, the imperial household offices, the privy council, the house of peers, and the political parties within the house of representatives, each of which was capable of obstructing cabinet policy.[58] The parliamentary parties had won a grudgingly conceded place in the intricate and unstable balance of powers constituting the government of the empire, and in alliance with important elements of the bureaucracy had come to play a nominally dominant role. The parties did indeed gain control of the cabinet, but not thereby control of the government. Party cabinets inhabited a no-man's land through which they pursued their tortuous careers until toppled by blows from the side of the bureaucracy or from the house of representatives. Naturally, the leaders of the parties (or at least of that party momentarily in power) found this condition intolerably frustrating and were eager to make control of the cabinet mean effective control of government.

Against this background, the implications of the proposals and criticisms he advanced in his essays on current issues were clear. He demanded curtailment of the privy council's interference with cabinet policy; he even suggested the abolition of the council. He insisted on rigid delineation of the competence of the military commands and the subordination of the military ministers to cabinet discipline on defense matters; he even advocated "civilianization" of the posts of minister of war and minister of navy. He proposed reduction of the legislative powers of the house of peers. All of this was certainly to the advancement of the cause of party government: his critical essays on the house of peers, the privy council, and the military command were engendered respectively by the presumption of the Kenkyukai (a faction in the house of peers) in establishing a nonparty cabinet in 1923; by the privy council's wrecking of the Wakatsuki (Kenseikai) Government in 1927; and the attempt of the navy staff to exclude the Hamaguchi (Minseito) Cabinet from defense policy determination in 1930. In contrast to the cautiously correct language of his formal constitutional commentaries, in these essays he joined the party publicists in the identification of normal constitutional government with party government. It is hardly surprising that his constitutional doctrines evoked disapproval among opponents of parliamentary government, especially the military, and among elements of the bureaucracy in the privy council and house of peers who saw the salvation of Japan in a strong authoritarian regime based on military-bureaucratic coöperation.

Minobe's faith in party government was by no means unqualified, however. He recognized weaknesses and dangers in it, and he regarded with favor some of the legal and conventional checks upon it. His belief in bicameralism has already been noted; it stemmed from fear of the abuse of majority rule—the despotic behavior that might come from a government based on a rigidly disciplined party majority in the house of representatives. His attack upon the house of peers was not upon its function of legislative review, but upon its power to veto legislation absolutely and to overthrow cabinets without responsibility. Of the privy council he complained that at best it merely duplicated the proper function of the upper legislative chamber.

It is in the context of his concern that there be checks upon the willfulness of party government that he made some apology for the rank and file of the civil bureaucracy in their pretended independence of the political heads of the ministries. According to his analysis, the phenomenon of official recalcitrance reflected a basic change in the outlook of public officials resulting immediately from the economic depression of the official class and the attendant loss of social prestige. Official psychology had, moreover, been penetrated by the same spirit of economic competition and the same attitude of opposition to authority which had infected postwar Japanese society generally. Underlying and aggravating these possibly transient factors was the fact that the rise of party government had destroyed the close paternalistic relationship between the government and officials which had characterized the pre-party regimes.[59] Not only was bureaucratic independence, in part at least, a "natural" result of party government, but "as a counterweight to the defects of party government it should be looked upon as something welcome."

> It must be deemed harmful to the nation that when the government has support of the diet majority it has no fear of attack and can abuse its great power with impunity. . . . Under party government there is no permanency in administration and this too is harmful to the people. . . . When the bureaucracy under party government enjoys a degree of independence it restrains the excessively arbitrary acts of the government and provides continuity in administrative affairs . . . and this may be considered somewhat corrective of the shortcomings of party government. . . .[60]

Thus he found justification for preserving the capacity of lower echelons of the civil service to make concerted resistance to the government.

It should be noted that he was not speaking here of the powerful bureaucratic figures who constituted the "political" bureaucrats as in the house of peers and the privy council. The bureaucrats of which he spoke were not the small group of top civil officials who occupied positions in which political and administrative functions were mixed and whose careers depended on individual connections with one or another of the parties. Rather they were career officials adversely affected by the Minseito government's policy of civil payroll reduction. Their opposition to this policy brought to a head a long-standing complaint of the party ministers that the policies of party cabinets were being consistently obstructed by the noncoöperation and hostility of career civil servants. Minobe did not, of course, condone willful disobedience of superior commands; nor did he sympathize with the bureaucratic opposition to the government on the specific issue of salary reduction. On the other hand he could not welcome strict subordination of the civil bureaucracy to the leaders of the parties.

In this context, his ideas on electoral reform also achieve fuller significance. Party government, for all its inherent shortcomings, was the practically inevitable and, on the whole, preferable corollary of constitutional government. It was proper that it should be subject to checks and restraints, as should every government of whatever type. But it was perhaps even more important to avoid and correct the adventitious imperfections of the system—for example, the inadequacy of party responsibility to the electorate, or corruption, or subservience to special interests. It was because he supposed that it would meet these requirements that he came to advocate the strict list system of proportional representation.

In all, then, Minobe's reasoning showed that the rule that constitutional government is popular government led necessarily to the principle of government responsibility to the people through the parliament in all aspects of state administration. Since the only constitutional link between administration and the diet was the cabinet, it was logically and practically necessary that the cabinet have full control of state administration. This meant, moreover, that the government was bound to maintain harmonious relations with the diet majority, and led logically to the institution of party government. Democratic party government was therefore defensible and, indeed, deserved support despite its admitted drawbacks. Moreover, of all the political forces which might seek to control administration, that which most nearly met the constitutional requirement of popular government was the political force represented by the party commanding an electoral majority. And it was to justify the legitimacy of the parliamentary majority that the problem of effecting a proper representative relationship between the electors and the parliamentary parties was so important.

The Rule of Law and Civil Liberty

After the provision for a representative legislative body, the Imperial Constitution's most important gesture toward western constitutional tradition was its "bill of rights." Chapter II was a direct translation of European form, and its substance was patterned on the corresponding portions of the Prussian Constitution of 1850, which echoed French revolutionary themes as filtered through the Belgian Constitution of 1831, and the Declaration of the Rights of the German People made by the Frankfurt Congress of 1848.

The complexities of the area of civil liberties and its particular importance in Minobe's work call for some general observations at this point. The parallel between Chapter II and its German model also included a rough circumstantial similarity in the enthusiastic but politically ineffective revolutionary agitation, and in the cautious official response to that agitation, which led to the inclusion of such provisions in the new fundamental law of the state. The rights and duties of Japanese subjects were stated in language indicative of the regressive spirit in which the concession was made. An imported juristic exegesis, dominated by the *Rechtsstaat* concept and but narrowly solicitous for the individual's claims to liberty, contributed to the circumscription of the practical legal meaning of these provisions. But official hostility was not the only, nor, in the long run, the chief impediment to the realization of personal rights and political liberty in Japan. The Japanese social climate during the era of the Imperial Constitution was not congenial to the notion of a defined area of individual freedom. The absolutism of the governmental apparatus repelled and the authoritarian traditions of the social order remained relatively unresponsive to the libertarian and equalitarian doctrines which had inspired revolutionary agitation in Europe. Japan lacked a counterpart to the empirical, prescriptive experience of the English in the limitation of governmental power over the individual. It had no politically conscious class prepared to advance the idea that individual freedom is an essential condition of a good society.

Still, the progress of social and political revolution in Japan under the Meiji constitutional system was manifest in the increasingly wider range of Japanese society responsive to new and expansive notions of liberty. This was evident in, for example, outspoken criticism of bureaucratic and police restrictions and surveillance in the areas of economic enterprise, intellectual pursuits, and political associations. But even when the fever of freedom ran high in the decade after 1914, it produced very little substantial advance in legislative implementation of the provisions of Chapter II of the constitution. Widespread verbal subscription to various liberal principles apparently did not reflect solid commitment to them, or even a common appreciation of their meaning. After 1925 anti-liberal tendencies again dominated, not only in administrative and police practice, where they had never abated significantly, but in the law and in the social atmosphere. The retreat from liberalism seems to have followed from recognition of the perversions and failures of capitalistic individualism and from the draining off of social discontent toward the revolutionary extremes. It was hastened by the frightened, fumbling reaction of the "middle-class" champions of freedom to the rise of intellectual radicalism and proletarian political activity. The eclipse of liberalism paralleled the failure of the institutions of parliamentary government, for the two were bound in a common, interdependent fate.

The promotion of the ideals of a free society in the Japan of Minobe's mature years may appear in retrospect to have been a forlorn effort. It is difficult, in the light of the discouraging evidence of the years after 1920, to avoid this gloomy construction.[61] On the other hand, the problems of recent social and political reconstruction and development have given new significance to elements of liberal, democratic experience which may have survived the transition from 1930 to 1950.[62] The cause of freedom may have been forlorn in that earlier time and there may be reason, even now, to doubt that the basic obstacles to 'its success have been certainly eliminated; Minobe, in any case, stands out among the prewar constitutional theorists and teachers for his devotion to liberal democratic principles. If there were others of greater depth and sophistication of insight, few if any of them were in a position to influence as Minobe did the thought of the class and generation of men out of whose ranks have come, by bureaucratic or political preferment, the custodians of political and administrative power in the new constitutional era.

Minobe, to be sure, does not fairly represent the prevailing attitude toward individual rights and civil liberty in the prewar period. Indeed, his importance is largely precisely a matter of his holding to unorthodox lines of thinking in this as in other constitutional matters. Moreover, it was not only in his more popular writing but in his professional academic capacity that he marched in advance of the main ranks, so far, it would seem, that despite his eminence and the considerable emulation accorded him by his students he failed to persuade any significant number of academicians or bureaucrats to adopt his positions. In this, as much as in any other aspect of his work, it was apparent that his interpretation of the constitution was a "political interpretation" and that his political creed was that of "bourgeois liberalism."[63] In holding to this position he found himself increasingly isolated as the forces of liberal democracy disintegrated under the test of leadership, responsibility, and opposition.

Minobe's rejection of the term "liberal" as applied to himself need not be taken too seriously:

I have commonly been referred to as a liberal, and, indeed, those who attack me do so generally on the ground that I am a liberal. If by liberal you mean one who respects the freedom of others and cherishes his own freedom, then in that broad sense I am undoubtedly a liberal. Surely everyone loves liberty in that sense. . . . But liberalism has come to be used from time to time in various special senses other than this broad sense. In an early period religious freedom was strongly asserted, and at the time of the French

Revolution it was political freedom which was emphasized. In the burgeoning era of capitalism the central theme became *laissez faire* in economic life. If we are speaking of liberalism in any of these particular senses, then I have never been a liberal nor have I ever represented myself as one. . . .[64]

This statement expresses his characteristic individuality; it cannot conceal, nor did it conceal from his contemporaries, Minobe's status in the front ranks of political liberalism in Japan at that time (1934). He was spokesman for a "purified constitutionalism," the residue of liberal ideology from which the element of economic liberalism had been purged.[65] Minobe spoke of free capitalism as having outlived its time; he did not suggest that it was incompatible with the imperial tradition or with constitutional government, and he did not share in any way the aspirations of those who sought in fascistic doctrines, or in something they called "imperial socialism," the salvation of Japanese society. In his advocacy of the liberties of Japanese subjects he transcended the bias of middle-class politics in its concern for property and its hostility toward proletarian interests and action.[66]

The principles of law and constitutional theory set forth in Minobe's works under the rubric of the rule of law and civil liberty are not readily reduced to neat and comprehensive statement. They were evoked frequently and in great diversity of form by the daily operations of government. If the specifics at issue on such occasions were of lesser dimensions than those which turned upon the questions of popular government and the responsibility of administration, they nonetheless seriously engaged Minobe's energies and talents. The various explications of his outlook turned upon a single fulcrum: "Constitutional government is government by law, government in which the administrative and judicial powers can be exercised only within the limits of the legislatively determined rights and duties of individual subjects."[67] In this idea of the rule of law (*hōchishugi*) Minobe found the third of the three essential ingredients of his formula for constitutional government, assigning to it perhaps an even greater importance than he gave to the "formal" principles of popular government and responsible government. The idea of the legal state was, in a sense, the essential part of his constitutionalism, the juristic expression of an ethical imperative that the individual be liberated from all despotic authority.[68] It found formal expression in constitutional guarantees of liberty and in the codes of judicial and administrative procedure.

The idea of the rule of law had been received as a positive norm into the fundamental law of Japan. This was explicitly indicated in the preamble: "We now declare to respect and protect the security of the rights and property of Our people, and to secure to them the complete enjoyment of the same, within the extent of the provisions of the present constitution and of the law." Interpretations of Chapter II proceeding only from its own clauses and ignoring this statement had led, Minobe noted, to serious misunderstandings. The idea of the legal state was fundamental to a correct notion of the meaning of the rights and duties of Japanese subjects.[69]

The major points of divergence among the authoritative interpretations of Chapter II centered of course around the nature of the individual's rights under the constitution and the relation between those rights and the legislative power of the state. Minobe's position regarding both issues followed closely from his premise that the principles of the legal state governed the relations between the people and the state under the Imperial Constitution.[70] It was a dictate of the corporate theory of the state, and particularly of the idea of constitutionalism, that the individual be regarded as the subject (*shutai*) of both rights and duties in respect to the state. In determining the nature and scope of the public rights (*kōken*) and the public duties (*kōgimu*) of Japanese subjects, he said, not much reliance could be placed in the language of Chapter II. For instance, it placed upon Japanese subjects the duty of military service and the duty of paying taxes, yet no one would pretend that these were the only duties owed by individuals to the state. Similarly, the enumeration of rights was certainly not inclusive of all of the rights of individuals in respect to the state—there was no mention of such important rights as physical security, marriage, contract, education, communication, academic freedom, and so on.

Minobe pointed out that the obligation of the individual to the state could not be defined simply as the sum of the specifically enumerated duties. The subject had one primary duty to the state: obedience (*fukujū gimu*), the duty to obey the commands of the state and to submit to its coercion. The duty of the subject was not, however, absolute; it existed "only within the limits recognized by state law." It was, then, the duty to obey the lawfully made commands of the state. "All of the duties borne by the people are determined by provision of law as a general rule. Modern constitutional states conform with the requirement of the legal state in making the imposition of specific obligations upon the people an exclusive function of the legislative power, and in forbidding the judicial power and the administrative power to command and coerce the people except in accordance with the provisions of law. Japanese public law is governed by this general rule. . . ." Normally all of the particular duties of Japanese subjects required statutory definition.[71]

Within the area of individual rights, troublesome problems of interpretation arose for Minobe chiefly in respect to that category of rights he labeled the rights of freedom (jiyūken), the right not to be subjected to state command and coercion except according to the provisions of state law.[72] Since the right of freedom arose from a limitation on the power of the state by state law, some authorities reasoned that it was not a right (kenri) in the true sense of the word.[73] But freedom, Minobe asserted, means more than mere restraint by the state of its own administrative power: if a person's liberty is invaded illegally, that person has the right to sue on the illegality, and when the law permits a person to plead a specific cause to his own advantage, it recognizes the person to be the subject of a right. The right of freedom does not exist "positively," as a right to do certain things, but "negatively," as the right not to be commanded or penalized except as provided by law. Thus the right of freedom is indeed distinguished from a right (kenri) in the general sense of the word.[74]

This negative definition of jiyūken as the converse of duty precludes an interpretation which sees the individual's freedom as the sum of the several particular rights enumerated in Chapter II of the constitution. Speech, assembly, and residence were, for instance, like eating, sleeping, walking and conversing, only components of natural freedom (tenzen no jiyū), and the latter, though not mentioned in Chapter II, were as surely guaranteed against unlawful restriction as were the former. The enumeration of particular rights, as Minobe explained, only reflected the traditions of constitutional history, out of which certain particular rights and duties had acquired special significance and were for that reason customarily mentioned in bills of rights. Chapter II was a declaration of the acceptance of the rule of law, according to which the liberty of the people extended to every phase of their private and social existence and could be restricted only by the legislative power of the state.[75]

It should be noted that there was nothing in the concept of the legal state which ensured to the individual an area of freedom inviolable by legislative action. It did not contain the notion of natural rights guaranteed against the state. To say that freedom can be limited only by law does not mean that it could not be limited by law. Japanese subjects enjoyed their liberties "within the limits of the law," within the limits laid down by legislative provisions.[76] The question of individual liberty thus came into direct relation to the problem of the definition of the legislative power and of the role of the diet in its exercise.

Most leading commentators held that the enumeration of rights in Chapter II was a catalog of "legislative items." As we have seen, they meant by this that the formal legislative power—the power in which the diet participated—extended only to matters specifically set forth in the constitution as requiring diet action. This view of Chapter II led to the assertion that only those rights enumerated were guaranteed against non-legislative restriction. Minobe rejected this interpretation *in toto*.

As we have already explained in connection with Article V, that article requires that the legislative power be exercised with the consent of the diet, which means that every new determination of the rights and duties of subjects requires, as a general rule, the decision of the diet. What is required, therefore, is not that only certain matters be determined by law as legislative items; rather, on the contrary, that only certain matters may be determined by ordinance, and that in all other matters in which the rights and duties of subjects are concerned, determination must be by law. . . . There could be no interpretation more destructive of the fundamental spirit of the constitution than that according to which only those matters listed in this chapter are to be determined by law. . . .[77]

But now Minobe took away with one hand some of what he had given with the other, for he was bound to acknowledge that the legislative power was not the exclusive province of the parliament:

An associated error in interpretation is that which holds that the rights and duties listed in Chapter II can be determined only by law (*hōritsu*). . . . This chapter is not intended to be a definition of the respective spheres of laws and ordinances, but to establish the principle of the legal state, emphasizing that the rights and liberties of the people can be invaded only by law. But, as we know, the principle of the legal state has many exceptions under the terms of our constitution. . . . This chapter does not mean to deny those exceptions.[78]

There could be no doubt, for instance, that the emergency ordinance power and the treaty power operate as exceptions to this chapter. A further constitutional exception existed under Article IX, according to which the emperor's prerogative extended to the issuance or ordinances restricting the freedom of the people for the purpose of maintaining public order and advancing the welfare of the nation, so long as such ordinances did not conflict with any law. This so-called "police-ordinance prerogative" was, in fact, fortified by a law antedating the First Diet and subsequently unamended, which authorized the enforcement of such ordinances by substantial penalties.[79]

Minobe did not say so explicitly, but it may be inferred from his expansive definition of the legislative competence of the diet in respect to the imperial prerogative that he considered the substantial *de facto* invasion of individual liberty by administrative action under the emergency-ordinance and police-ordinance prerogatives to be the result of the failure of the diet to exercise its legislative authority to the full. It is more than probable that no substantial or persistent membership (not to mention majority) in the diet was committed in principle to the reduction of police and administrative discretion in these matters. For instance, while the diet objected to the method of extension of the Peace Preservation Law, it did not insist on modification of the substance of the changes. Actions taken by the government in the form of emergency imperial ordinances and police ordinances were, in effect, taken with the consent of the diet. By and large, the diet made little attempt to restrict the scope of official action based on constitutional exceptions to the general rule that the legislative power was exercised with the consent of the diet. Indeed, the over-all record of the diet (as distinct from some of the dissents expressed in the course of its deliberations) does not show it to have been significantly more considerate of the rights and freedom of the people than were administrative officials.

While refusing to accept Chapter II as a definitive statement of the rights of Japanese subjects, Minobe did not put aside the necessity of analyzing and interpreting its several provisions. The characteristic individuality of his treatment of Chapter II can be indicated by a review of his commentary on Article XXVII: "The right of property of every subject shall remain inviolate. Measures necessary to be taken for the public benefit shall be provided for by law." "Right of property" (*shoyūken*) here, he stated, meant all property rights; it was a direct translation of the Prussian constitutional phrase *Das Eigentum (ist unverletzlich)*. It was taken to embrace the whole system of private property, which this article guaranteed against arbitrary violation at the hands of the state. With the overthrow of feudalism, private property and freedom of contract had become key features of the Japanese social order.[80] The effect of Article XXVII, Minobe pointed out, was only to guarantee that property rights would be defined by statute and not by administrative fiat or judicial decree; it did not protect property rights against legislative limitation: the legislative power could circumscribe them in any degree required by the public interest, even to the extent of extinguishing them.

Up to this point Minobe differed from other constitutional authorities only in making his restrictive definition of the imperial ordinance power relevant to the issue. He declined, however, to go along with the prevailing position among his contemporaries: that the customary equation of property rights with the capitalistic social order was required by the constitution.[81] Indeed, he considered it a grave defect of the controversial Peace Preservation Law that it viewed an attack upon private property (capitalism) to be an attack upon national polity.[82] He did not deny that Japanese law had, in fact, established capitalism. But he did deny that either national polity or the constitution forbade modification or even abandonment of the capitalistic system. Whatever justification there may have been for linking Minobe with the capitalistic camp in Japanese politics—usually on the basis of the actual and assumed relationship between parliamentary democracy and capitalism—he was, as we have already noted, no defender of economic individualism and free enterprise *per se*.

Much as the essential liberalism of Minobe's position is evident in his formal commentary on the articles of Chapter II, further review of that commentary cannot highlight it so dramatically as do his reactions to some of the celebrated causes of his day, particularly those concerning police and administrative procedures and political and intellectual freedom.

Police and Administrative Procedures

On January 23, 1935, Minobe rose in the house of peers to deliver a tardy maiden speech. His address took the form of an interpellation of the minister of justice concerning an alleged violation of the rights of a number of prisoners being held by the police for the office of the procurator general as material witnesses in the prosecution of the Imperial

Rayon Corporation scandal. It was a climactic moment in his career, his first fully public appearance as a cog in the constitutional superstructure of the Meiji state. It was also his penultimate appearance, for when next he rose to speak in that chamber, not two months later, it was to defend himself against the charges which shortly drove him from public life.

If this moment on the parliamentary stage was brief, it did not lack attention. The circumstances which exacerbated his professional sensitivities were of a sensational order. Public passions had been aroused by disclosures of official corruption. There was much partisan grist in the situation—between the parties severally as such, and between the parties and antiparliamentary forces. Among the prisoners were members of the diet and prominent members of the preceding Saito Government.[83] The interpellation was scheduled three days in advance, which enabled the press to build up dramatically the approaching spectacle of the learned scholar taking up the cudgels in a "last ditch defense of the constitution" against police and procurators who operated in high-handed disregard of personal rights and deprived subjects of fair judicial process. That many officials in the ministry of justice had been students under Minobe did not escape the notice of the journalists.[84] The interpellation was made before a full gallery and was reported by the press as "a masterpiece of oratory on the constitution" under banner headlines referring to "the trampling of human rights." One observer described it as "well organized and unambiguous, like his writing, clear, to the point of artistry, and dignified, with all bitterness restrained, nevertheless unequaled in the forcefulness of its attack. The substance of the speech was commonplace; what gave it force was Minobe's character and learning."[85]

The incident offers a dramatic caption to one of the most important phases of Minobe's work—his war against official presumption and willfulness, his unflagging promotion of the legal state. His chief obstacle was the general attitude, rooted in the authoritarian past, of which the official behavior he detested was but one manifestation in Japan. Officials of all sorts tended to assume the overriding importance of official purposes and to ignore—even despise—the interests and rights of the private individuals. The countercoin of this bureaucratic authoritarianism, the acceptance of official arrogance by the citizenry, only reinforced its effects. Moreover, the justices of the courts and the lawyers who practiced before them were greatly influenced by it.

It was particularly against the partiality toward official authority (*kan-*

ken henjū) on the part of those concerned with the administration of justice that Minobe directed his criticism. In his textbooks and case books he sought to indoctrinate students against the evils of a narrowly literal construction of the written law, to impress upon them the obligation to give weight in the application of the law to considerations of social justice and social advantage. He argued for the application of private-law principles to the operation of state enterprises and for the right of appeal against acts of official discretion required by law to be based on a finding of public necessity.[86]

Minobe's concern was expressed chiefly in his work in administrative law, which as such lies outside the scope of this study. But it relates intimately to the problem of the rights of individuals under Articles XXIII and XXIV of the constitution, for those rights were inevitably affected by the exercise of police authority and the behavior of procurators and judges.[87] The first of these constitutional provisions purported to protect the individual against unlawful arrest, detention, trial, or punishment. This freedom of the person, Minobe insisted, constituted a strict limitation on the power of the police. While the police might properly expect coöperation from the public, people were not obligated to fulfill that expectation except as the law required. Nor could punishment be inflicted except as the law provided. The principle "no law, no penalty" ought, Minobe insisted, to be held as sacred as the constitution itself. The second constitutional provision fortified the first by guaranteeing that no subject could be burdened with any punishment or penalty except by judgment of a legally constituted tribunal. Minobe said of Article XXIV that it had "somewhat the same meaning as the due process clause of the fifth amendment of the American constitution."[88]

Minobe's preachments of respect for individual rights were aimed primarily at the student of law and the public official, but he also sometimes addressed himself to the citizen on this issue, as when he wrote for the university newspaper in 1927 an article on "The Limits of Police Detention."[89] That article was aimed at the student not merely as a student of law but as the object of police attention. "Without challenging the police action in this particular instance," Minobe stated, "I want to take this occasion to discuss the proper limits of police detention . . . so that its legal limits will be made clear, and the people, being familiar with them, may check its abuse. . . ." To be sure, his elaboration was in itself a challenge to the police action.

The occasion was a holiday declared by the university authorities to facilitate a police investigation of suspected subversive political activities among the students. Police detention, he observed, was authorized by the Law of Administrative Performance. Since it was a judicial-like action at the discretion of administrative authority, it ought to be exercised strictly within the terms of the law, which permitted detention only for protection of the detained person and prevention of threats to public order. But the only remedy open to persons illegally detained was the impractical one of placing a criminal charge against the offending official. This circumstance did little, Minobe noted, to restrain official arbitrariness; there were frequent violations of personal rights. Abuse was most frequent in connection with preventive custody, which police officials employed without regard for the requirement that such detention was permissible only when it was possible to suppose a person was not merely capable of breaking the public peace but was preparing to do so.

The temper of Minobe's concern for evenhanded justice is demonstrated further in another case of a quite different order.[90] In this he protested against a discrepancy in treatment as between civilian and military persons accused of similar offenses. His indignation was aroused by the treatment of military officers implicated in the May Fifteenth Incident of 1932 in which Premier Inukai had been assassinated. These officers were charged with and convicted of the offense of insurrection (hanran), and sentenced to fifteen years of penal servitude.[91] Minobe contrasted this development with the case of the civilian who had made the fatal assault on Premier Hamaguchi in 1930. He had been tried and convicted on a charge of attempted homicide (Hamaguchi did not die until the next year and then of "complications") and sentenced to death, a sentence which was not, however, carried out.

With this latter disposition Minobe had no quarrel. He approved of the court's rejection in such cases of pleas for the mitigation of the sentences on the ground that the purpose of the crime was not accomplished, or because of the disinterested motivation of the felons, or because of the convention against capital punishment for offenses based on political motive. "Legally and morally the crime was reprehensible," he asserted. "Courts should consider motives, but that does not mean that they should endorse such motives. Political motivation would be as valid a defense for communists as for these men. Their actions in themselves were criminal regardless of their motives. . . ." For Minobe, the injustice lay in the more lenient treatment of the military assassins. They had been charged with rebellion against military authority rather than with murder. The court martial, considering among other factors their "patriotic" motivation, had meted out a minimum sentence to the naval officers. It was little wonder Minobe felt, that such events as these should shake the faith of the people in the justice of the state.

Minobe's interpellation in the matter of the Imperial Rayon scandal was not, then, an expression of momentary interest. It flowed directly from his philosophy of constitutional government. The forum and the medium were novel to him, but the cause was one to which he was enduringly devoted.

Political and Intellectual Liberty

The chronicles of political affairs in Japan for the decade and a half following 1920 give prominent place to the development of troublesome, sometimes violent interactions between the pressures and movements militating against sanctioned social and political patterns and the conservative resistance to these revolutionary currents. The latter forces sought to erect a double barrier against subversion of old attitudes and institutions by mobilizing the law and the administrative agencies of the state against abhorrent doctrines and practices and by generating and nourishing general social opposition to them. A number of factors favored their tactics. Political censorship as a governmental policy and extralegal agitation in defense of alleged national ideals had ample precedent in Japanese history. On the other hand, the concept of an open society had barely established itself in the Japanese mind. It came naturally—one cannot say painlessly—to the Japanese to meet social disturbance with police surveillance and repression. There was a less than meager reservoir of social conscience, so to speak, to resist the passage from milder, partial measures to full-scale, officially supported "thought control."

The policy of repressing objectionable ideas was not in this period merely a recurrence of the high-handedness of clan oligarchs which characterized the early Meiji era. The target of censorship in the 1920's was bolshevism and kindred errors, and the suppression of

Marxian heresy was approved and abetted by regimes emerging from the diet. Later, parliamentary democracy itself became the evil to be exorcized, and when official agencies moved too slowly to silence its leaders and defenders, the techniques of villification, incendiary agitation, and terroristic violence were brought into play by elements, old and new, which merged in Japanese fascism.

These developments challenged Minobe's liberalism. They provoked him to frequent expressions of alarm and criticism. Constitutional issues, in the narrow sense, were seldom involved, since the words of the constitution offered little obstacle to the curbing of intellectual heterodoxy and political radicalism. But he saw that the issues of free political agitation and association and intellectual freedom went right to the heart of the philosophical bases and the mechanics of constitutionalism and parliamentary government. By the early thirties, when the attacks of the right extremists and finally the weight of the law and the police were brought home directly against his personal position, he had already shown himself a constant champion of free thought and free political activity within the limits of social responsibility as he understood it.

The single provision of the constitution which related directly to these problems was Article XXIX: "Japanese subjects shall, within the limits of law, enjoy the liberty of speech, writing, publication, public meetings, and associations." Minobe said that this article was merely an expression of legislative policy, putting the definition of these rights normally outside the ordinance power and exhorting the legislature to treat them with great respect.[92] The diet had exercised its power to define the area of liberty in respect to some of these rights by enacting such statutes as the Publication Law (Law No. 15 of 1893), the Peace Preservation Police Law (Law No. 36 of 1900), and the Newspaper Law (Law No. 41 of 1909). Strictly construed, the limited coverage of these statutes left to police ordinance the regulation of such important media as radio, theater, cinema, and music, as well as all associations other than those covered by the corporation laws. Moreover, the diet's definition of the zone of freedom was not notably liberal, and Minobe's critical observations on problems involving free speech and association were aimed, not merely at abuses of police authority, but at legislative policy itself and at vigilantism by civilian and military groups. He had, of course, a special interest in restrictive measures and pressures aimed at the academic community.

Minobe questioned the efficacy of police measures as a means of defending society and the state against social unrest and political agitation. As early as 1919 he wrote:

Freedom of speech is both the basis of social progress and a source of social disturbance. . . . [But it is] discontent with society that constitutes the chief threat to the peace and order of society. If discontent mounts steadily and all society is consumed with it, then to limit free discussion in an effort to maintain social order will, on the contrary, strike at the very basis of order. Furthermore, since social progress usually results from the stimulus of a variety of ideas, if the expression of ideas is restricted, very likely social progress will be checked. A society which does not have freedom of speech . . . is a dead society. . . . [Under the present law] penalties are fixed for persons who publish articles which are disrespectful of the imperial household. It is unnecessary and dangerous that there should be additional sections fixing penalties on persons responsible for articles which disturb public order. Since men will differ according to their individual positions on what constitutes a disturbance of public order . . . it is very disquieting to find such a matter left to the discretion of the police. Some will say that those who advocate democracy menace public order; others will say that the supporters of Shinto and the defenders of national polity are a threat to public order. . . . To put this question in the hands of a police court with power to give a prison sentence up to six months means that no one can take up the pen in peace.[93]

This passage discloses the focal elements of his often voiced protest: Attempts to resist disorder by suppressing free expression of opinion and free association are futile since they aim at the symptoms rather than at the underlying social discontent. But they are worse than futile; they are a positive danger, for they block normal channels for release of the pressure of discontent and they destroy the process by which society achieves consensus. They impose the deadening stamp of official orthodoxy on the intellectual processes, foster stagnation and inertia, stifle challenge and progress. The proper role of government, he said, is not to repress (except for the punishment of overt attacks on public order, the defense of public morals, and the prosecution of lese majesty) but to exercise the state power and official ingenuity for the rectification of social, economic, and political wrongs which create the discontent on which subversion flourishes. Police action is particularly harmful when its purpose is to harass and destroy proletarian political agitation and when it seeks to eradicate dangerous thoughts as distinct from dangerous actions.

It is not surprising, then, that Minobe was entirely opposed to the so-called peace preservation legislation of 1925 and 1928. Stringent political security regulations had been in effect continuously since early in the Restoration, but they were cast in general terms and were capriciously and unevenly enforced. In 1922 the government introduced new legislation, aimed particularly at the suppression of anarchist and bolshevik activities, but the diet failed to pass it. The government enacted this legislation provisionally by emergency ordinance during the crisis of 1923. In 1925 the diet was finally induced to adopt the Peace Preservation Law, effective in May, 1925. This law prohibited and severely penalized associations and organizations devoted to the subversion of national polity or to the overthrow of the system of private property. The faculties and students of the universities were among the first to have the terms of this law visited upon them, and when in 1926 a number of students were prosecuted, Minobe attacked it as "a law of rarely equaled iniquity in modern constitutional government," one "under which the beliefs of the class currently holding power are viewed as correct and the opposing views are deemed heretical and are suppressed by force. This is a war of ideas against ideas . . . not by reason and education but by law and penalties. . . ." Illegal actions aimed at subverting the political and social order were one thing. But this law sought to punish as subversive acts of association and discussions leading to the formation of associations. It fixed on such acts penalties more severe than those applied to outright revolt.[94]

While it was actually a law to destroy the Communist Party, and although the police no doubt were charged to use it as such, "still it greatly betrays the spirit of constitutional government, and I cannot concur in the attempt, to suppress thought itself by penal law. This is an extremely despotic idea such as is known only in dictatorships as in Italy and Russia. It can be said that it resembles the policies of the very party at which it is aimed." He asserted that the makers of the law knew well that national polity was fully protected against attack by the provisions of the penal code, the press laws, and the security-police law. It was not to duplicate these provisions but to protect the system of private property that they had brought forth the Peace Preservation Law, ignoring the fact that there was nothing especially Japanese or eternal about the system of private property, and that it was "just as wrong for those in authority to suppress opposing thoughts as for those without authority to attempt to impose their ideas by force." Such a law could not possibly achieve its purpose except temporarily; meanwhile its consequence would be "spy government" and stultification of the intellectual life of the nation.[95]

When the diet refused to approve proposals for tightening the penal provisions, the government again accomplished its purpose by emergency ordinance (June, 1928) and launched a full-scale campaign against the Communist Party. At that time, Minobe reiterated his criticism.[96] Quite apart from objecting to the "unconstitutional" procedure employed by the government in amending the law, he found grave defect in the substance of the amendment. In spite of the currency of revolutionary thought among students in recent years and the shocking development of the Communist Party,[97] he held to his belief that purely penal countermeasures were not an adequate answer to the problem, for "there can be no doubt that the cause of the unfortunate increase in the influence of foreign intellectual currents in Japan since the World War is to be found in the economic system and in attendant political evils. . . ." A policy of forceful suppression without constructive remedies was more apt to increase than to lessen the chances of revolution. Indeed, the government which sponsored the amendment of the law was itself culpable in the extreme. In the administration of local government, the colonies, the railroads, and special banks, in electoral interference, in the suppression of speech, in the use of gangs, in the corruption of diet members, in the selection of cabinet personnel—in almost all its behavior it demonstrated a brazen and arbitrary use of authority in private and partisan interest.

Minobe was, however, shaken and somewhat chastened by the evidence of Communist Party activities disclosed by the police campaigns of 1928–1929, and especially by the revelation of the close relationship between the Japanese communists and the Communist International. Under the influence of that intelligence he wrote for the university daily newspaper an analysis of the problem of subversion.[98] He conceded that the scope of the conspiracy was alarming, and that even though there was no indication of a mass defection from national polity the matter required serious consideration. Careful analysis, he declared, made clear the necessity by distinguishing between basic cause and immediate cause. The basic cause lay in the imperfections of the economic, social, and political order, specifically in the maldistribution of wealth, the depression of agriculture and unskilled labor, the social influence of money, and the failure of the parties to rise above clique politics, corruption, and collusion. None of these defects was directly attributable to national polity, and the fact that attacks on national polity were apparent in the literature and programs of the radical left had to be explained by other, immediate causes. But, he went on, these other causes would have had little effect were it not for the underlying discontent, for ideas have force only against a background of social reality.

Of immediate causes two were of particular importance. One of these was the penetration of the social sciences by Marxist doctrines. As an honest academic position, Marxism was inextricably bound up with revolutionary doctrines of class struggle, violent overthrow of capitalism, dictatorship of the proletariat, and proletarian internationalism. Marxist-Leninist theory was undoubtedly the immediate intellectual source of the communist problem, but it was not the sole source of intellectual disturbance in Japanese society. It was only part of a broader, worldwide revolutionary ferment against which there was no insulation. Nor could the observer ignore the continuing influence of Japan's own revolutionary tradition stemming from the Restoration, for many of the revolutionaries of early Showa aspired to the glories of the canonized leaders of the Restoration. The other immediate cause of communist threat was the policy and activity of the Russian government in attempting to subvert the governments of other states through the agency of the Communist International. This was a serious problem indeed, but Japan was not alone in suffering its effects. Only collective international restraint on Russia could truly cope with this problem.

What, then, should be the policy of the government toward the revolutionary peril? Minobe apologized for his failure to conceive of a comprehensive solution to the problem. The policy of repression, while dealing effectively with symptoms, was not in the least an answer to the deeper problems; it served, indeed, to incite resistance to the government's presumed ultimate purposes. Equally futile and objectionable were official attempts at "rectification of thought" (*shisō zendō saku*): "It is altogether beyond the function of the state to attempt such a thing as the rectification of popular thought. Not only is such an attempt bound to fail of its purpose, but it will obstruct cultural development. . . . These are times of expectancy of great change in all aspects of society and government . . . and it flies straight against the times to attempt to reform the thinking of the people by a revitalization of feudal ideas or by an infusion of theocratic notions. . . ."

If there were those who hoped that the increasingly militaristic bent of national policy after 1928 would submerge internal conflicts under an overwhelming patriotic unity, Minobe felt they overlooked the fact that wartime solidarity only concealed the bases of domestic strife. A positive military policy would probably serve to aggravate rather than allay the threat of internal disorder; certainly it would preclude determined and resourceful attack on the social and political problems which nourished that disorder.[99]

The one positive step Minobe proposed was reform of the electoral system in order to improve the opportunity for minor party representation in the diet, as discussed earlier in this chapter. He believed that augmentation of the proletarian voice would constrain the most serious abuses of capitalism and expedite peaceful parliamentary achievement of social reform based on humane and democratic ethics.[100] But if enlargement of the role of political dissent was essential to the health and popular credit of the parliamentary system, there was need he emphasized, also for an end to political censorship and renunciation of the official attitude of suspicion and hostility toward proletarian politics and personalities.[101]

The academic community was, as we have noted, the source of much of the radical thought and agitation which excited official alarm. The universities were widely advertised in the press and from the platform as seats of communist conspiracy and propaganda. These circumstances understandably gave rise to issues of academic freedom. In his articles on the peace preservation legislation and in others, Minobe dealt to some length with the question of the relation of the academic community to state and society in a period of ideological conflict. In these writings he pursued a difficult course, attempting to maintain a balance between his devotion to intellectual freedom and his scholarly skepticism of scientific materialism; between his professional interest in preserving the hard-won autonomy of the university faculties and his recognition of the special public obligation incumbent on the faculties of state educational institutions.

The high rate of arrests among university students and graduates encouraged the public to fix the blame for the shocking phenomenon of revolutionary radicalism upon the university administrators and teachers. This tendency was reflected in statements from the ministry of education itself in 1926. Minobe's defense of the universities was not altogether persuasive. It was true, he said, that the faculties were familiar with Marxism and that Marxism was studied at the universities along with an analysis of the existing social and political structure and its defects. But the universities could not be blamed for those defects. Nor could they be held accountable for the fact that some of their students were only nominally enrolled and paid little attention to their bourgeois instructors. As a matter of fact, the dispassionate study of Marxism in the universities was not nearly so important a source of revolutionary activity as was the publication of communist literature for nonacademic distribution. However patriotically inspired his teaching may be, the teacher has no other control over what intellectual sources the student may probe. The only way to escape this problem would be to abolish education outright. Even assuming that closer professorial supervision of students outside of class would have the salutary effect so often asserted, it was patently impossible to realize such a purpose in view of the swelling size of the student body.[102]

Minobe's general position on the question of student participation in reform movements was somewhat ambivalent. He held it to be only natural that students as members of society should be concerned with its improvement, and he saw no reason why they should be denied connections with movements to that end. Since there was no danger to society in a movement to achieve a goal generally approved by society, student participation in such movements should not be restricted except in the interests of scholarship. On the other hand, the student betrayed his primary responsibility when he committed himself prematurely to controversial movements, and especially when he participated in movements actively engaged in promoting social revolution. For this reason he declared himself opposed to the student socialist movement and to its communist phase in particular.[103] But there is no evidence that Minobe participated in or was sympathetic with right-wing counterorganization among the students and faculty at To-Dai. Indeed, his general and incidental opposition to Uesugi and others of the conservative camp in constitutional and political matters no doubt gained him popularity among students of leftist inclination. On the other hand, he cannot but have shared in the defensive antipathy of the interpretive school for the harsh and damaging criticism of the Marxists and for their condescending patronage of the old liberals.

By and large, he spoke sympathetically of the problems of the university student. Unlike earlier generations at the universities, who had little concern except for the superficialities of deportment, students of the Showa era were bombarded by stirring, revolutionary appeals and challenges from the extreme left and right, all the while threatened by an official policy of harsh repression of opposition thought (potentially almost any thought) and collective agitation (potentially almost all action). These students were indeed beset by "fear lest by some intellectual corruption they be cast forth from society." Minobe took stock of the consequences of falling afoul of the political security regulations—termination of schooling and foreclosure from one's chosen career, possible penal servitude, and certainly disgrace for one's family—and admonished students as follows:

It is fitting to be anxious about the shortcomings of the organization of society. And it is permissible to discuss the contradictions of capitalism, and even to apply oneself to the problem of how they may be corrected. But it is of the greatest importance that you guard well your role as scholars and that you respect the constitution and honor the laws, at no time transgressing their bounds. While you are still in the midst of your academic activities as students, to assume the position of a social pioneer, to embrace the spirit of some revolutionary or other and to enter into unlawful movements, even though your intention may be to your heart the improvement of society, such behavior is sufficient only to your own glorification. From the point of view of society it is but a poor joke, bringing grief not only to yourself but to your family. That is no way to reform society. . . .

It was up to each student to discipline and control himself, Minobe concluded.[104]

The prosecution of campaigns against dangerous thought brought distress to professors not only because of the effects on their students. Some academicians came to be suspected as the supposed authors of subversive ideas, or at least of incompetence in supervising youthful intellect. Occasionally professors were fetched up in the police nets, usually under the terms of the press laws. When in 1933 the ministry of education forced the resignation of a member of the Kyoto Imperial University law department, the issues of free speech and academic freedom became mixed up with the parochial problem of university autonomy. The triumph of the ministry in the case of Dr. Takikawa Yukitatsu was an omen of the closing in of the police state upon academic institutions which was to run its full course in the academic purges of 1936–1940. Takikawa had written a textbook, *Keihō Tokuhon* (*Criminal Law Reader*), to which official exception was taken on the ground that its sections criticizing the law of adultery and the law of rebellion threatened the state and its national polity. Following court action banning the book, the ministry of education forced Takikawa's resignation from the Kyoto faculty against the stiff opposition of the president of the university and its faculty. At one time a mass resignation of the Kyo-Dai law department staff was threatened, with the possibility that the faculties of other imperial universities would join in the walkout. As it turned out the resignations of several of the senior members of the Kyoto law faculty were accepted, including that of Professor Sasaki Sōichi. Takikawa was not reïnstated, however, until 1946.[105]

Takikawa was by no means the first academician to get into trouble with the political censors. Precedents dating as late as 1926 were well known to the academic community.[106] But Takikawa's was the first dismissal since 1920 in which the ministry prevailed despite the opposition of the university administration and faculty.

In May and June of 1933 Minobe went to the pages of *Teikoku Daigaku Shimbun* to air his views on the Takikawa affair.[107] He condemned the action of the ministry of education on three grounds: for declaring something that was hostile neither to the state nor to national polity to be dangerous thought; for transgressing the bounds between administrative and academic competence; and for violating the organic law of the university. Umbrageously he asserted: "A university is not an assemblage of government officials established to carry out government policy . . . and university professors are not, in respect to academic matters, bound by the policies of the government of the day. They must be free to investigate and to teach in scholarly good faith and to publish what they believe to be the truth." But, if professors were not indeed to be likened to servile *bakufu* scholars, they nevertheless were responsible under the University Ordinance not only for teaching according to the needs of the state, but also for cultivating student character and patriotism. Should a professor embrace ideas incompatible with those obligations, then he forfeited his status, and a plea to academic freedom was no defense. In this case the ministry had ordered dismissal on the basis of the writing of Professor Takikawa. It appeared, however, that the book was hardly offensive, except perhaps in the intemperance of its language, and the faculty at Kyoto had unanimously declared the book innocent of the charges made against it. Surely, Minobe concluded, the ministry's action constituted a gross infringement of academic competence.

While it was undoubtedly within the power of the ministry to order the dismissal of a professor who was clearly disqualified by reason of personal delinquency, lack of training, or criminal behavior, no such disabilities had been laid against Takikawa. The charges ran rather to the content and meaning of the product of his scholarship, which in the judgment of his colleagues—and in the opinion of Professor Minobe they were the only proper judges on the matter—in no way offended against the state or society. It was provided in the imperial ordinance establishing Kyoto Imperial University (and similarly for all imperial universities) that: "The president shall report to the minister of education concerning the appointment and dismissal of superior officials." And the ministry of education had "finally concurred" in the position of the universities, in the aftermath of the Morito case (1920), that this provision should be construed to mean that if the minister of education proposed to discharge a professor he would wait upon a report from the university president before doing so. If the president failed to comply with the proposed action, then the minister would suspend or dismiss the president and appoint in his place one amenable to the minister's proposal. Minobe pointed out that, in failing to adhere to this understanding, the ministry was guilty of violating at least the spirit of the ordinance.[108]

In a lengthy article in *Chūō Kōron* Minobe repeated his criticism to a wider audience and upbraided the ministry further for its misguided and insulting action in accepting the resignations of only a select few of the senior members of the Kyoto law faculty. He predicted that the affair would wreck that law department and damage the morale of its students. To those who were pointed in asking why the To-Dai law faculty had not joined their Kyoto brethren in submitting resignations he replied:

I believe that I can say definitely that the professors of the To-Dai law faculty, or at least a majority of them, are devoted to academic freedom and are in accord with the Kyoto professors in holding that the action taken in respect to Professor Takikawa constitutes an illegal invasion of his liberty. Their failure to act jointly with the Kyoto professors and to adopt an attitude of antagonism toward the ministry of education is due chiefly to the fact that since imperial sanction has already been given to the acceptance of the resignations, there seems little possibility that the action can be rescinded. As a consequence, a fight with the ministry could only result in precipitating To-Dai into the same disorder that prevails at Kyoto. And if professors resign it would only serve to jeopardize the future of the students at To-Dai.

If it becomes the accepted idea in society to oppose abuse of power with concerted force, then it becomes a matter of force against force, and the destruction of the social order will be inevitable. Even if such a recourse is sometimes unavoidable, we are bound to make every possible effort to avoid it. . . .[109]

Minobe realized that official concern over Takikawa's teaching had been motivated in the first place by pressure from outside the ministry of education, and that the ministry had adopted its adamant position *vis-à-vis* the university faculty in response to this same pressure, which, he said, came from extremely prejudiced persons who habitually made reckless attacks on academic theories on the ground that they were bolshevik in character.[110] He was frequently exercised by the increasing use of intolerant and intemperate name-calling, blacklisting, bullying, and censorship as regular weapons of conflict between opposing groups in Japanese society. As the years of Showa unfolded and the social crisis in Japan and the world deepened, these attitudes and tactics became especially prominent on the right. And as the old lines of authoritarianism, militarism, and patriotic mysticism merged with newer strains of social and nationalistic radicalism, they matured in virulent journalism, vigilantism, and terror. The atmosphere engendered by these habits of thought and tactics were, in a sense, a greater threat to political and intellectual freedom than were the legal and police apparatus of the state. Minobe's interest in this problem was not impersonal. He had emerged rather handsomely from the ordeal of such an attack at an early stage of his career, but as the blows of the new reaction came closer and with increasing intensity and recklessness upon his own position it was clear that the "objective conditions" of society were not in his favor as they had been in that earlier period.

In 1929 he found occasion to inveigh against the return to the old national polity clamor as a means of confounding opposing opinions.[111] He deplored the intensification of nationalistic (*kokusui*) thought which had developed as an antidote to communism, and the growing influence of this type of thinking among officials and the public at large. The extent to which the national polity argument had indeed become a convenient and apparently effective weapon was illustrated by its use in interparty warfare. In August, 1928, for example, the Tanaka (Seiyukai) Government put Japan's signature to the Kellogg-Briand Anti-war Pact in Paris. In so doing it precipitated an extended attack by the opposition (Minseito). The basis of the Minseito complaint was the alleged incompatibility between the phrase "in the names of their respective peoples" in Article I of the treaty and Japan's national polity as expressed in Article IV of the constitution.[112] Minobe denounced the Minseito's complaint as specious and mischievous: "The answer to this charge is very simple, and outside of Japan the problem could not conceivably arise. That it has come up in Japan is a disgrace to our national dignity. It is impossible to believe that either party has any other intention than to protect national polity, the unshakable faith of our people. But to use national polity as a political weapon is not to preserve national polity." He cautioned his readers to keep in mind that Japan had not drafted the convention unilaterally and that the problem of translation was difficult. He reminded them that Japan had frequently used different language in international documents than was used for promulgations to the Japanese people.[113]

However disgraceful the behavior of the Minseito in making this an issue against the government, it was in a sense only giving back what it had gotten, in kind. When the Minseito (*Rikken Minseitō*, Constitutional Democratic Party) was founded in 1927, through the merger of the Kenseikai and other anti-Seiyukai groups, it was almost immediately subject to abuse by the *kokutai*-mongers. In 1928, Seiyukai home minister, Suzuki Kisaburo, a bureaucratic party man with long affiliation with the ultranationalist movement, and later president of the Seiyukai, joined in this attack, advertising that the very name Minseito was an affront to national polity. One of the slogans of the Minseito, one dating from the Taisho Political Reform, proclaimed the party's dedication to *gikai chūshin shugi* (literally, parliament-centered government), and this was denounced as a direct contradiction of the emperor-centric principle of the constitution and national polity. This attack came close to home for Minobe and he was alert to meet the charge.[114]

Patiently he recited the constitutional premises essential to the position of the parliamentary parties, addressing himself to those who were thickheaded enough not to recognize, even at that late date, the necessity of distinguishing between the legal and the political reference to *chūshin seiji* (center of government). Legally, Japan's was an emperor-centric polity and no one, certainly not the Minseito, would deny it. But neither would any thinking person suppose from this legal principle that the emperor governed immediately in his own person, for that would be contrary to the constitutional principle of the inviolability of the throne. The emperor governed through the advice of the cabinet, the consent of the diet, the counsel of the privy council, and so on. The tenet of the Minseito was simply that among the several instruments of imperial rule the central position belonged to the diet.

Constitutionally the cabinet is exclusively responsible for advice on the prerogative, but in actual practice, politically, the cabinet is under the sway of the clan cliques, the military clique, the bureaucrats, the peers, or the majority group in the house of representatives. *Gikai chūshin seiji* contrasts, then, not with *Tennō chūshin Seiji*, but with clan oligarchy, military oligarchy, etc. . . . constitutional government is *gikai chūshin seiji*, and in the west constitutionalism and parliamentarism are used interchangeably. . . .

Whatever the fault of parliamentary government it was clearly superior in merit to any of the alternatives known to the contemporary world. Whatever the faults of the Minseito, they certainly did not merit this calumny.

By reason of their indulgence in mutual vilification, their recitations of extreme slogans designed to exploit popular distemper, the parties themselves bore a heavy burden of responsibility for the deepening atmosphere of frustration, hate, and distrust from which emerged the monstrous spectacle of their own demise in shattering bursts of bullets. As we shall see, Minobe's understanding of the morbidity of parliamentary government in Japan extended beyond the omen of extremist direct action. But the aberrant behavior of the revolutionary right was a palpably serious phenomenon in itself, even though it appeared in his diagnosis of it to be symptomatic rather than causative. True, the tendency for opposition to take the way of conspiracy and violence was a familiar pattern in Japanese political history, and might even be thought to have a "natural" and efficacious part to play under authoritarian regimes. But, by the same token, such tactics, and the philosophical and psychological bases of their being, were, as Minobe time and again maintained, absolutely incompatible with constitutional government.

Writing on the occasion of the assassination of Inoue Junnosuke early in 1932, Minobe in no uncertain terms castigated the parties for their contributions to the climate of violence.[115] Their guilt was the more damnable because it involved betrayal of the very principles of government upon which they based their pretensions to political power. They had demonstrated a complete lack of appreciation of the fact that "constitutional government is tolerant government," that "its fundamental spirit lies in treating opposition thought magnanimously" rather than in suppressing it by authority and force. They had forgotten that "constitutional government requires discrimination in the choice of means; that it is a denial of constitutional government to seek proper ends by illegal use of authority and by violence." He continued ironically:

Party politicians today are forever calling for political education and civic indoctrination. Now this is not unreasonable in itself, but, to speak the truth, it is not the people generally who are in such urgent need of political education; rather it is the leaders of the country. . . . Before demanding political indoctrination of the masses they would do well to reflect upon themselves and the necessity of cultivating in their own minds a deep faith in constitutionalism and the abjuration of force. . . .

Specifically, the error of the parties was that they had become habituated to argument by slander, seeking always to comfound their opponents by calling them "traitors, rebels, blackguards, etc." There were among the leaders of the parties men who were willing to sponsor or encourage the publication of incendiary posters, pamphlets, and news sheets openly inciting physical violence against opposition personalities. And if these charges could be turned aside as applicable only to a few miscreant individuals, certainly the parties could not escape responsibility for the fact that they had tolerated such behavior when it had been in their power to prevent it. The policy of party governments had been to suppress the left, but to leave unhindered, whatever violence or illegality they proposed, those operating from "patriotic" platforms. "When it comes to identifying violent ideas dangerous to society and the state, the left has no monopoly of them. The government's toleration of right-wing extremism is certainly a contributing factor" in the degeneration toward political darkness and violence.[116]

Earlier, in commenting on the tactics of the government in the electoral campaign of 1928, he had predicted that a continuation of official policies of violence and corruption would serve only to provide a substantial social basis for the very radicalism which the government sought to suppress.[117] In 1934 he spoke as though observing the fulfillment of that prediction:

but if [ideas] find in society a background of actual social conditions receptive to them, then their power to move society will be very great, and they will be converted into action giving rise to very real dangers to society and the state. Herein lies the real danger of extreme rightist thinking. . . . The principle plank in their platform has been a denunciation of the parties and the *zaibatsu*, and so deeply have the evils perpetrated by politicians and capitalists been felt, that this advocacy is very readily accepted. Thus the danger is great. How far this thought has moved society can be inferred from the manifestations of public sympathy at the news of the Five Fifteen Incident. . . .[118]

Thus, the parliamentary ranks themselves, by reckless disregard of vital constitutional principles, had helped to nourish the flames of revolutionary violence against which even the administrative power of the state could not protect them.

VI

Constitutional Government in Crisis

The essential components of "Minobeism" in general have been drawn mostly from writings and events predating the period of constitutional crisis following 1930. Minobe's work following that turn in Japanese (and world) history has been largely ignored by Japanese as well as foreign writers, possibly because it constitutes an awkward twist in his position. His career up to 1930 gives a less than complete, perhaps even misleading, impression of the depth of Minobe's attachment to democratic liberalism. Some consideration of its tenability and his tenacity under adverse conditions is needed to fill out the picture.

The thirties was an era of trial for all those who professed to find in responsible representative government the necessary and proper ordering of the Japanese state. Under the harsh conditions of the period—the rough rejection by his own society of his liberalism and constitutional doctrine—Minobe was not insulated from prevailing humors of that society. Its fears, anxieties, and revolutionary pressures were contagious; in Minobe's wrestling with the constitutional problems of those years he did not escape confusion, contradiction, and compromise. What earlier had been mere shadows of doubts and reservations now became dark clouds; what had been maximal dimensions in his liberal interpretation of the Imperial Constitution shrank to minimual proportions. It is impossible to say how far he might have gone in "adjusting" his position had he not been silenced by the events of 1935. Meanwhile, at least relatively, he remained preëminent among the handful of scholars who, in the words of Tsunego Baba, "consistently braved the reactionary storm to stand by their plea for the cause of parliamentarism." When he departed suddenly from the lists, he was still the symbol of the liberal constitutional cause.

Indeed the so-called Minobe Affair (with which the next chapter deals) arose out of the stormy scenes of 1930–1935. Although the charges made against him in 1935 referred chiefly to his pre-1930 works, other and very cogent factors behind those charges were prompted by his resistance to the drive toward dictatorship in the more immediately preceding years. The isolation in which he was to find himself in 1935 was foreshadowed by his singular position during those years. Committed to defense of the parties as instruments of constitutional government, he was, nevertheless, almost completely alienated from the existing parties by his criticism of their undemocratic character and the power orientation of their thinking and action. Similarly, the bond between himself and important elements in official and business circles on the issue of preserving constitutional government was really very tenuous, for he was devoted to constitutionalism for its own sake, and not merely as a means to preserve the social and political *status quo*. Professor Maruyama has asked, "Whom may we regard as having been right wing [before 1945]? If we overlook an extremely small number of heretics, the answer is—everybody." Minobe was probably not among the heretics Maruyama had in mind, but it may be suggested that even in this retrograde period he did remain relatively more true to the principles of normal constitutional government than did the important public figures with whose causes and concerns he was linked.[1]

The years 1932 to 1940 saw a full transition from constitutional parliamentary party government (however ambiguous) to the firm establishment of the military-dominated, authoritarian regime under which the empire was to pursue its course to disaster. It was the time of "the dark valley" when the "still delicate plant of liberalism and personal freedom which had sprouted during the twenties was effectively killed."[2] Minobe's connection with this course of events ended abruptly in 1935. His writing up to that time did not, to be sure, manifest explicit awareness of the inexorabilities that seem clear in retrospect; nevertheless, reflections of the ominous context of the time are evident enough in the ambivalence of his response.

The Agony of Parliamentary Parties

It has been customary to fix the period of the crisis and transition between the assassination of Inukai in May, 1932, and the dissolution of
the parties in the latter part of 1940. These events are fairly obvious
terminal points, but the usual *caveat* against such chronological compartmentalization holds. It is especially deceptive to look upon the Five
Fifteen Incident as the beginning of the trouble. In a sense, the roots of
the phenomenon were as old as the Restoration itself, and indeed even
older if the endless threads of causality were to be fully unraveled. As a
pivotal event, however, Hamaguchi's Pyrrhic victory in 1930 in the matter of the London Naval Treaty is probably the most significant signal
of the crystallizing crisis, although Minobe, ignoring that event in which
he had himself played a part, elected the opening of the Manchurian
trouble at Mukden in September, 1931, as "the first and most obvious"
point of its origin. He, however, was more concerned with underlying
causes than with events, and he gave greatest weight to the tensions in
Japanese society dating from the period of World War I, seeing in them
and the resulting cleavages in Japanese society the revolutionary potential
which materialized in the economic and international crises of the
1930's.[3]

Although parliamentary government was virtually defunct with the
lapse of party government in 1932, the formal vestige of parliamentary
government persisted in the being of the diet. Among the various explanations of this, probably first consideration must be given to the fact
that the diet could have been abolished or altered only by constitutional
amendment. Accordingly, only the most extreme revolutionary proposals
called for its abolition or reconstitution. The effective attack on parliamentary government was aimed, instead, at the vitals of the system, the
political parties, and at the whole complex of "liberalism" which sustained it. Once that liberalism had been exorcized and the old parties
finally extinguished, the parliament itself ceased to be an obstacle to
military-bureaucratic despotism.

The protraction of the life of the political parties after 1932 is of
particular interest in this narrative because Minobe's work in the early
part of the period undoubtedly reflected the psychology which served to

sustain the parties' expectation of redemption and contributed ammunition and inspiration to those outside the parties who hoped to preserve a constitutional order in which the parties had a necessary function. The apparent durability of the parties can be explained in this context, in terms of institutional inertia. For all their weakness, the two major parties represented a considerable political force; even as it dwindled, it gave them a relative advantage over their opponents, who were divided and even less endowed than the parties with popular support or the means of mobilizing such support. However hollow the pretensions of the parties to participation in governmental power, they maintained an appearance of vigorous activity so long as the electoral law and party machinery remained even nominally viable.

The appointment of Saito (May, 1932) was a blow to the parties. But they were aware of the obstacles to their own succession to power and endorsed it, albeit reluctantly. They had (they thought) reason to believe that they had not yet lost the game. The composition of the Saito Government and the auspices under which it had been established permitted a supposition that the retreat of the parties might be only a temporary deviation such as had punctuated the course of party government in the past. The national unity slogan of the Saito Cabinet recalled previous political "truces" invoked in time of crisis without signifying an end to the parties' struggle for power. There were, moreover, still other meliorating conditions. For one, while party leadership had been sidetracked, the new regime was not transcendent, strictly speaking. Saito sought party support and got it, at least nominally, with both parties holding seats in his predominantly bureaucratic cabinet. Second, the parties had no reason to believe that the men who chose Saito (and his successor, Okada)—that is, the Genro Saionji and the officers of the imperial household—really wanted completely to destroy the parties. Thus the parties although helpless to prevent their displacement from nominal control of the government, still continued to look upon themselves as the proper custodians of political power. They continued business-as-usual interparty warfare and, even more literally, business-as-usual brokerage between business interests and administrative authority.

Thus, the parties, no longer strong enough to control government, were still too strong to be ignored by those who did. At several critical junctures in 1932–1934, so long as the most articulate and active anti-party movements were closely tied to radical social revolutionary pro-

grams (which remained the case until 1936), important financial and
official elements having no great attachment to democratic principles
clung to the idea of parliamentary government as the best hope of fore-
stalling full-scale revolution. Such is the motive imputed to the inner
court circle in its effort to prevent a complete subversion of the parliamentary system.[4]

A Forlorn Advocacy

Minobe was not one of those few perceptive enough to realize the
finality of the interruption of party government in May, 1932. There
was to be sure at this stage, a growing minority of opinion which advertised forthrightly its rejection of parliamentary government in principle and drew great comfort from the sight of normal constitutional
government floundering to a standstill. On the other hand, probably a
majority of those whose views found access to the public through the
normal channels of communication were by no means ready to write off
the recent past as a total loss. There were many who, if not convinced
champions of parliamentary government, nevertheless continued to assume that is was the normal order in the state, the one to which their
fortunes were tied, and who consequently clung to it, for all its faults,
as the better part of what was yet to be. For them the hope of parliamentary revival persisted. It was a time, however, not only for continuing
the fight against old enemies but for reassessing the qualities of parliamentary government, for identifying its inherent defects, and for seeking
the means of purging its adventitious failings. For those most seriously
concerned for its survival, it was a season for seeking a new concept of
the role of parliament in constitutional government, for projecting reforms which would revitalize the parliamentary institution. Minobe's
writing in these years attests to his participation in such exercises and to
his involvement in the confusions and anxieties of the times.

Premier Inukai is reported to have protested to a public audience a few
days before his assassination of the tendency in certain quarters to negate
the diet: "this is unrealistic under the actual political conditions, and it
is an opinion which concludes that thorough reform is impossible. Opposed to this, we believe in the wise use of parliamentary politics to the

greatest degree, and we believe that sufficient reform is possible."[5] These sentiments closely parallel those expressed by Minobe a month later:

I do not join with the many who have abandoned political parties, nor can I find much to agree with in the so-called fascist movement. I desire to maintain the principle of constitutional government as far as possible, and above all I cannot assent to a return to the old despotism. On the other hand I fully recognize the insupportable evils manifested by the parties to date, and I do not doubt that the principles of constitutional government must be amended in some way if these faults are to be avoided. . . .[6]

Scalapino has said of Inukai's remarks that they signified the "defensive and forlorn" psychology which gripped the leadership of the parliamentary parties. Should Minobe's words be construed in the same sense? There can be no doubt that he was on the defensive, but he was not passive, and his thinking was certainly not dispirited. To be sure, he was prepared to admit that the cause of party government in the pattern of the 1920's was lost, and he accepted the recourse to nonparty leadership in government as a temporary necessity. But he remained firm in his conviction that a continuation of parliamentary government, albeit in a modified form, was constitutionally necessary and politically desirable, and he continued to denounce those steps by which, openly or covertly, the scheme of government was being shifted in the direction of dictatorship.

If Minobe's experiences and convictions were not impervious to the perplexities and anxieties of those days, still, throughout the doubts and confusions, the improvisations, the backing and filling, ran a single theme: the necessity of preserving the constitution in the form and, as nearly as might be possible, in the spirit of his liberal interpretation of it. This purpose he shared with powerful elements—the *genrō, the jūshin,* and the magnates of monopoly capitalism. Did he also share their previously mentioned motives? The answer must be in the negative. To be sure, Minobe was no revolutionary; he was neither temperamentally nor intellectually capable of espousing a radical program. On the other hand, all that has been shown about his work indicates that he was a vigorous critic of the social and political structure. And his writings during the crisis years suggest his continued receptivity to social reconstruction. For example:

For us Japanese too, the most important thing today is to grasp firmly the fact that the so-called crisis is not a temporary thing but is deeply rooted in society, and that we must combine our efforts to establish a new social order, undertaking the necessary social reformation by peaceful and legal means, shunning all force.

[When we have identified the immediate cause of the crisis we still come back to the ultimate fact that] the social order as it stands no longer works, that great and fundamental changes in that order are required. . . .

Just as the decline of the feudal system necessitated the Meiji Restoration, so the impasse in the capitalistic economy today brings us face to face with an era of social change. To use stronger words, I wonder if these times do not require a revolution comparable in dimensions to the Meiji Restoration. . . .[7]

Such statements in themselves might, of course, be compatible with a reactionary interest in national reconstruction, and, unfortunately for the argument, Minobe was not explicit in his talk about social and economic reform. The case must rest upon the fact that it is impossible to reconcile his position with either a bolshevist or fascist solution to the problem. There can be no doubt that authoritarianism of whatever complexion was repugnant to him, that he attached the greatest value to the institutions, processes, and spirit which he identified with constitutional government. Thus, his constant demurer that "we must hope that even in this present hour of crisis we can abjure the dangerous path of dictatorship, and even if it does not seem the appropriate means of carrying out a great reform, we can pursue the normal path of constitutional government. . . ."[8]

For Minobe as well as for those more directly involved in the fortunes of party government the advent of the Saito Cabinet was a baleful event, an open retreat from what had been thought to be an irrevocable succession from transcendental to responsible government. He had willingly followed the logic of his constitutional theory to welcome party government as the natural and effective expression of constitutional democracy, entirely compatible with the monarchical institution. On the other hand, he himself stood outside the party movement and his attachment to the theory of party government had never dulled his observation of the seamy side of party government in operation. One detects in his reaction to the downfall of the parties in 1932 that it was not so much the unlaid ghost of the parties as the rising spectre of despotism which alarmed him.

The all-important constitutional problem was to secure an administration strong enough, within constitutional limits, to control all the lines of state administration, to bring firm decision and vigorous execution in all aspects of domestic and foreign policy—in all, to check the drift toward authoritarian despotism. This was, in a sense, an intense urgent manifestation of the chronic problem of modern Japanese government. Conspiring against its solution were all the time-proven weaknesses of the constitutional structure itself. It was embarrassing to Minobe that as he himself insisted, the constitutional order which he defended was inseparable in theory from party government, inseparable in the public mind from the recent unhappy performance of the parties. The existing parties were really indefensible; they were not at all inclined to coöperate in schemes relegating them to a secondary status. But Minobe, determined to defend parliamentary government, was forced eventually to do so with a program in which the role of parties was sharply curtailed.

He conceded at once that under the circumstances the *genrō's* choice of Admiral Saito was "the coolest and most acceptable" one that could have been made.[9] Since the Seiyukai had a clear parliamentary majority, the *genrō* might have been expected under normal circumstances to have continued that party's administration with its president as premier. But the military had announced opposition to that choice, and even if they could have been induced to supply service ministers for a Seiyukai Government the result would undoubtedly have been to precipitate further acts of violence on the part of the anti-parliamentary extremists. Neither the Seiyukai nor the Minseito could claim public confidence, and—more important for a successful administration—neither could claim the confidence of the military or the bureaucracy. The *genrō's* decision was all the more to be appreciated, Minobe observed, in view of the fact that one of the alternatives reputedly urged upon him was the establishment of a transcendental military cabinet headed by Baron Hiranuma.[10]

As Minobe saw it, the immediate cause of the elimination of the parties from governmental leadership was the demonstrated ability and willingness of the revolutionary opposition to wreck party governments by violent direct action. What made terrorism fruitful was the general indifference or acquiescence of the public, which had long been subjected to left and right propaganda fixing the blame for Japan's troubles on parliamentary government and on the alliance between capital and the parties. The people had observed the open spectacle of corruption in elections, cabinet arrogance toward the diet, the undemocratic attitude and behavior of party leaders, and the inability of party cabinets to cope with bureaucratic and military intransigence. They had watched the diet consume its time and energy in passionate debate over formalistic matters, such as the question of the treaty power or the issue of national polity, having nothing to do with the problems of livelihood. They had been conditioned to appreciate the aptness of such epithets as the homonymic *shūgi-in* (bawdy house) applied to the house of representatives, or *bōryoku dan* (strong-arm gangs) applied to the parties.

But it was possible to make too much of the sins of parliamentary politics. Without apology for his own contribution to the chorus of indictment, Minobe deplored the constant harping on faults of the parties and of parliamentary government which he feared was smothering public faith in them. It availed little, however, to recapitulate the positive accomplishments of the era of party government, or to point out that the parties were as much sinned against as sinning, that they had labored under extremely adverse constitutional arrangements, that their vices were not worse but only more public than those which flourished under authoritarian regimes. Minobe's task was helped not at all by the prominent display of parallel parliamentary evils abroad, which seemed to confirm their inevitability. All in all, he observed, general circumstances and specific events nourished growing sentiment for the establishment of a strong government, a longing for the despotism of sages or heroes. The general public was certainly not notably dismayed at the advent of the Saito Cabinet; they were subsequently to show even greater indifference to the threat of a complete eradication of the party system.[11]

Minobe was hardly enthusiastic in endorsing the so-called national unity governments of Saito and Okada. Use of the term "national unity" (*kyokoku itchi*) was intended to draw upon the credit owing to the supposed merits of the similarly designated governments of the periods of the Sino-Japanese and Russo-Japanese wars. The analogy was not very close. In those earlier instances there had been no problem of accommodating party men within the administration. Moreover, there had been then, in the presence of actual warfare, a cessation not only of intragovernmental quarreling but of opposition in the diet. Underlying the official harmony was a substantial unity of public opinion on the issue of war. No such felicitous conditions or consequences had attended the more recent careers of the transcendental cabinets of admirals Kato and

Yamamoto and Baron Kiyoura in the 1922–1924 period. Minobe did not believe that the result would be different in the present instance.

As time passed, he became increasingly skeptical of their efficacy. His attitude was hardly surprising in view of his old animosity toward bureaucratic absolutism. Too much of his life had been consumed in the advocacy of normal constitutional government to allow him easily to welcome a step suggesting return to earlier patterns of military-bureaucratic arrogance, irresponsibility, and secrecy. Little wonder if he perceived in the background the mocking ghosts of old foes claiming vindication. This psychology showed clearly in his tendency to draw unfavorable parallels from the past and in his refusal to admit that parliamentary government was permanently defunct in Japan. But it was not only, or even primarily, defense of his own reputation or loyalty to old symbols and slogans that made him critical of the Saito and Okada efforts at national unity. The trouble with those cabinets was that they were weak. Possibly his constitutional qualms would have been assuaged had these governments dealt even somewhat effectively with the problems of social reform or had they recovered for the cabinet central control over foreign and military policy.

Indeed, even as the *genrō* was reaching his decision to nominate Saito, Minobe anticipated the weakness of a nonpartisan or suprapartisan administration. The press had been agitating for the establishment of a strong national unity government; there and elsewhere proposals frequently appeared for such diverse formulas as a cabinet based on a coalition of factions or a cabinet of experts. Minobe scoffed at such ideas: a strong national unity government was an ideal more easily spoken of than realized. Were such a government truly devised it might go far to satisfy the nation's need, but it could not be expected that a mere formal gesture of unity would produce the singleness of purpose, the coöperation on vital matters of policy without which such a government would be very weak.[12]

In Admiral Saito the *genrō* had found the ideal "harmonious and affable" type, without partisan connections, under whose unsullied reputation to attempt a reversion to the pre-Hara pattern of supraparty administration. But the hollowness behind the shell of unity was apparent from the beginning. Without being either a coalition of parties or a cabinet of experts, the Saito and Okada cabinets traded on the pretense of embodying the presumed virtues of each of them. Both consisted of bureaucratic, military, and party men, reflecting the effort to produce harmony with the house of representatives, the house of peers, the privy council, and the military. The unity was precarious and probably satisfactory chiefly to the bureaucrats. Certainly neither the majority party (Seiyukai) nor the army was content with the compromise arrangement. It was only with difficulty that the military were kept in the fold, and the Seiyukai went into opposition in 1934, leaving the Minseito as the "government party."

In September, 1932, Minobe found his earlier apprehensions more than fulfilled. The Saito Government, he asserted, "goes under the banner of national unity, but it is a far cry from national unity in the true sense of the word. . . . Without settled goals and without unity of principle, even though the various factions have been brought together to constitute a cabinet, suddenly and without regard for different backgrounds and different sentiments, it is only a mechanical combination with little hope of organic unity. . . ." Division of purpose within the government was the certain consequence of the mutually exclusive ambitions of the Seiyukai and the army.[13]

Minobe appreciated, however, that those who were fighting to preserve constitutional government were stuck with this improvisation, that whatever its inadequacies it was the most hopeful of a number of unhappy alternatives: "There is nothing else to do," he admitted, "but to hope that the [Saito] Cabinet will continue as long as possible, and to strengthen it. . . . For if this cabinet should fail, the nation would be face to face with an even more serious political peril. . . ."[14] And if the so-called national unity government should not achieve a positive program of economic and social reform, it was essential that it at least perform the caretaker function, preserving the constitution against the day when normal constitutional processes could be restored. Indeed, it is not unreasonable to believe that Minobe considered the prime mission of the Saito and Okada cabinets to be to prevent a *coup d'état* from the right. In this role, too, their performance was disappointing. Their ineffectiveness, their blunders and scandals might serve to deflate naive notions of the virtue of transcendental administration, but they in no way inspired a revival of popular faith in responsible representative government. Instead, they evoked ever more urgent pressure for further retreats from constitutional principles—even for the establishment of an outright dictatorship by force if necessary.

The Menace of Militarism

The most explicit threat to constitutional government was presented by resurgent militarism, an old and familiar enemy now made more virulent by the accretion of fascistic and national socialistic overtones. The social and professional traditions of the military arm of the Japanese state, particularly in the army, was basically hostile to responsible parliamentary government and to capitalism.[15] Military officers in general were oriented toward nationalistic ideas and programs; many were prominently active in non-military patriotic and ultraconservative organizations. The authoritarian cast of the military mind was hardly disturbed by such contacts, for it tended to infuse its own characteristics rather than to absorb those of their civilian associates.

The position of military authority within the constitutional system had long aggravated civil-military conflicts, especially as civil authority came under the influence of parliamentary politics. Senior military officers had, of course, played important roles in government during the era of Satcho domination. As the early clan military power began to wane, the newer generation of the officer corps developed an active interest in politics and economics as these related to armaments and national defense. The tendency toward extraprofessional interest in matters of state policy became more intense in both services under the disarmament and military economy policies of the party governments of the 1920's, especially after 1925. Underlying this common general inclination were intense interservice rivalries, personal factions, and a wide difference of attitudes on political and social questions ranging from very conservative to quite radical, but uniformly unfriendly toward the axis of political and economic liberalism.

The 1920's was a period of low ebb in the popular prestige and political influence of the military, a time when anti-militarist sentiments prevailed among the general public. In the 1930's the military achieved hegemony in the Japanese state. The explanation of this change is exceedingly complex and only the barest outline of the main points can be made here. First, there was the already noted fruition of the liaison between military personnel and the civilian nationalist movement. Prior to the late 1920's their associations had amounted to little more than rearguard actions against apparently triumphant liberal forces, and their overt attacks were directed chiefly at Marxism. By 1930, however, a new revolutionary element had entered the scene; older lines of conservative, authoritarian nationalism were fused with and, in some cases, more or less dominated by actionist revolutionaries of national socialist or fascistic character. The avowed purpose of these was to bring about a national reconstruction involving the extirpation of parliamentary government and private capitalism. The long-standing contacts with the civilian right-ists exposed the military to the growing revolutionary tendencies and multiplied the opportunities for the military to exploit the violent actionism of the civilians. Deepening economic depression seriously affected the temper of the predominantly peasant conscripts in the army; the junior officers of that service were especially sensitive to agrarian discontent and hence were particularly vulnerable to the appeal of radical movements. The military now stood to profit from close relations with the rightist associations and action groups, whose aggregate political significance mounted in proportion to the decline of the credit and vitality of the parliamentary regime. And Japanese "fascism," lacking unity, organization, and leadership of its own, stood to gain these, as well as encouragement and subsidy from participation of the military.

Second, the military, playing on the peculiarities of the imperial constitutional system and the geographic circumstances of the empire, found the opportunity they required in Manchuria. The result, if not the purpose, of their unilateral action there was to create and perpetuate a state of international crisis which catapulted military urgencies to domination of national policy. The role of military personnel in government soared, nationalist passions and patriotic apprehensions flamed—all to the further embarrassment of capitalism and constitutional liberalism. But the situation was still far from satisfactory so far as the ultimate aims of the military leaders were concerned. For one thing, the military threat alarmed party leaders, moderates in the bureaucratic hierarchy, and some financial and industrial circles. Moreover, the Manchurian adventure and the general enhancement of the military role, tended to exacerbate the conflict of interest between the army and the navy as well as intraservice factionalism, and to expose those divisions to public view.

The third factor contributing to the establishment of military hegemony in the state was the success of military leaders in turning the pattern of factional struggle within the army to the service of military ambitions. The division within the army, seemingly bi-polar in character, was in fact quite complex.[16] The army command structure was divided on the issue of technical modernization which vitally affected the careers of officers, particularly of those among the imperial military graduates fortunate enough to be selected, on the basis of professional competence, for advancement through the War College. Upon this division was superimposed a revived Choshu-anti-Choshu rivalry in which the anti-Choshu (i.e., pro-Tosa and -Hizen) group tended to champion "spiritual" as opposed to technical values. The ideological proclivities of this element were symbolized in the designation Imperial Way Faction (kōdōha). Over against the Imperial Way Faction there emerged in 1934 the Control Faction (tōseiha), a less homogeneous group made up of those who regretted the han factionalism issue. Chief among these were those who pushed for rigorous professionalization along advanced technical lines. In the course of this struggle the Imperial Way Faction openly advertised its authoritarian and ultranationalist beliefs and thus attracted the admiring and expectant attention of the junior officers, those passed over or not yet eligible for staff and command training, who were very much affected by various doctrines of extreme social radicalism and direct political action. The most self-conscious and activist of these young officers, a group known as the National Principle Faction (kokutai genri ha), eventually came into direct relations with the Imperial Way Faction in 1935. While no less interested in military ascendancy in the state, the Control Faction was less extreme in its reconstructionist aims and determined above all to keep control of the revolution in the hands of senior military leaders. The Control Faction exploited the radicalism of the Imperial Way Faction to induce conservative bureaucratic and business interests to play the Control Faction game. This liaison was broadened and deepened with the progress of continental expansion. By mid-1936 the Control Faction had established firm control within the army and made itself thereby the dominant force in the constellation of powers controlling the state. From that position it was to advance step-by-step, by "constitutional means," to the establishment of military rule in the empire.

The Case Against Dictatorship

By 1932 it was too late for Minobe to dwell upon the constitutional weaknesses concerning the military power which had earlier concerned him. It seemed perfectly clear that a *de facto* military or fascist dictatorship could be brought about within the letter if not the spirit of the Imperial Constitution, and the vacuum created by the failure of the parties disposed many persons to welcome such a development.[17] Only the prevalence of an enlightened sense of general public interest, informing and strengthening the councils of the national unity government could prevent it.

PRAGMATIC DANGERS

Minobe sounded the alarm of common sense against the siren calls from the right. He warned of the loss of freedom and of the danger of disastrous war. He warned that the military would end neither corruption nor social inequities. He pointed to the political naiveté and the technical incompetence of the military regarding economic and social policy and administration. He noted the absence of leaders of popular standing among the military and bureaucratic groups who proposed to assume command of the state.

Minobe believed, moreover, that dictatorship ought to be shunned because despotism is itself an evil thing. To strike down parliamentary government in favor of dictatorship would be to give up freedom of political choice and a method for peaceful and legal transfer of power in exchange for a monolithic system in which dissent would be treason and spying and naked force would be the routine instruments of power: It would be to give up a system whose operations were public and subject to criticism for one of secret deliberations and unchallengeable commands. It would be to give up a system in which the people had an indirect influence on the choice of governmental leadership for one in which they would have no influence.[18] It was no use pretending that a modern dictatorship would be any different in this respect from the despotism of Japan's recent past. "While the name fascist is new, fascism itself is no novelty," Minobe noted, citing the Satcho regimes as essentially fascistic. Whatever the historical justification for the Satcho tyranny, there was no denying its violence, counterviolence, and assassination, and there was no reason to expect that a newfangled dictatorship would be any different.[19] In short, advocates of dictatorship were asking the Japanese people to make a doubly bad bargain: sacrifice of liberty in exchange for the benefits of a strong military government despite evidence that a cabinet based on military power would be incapable of providing strong government.[20]

CONSTITUTIONAL ARGUMENTS

Understandably, Minobe reinforced much of this concrete, "pragmatic" opposition to military dictatorship with constitutional steel: such a government could not be established without departing from the essential purpose and spirit of the constitution. One of the principal aims of the constitution had been to break up the union of civil and military power which existed under the clan despotism. The revival of such a union would be tantamount to a suspension of the constitution.

Only the utterly naive, he protested, could suppose it to be consistent with national polity that the emperor himself occupy the center of political power. The frequent cries for restoration of direct imperial rule were either purely innocent or masked the assumption of governmental authority by some irresponsible group. Slogans such as "the restoration of imperial rule" could not lessen the repugnance to the constitution of a fascistic military dictatorship. And, Minobe observed, the one-party scheme fundamental to dictatorship could not be achieved or maintained for any length of time except by means of military force. Under the constitution, all military force was monopolized by the emperor as supreme commander; by the emperor's own decree, the supreme command could not be prostituted to the service of any party or faction. On the other hand, within its constitutional powers the diet was not subject to any external controls, and its regimentation by a military (or other non-party) regime would make a pure fiction of any pretense of constitutional validity. A regime raised up by force would last only as long as its physical power was greater than that of those who opposed it. It was indeed foolish, Minobe warned, to credit the claims of the right revolutionists that what they sought was a second Restoration. They liked to cast themselves in the glorious part of imperial loyalists, assigning to their opponents the role of the wicked *bakufu*. There was no basis at all for such a comparison. The revolt against the *bakufu* had been constructive, but the self-styled latter-day loyalists were merely destructive in their purpose. Neither alone nor in combination with the so-called new bureaucracy did the military have the constitutional right or the political capacity to take over the helm of government.[21]

INTERNATIONAL CONSEQUENCES

Minobe advanced yet another reason for abhorring a military regime: its rule would greatly increase the prospects of war. The military adventure in Manchuria had already proven to be an unmitigated disaster. More than any other specific thing it had served to break the back of normal parliamentary government. It had brought the evils of dual government to national administration; it had brought Japan to a state of perilous international isolation. If Japan's peril did indeed stem from the Manchurian situation, then there was every reason for seeking not the end of parliamentary government but its restoration to good health and normal operation. To be sure, if war was inevitable, then sacrifice of constitutional regularity might be necessary,

but even under the circumstances today, with the danger of war present and pressing, it is difficult to accept the idea that it is absolutely inevitable. Certainly . . . from the point of view of social conditions at home and abroad there could be nothing more dangerous than to go ahead with the object of war as the basis of our national policy. To do so would carry the danger of bringing us into complete international isolation and finally to the necessity of a struggle with the whole world as our enemy. . . . It would be like throwing oneself into the fire, clutching bundles of fagots. I believe, as deeply as one may feel, that our national policy today ought to be to maintain peace to the utmost and to bend every effort to avoid war. To the extent that peace is our basic policy, then the most effective measure that we can take is to restore parliamentary government to its normal condition as rapidly as possible . . . the main reason for the degeneration of our international standing . . . is the mistaken belief abroad that we are an aggressive nation. And the basis for this misconception abroad is that since the Manchurian Incident the primary influence in our governmental affairs has been wielded by the military. If we are to improve international relations and avoid the danger of war, we must destroy that false impression. To that end the most effective measure we can take is to restore our governmental system to its former condition, thereby manifesting to the world that our national policy is indeed a policy of peace.[22]

When the press section of the war ministry in October, 1934, published a pamphlet on "The Essence of National Defense and Proposals to Strengthen It," advocating national economic planning,[23] finance minister Baron Takahashi Korekiyo counterattacked vigorously. Takahashi, a bureaucrat turned party man, a protégé of Hara, and one-time Seiyukai premier, had been, as a member of the Saito and Okada governments, a constant and outspoken critic of military highhandedness and recalcitrance. Minobe applauded Takahashi's denunciation of the "trumpet blowers" and warmly endorsed his defense of civilian-directed diplomacy. That there were those who wanted to upset the enlightened policy of "peace with diplomacy before national defense," was "a matter going to the very foundations of the state, a real danger to the life of the state." In February, 1935, he wrote in the journal, *Keizai Ōrai*: "On these issues [Japan's maintenance of Manchukuo and her coöperation with that country, and Japan's retention of the South Sea mandates] Japanese public opinion is wholly united. A war is inevitable, therefore, if any nation should challenge such determination by armed force. . . . [But nobody is going to fight Japan over Manchuria or the mandates.] If there is any possibility of war, it would be due to Japan's seeking through aggression further extension of her power, not satisfied with accomplished facts and rights already acquired."[24]

Confronting the Political Anomaly

However earnest, these critical reactions to actual or anticipated threats of dictatorship were secondary to Minobe's concern. The central theme in his writing in this period involved a quest for a correction of the anomaly he referred to as *chūshin ga nai seiji*, "centerless government."[25] The problem for the constitutional loyalists as he saw it was this: How to refill the void left at the crucial center of the governmental mechanism, the cabinet, by the forced retirement of the old parties; how to reconstitute the center in such a way as to preserve the integrity of constitutional government. He held as prerequisite to solution of this problem, either provisionally or for the long run, a reformation of the constitutional role of the diet and the political parties.

The inadequacy of Minobe's formalistic conception of constitutionalism and the limitations of his social science were fully exposed in his perception of the problem and in his approach to its solution. We have seen that he had always recognized the obstacles to responsible and integral control of state administration through the cabinet to be a major difficulty under the Imperial Constitution. He had envisaged the correction of that weakness through the development of conventional practices and legislative provisions which would have centered in the cabinet full control over all matters of state and would have made the cabinet politically responsible through the house of representatives. His sharp criticism of the existing parties and his advocacy of various reforms of them were aimed at making them fit instruments of constitutional government. But the reforms had never been seriously attempted.

Indeed, apparent progress toward this objective was reversed on all fronts after 1930. The fall of party government in 1932 could not be taken merely as an interruption in the course of normal constitutional government, nor as a temporary return to the pre-1924 or even pre-1918 situation. For it was no longer possible to believe that the parliamentary parties were emergent and capable of exercising power effectively and responsibly if only permitted to do so. Minobe concluded that party government as the norm of constitutional government had failed. He was quite aware that the Saito and Okada governments represented at best makeshift arrangements pending the evolution of permanent constitutional adjustment. The difficulty that confounded him was akin to that which confronted the imperial advisors: how to maintain a moderately conservative, nonparty, civilian administration against the sapping operations of the mutually hostile forces of the parliamentary parties and the military, each of which aspired to hold the reins of government, each of which had the constitutional power to wreck any government attempt to deny its ambitions, and neither of which was loath to exploit the extralegal, terroristic inclinations of the revolutionary sectors of society. He was no more able than the statesmen of the day to find an answer to that problem. The net product of his labor was a revised concept of the role of parliament which, although it testified to his earnestness to salvage the essentials of constitutional government, was devoid of practical political significance.

From his various writings of the early 1930's, certain persistent themes emerge in an inchoate reformulation of his constitutional thesis. We may begin with his proposition that the real measure of the effectiveness and durability of any system of government in an age when highly complex economic questions constitute the greater part of the governmental problem is the adequacy of its machinery for the development of state policy and the direction of state administration. From this point of view, the customary formula according to which constitutional government had been identified with parliamentary government was misleading, for it was actually not the parliament but the cabinet which made state policy. Universally parliaments exercised only indirect influence on policy, by supporting or obstructing executive policy: "In constitutional government it must be said that it is the cabinet and not the parliament which really exercises the controlling power in government. Thus the question whether constitutional government is being well conducted or not comes back to the question whether or not there is a healthy constitution of the cabinet."[26]

Moreover, government in Japan suffered from failure to recognize that the making and administration of state policy was a matter for experts and that, in the interest of policy continuity, the policy-making and administrative processes ought to be insulated from the disrupting effects of partisan struggles.

During the era when economic *laissez faire* prevailed, there was barely any connection between government and economics, and . . . even if the cabinet changed occasionally the weakness of the government did not greatly affect the people's livelihood. But . . . the area of the national economy affected by the government has become much larger. Since control of economic life requires specialized knowledge and experience, party government is not satisfactory. And since control must be based on continuity of policy, not subject to frequent change, if the cabinet changes from time to time and each time there is a change in policy, the result is most unfortunate.

Not only a party executive, but the representative legislature suffered by the same standard. When the business of parliament was principally political, any intelligent man could function well as a member. There were serious doubts, however, that parliamentary talents were sufficient to deal with the highly technical and far-reaching economic issues of the era of social revolution.[27]

RETREAT FROM THE PARTY PRINCIPAL

The history of the early years of the Meiji Constitution made clear the practical impossibility of maintaining a cabinet without the support of the diet, and at one time Minobe had insisted that parliamentary government is party government. Now he was prepared to question whether harmonious relations between cabinet and diet did indeed depend on the existence of party government. To be sure, political parties were an unavoidable and indispensable concomitant of the electoral system and the internal operations of the house of representatives; as long as the diet was a constitutional organ of the state the parties could not be destroyed without violence to the constitution.[28] On the other hand, neither under the specific terms of the Imperial Constitution nor under the general principles of constitutional government was party government a necessity.

Minobe wrestled with the dilemma he had thus contrived for himself. He observed that the experience of the Saito and Okada cabinets revealed clearly that, whatever virtue might lie in the mobilization of "nonpartisan" leadership and expert talents to form a cabinet, such persons had no political strength nor the means of building any. The demonstration of political strength rested in elections to the house of representatives. Constitutionally, neither the imperial household officials, the ministerial bureaucrats, nor the military could enter the electoral struggle except indirectly and as individuals in alliance with a political party. Alienated from party, such regimes were by the same token alienated from the diet and therefore deprived of healthy political central force. Thus they were weak and ineffective. They constituted an invitation to dictatorship.[29]

When he had followed such considerations as these to the conclusion that "sooner or later we must inevitably change to a cabinet based on the diet," Minobe went on to talk as though such an arrangement were possible without a reversion to party government: As a matter of historical fact, party government was a late development. Granting a constant inclination for the operations of parliamentary bodies to lead to parliamentary party governments, there were apparently insurmountable obstacles to the fulfillment of that inclination. The customary identification of party government as the normal condition of constitutional government might have to be abandoned.

After all, if constitutionalism were not to become a mere meaningless formula, it had to be adjusted to changing conditions. Party government undoubtedly could claim some distinct advantages, but there were sound reasons for doubting its capacity to govern effectively under conditions of social crisis. "Generally speaking . . . the party cabinet system should not be rejected in principle. . . . It seems to me that when the political condition of the state is on the normal track the party cabinet system is relatively the most appropriate mechanism. . . . But these times are certainly not calm and without peril. I believe that even in the realm of government this is not the time to cling to the conventional. . . . The impasse in the capitalistic economy confronts us . . . today with a turning point in society. The real problem in respect to the party cabinet is that it is not capable of taking charge of the needed reformation. . . ." Consequently, even though the parties were an unavoidable feature of representative government, and even though the constitutional requirement of cabinet responsibility to the diet were retained, party government as it had been known and practiced was not feasible under the prevailing circumstances.[30]

The abrupt termination of Minobe's contributions to the debate on the issues of the constitutional emergency left his ideas on this problem unsettled and unintegrated. Generally his remarks were cast in the context of the immediate impasse. Even when they were phrased in terms of a long-run constitutional settlement they were exploratory rather than committal. The few fragmentary proposals that he made at that time must be considered in that light.

THE SUPER-CABINET CONCEPT

In an attempt to overcome the conflict between his insistence on cabinet responsibility to the diet and his low estimate of the capabilities of statesmen emerging from the parliamentary parties, Minobe proposed, in June, 1932, that the competence of the cabinet be reduced and the area of government not affected by cabinet changes be enlarged. Thus, vital matters of policy would be lifted out of the realm of partisan control, just as judicial and military matters had been long since. "What is needed is . . . a permanent supraparty council, insulated from cabinet changes, with the power to make policy in the areas of national defense, foreign affairs, finance, and economic matters. Its decisions would be

binding on the cabinet which would be required to execute them. . . ."[31]
His idea was offered, in this instance, as a means of making a party
cabinet safe for Japan. The idea was equally applicable to the conditions
of the Saito and Okada cabinets. In any case, in January, 1934, when
he no longer contemplated an early restoration of party government,
Minobe reiterated the proposal, modified, however, to the extent that the
supercabinet's relation to the cabinet would be advisory rather than
directive, "a strong commission . . . outside the diet to assist and support the government. It will suffice if it is legally only an advisory adjunct
of the cabinet, but in practice it would be the organ for deliberating on
and drafting the most important state policy on economic problems. As
for its composition, it would be appropriate to make it an assembly of
important representatives of critical industries, finance, labor, etc., from
every sector of the national economy."[32]

The idea of such an extraparliamentary policy-making body was not
original with Minobe. Aside from well-known European theories and experiments along the same line, there had been various bureaucratic,
business, and military leaders discussing similar proposals. The core of
the several variant notions reflected a faith in bureaucratic efficiency,
perhaps, and certainly a loss of faith in the leadership of the parliamentary parties. Even in Minobe's case, the idea must be accounted as evidence of some degree of sympathy with the authoritarian inclinations of
the rising military-bureaucratic alliance. Was there not an echo of "Yama-
gataism" in his call for a reduction in the competence of the cabinet?
Nevertheless there were notable differences between his concept of such
a policy council and the concept espoused by the men who eventually
had their way in the matter.[33]

Minobe thought of the special policy-making body not as a bureaucratic superministry, but as a kind of economic superparliament. He
seemed to be interested largely in the technical capacity of an assembly
of economic specialists. But there was also a clear suggestion that he saw
it as a function of the group to produce a harmonization of interests. His
failure to say how "the important representatives of each sector of the
economy" would be chosen left his position quite nebulous.[34] Presumably the product of the deliberations of this body would be authoritative
simply because no other body of equal prestige, qualification, and official
sanction would be prepared to present a comprehensive national economic policy. It would supply the cabinet with a policy which it could

not produce itself and would fortify cabinet efforts to administer the policy against attack and resistance from whatever quarters.

PARTIES WITHOUT POWER

But this was only part of the problem, for the best considered arrangements for the development of national policy would prove futile so long as the vital matter of the relations between diet and cabinet remained unsettled. As has already been remarked, the record show his thoughts on this question to be more notable for perseverence in behalf of constitutional regularity than for practical political cogency. He offered a very sketchy statement of his notion of the revised role of the parliamentary parties in two articles published in January, 1934.[35] The gist of these follows: The main task of government today is to regulate and harmonize the conflicting interests making up the national economy. Only if the regime is strong enough to control all of these interests can it hope to achieve domestic order and prosperity or to succeed in international economic competition. Strong government need not mean government based on military power. Strong government is to be found in the form of a national unity cabinet. It has to be recognized that the role of the diet as a legislative and budget-making agency has become negligible, and that there is no prospect that the causes of this can be overcome.

There will, however, remain to the diet several important functions, "most importantly in its role as an organ for public criticism of state policy, as an organ for manifesting popular sentiment as representatives of the people, and as an organ for protecting, indirectly as it were, the rights and liberties of the people." Insofar as the parties have fixed their eyes on political power, however, they no longer have a useful purpose, for "we have reached a point where the several parties must be spiritually renovated. This does not mean abolition of the parties, nor does it mean 'one country-one party.' It means that the parties cease thinking of themselves as machines for seizing government authority, that they think of themselves rather as chiefly organs for making the people's will known through the diet, and as organs for criticizing the government."

The only alternative to dictatorship, then, he saw, was a cabinet, composed of men of sufficiently eminent qualifications to command the confidence of the people, and at the same time based on the support of the majority in the diet. Party men would not be excluded from such a cabinet, but the parties themselves would not determine its make up or its policy. "The best way to preserve the constitution is for the parties to give up voluntarily their desire to occupy responsible positions of authority, to be content as superintendents and critics of state administration, and to take a position supporting and assisting a suitable cabinet of talent. . . ."

It cannot be supposed that what Minobe had in mind was the course of "self-liquidation" actually pursued by the parties after 1937. On the other hand, even if there had been a will and a way for the parties to follow his counsel of self-abnegation, it seems hardly likely it could have saved them. It might have saved the constitution, but it could not have saved constitutionalism as Minobe himself defined it. Despite his effort to salvage his original position, all that remained was an emasculated vestige of constitutional form and a truncated and bootless democratic process. Events had driven him from the high and felicitous plateau of confident, dogmatic liberalism, had forced him into an increasingly desperate and sterile conservatism, a position as uncongenial to his temperament as its results are ungratifying to our observation.

The Minobe Way

The examination of Minobe's work as a constitutional theorist and expositor of Japanese public law is now complete. Before proceeding to consider developments of 1935 and later, it is well to bring together the several threads of the account up to this point and to sum up various conclusions concerning his relation to the constitutional history of Japan before World War II.

The measure of Minobe's importance was not in his breadth of vision or depth of insight in the realms of political science and jurisprudence. The external circumstances of his career may make a modest claim on the attention of students of modern intellectual and social history, but it is only within the narrower framework of the political evolution of modern Japan that his constitutional theory has importance. To say this is not to belittle his ideas or to deny their influence within that parochial context. After all, his mission was not to explore or to create, but to translate, to interpret, to instruct the minds of bureaucrats, judges, pedagogues, and politicians in what he understood to be the necessary and salutary consequences of the establishment of constitutional government in Japan.

The public law professors of Tokyo Imperial University were inevitably drawn into the constitutional struggle which tormented the Meiji state for more than three decades from the opening of the Imperial Diet. Reduced to its simplest terms, it was a conflict between bureaucratic authoritarianism under the banner of imperial autocracy, and the parliamentary opposition, which sought power for itself under the banner of responsible parliamentary government. Underlying the strife, and ultimately determining the outcome of the contest, were deep social and economic changes and dislocations. The constitutional legislation of 1885–1890, which had been intended to resolve the political issue on the side of bureaucratic authority, had only succeeded in guaranteeing a perpetuation of the conflict by conferring rigid constitutional sanction upon an unhappy union of a representative legislature with an overwhelmingly despotic administrative structure. No professor could address himself to the interpretation of state law without consciously serving one side or the other in that conflict. The lines between the resulting academic factions, aggravated by parallel conflicts of temperament and personal ambition, were already drawn in the To-Dai law faculty when Minobe was yet a student.

Already confirmed in opposition to the orthodox, authoritarian interpretation of the constitution when he took up his professorship in 1903, Minobe brought to his task inexhaustible energy, a direct and lucid manner of thought and expression, and a somewhat arrogant self-confidence. The intellectual climate and the practical political developments of the Taisho era greatly favored the prosperity of his scholarly professions. For the greater part of his career he dedicated his talents and the influence of his ascendant position to the construction, propagation, and defense of a constitutional intepretation in support of parliamentary democracy. Minobe was undoubtedly more a beneficiary of than a creator of the Taisho political revolution, but it must be accounted highly significant that the emergence of parliamentary party government was readily and effectively supported at the imperial law school by a man whose position gave him great opportunity to shape the attitudes and habits of thought of the civil bureaucracy and whose words carried with the weight of official sanction into even wider ranges of society.

It was probably a necessary condition of his rise to academic eminence and official influence, that when Minobe challenged the orthodox constitutional position at To-Dai he did so within the very respectable state-science framework of his opponent's own thinking. Conditioned by Ichiki's precept, Minobe profited by his brief and intensive experience in Germany. He brought back from Heidelberg a superficial but sympathetic acquaintance with the "march of constitutionalism" in the west, a a thorough indoctrination in the universal propositions of the *Staatslehre*, and an appreciation of the sophisticated methodology of positivistic *Staatsrechtslehre*. On the basis of the corporate theory of the state he contrived a constitutionalized version of the monarchy. It has been truly said that his teachings "were of epochal significance in the development of constitutional state theory in Japan," and that Japanese constitutional scholarship found in them "a guiding star leading toward constitutional theory of the state."[36]

It was on the basis of the Jellinekian method—rigorous positivism in juristic analysis combined with a sense of institutional development, clearly biased in favor of political freedom—that he succeeded in finding in the law of the Meiji state the necessary juristic basis for the emergence of "normal constitutional government." Coached in the language and forms of legal erudition, his teachings were well conceived to influence the minds of the politically important groups educated in the faculty of law and political science, and to condition them to accept, if not to approve, the development of political leadership in the state through the parliamentary parties. At the same time he made it possible for those who espoused the cause of parliamentary government to believe that the Imperial Constitution was not necessarily an irreducible obstacle to their goals.

Since "liberal" implies values of imprecise connotation, its use in relation to Minobe deserves some clarification. In calling Minobe a liberal I have not merely echoed the practice of his contemporaries. My usage hinges upon a major assumption underlying this study and a conclusion I bring from it; that Minobe represented the most advanced, the most thoroughly rationalized, and most influential attempt to support a liberal political order upon the basis of the Imperial Constitution. I have not, moreover, subordinated my use of the term to a dogmatic definition of liberalism, but have taken advantage of the latitude which it allows. In short, relative to his time and place, and despite the conceptual inhibitions associated with his academic orthodoxy, Minobe was a liberal.

The philosophical basis of his liberalism lay in the ethical necessity of the moral and intellectual freedom of the individual. But Minobe was not released thereby from the inclination he shared with most of his contemporaries to value social integration and social responsibility, defined and enforced by state processes, over individualism—both in social relations and in the market place. He accepted in principle the democratization of the electoral processes of the state as an integral aspect of constitutionalism, and he concerned himself with the problem of ensuring that the electoral results should faithfully reflect popular sentiment. But he was, notwithstanding his formal commitment to democracy and his long war against official irresponsibility and tyranny, captive to the elitist psychology of the professional bureaucracy. Despite his hostility to plutocratic influence in government and his defense of proletarian political action, it is difficult to detect in him any real sympathy for popular interests. He never did resolve for himself the conflict between the imperatives of his constitutional theory and his predisposition to look upon government as the business of experts.

Serious demurrers remain, all coming down to the basic one, his identification with the objectively hostile constitution of the empire. The Meiji constitutional system was intended to be, and was in fact, a thoroughly reactionary structure designed to sustain, on the basis of an absolute autocracy, a conservative, oligarchic regimentation of Japanese society. It imposed on the Japanese nation an anti-democratic legal straitjacket having at its core a constitution vested in a sanctity which foreclosed popularly inspired attempts to change its terms. How, then, can we say that any man was a liberal, who did not recognize the hopelessness of the liberal democratic cause so long as the letter and spirit of that constitution were perpetuated? How can it be said that he was a liberal when his conception of the constitutional problem in Japan did not compel foreswearing the Imperial Constitution and the sterile juristic manipulation of its clauses so that he could genuinely pursue the path of liberal reform from the position of critical opposition? What sort of a liberal is it who could not see that the sickly and fraudulent parliamentary democracy of the 1920's was the best that was likely to be realized under the Meiji constitutional system?

Minobe did, indeed, accept the Imperial Constitution and he professed his loyalty to the historical monarchy. Whether or not he harbored sincere faith in the sacred and immutable qualities imputed to it, it was the politic thing to do and, in view of his professional position, it was inevitable that he accept it as a juristic fact from which his juristic interpretation must proceed. But, if he honored the Imperial Constitution, he did not defend the constitutional system in the broader sense. Certainly he felt no awe for the structure of rescripts, ordinances, and statutes which brought the constitution down to hard cases, for he recognized that it was this supplementary legislation which gave it real, practical meaning. He probably did not write a single article or book in all the period up to 1935 which did not contain an attack upon, or at least a criticism of, the constitutional structure of the empire. The whole sense of his life's work was to point the way to a legally legitimate, historically sanctioned transformation of that system in accordance with a liberal, democratic constitutional ideal. He was no radical; by temperament he shunned extremism, by professional conditioning he abhorred revolutionary ruptures in the continuity of the law. But his philosophy was confidently progressive, and he was not at all backward in making positive application of the imperatives of that philosophy, not only in political analysis and criticism, but in commentary on the law.

It is irrelevant to speculate on the position Minobe might have occupied in the context of a liberal-conservative polarization of politics under a condition in which parliamentary democracy was the firmly established constitutional mode. The political struggle in this era was a struggle to realize "normal constitutional government." Minobe was certainly aware of the fact that that goal had not been attained. It is not necessary to pretend that his was the true and perfect liberal position. There were doubtless many arenas in which the battle was being fought. If his field was restricted, I think it must be allowed that within it some real and durable advances were made and that he took precedence second to none in the vigor and direction of his efforts. If it is said that Minobe's liberalism shone brightly only in contrast to the reactionaries of his day, it must also be said that reaction was a real enemy of liberalism in his day. If, by a broader, more advanced definition of liberalism, he be judged a conservative, still "his conservatism was liberal enough" for the occasion.

It was not the law of the Meiji state which destroyed the world of Minobe's aspiration; it was the political inadequacy of the governing classes, their inability to absorb and prevail over the concurrent and protracted shock of political and social revolution. Minobe was not ignorant of the political obstacles to the realization of his constitutional ideas, and although he was intellectually and psychologically unequipped to meet those problems effectively he bore no complicity in the irresponsibility and opportunism of the political leaders of the right and left. He must be numbered in the company of the real friends of liberal parliamentary government in Japan. His retrogression after 1932 must be discounted as a rearguard action, giving the greater weight to his efforts, unrealistic and inconsistent though they were, to resist in his way the final and complete capitulation to authoritarian despotism and militarism.

VII

The Minobe Affair

When Minobe Tatsukichi closed out his long academic career with retirement in 1934, his name was not widely known. Except for some few among the general public who might have identified him vaguely as the author of several rather controversial magazine and newspaper articles of recent years, his reputation was limited to academic and official circles. Then suddenly, in the first half of 1935, his obscurity was replaced by a blaze of publicity. He became a focus of popular attention throughout the nation.

Minobe drew the limelight to himself, as we have seen, by his interpellation in connection with the Imperial Rayon Scandal. Even then, he might have lapsed into his customary anonymity had not the dying echoes of that incident been succeeded almost immediately by the notoriety and obolquy of the Minobe Affair—or, more broadly, the Organ-Theory Affair.

The events making up that unhappy, at times ludicrous, story caused a great deal of official and public agitation, more perhaps than their intrinsic significance warranted. They appear in retrospect rather as a diversion obscuring from the nation the rapid movement toward military dictatorship and the further evolution of the factional strife within the military. The assassination of General Nagata in August, 1935, exposed briefly, but sharply, the serious intentions and reckless temper of the military radicals and foreshadowed the attempted *coup d'état* of the following February. In 1935 Japan reaped the full measure of her international isolation following her withdrawal from the League of Nations and also committed herself by the perilous processes of dual government to a further extension of power in north China.

Meanwhile, not a breath of reformative spirit stirred the parliamentary parties. Indeed, their unregenerate behavior in the course of 1935 obliterated whatever prospect of a restoration of party government had persisted through "the afterglow of Taisho democracy."

In this context, the Minobe Affair was more than a mere sensation. It was an important incident in itself, significant beyond biographical dimensions. In intellectual and political circles, Minobe was the symbol, nonpareil, of constitutional liberalism, of responsible civil government, in Japan. Even though the constitutional regime for which he stood seemed to have failed beyond redemption, there was still—from the point of view of destroying permanently the remaining elements of "normal constitutional government" and the economic order with which it was associated—much to be gained attacking the vulnerable position which Minobe occupied. It has been said that "defeat in this peculiarly Japanese 'debate' is what destroyed the intellectual basis for resistance to fascism in Japan."[1]

As important as the destruction of the man himself was the blow that his downfall would deliver to the influence of various political and bureaucratic personalities who could be shown to bear the taint of sympathetic association with his heresy. The attack on Minobe and the organ theory marked the outset of the closing action in the campaign to eradicate the remnants of the anti-militaristic, parliamentary position. It had also a forward-reaching meaning, for it was the opening phase of the movement to "clarify national polity," in the process of which, over the next two years, there was to be a grand purge of academic and bureaucratic ranks. It paved the way for the successful promotion of an intensely nationalistic, authoritarian, and totalitarian view of the Japanese state and society. The organ-theory issue made the middle class for the first time in a meaningful degree responsive to the call of Japanese fascism.

The various episodes which comprised the affair are also of interest in providing a relatively well-recorded case in Japanese politics. Before launching a chronicle of the events, however, a somewhat closer examination of the roots of the opposition to Minobe and his legal theory and of the circumstances of his isolation is in order.

Sources of Opposition to the Organ Theory

Among the various groups joining in the assault on Minobe and the organ theory in 1935, the parliamentary opposition party, commentators are generally agreed, played an important role. Maruyama asserts that the organ theory became a serious political issue when the Seiykai used it to promote the collapse of the Okada Cabinet. But he goes on to say that, however important the tactics of the Seiyukai in pushing the matter to the extremity, they only exploited an already ripening temper in the general public. The question of the emperor-organ theory had become a subject of discussion among the middle classes and thus had been rendered significant as a political and social issue even before the Seiyukai launched the drive for clarification of national polity.[2] General public interest grew as spokesmen of a number of conservative, patriotic, and fascistic groups turned from desultory sniping to vigorous, confident attack.

A great diversity of forces were mustered among the several quarters of anti-Minobe thought and action. Some of the parties involved were old enemies, others had only recently acquired their concern in the matter. Some were seriously concerned with the specific issue of heresy, others pursued the theoretical question only as a means of striking at remote and collateral objects of antipathy: Some represented small and particular interests, others moved at the front of large and powerful forces. Some were dedicated and purposeful; for others the animus was ephemeral and inconstant. There was, moreover, much overlapping in the affiliations of particular individuals, and at some stages a degree of communion among them all. Out of such a congeries, the leading elements of the anti-Minobe coalition fall into three rather distinct categories: the academic opposition, the bureaucratic opposition, and the military opposition. A review of their machinations tends to confirm the comment of the contemporary observer who wrote that while the Minobe Affair "turned ostensibly on a point of doctrine as obscure as any of the questions of dogma which had set the fires of bigotry burning in the past . . . yet a practical purpose was pursued behind the mystical rhetoric."[3] Their convergence points up the retrospective judgment of another, himself but once removed from the center of the controversy, that "the Organ-Theory Affair was not so much an incident in the history of Japanese public law as in Japanese political history."[4]

ACADEMIC OPPOSITION

Academic authorities in the fields of law, political science, political history, and social ethics stand large in the record of opposition to Minobe and the organ theory. This is hardly surprising considering that the organ theory was of almost exclusively academic interest prior to 1930 and in view of the propensity for academic disputes to take the form of voluminous literary exchanges. For the small specialized audience of theoreticians and knowledgeable civil servants and lawyers, the charges and counterarguments which came before the diet, the judicial authorities, and the public in 1935 were familiar. They had existed in the literature of public law and constitutional theory for many years. For most legal scholars, however, the organ-theory debate had lapsed into the realm of forgotten causes. Rank-and-file teachers of public law presumably held their commitment, if any, to the organ theory lightly and without personal conviction. In any case they were easily persuaded to abandon it, even to join in purging it, once public and official hostility became manifest.

Because of the relationship which their actions and their attitudes bore to the situation in which Minobe found himself in 1935, two groups of legal scholars merit attention. To one of these, the small but persevering group which carried on the academic tradition of the *kaminagara* school after its eclipse in early Taisho, the anti-parliamentary forces of the 1930's were greatly indebted. Their long-unrewarded efforts provided ready at hand the stuff with which to charge the mine and sap the last remaining barrier to military-fascist power. Apart from the fanatical core of opposition, the relatively few legal specialists—of both the liberal and orthodox schools—who concerned themselves with the theoretical foundations of constitutional jurisprudence, included men whose rejection of the theoretic basis of Minobe's position was based on sober intellectual persuasion, untainted by hysteria, mysticism, or personal animosity. Others, accepting his basic theory of the state, did not find in it a foundation for the liberal democratic interpretation of the constituton Minobe advanced. Even those among this company who would defend

Minobe (if they dared) against charges of subverting national polity could not be counted on to endorse his theory or to resist its displacement in the schools.[5]

The Organ-Theory Affair was, in part, merely a revival of the unresolved quarrel between Minobe and Uesugi. The firm establishment of the liberal school with Minobe's appointment as professor of constitutional law had not meant the extinction of the orthodox-historical tradition, which "continued to oppose . . . and remained strong at its roots."[6] Despite the high repute and preferment enjoyed by the liberal school, the orthodox tradition continued to be strongly represented in the universities. The ministry of education's classification of the thirty leading academic lecturers and publicists in public law active in 1935 described twelve as adherents of the *tennō shutai setsu* (theory of the emperor as sovereign) and eighteen as advocates of the *tennō kikan setsu* (theory of the emperor as organ of the state).[7] This classification apparently was purely formal, depending simply on the use of particular phrases and lines of reasoning in describing the constitutional system and not on the content of the constitutional interpretation. It was, of course, quite possibly to accept and expound the state-personality theory without explicitly stating a state-sovereignty formula or speaking of the monarch as a state organ. Endorsement or rejection of the organ theory was, however, a good index of the general attitude of the individual writer or teacher toward "normal constitutional government." Invariably the *tennō shutai* men were unenthusiastic about or hostile toward, and tended to negate the significance of the advance in the direction of parliamentary democracy and responsible civilian government.

Of the leading representatives of the *tennō shutai* group in 1935, Sato Ushijiro at Tohoku Imperial and Shimizu Toru at Chuo University were the outstanding authorities in the tradition of Hozumi. Both taught and published a pedestrian conservatism without theoretical speculations and without becoming involved in polemic exchanges with the liberal school. Their works were colored by the dogmatic obscurities inherent in the literal application of the myths of the imperial tradition and the mystical concept of national polity. The burden of imperial orthodoxy was even more evident in the case of To-Dai Professor Emeritus Kakehi Masahiko, who in 1935 was teaching concurrently at the Tokyo University of Commerce, Hosei University, and the Kokugaku-in. Kakehi had begun teaching at To-Dai the same year that Minobe did; he taught jurisprudence and administrative law, sharing the latter field with Minobe. Kakehi was opposed to the organ theory from the beginning, but his participation in the Uesugi-Minobe debate had been marginal since that argument was primarily in the realm of legal theory while his objections were raised from theological considerations. Indeed, Kakehi was known chiefly for his writing on the moral bases of the Japanese state, in which he was strongly influenced by Shinto doctrines.[8] The peak of his activities, professionally and in the conservative political movement, had passed before 1935, but his works still commanded great respect and were frequently cited as authority against Minobe. Shintoist hostility toward all manner of alien corruption extended, naturally, to western political and legal theories. Even at the height of its favor the liberal school was attacked on the ground that it undermined the familial, patriarchal, and theocratic qualities of the Japanese state and society.[9]

As was mentioned earlier, Uesugi Shinkichi, the individual most responsible for pressing the attack on the organ theory since 1910, had departed the scene before 1935. He had diverted Hozumi's orthodox interpretation along lines emphasizing and elaborating the theological and ethical qualities of the imperial tradition as distinct from the positive legal character of the constitutional system. We have noted that Uesugi assimilated the historical ethical tradition to an Hegelian conception of the state as the highest ethical norm. His insistence on the supreme normative character of the historical national polity was ancillary to the idea that for the Japanese the highest fulfillment of individual personality depended on the individual's identification of self with the personality of the state. In his late writing he resolved the contradictions arising from his attempt to harmonize Jellinek's rudimentary pluralism with a state-centered ethic tacitly abandoning all reliance on Jellinek.

Rejection of Jellinek and the identification of Jellinek as the source of the liberal heresy was more explicit and positive in some of the younger members of the orthodox school writing at the time of the clarification campaign.[10] These writers claimed that the individualistic democratic values which underlay the constitutional theory of the liberals could be traced to Jellinek's influence. Not, to be sure, that he was the originator of those abhorrent doctrines, but he it was who caused the intrusion of their corrupting influence into the *Staatslehre* and the *Staatsrechtslehre*.[11]

Uesugi's importance in relation to the Minobe Affair did not derive simply—perhaps not even primarily—from his work as a teacher and writer in constitutional law. In fact not a single disciple of his held any academic position of importance in 1935. Minoda Kyoki, self-appointed perpetuator of Uesugi's attack on Minobe, was in no sense the heir to Uesugi's mantle as scholar and teacher. But Uesugi had extended his influence beyond the academic sphere by his leading participation in conservative, nationalistic political movements, where he supplied a theoretical basis for the merger of Japanistic and socialistic thought.[12] He had undertaken to mobilize and revitalize nationalist sentiment among students at To-Dai at a time when democratic-socialistic fervor was still high. Under his aegis the Kōkoku Dōshikai (Association of Those Devoted to the Advancement of the State) was organized among the law school students at To-Dai in 1920, with Hiranuma Kiichiro as its extra-academic patron and advisor. An early project of that group had been the purging of Morito Tatsuo from the economics faculty.

The Kōkoku Dōshikai was the progenitor of two distinct lines of development on the right of Japanese politics.[13] The one with undoubtedly more significance in the overall political history of the period consisted chiefly of the fascistic movement in which Hiranuma played a leading part through his group, the Kokuhonsha, founded in 1924. The Kokuhonsha (State Foundation Society), stemmed directly from the Kōkoku Dōshikai and Uesugi was a member of it. But the role of the academics generally, and the influence of Uesugi specifically, was submerged in that organization under the weight of the numbers, prestige, and influence of bureaucratic, business and military members. Uesugi continued active in the Kokuhonsha and its satellites, especially in the so-called "new bureaucratic" groups. In 1926 he sponsored the founding of the Kenkokukai (State Construction Society) to provide a meeting ground between bureaucratic and national socialistic circles. Though he had broken off direct connections with this group in 1927, he provided in his own home an office for its director, Akao Bin.[14]

The second line of succession from the Kōkoku Dōshikai remained closer to Uesugi's thought. The original society had dissolved in 1924, but right-wing sentiment among To-Dai students and faculty soon found expression in a number of successor organizations combatting leftist manifestations in the academic community and outside and perpetuating

Uesugi's authoritarian and nationalistic constitutional doctrines. Uesugi, however, no longer participated directly in these groups. Similar right-wing societies also appeared in other state and private schools. Cross-affiliation of members was widespread and many groups were connected with one or another of the fragments of the revolutionary movement of national reconstruction begun by Kita Ikki and Okawa Shumei, and, consequently, were kept in contact with the main currents of evolving fascistic thought and action. Out of this milieu Minoda Kyoki emerged as a leading pamphleteer and organizer of academic vigilantism.[15]

Minoda's career as a rightist agitator began in 1925 when he participated with Mitsukawa Kametaro, an erstwhile follower of Okawa Shumei, in founding the Genri Nihon Sha (The True Japan Society), which in 1927 affiliated with other groups headed by followers of Uesugi in establishing the Zen Nihon Kōkoku Dōshikai (All-Japan Society for the Preservation of the State), with Minoda as president. By 1930 he and his collaborator, Mitsui Kayuki, were grinding out a steady parade of extremely anti-liberal, Japanistic diatribes under the banner of the Genri Nihon Sha.[16] The potency of his weapon and his allies was demonstrated when, in 1933, he launched through his press organ, *Genri Nihon,* and through the Kenkokukai, which he now headed, the attack which led eventually to the earlier discussed dismissal of Professor Takikawa.[17] By then, however, Marxian radicalism had been largely exorcized from the universities and the time was right for assigning a higher priority to the eradication of the vestiges of parliamentary liberalism. The time had come, too, to shift the hunting ground from Kyoto to Tokyo, and to focus upon one long-deferred target in particular. Minoda and his associates trained their sights on Minobe as the leading residual symbol of the tolerant, decadent, and socially irresponsible philosophy of liberalism, which they identified as the seedbed of the Communist threat to the state.

As early as 1930 an article by Minoda on "Dr. Minobe the Anarchist" ("Museifu Shugisha Minobe Hakushi") appeared as an appendix to a book by Mitsui Kayuki. In 1935 he published a collection of his articles from the regular series of *Nihon Genri* and from the newspaper *Nihon Shimbun* under the title *Minobe Hakushi no Taiken Jūrin.*[18] In 1933 Minoda had personally filed the charges which he expected would lead to Suehiro Iwataro's prosecution for violation of the Peace Preservation

Law and the Publication Law. The prosecution was quashed, but Minoda could claim some credit for having moved censors to ban further publication of one of Suehiro's works.[19]

Minoda relates that his efforts to draw Minobe into a debate were frustrated by Minobe's repeated declaration of "academic nonintercourse" (*gakujuteki muhannō*) with him.[20] Minoda nevertheless could take some satisfaction in observing that his criticism, when repeated in the diet, did draw a formal rebuttal from Minobe. On February 7, 1934, Baron General Kikuchi Takeo, in the course of an interpellation of the home minister in the house of peers, denounced the government for failure to suppress several textbooks in use at To-Dai.[21] He named works by Minobe (*Kempō Satsuyō*) and by Suehiro, without naming the authors. These works, he said, advanced ideas contrary to national polity and inimical to the prosperity of the state. Minobe responded in defense of the "good name of the university" with an article in the *Teikoku Daigaku Shimbun*.[22] The main outline of Minobe's defense throughout 1935 was indicated in that article: an appeal against the impropriety of his critics' intemperate and groundless aspersions of disloyalty; protestation of his complete devotion to the emperor system; a plea that his writings be judged in their whole context rather than by reference to isolated excerpts; and an assertion that the debate over the emperor-organ theory had been "fought out and settled long ago," and that his critics only exposed their ignorance in returning to long-refuted charges.[23]

The oblique opening attack on the organ theory in the diet, designed to arraign Minobe before a greater forum than any available to Minoda, proved premature. A full year elapsed before Minoda saw that objective achieved. Meanwhile, he continued to make his inimitable contributions to the literature of the day. He found a further use for his talents in the work of the Kokutai Yōgo Rengō Kai (League for the Defense of National Polity), which was at that time mounting an intensive campaign against Minobe.[24] Under the name of that organization, and showing the subscription of some sixty patriotic societies, in February, 1935, Minoda issued a broadside "Concerning the Ideas of Dr. Minobe Tatsukichi, Dr. Suehiro Iwataro, *et al.*, Which Put National Polity in Disorder."[25] This sheet presented a series of questions of which those concerning Minobe may be summarized as follows:

(1) To each minister of state: Do you agree with Minobe when he says that the peculiar responsibility of ministers of state is a political responsibility to the diet? Does it not violate the imperial rescripts to say as he does that since the emperor does not bear personal responsibility it is constitutionally impossible for the emperor to exercise the state prerogative except on the advice of ministers of state?

(2) To the president and members of the privy council: Do you agree with Minobe when he says that the privy council is an unparalleled anachronism and will probably be abolished in the future? Is it not an offense against imperial government to pass such a judgment on the privy council by reference to the practice of other states?

(3) To officers and members of the houses of the diet: Do you agree with Minobe's description of the diet as an organ to represent the people independently of the emperor and not, in its legislative capacity, subject to imperial command?

(4) To judges and procurators: Do you agree with Minobe when he says that the courts are completely independent in exercising their competence, and are not bound even by imperial commands? Does he not strike at the authority of the judicial power when he says that the Peace Preservation Law is a thing of unparalleled wickedness and that it is contrary to the spirit of the constitution?

(5) To active duty and reserve members of the army and navy: Does Minobe not subvert military discipline and the supreme command when he says that there is no basis in the text of the constitution for the independence of the supreme command and that the independence of the supreme command is contrary to the general principles of constitutional government?

(6) To scholars, educators and intellectuals: Does Minobe not undermine education and science itself when he says that schemes for the rectification of thought are futile and that the only way of stifling revolutionary thought is to cut off popular education entirely?

(7) To Shinto officials and devotees: Does Minobe not defile the Shinto bases of national polity when he says that the rectification of popular thought on theological lines is contrary to the requirements of the times, and will serve rather to worsen the evils of the day?

(8) To the members of the cabinet: Does it not violate your obligation to the throne to tolerate the continuation in office as a professor at

the imperial university, as a member of the house of peers, and as a member of the higher civil service examination board a proponent of such disloyal thoughts as those of Minobe?

(9) To the *genrō* and *jūshin*: Can you reconcile your obligation to the throne with the continuation in office of such subversive thinkers as Minobe?

The broadside concluded with a declaration setting forth the persuasion of the subscribers that the continuation in office of Minobe and the others was a "basic cause of the manifold evils recently besetting the country," and their determination that legal and social measures against the offenders should be speedily and vigorously prosecuted. The Kokutai Yōgo Rengō Kai broadside contained no mention of the emperor-organ theory, however. That presumably is to be explained by its attempt to play on the self-interests and vulnerabilities of the particular public officials and personalities to whom it was addressed, rather than to document a complete indictment of Minobe. Implicit in the questions was the assumption that all of the offenses set forth derived naturally and unavoidably from the fundamental sin of ignoring the historical traditions of the empire in applying universal juristic principles, the corporate theory of the state in particular, to the interpretation of the Imperial Constitution,[26] The appeal was really the old Hozumi-Uesugi argument updated. But it also demonstrated that what aroused the antipathies of the patriotic reactionaries was not so much the organ theory itself, as the corollary propositions respecting "normal constitutional government"—that is, representative, responsible, civilian, limited government.

Whether Minoda's role in precipitating the Minobe Affair was fundamentally important as well as conspicuous is not easily decided. He has been dealt with here as part of the academic opposition to Minobe even though his academic credentials were most tenuous. Minoda was not himself an ideologue; he was a journalist engaged in propaganda and agitation. He made some pretense of addressing the intellectual class but it may be supposed that his audience was of the "pseudo-intelligentsia" of Maruyama's sociology of Japanese fascism.[27] Minoda falls under the academic heading largely because the organizations he fostered and managed represented a projection from Uesugi's organization work among right-wing university students and because his attack on Minobe was almost literally a duplicate of the charges Uesugi had leveled at the same target years before.

That Minoda's assault eventually met with the reward that had been denied to Uesugi's efforts is to be explained by the relatively more favorable circumstances under which Minoda operated. In the mid-thirties the soil was fertile, the harvesting equipment was primed. For Minoda was working in harmony with bureaucratic and military forces even more impressive than his academic legions.

BUREAUCRATIC OPPOSITION

The close connection between the law faculty of the imperial university and the higher echelons of the civil bureaucracy, especially the leading groups of officials in the cabinet secretariat, and in the justice, education and home ministries, ensured a reciprocal sensitivity to factional disputes arising in either camp. The conflict between the orthodox and the liberal schools at To-Dai tended to reinforce and complicate the personal and factional rivalries among these civil servants and among the "political bureaucrats" in the house of peers and the privy council, and among the ranks of the parties.

During the 1920's the influence of the orthodox school had been weakened but by no means eliminated among the bureaucrats. But that trend was, as it were, unnatural. It was more in character for civil bureaucrats as a class to feel hostile, or at least unenthusiastic, towards the liberal school, whose emphasis on responsible representative government threatened bureaucratic influence. They were, by "reflex," suspicious and unappreciative of those who defended individual rights against official abuse, who attacked as irresponsible the influence of the high bureaucrats in the house of peers and privy council. The orthodox position on constitutional issues was "naturally" more comfortable to them. And the preachings of authoritarian nationalists were hardly uncongenial. In many cases the attitude of the individual bureaucrat was determined by his professional dependence upon the fortunes and favor of one or another of the powerful figures at the summit of the official hierarchy. Among these seniors were men whose position on constitutional questions bore the imprint of the original Uesugi-Minobe debate.

Best known among the bureaucratic foes of the liberal constitutional regime after 1925 was Privy Councillor Baron Hiranuma Kiichiro. A graduate of the To-Dai law faculty, Hiranuma rose to the heights of the judicial bureaucracy and sat as a member of the privy council from 1924. He was known to have great ambitions of becoming premier and was encouraged by various civilian and military reconstructionist elements.[28] Hiranuma's retirement as minister of justice in 1924 and his assumption of the less demanding dignities of privy councillor gave him the opportunity to expand his activities as an organizer and leader of conservative nationalistic thought. He had been a councillor to Uesugi's Kōkoku Dōshikai at To-Dai and he now drew upon former members of that group to provide the nucleus of an extra-academic educational society known as the Kokuhonsha (State Foundation Society). The Kokuhonsha exalted the essence of national polity in order to foster national spirit and strengthen the foundations of the state. It sought to purge the people of fickle irresponsibility and to deflect them from pursuit of eccentric and extreme ideas. Whether it was a fascist organization or not depends on how fascism is defined. So current was the allegation in 1932 that Hiranuma took pains to deny it specifically. The professed principles of the society seem reactionary rather than revolutionary. In the beginning its more prominent members were men whose political and social orientation was inherited from the old oligarchs of early Taisho. On the other hand, after 1928 many of its members were associated with the civilian social reconstructionists, the military radicals, and the so-called "new bureaucrats."[29]

The Kokuhonsha gave Hiranuma a wider sounding board than that afforded by the dignified, and indeed decisive, but unpublicized proceedings of the privy council. It gave him wide contacts and support throughout the bureaucracy, the military, and the business world. On the other hand, his temperamental and doctrinal conservatism, his open sympathy for the military, and the jingoistic tone of his public pronouncements gained him the suspicion and hostility of the genrō and the court officials. As a consequence, he was passed over in favor of Saito when Inukai's successor was chosen in 1932. A more stinging personal defeat came in 1934 when the jūshin advanced Ichiki Kitokuro from the imperial household ministry to the presidency of the privy council. Hiranuma, who had been serving as vice-president, had a presumptive claim to the chair. These circumstances strongly intimate that Hiranuma and his associates promoted and supported the attack on the organ theory not simply on the basis of ideology but because they hoped to destroy the influence of the "liberal" *jūshin* by convicting them of responsibility for the origin and spread of the parliamentary doctrine and system. When Ichiki retired in the aftermath of the Minobe Affair, Hiranuma at last became privy council president.

The conspiracy theory of the cause of the organ-theory crisis, while it doubtless oversimplifies the situation, was given much credit by some contemporaries. Saionji's amanuensis gives ample evidence of the currency in government and palace circles of the view that the affair was a product of Hiranuma's deliberate and vindictive purpose and of Saionji's adamant resistance to Hiranuma's personal advancement. Premier Okada is quoted as advising Harada (September 26, 1935): "Their idea after all is to get Ichiki and Makino into hot water. This is a result toward which they have conspired for years. After all, the right-wing group centered on Hiranuma uses the organ theory as a means to thoroughly harass the *genrō* and chief ministers."[30]

Another important manifestation of bureaucratic opposition to parliamentary government was the "new bureaucratic movement," a term loosely applied to various groups of officials more or less agreed on the assumption of a harmony of interest between the younger generation of top ministerial career officials and the military. This group focused on integral control of the national economy as the area in which the accommodation would take place. While these new bureaucratic forces were uncommitted in the old constitutional quarrel, or at least not involved in the personal vendetta of the Uesugi-Hiranuma groups against the Minobeites, they nevertheless contributed to the accumulation of opposition under which the idea of normal constitutional government was liquidated. Authoritarian inclinations at the core of official psychology throve on contact with military counterparts under the auspices of the new bureaucratic societies.[31] In time, their contact with the military oligarchs, especially with the Control Faction of the army, assumed the character of a collaboration.

The new bureaucrats did not participate directly in the attack on Minobe, but that was not because they harbored the least sympathy for his constitutional theory or for the parliamentary system. Indeed, the existence of the movement constituted a large albeit mostly amorphous dimension of the official isolation in which Minobe found himself in 1935. Thus the active hostility of senior political bureaucrats in the house of peers and the privy council had a broad base in the "passive" hostility of Hiranuma's following in ministry of justice and of strong elements of new bureaucratic sentiment in the home ministry and the education ministry, the departments most immediately concerned in the Minobe Affair.[32]

MILITARY OPPOSITION

It is not surprising that some observers close to the events saw in the military the driving force behind the Minobe Affair. Certainly in the denouement following March 1935 the role of the army was all important. It is also clear that the ambitions of the military were most substantially advanced as a consequence of the Affair. Nevertheless, to see the Minobe Affair as a military contrivance would be to adopt an oversimplification as gross as laying it all to Hiranuma's machinations. There were, in fact, several military viewpoints on the organ-theory issue, all negative views, to be sure, but differing in degree and in tactical preference. The military interest in the constitutional question was collateral to the factional struggle inside the army, and the attitude of the various military factions diverged according to conflicting views regarding the coming military hegemony in the state.

Military opposition to the organ theory proceeded from basic tendencies paralleling those noted in the case of the bureaucrats. Many of the senior military officers had never been reconciled to the Taisho Seihen; they continued to cherish authoritarian, elitist, hyper-loyalist concepts of the state as idealized in the golden era of the Satcho oligarchy, when the civil and military arms of the empire were the common and exclusive preserve of the post-Restoration nobility and when capitalistic-parliamentary politics had not yet cracked the citadel of military and bureaucratic autonomy erected by the genrō Yamagata. Indeed, even during the period of parliamentary party ascendency the sanctuary of the supreme command was breached but slightly. It remained a haven into which the military bourbons retreated from the greater political world, leaving it to a few "adventurers" such as Tanaka Giichi and Ugaki Kazushige to play at the party game.

The military reactionaries were not unmindful of the relationship between the capitalistic-parliamentary regime after 1918 and the constitutional theory expounded by Minobe. The prevailing "liberal" psychology of the time and the cross purposes among the oligarchs themselves had doomed the effort to purge Minobe during the 1912–1918 period, but it was Uesugi's teachings which were required at the military schools. And it was with Uesugi and Hiranuma that the senior military barons made common cause in the ultranationalist movement of the 1920's. The dean of all the emperor's military advisors after Yamagata's passing, Field Marshal Uehara, was known to have opposed the teaching of the organ theory under any military auspices.

The ultraconservative military position of unqualified affirmation of the doctrines of divine and absolute imperial rule was clearly in close harmony with the material and professional interests of the military as a class. The military hostility to Minobe and what he represented was, then, merely the reflection of an antediluvian ideology. The rise of the parliamentary party system had meant a substantial curtailment in the political and social influence of the military and a departure from reliance in state policy on strong military power and its active use. The ideology of the senior military leaders mustered support through all levels and branches of military service because of the budgetary parsimony and "weak" foreign policy of the party government. Further reinforcement came from the alienation of popular affection and deference caused by the corrupting psychology of democratic liberalism. Constitutional conservatism, under the banner of imperial loyalty, was an expression of the determination to reassert the authority of the military councils in the formulation of economic, educational, and defense policy against the unsympathetic attitude and unmilitaristic impulses of governments centered on the diet.

The running conflict between the military staffs and the "economy minded" and "politically motivated" party governments over specific issues of national defense policy was raised dramatically to the level of major constitutional argument on the occasion of the ratification of the London Naval Agreement in 1929. The government's action was based implicitly on the minimal view of the autocratic prerogative and the particularly restrictive view of the scope of the autonomous supreme command which Minobe had asserted, and the military outrage was, consequently, focused on him. The connection between Minobe's theory and the frustration of military pretensions was made explicit by his open participation in the public debate. There can be no doubt that from that time some military circles, including significantly some of the officers of the navy, harbored serious resentment toward Minobe.[33] Military leaders may not have consciously inspired the 1935 attack on Minobe, but they were clearly and importantly involved in it, and the military establishment welcomed, abetted, and profited by the attack.

Until this period, active opposition to liberal constitutionalism had generally been limited to the higher military echelons, finding expression through the policies and actions of the military command and administrative organs in relation to the civil government and in the behavior of individual military men and their civilian partisans occupying nonmilitary governmental positions or participating in conservative nationalist organizations. But from the early 1930's an additional force of great consequence arose in the lower ranks of the officer corps of the army. Their consciousness of the common professional grievances of the military class was sharpened as a result of their sympathetic understanding of the great discontents of the depressed and socially dislocated agrarian communities out of which most of them had lately emerged. Their outlook was clouded with apprehension as they witnessed the clash of personalities and policies among the senior ranks. Professional insecurity, impatient ambition, a sense of widespread social injustice—all made these military juniors receptive to various revolutionary doctrines and ready to engage in direct action against the existing regime, against their own military superiors if necessary.

In some measure, most responded to one or another of the renovationist appeals, to the agrarian fundamentalism of Gondo or Tachibana or to the nationalistic socialism of Kita, Nishida, or Okawa. Many actively joined civilian revolutionary agitators and conspirators, who in turn encouraged their inclination to look upon the imperial army as the ordained instrument of national salvation. The sanction for their seditious behavior was the promise of a reëstablishment of uncorrupted, direct imperial rule—"the Showa Restoration," and the purging of the perverse doctrines, the social evils and the usurpations of power by which the promise of the original Restoration had been vitiated. Not only on grounds of professional interest, then, but on ideological grounds and as a matter of tactics in political action, the radical element in the military came to look upon Minobe and his doctrines with exceeding malevolence. It was from among these disturbed young officers that were recruited the members of the Kokutai Genri Ha who participated in the acts of assassination and rebellion in May, 1932, and February, 1936.[34]

A significant feature of military politics at this time was the fact that many leaders of the military reservist associations sympathized enthusiastically with the more radical renovationist sentiments in the army. The reservist organizations played a double role. On the one side, as semi-civilian groups they constituted a part of the complex of associations making up the right-wing movement. On the other side, as semi-military groups they had direct access to leaders of the army and navy. In the period under view the reservist associations seem to have functioned conspicuously as agencies for putting radical pressure on the minister of war and the general staff rather than as agencies for conveying the official army line to the civilian realm.

How the various elements of military opposition to the liberal constitutional order played their part in the events of 1935 becomes clear only if they are viewed in relation to the factional struggle within the army. The evolution of this conflict was probably the most portentous political development between 1934 and 1936. The army had found in the deliberately provoked military crisis in Manchuria a lever for extorting an increasingly important voice in state policy. Failure of the civil government to support the military program fully increased the drive toward military supremacy in the state. Within the context of this common objective, however, the army leadership was riven by the power contest discussed earlier.[35] Reputedly grounded in old *han* rivalry, this contest now turned upon the issue of asserting military predominance for the purpose of achieving full national mobilization behind a policy of overseas expansion versus subordinating the program of expansion to internal social revolution.

At stake in the strife were not only careers and power but issues of policy concerning the timing and direction of continental development and concerning the choice between national mobilization and social revolution. On one side was the Control Faction, a group of senior officers including the modernizers, notably Nagata Tetsuzan, and those primarily concerned about discipline and order. This group had the support of the tenuous remnants of the Choshu clique.[36] The Control Faction was made up of relatively conservative officers, somewhat more committed than their opponents, by both social connection and the experience of military-civilian politics of the 1920's to the existing order of Japanese society, but having nevertheless considerable affinity for totalitarian ideology. Bent on military domination and willing to exploit the violent inclinations of the military radicals to the detriment of civil authority, they were, however, disinclined to make a direct attack on the traditional seats of civilian power. They were above all concerned to ensure their own control of the army, and utilized their campaign against the military radicals as the basis for an alliance with the leading economic and bureaucratic circles. The alliance ensured their final ascendancy in the army and, in due course, virtual military dictatorship.

Opposite the Control Faction and constituting the force to which, in a sense, it appears as a reaction, was the second great camp in high army politics, the Imperial Way Faction (kōdōha). The chief officers of this group were identified one way or another with Tosa and Saga. As heirs of the grievances of minority military interests, this generation of anti-Choshu men "naturally" tended to oppose prevailing authority. Perhaps for that reason they developed an ideological affinity with the social radicalism of the young officers. Since they had not been in the leading positions of responsibility in the army prior to 1931, these men were untainted by the onus of the unfavorable national defense policies imposed by cilivian governments between 1921 and 1931. Hence the young radicals looked to these men for leadership. Moreover since they were opposed by the modernizers for having revived the old hanbatsu factor in the selection of staff and command personnel, the Imperial Way Faction tended to emphasize ideological zeal instead of technical proficiency in its pronouncements. It is not surprising that the radical young officers looked to these men for leadership. The appointment of Araki Sadao as minister of war in December, 1931, initiated the leaders of the Imperial Way Faction into the top of the army administration and command.

General Araki's tenure as minister of war extended to January, 1934, bridging the transformation from the Inukai party government to the transcendental cabinet of Admiral Saito. The Manchurian Incident, the personnel shifts enforced by the new leadership, and the counter-tactics of those whose careers and policies were threatened—all created grave unrest within the army during this period.[37] Araki gave way at last to General Hayashi Senjuro, reputedly a man with friends in both camps. Other top posts in the army were divided between kōdōha and *tōseiha* adherents. In time, under constant encouragement from civilian circles and assiduous pressure from the Control Faction, Hayashi lent his support to a move to expel Imperial Way men from positions of importance and to isolate and suppress the radical elements among the young officers. This program was carried forward during 1935 under the inspiration of General Nagata Tetzuzan, chief of the military affairs bureau, until in July of that year General Mazaki Jinsaburo, the reputed brains of the *kōdōha*, was relieved of his post as inspector general of military education.[38]

The *kōdōha* officers, the leaders of the young radicals, and their civilian and reservist sympathizers were brought by this policy to a state of desperation.[39] From the assassination by Lieutenant Colonel Aizawa, a member of the Kokutai Genri Ha, of General Nagata in August until the abortive *coup d'état* of February, 1936, it was touch-and-go whether the army radicals could be checked and liquidated. The *genrō*, the palace bureaucrats, and the business magnates were forced to commit their support to the Control Faction.

The contest between the Control Faction and the Imperial Way Faction was at heart a matter of professional preferment and antipathetic personalities, not of fundamental purposes. The higher Imperial Way officers were probably not altogether happy about the social radicalism that moved the lower ranks of the army. The Control Faction, on the other hand, was not nearly so charitable toward the political and social *status quo* as its suppression of the radicals would suggest. Nevertheless, the behavior of the army leaders with respect to the Minobe Affair was significantly influenced by the approaching denouement in the army.

The Clarification Campaign

Within this context of academic, bureaucratic, and military opposition to the liberal constitutional system, the Minobe Affair was enacted. It will appear that there were personalities and groups other than those accounted for in the preceding pages—certain parliamentary party men, for instance—whose actions were important in relation to the organ-theory question. The diversity of motivation and tactics represented in this miscellany was such as to make impossible a generalization of the bases of their opposition. The more important of these will be treated individually as they enter the account. It will also appear that some of the best known of the anti-parliamentary agitators (e.g., Okawa, Kita, Nishida) took no overt part in the attack on Minobe or in the clarification movement so far as we are concerned with it.

It may be well to elaborate somewhat more fully on the relationship between the Minobe question (or the organ-theory question) and the question of the clarification. It was, as it were, a play within a play, of which our main interest here is in the lesser drama. The connection between the two was more than coincidental. The attack on the organ theory advanced the destructive theme of the larger drama, sweeping away symbolically the vestiges of political and social liberalism. The attack on Minobe was but an episode in the progress toward clarification. Maledictions on Minobe were linked always with cries for clarification of national polity.

But the driving purpose behind the clarification movement considerably antedated the Minobe Affair and continued to run its course long after the echoes of 1935 were silent. "Clarification" was a euphemism for "renovation," which in turn was but another euphemism for the establishment of a fascistic military despotism. The movement proposed to use every educational and propaganda agency of the state to create a public psychology receptive to a new totalitarian tyranny. In the process of bringing the new order to Japan, the fate of Minobe and of the organ theory was of minor consequence except as a matter of temporary tactical advantage. During the nine months from February 1935, however the renovation daemon was mostly destructive, and focused largely upon the organ theory and the man who most fully embodied it.

ATTACK IN THE DIET AND COURT

The offensive against Minobe developed swiftly and almost simultaneously from three quarters. Within less than a month he was subjected to unrestrained and undisguised denunciation in both houses of the diet and to a charge of lese majesty in Tokyo district court. The circumstances suggest that there was some degree of collusion between the parties to the several attacks, all of whom were identified with the renovationist camp. This initial onset persuaded leaders of the Seiyukai majority in the house of representatives, apparently not involved in the opening phase, that they could not afford to pass up this issue as a means of unseating the government. Consequently, the government, too, was forced to take a stand on the issue. Having raised this "academic question" to the level of a major political issue, the attackers reaped the benefit of the great public excitement which ensued.[40]

The first guns were fired on February 7 and 9 by Eto Genkuro, a reserve major general and a member of Minoda's Genri Nihon Sha, elected to the house of representatives from Nara. In the course of the proceedings of a budget subcommittee, Eto demanded of Home Minister Goto an explanation of the government's failure to suppress Minobe's *Kempō Seigi* and *Kempō Satsuyō*. These works, he said, contained passages contrary to Articles I and IV of the Imperial Constitution, passages likely to mislead young students into communistic ideas. Goto, under whose jurisdiction the censorship bureau functioned, evaded Eto's challenge by recourse to a typical bureaucratic dodge: he refused to engage in controversy concerning the constitution in the house of representatives.[41] This action by Eto might typically have come to nothing, might have been passed over as just another tiresome heckling by the lunatic fringe. But it was soon apparent that such was not to be the case. The climate of the forum had changed. The extremist literature attacking everything that stood in the way of militarist renovation had by this time cumulatively ensured favorable reaction to any patriotic declaration. The dissatisfied parliamentary majority was, moreover, more than eager to seize upon any issue likely to embarrass the government. Some of the Seiyukai leaders were quick to see the profit to be made.

And Eto's blow, it soon became evident, was not an isolated act. The second shot was fired on February 18 when Baron Kikuchi delivered in the house of peers what was essentially a repetition of his attack of the previous year. That attack, it will be remembered, was based on the Genri Nihon Sha's documentation of Minobe's purported offenses against the constitution and national polity, a reworking of the old Uesugi brief. Kikuchi's address on this occasion was in the form of an interpellation of the home minister and the education minister demanding that positive steps be taken to ensure a reform of political education and the banning of "reprehensible literature." He abandoned

the amenities of the house, naming Minobe as the author of the treason-
ous works, and charging Privy Council President Ichiki with responsibility for the importation of the hateful doctrines.[42] Kikuchi, long a
leading member of the Kokuhonsha, had already some laurels as a
minister-slayer, having precipitated the resignation of Commerce Minister Nakajima Kumakichi in February, 1934, by charging him with
a seditious utterance.

On February 25 Minobe took the rostrum in the house of peers to
defend himself:

> I regret that I cannot refrain from saying a word in my own behalf in regard
> to certain remarks made concerning my writings by Baron Kikuchi and
> others. . . . Baron Kikuchi last year in the 65th Diet said that it would be
> well to expel from the higher civil service examination board persons who
> harbor such ideas as he attributes to my writings. He spoke also other harsh
> words of criticism then and in this diet: that these are clearly treasonous
> thoughts, that I am rebellious man, and even that I am an academic tramp
> (*gakuhi*). For a Japanese there is nothing more shameful than to be called
> treasonous or traitorous, and for a scholar to be called an academic tramp
> is an equally serious insult. He has said these things . . . openly in formal
> session of this house, without an order for retraction from the chair. There
> are those who doubt that these things are permissible. One may question
> whether the dignity of this house has not been violated. I cannot overlook
> the shame that has been brought upon this house. Thus, though I feel that
> it is entirely improper that these matters he discussed here, and though I
> regret taking your time with them, I must beg your attention, however un-
> pleasant it is. . . .[43]

With these words, at once apologetic and resentful, he opened his
confident defense. He went on to display a remarkable blend of un-
common tenacity on points of personal dignity and of skillful sophistry
on points of doctrine—characteristics which persisted in his behavior
through the months of trial ahead.

Minobe was not without sympathetic and admiring listeners as he
spoke; he was interrupted several times by applause, a rare thing in
that chamber.[44] His argument that day followed more or less faithfully
the line he had pursued in his written rebuttal to Kikuchi's charges
the preceding year. First he challenged Kikuchi's qualification to criticize
an expert legal opinion, noting that "if an academician trained in the
law as I am should meddle in a military school and criticize the sayings
and writings of military specialists there, it could only be a laughing
matter in the end. I do not know what attainment Baron Kikuchi has

in respect to constitutional questions, but judging from the stenographic record of what he has said concerning my writings ... he has either failed to read them or has read them without understanding. . . ." He asserted his faithfulness to the emperor system: had Kikuchi considered the full context of the selected passages he cited, he could have seen that they implied no disparagement of the principle of monarchy as set forth in the constitution.

There were two points, Minobe admitted, over which there might be dispute: (1) whether the emperor's governmental prerogative was a right pertaining to his person, or a power he superintended in his capacity as chief of state; and (2) whether the emperor's governmental prerogative was an absolute power, or a power whose exercise was limited by the constitution. Minobe did not equivocate before the assembled peers in rejecting the absolutist side of these issues. Indeed, he was bold to profess the organ theory: In juristic terms, "the subject of governmental powers is the state conceived as a corporate body, and the emperor as chief of state, in other words as the supreme organ of the state, has the superintendence of the whole power of the state, and he is conceived to be the highest source from which issues every action of the state, legislative, administrative, and judicial." Those learned in jurisprudence, he asserted, would know these words were not in any way derogatory of the emperor's sovereignty.

Minobe's disclaimers of disloyalty to the emperor provide documentation for Maruyama's neat generalization on the defensive psychology of prewar Japanese liberals:

When [the rightists] raised the imperial standard of "national polity" (*kokutai*), none of the parties and circles in Japan, with the exception of a handful of anarchists and communists, had any legitimate grounds for offering frontal resistance. In the face of rightist attacks Japanese Christians, liberals, and democrats always had to begin by vindicating themselves, that is, by pleading that their own thoughts and deeds were in no way opposed to the "national polity." Their arguments, accordingly, always tended to be passive. It is these conditions that explain developments like the Minobe Incident, which swept over Japan like a typhoon in 1935. . . . During this time almost all academic and journalistic circles remained silent; furthermore, despite the fact that these victims of rightist onslaught had close connections with the upper levels of the bureaucratic, political, and business worlds, hardly a single person, even among their friends, dared to come to their support. . . .[45]

But there is also a hint of defiance in Minobe's posture before the house of peers, a token of the self-confidence and aggressiveness under attack which became more evident later. Minobe did not succumb to the resignation reflected in Premier Okada's explanation of the government's failure to take the offensive against the rightist: "We cannot afford to make a mistake; there is nothing to do but to accept the situation."[46]

Minobe clearly won the debate on points against the outclassed Kikuchi.[47] But it only seemed that the liquidation of this gaucherie from the right had beheaded the dragon. The beast was soon to sprout new heads. Again General Eto comes to stage center. Undaunted by the failure of the house of representatives to take up his lead at once, Eto had proceeded with his campaign, putting his questions not only to the home minister but also to Premier Okada, demanding suppression of the published notes of Ichiki's university lectures (1900) and the dismissal of Ichiki from office. On February 27 Okada informed the house of representatives that the home ministry had no intention of suppressing Minobe's works.[48]

On the following day, still armed with the materials put out by the Genri Nihon Sha and by the Kokutai Yōgo Rengō Kai, Eto filed in the Tokyo District Court a formal complaint of felonious lese majesty against Minobe. As fantastic as the content of his information was, it ensured that from that moment the ministry of justice was brought into the conflict. Justice Minister Ohara was thereafter constantly pressed in the diet for an accounting of the progress of the procurators in pushing through an indictment of Minobe on these charges.[49] Eto's legal action was clearly aimed at the Okada Cabinet as much as at Minobe. The judicial test was intended to force the government's hand and to demonstrate to potential allies in the diet that the charges were seriously made.

THE CIRCUMSPECT BEHAVIOR OF THE MILITARY LEADERS

Up to this point there is no indication of any official military participation in or reaction to the issue posed by Eto and Kikuchi. Neither War Minister General Hayashi nor Navy Minister Admiral Osumi Ginsei had taken part in the debates or publicly indicated an official military position on the question. In view of the prominent role the army came to play in succeeding stages of the affair, this may appear surprising. The apparent incongruity can probably be explained in terms of the internal politics of the army.[50] In February, 1935, the Imperial Way Faction was still highly potent. Although the purge of the young radicals was already under way, the Mazaki group had by no means abandoned hope of regaining control of the army and, presumably, pushing on to radical renovation of the state. The Imperial Way Faction fully appreciated that a vigorous campaign for clarification of national polity and the eradication of the organ theory was a prime weapon in advancing its revolutionary objectives and in weakening the *zaibatsu-jūshin-genrō* combination which dominated the government and encouraged the Control Faction.

For War Minister Hayashi, now committed to the Nagata policy, the problem of 1935 was to ride out the internal storm which attended the attempt to complete the displacement of the Imperial Way Faction, and he had to pursue a highly equivocal policy in respect to renovationist sentiment in the army. To ensure the support of the *jūshin* and of the economic magnates of the empire, he had to adopt a repressive policy toward the military radicals. At the same time, in carrying out the removal of Mazaki and other *kōdōha* heroes, he had to avoid any appearance of concession to the civilian moderates—indeed, he had to be prepared to meet as much of the radical demands as was necessary to keep them from moving into open rebellion. Both objectives— the destruction of the *kōdōha* and of its radical minions and the destruction of the remnants of constitutional liberalism—were quite consistent with the ambitions of the *tōseiha* for itself and for the army. The problem was to walk the razor's edge between the apparent contradictions until the intramural crisis was passed.[51]

While there is reasonable suspicion of military influence behind the launching of the attack on the organ theory, the evidence remains circumstantial.[52] The suspicion stems first of all from awareness of the intimate relation between the military and civilian radicals discussed earlier. In his memoirs, Premier Admiral Okada asserts that: "Behind them [Minoda *et al.*] was really a part of the military. In such an atmosphere the reservists in the diet, who were in collusion with them, acted to extirpate Dr. Minobe's theory. . . . At first this appeared to be an attack on an academic theory, but gradually the mask was discarded to reveal a major offensive by right-wing forces, and finally the army showed itself in the van."[53]

Indeed, there is considerable circumstantial evidence of military involvement in the actions initiated by Eto and Kikuchi in the diet. The most obvious connection exists in the persons of Eto and Kikuchi themselves. Both were high ranking reserve officers. Both were members of the ultrapatriotic society of reserve officers, the Meirinkai. Kikuchi was prominent in the Kokuhonsha and the Jimmukai. Both were members of the Teikoku Zaigo Gunjin Kai (Imperial Reservist Association), a quasi-official organization embracing all reservists. Some of the provincial sections of this association were hotbeds of agrarian renovationist sentiment, strongly oriented to the *kōdōha* and very active in agitating against the organ theory.[54]

On February 17—that is, between the date of Eto's opening in the lower house and Kikuchi's in the peers—the Kokutai Yōgo Rengō Kai issued the notorious manifesto described earlier in this chapter. True to their undertakings in that declaration to take legal and social measures against Minobe and his doctrines, at least two of the subscribing groups sent delegations to Minobe's residence on February 21 urging him to resign all his public offices. This was apparently a civilian gesture. Among the many groups endorsing this declaration, only the Jimmukai had a substantial military connection. But Maruyama claims that such groups were "mere subcontracting agents" for the Imperial Way elements in the military.[55] In any case on February 27 two reservists groups, the Meirinkai and the Kaikyokai (the latter a small group headed by Baron General Oi Narimoto of the house of peers), issued their own declarations denouncing the organ theory.[56] Moreover, a report had leaked to the press on February 23 that the army would soon publish another pamphlet on the virtues of the Imperial Way and the evils of western individualism.[57] This announcement presumably intimated a successor to the pamphlet *The Essence of National Defense and Proposals to Strengthen It*, issued by the army in October 1934. As we have already noted, that earlier pamphlet had been a plea for the adoption of economic controls in the interest of social justice and the advancement of national defense. It clearly implied that the capitalistic-parliamentary system was an obstacle to both. Since the attack on the organ theory in the diet was a blow for the Imperial Way, and more significantly a blow against the political *status quo*, it undoubtedly served the purposes of the military renovationists.[58]

Thus the presence of the military on the scene was palpable. Even though there is no evidence of deliberately concerted action between Eto and Kikuchi, or between either one of them and active military personnel in launching the affair, the lack of official military commitment was soon to be remedied. The maneuvers in the diet, constant speculation in the press, and the pressure of renovationist sympathies in the army were bound to force the ministry of war to bring the weight of the army to bear publicly and in the deliberations of the government as it sought to cope with this embarrassing and threatening political issue. Even if the army had no formal commitment to Kikuchi's denunciation of Minobe, all factions could see that Minobe's successful rebuttal posed a threat to the advancement of military objectives.[59]

THE ARMY TAKES THE FIELD

Thus it was that during the month of March General Hayashi made his first somewhat cautious pronouncements on the organ-theory question. On March 8 in the house of peers and on March 15 in the house of representatives, Hayashi denied that Minobe's views had had any effect on army personnel. He conceded, however, that the organ theory had gotten beyond the limits of the academic to become an important ideological question, and that it would have to be dealt with by strong measures to ensure that it would not have influence.[60] On March 15 Hayashi and Osumi received a deputation of fifty representatives of various patriotic organizations, who urged upon the ministers their conviction that Minobe's theory was contrary to national polity and a threat to the independence of the supreme command. The following day Hayashi and Osumi received from the councillors of the Imperial Reservist Association a resolution denouncing Minobe and others who subscribed to the organ theory.[61]

Press reports on Hayashi's conference with Premier Okada on March 19 indicated that a decision had been made to abandon the partly negative response made by Hayashi in the diet a few days earlier—and to move ahead of the cabinet in pressing for a positive policy of eradicating the organ theory.[62] According to the newspaper accounts, Hayashi expressed to Okada considerable concern in the army over the effects of the organ theory on the supreme command and on future military education and training. He reported that the army general staff had concluded, on the basis of a report from the inspector general of military education (Mazaki), that there was no room for official toleration of a theory that was contrary to national polity.[63] He said that in view of the public furor over the organ theory it was advisable that the army announce in both houses of the diet that it was opposed to the organ theory. He then advised Okada that "It is incumbent on the government to indicate clearly the limits of the scholar's freedom consistent with the vindication of the conception of national polity. After this has been done the government should proceed to consider steps to strengthen the supervision of the education ministry over the universities, to enforce a stricter censorship of publications, and to make better known to the nation the dignity of national polity." With this gratuitous intrusion of military advice on matters of education and intellectual freedom the minister joined the threat that army authorities were endeavoring to prevent ex-soldiers as well as actives from allowing themselves to be dragged into the quagmire of political strife.[64]

SEIYUKAI MANEUVERS

The move early in March by the Seiyukai Diet majority to seize the organ-theory question as the means to destroy Okada's regime had probably emboldened the army, in spite of its own internal difficulties, to challenge the evasive policy of the cabinet. The decision of the Seiyukai to exploit the issue is not difficult to explain. It has been too often marked up to mere suicidal opportunism.[65] Indeed, it was an opportune course—or seemed to be. That the Seiyukai attempted to bend it to purely partisan advantage is also beyond question. But to leave the explanation there ignores the fact that there were among the leaders of the party important figures who were sympathetic in principle with the attack on the organ theory, and these men were not without following in the rank and file of the party. Prominent names in the Seiyukai (and, for that matter, in the Minseito) appeared in the rosters of the nationalist organizations. Suzuki Kisaburo, successor to Inukai as president of the party, was a "Hiranuma man" out of the ministry of justice and a member of the Kokuhonsha. He and other party leaders were members of the Jimmukai.[66]

Moreover, even though as a parliamentary party it presumably bene-
fited by the constitutional doctrines of the liberal school of interpretation, the Seiyukai had in fact little cause to regret Minobe's distress.
Most of the specific constitutional problems upon which Minobe had
taken his stand since 1928 had been issues in which the Seiyukai found
its position more or less undermined by his criticism. Not that the
party was particularly sensitive of this fact. Presumably neither the
leaders nor the rank and file concerned themselves with academic theories or theorists, whether friendly or hostile. (Indeed, a Seiyukai administration had made Minobe a member of the house of peers.)
Nevertheless, it would not be difficult to arouse the party against a
man whose constitutional philosophy was so consistently hostile to the
now prevailing anti-liberal tendencies in the party and whose more
and more frequent comments on current constitutional issues so regularly redounded to the credit of the opposition party. The Seiyukai had
been for a long time relatively sympathetic with the demands for a
"positive" foreign policy. It had been strong for the suppression of
proletarian and intellectual radicalism at home. The traditional sources
of its electoral strength made many of its members sensitive to the
economic problems and political fundamentalism of agrarian society
and the small entrepreneur. The incumbent Seiyukai majority had
been elected in 1932 on a platform favoring an aggressive continental
policy and social conservatism at home. There was much reason to expect a relatively harmonious relationship between the Seiyukai and the
military. The apparent stumbling block to cordial relations was not
issues of policy but their mutually exclusive ambitions to control the
state.

In any case, as the 1935 regular session of the diet opened, the Seiyukai was ripe to play the renovationist game, unable in its avid fas-
cination to see the fatal flaw in the prize. Seiyukai President Suzuki
had been frustrated by the army and the Minseito in his expectation
of succeeding to the premiership following Inukai's assassination. He
had had little choice but to join the Minseito in grudging support of
Saito's national-unity cabinet. By mid-1934, however, he had led his
party into opposition, and since that time his personal ambition and
the eager expectations of his equally frustrated fellow partymen had
led him to exploit every conceivable pretext to embarrass and weaken the
Okada Government, in full confidence that the fall of that cabinet

would lead to the restoration of the Seiyukai to its rightful position.

The party did not, however, go into the sixty-seventh Diet determined on a policy of pushing the organ-theory issue. Its strategy apparently focused on a campaign to harrass Minister of Communications Tokonami, a veteran member of the Seiyukai who remained in the Okada Cabinet after his party went into opposition. As one writer observed at the time, "The flames of the organ-theory question rose up in the house of peers, and when the Seiyukai men saw it reach the point of a concrete proposal, they jumped on the bandwagon and mustered their strength to bring a decision."[67] Whether or not Eto was in collusion with the Seiyukai (it will be recalled that he was once a member of that party), some Seiyukai members certainly saw immediately the virtue and the advantages of his attack. Agitation within the party for a positive attitude on clarification of national polity and eradication of the organ theory centered in the activities of the Kuhara faction.[68]

On March 11, before a special committee of the house of representatives considering revision of the Peace Preservation Law, Okada, Ohara, and Kanamori Tokujiro (chief of the cabinet legislative bureau) were heckled by Takeuchi Tomojiro of the Seiyukai. Having gotten Ohara to define national polity in the Peace Preservation Law as meaning that the emperor was the holder and subject of sovereignty, Takeuchi demanded whether Minobe was not indictable under the law. Both Ohara and Kanamori replied that although the government did not subscribe to the organ theory, that theory was, *per se*, not in conflict with national polity. As academic theory, it was in any case beyond the control of the government. Okada promised that any published works which appeared upon careful examination to be contrary to national polity would be suppressed.[69] Takeuchi and two copartisans continued to obstruct the work of the committee through the rest of the session.[70]

The work of these lesser lights of the Seiyukai sparked a quickening interest among leading members. On March 12, Yamamoto Teijiro, a former minister of agriculture and forestry, demanded in the house of representatives that the government take positive steps to suppress the organ theory.[71] And in the house of peers the Kenkyukai, the largest faction in that chamber and the one most closely allied with the Seiyukai, joined on March 20 in pushing through a resolution calling on the government to act positively to establish the correct view of na tional polity through a reform of political education. Finally, on March 26, President Suzuki himself introduced a resolution, supported by the Seiyukai, and the Minseito, calling for clarification of national polity. It was, of course, adopted by a large majority.[72] With this the Seiyukai had come fully onto the stage and the cast of characters was complete. The action of the houses had by no means fulfilled the desires of the men who had spoken the opening lines, but it was too late to do anything further through the diet, for the Sixty-seventh Diet closed on March 26.

The resolutions which had issued from the diet were, indeed, rather mild. They expressed the diet's professed alarm at the flippancy and radicalism of popular thought and at the existence of theories contrary to the fundamental historical principles of the Japanese state, and they enjoined the government to undertake a "clarification of national polity" (*kokutai meichō*). In the words of the house of representatives "It is most urgent that the essential character of national polity should be made clear to the people so that they may be under no misapprehension. The government should take decisive action against speech and theories inconsistent with the noble and peerless national polity of Japan." There was no direct mention in either resolution of the organ theory itself and no identification of the particular miscreants who had propounded and propagated it (this dismayed Eto, Kikuchi and company); the diet merely assigned to the government the responsibility for eradicating a theory which had existed for three decades, unknown to nine Japanese out of ten until the previous year.

To be sure, the leaders of this action were not necessarily concerned with Minobe's theory. As we have seen, they were unhappy for a variety of reasons with the *status quo* in politics and believed that the organ-theory issue would force a change to their advantage. Reference to "clarification of national polity" was well chosen. It discreetly avoided direct attack upon powerful interests, it raised the issue from the narrow level of a single heretical utterance to embrace all errant philosophies, it meant all things to all men.[73] *Kokutai Meichō* was a venerable reactionary slogan, at least as old as the antidemocratic movement of the period of World War I.[74] For its earliest users it had a purely backward-looking sense and its evocation now invited endorsement by all who would reject the Taisho political change and all its fruits. But there were those also who could heartily support clarification, having in mind, not the reëstablishment of some bygone ideal, but the introduction of a new totalitarian order. It was, indeed, to this latter sentiment that the days and years ahead belonged.

The government might have breathed a sigh of relief when the diet adjourned. The session had failed to produce any of the action which the government wanted and had forced it to take a stand on the Minobe question, but the diet's final action had not presented an insurmountable obstacle to the disposition of that problem. Forced to abandon its original contention that the whole question was of purely academic significance, the government had moved nimbly to a defensive position, saying that although it did not approve of Minobe's theory it could not find that the organ theory as he expounded it violated the law.

By this time, however, the passions of the diet had communicated themselves to the general public. The emperor's simplest subject could see, once it was pointed out to him, that the organ theory was "contrary to common sense and blasphemous."[75] The diet had dispersed, but there remained in the cabinet, in the person of General Hayashi, an agent capable of exacting compliance with the purposes of the diet resolutions, even with the demands for destruction of Minobe, Ichiki, Kanamori, Makino Nobuaki (lord privy seal), and the Genro Saionji.[76] Should General Hayashi falter in discharging this duty, his subordinates of the Imperial Way Faction had a lever to use against him in the reservist associations and in such groups as the newly organized League for the Destruction of the Organ Theory (Kikan Setsu Bokumetsu Dōmei).[77]

On March 30 the cabinet council decided on the following measures: (1) the war and navy ministers were to issue instructions to the services warning them against the organ theory; (2) the home minister was to instruct the prefectural governors on the suppression of the organ theory; and (3) the education minister was to address a similar instruction to higher school officials.[78] The inspector general of military education and the minister of education, Matsuda, took measures accordingly in early April.[79] On May 3, Home Minister Goto's instructions were delivered to the prefectural governors meeting at the premier's residence.[80]

The Tokyo dailies reported that Goto's instruction was followed by an address by Justice Minister Ohara declaring that "It is fortunate that the Japanese have of late come to realize their glorious national polity. . . . At the same time, however, there are some who are resorting to violence under the fair name of loyalty to the Emperor and patriotism or protection of national polity . . . these undesirables intimidate and blackmail people in connection with trifling matters. . . . Furthermore, they declare that in the background of their unlawful actions is the influence of the Army and of various other powerful organizations. They also utilize religious faith. They try unduly to muzzle freedom of speech. Thus they are a source of trouble for innocent people. . . ."[81]

There was no little intrepidation in the making of such a statement. In the brief two months during which this question had been before the public the terroristic elements of the right had been at work. From late in March Minobe and some who presumed to defend him, notably Dr. Onozuka Kiheiji, former president of To-Dai, were subjected to invasions of their homes by abusive and threatening groups and had been put under police guard. The premises of *Asahi* and *Yomiuri* were the scenes of riotous disturbances. Threatening gestures toward Ichiki and Makino were reported. Even Saionji, in his country retreat, received abusive communications. On March 29 War Minister Hayashi himself had made ominous remarks to the press, observing that "Those who say that the Army is leading the Government against Minobe may be hindering the Army."[82]

Ohara's ministry of justice had, indeed, become a particular source of frustration to the anti-Minobe forces because of its failure to render up Minobe's head on charges of lese-majesty. The criminal action initiated by Eto had languished, due in part to a difference of opinion within the ministry.[83] At its meeting on March 30, the cabinet excused itself from immediate action pending reports on the findings of the procurator general's office and the censorship bureau. The ministers of justice and home affairs were ordered to speed up their subordinates.[84] Delay in official action presumably reflected the government's hope that Minobe would solve everything by making a voluntary recantation.[85]

Goto's department moved quickly then. On April 9 he published the findings of the censorship bureau, ordering the suppression of *Kempō Satsuyō*, *Kempō Seigi*, and *Nihon Kempō no Kihon Shugi*, and revisions in *Gendai Kensei Hyōron* and *Gikai Seiji no Kentō*.[86] It appears that this move was timed, somewhat ineptly, to tie in with the ministry of justice announcement on April 8 that Ohara and Procurator General Hayashi Raisaburo had concluded, after interrogating Minobe, that no prosecution for lese-majesty could be made "because of the absence of intent." This announcement advised that further study would be made regarding possible trial of Minobe for violation of the Publication Law.[87]

In their efforts to appease the demands for clarification, without springing a trap on the *jūshin* by a criminal conviction of Minobe, the ministry of justice and the cabinet found Minobe to be not an entirely reliable pawn. The differences within the ministry of justice were provisionally resolved on April 4 when it was decided to push the inquiry on the single point of Minobe's contention that imperial rescripts were subject to criticism. Accordingly Minobe was invited to present himself for interrogation at the Bar Association building on April 6. The interview was postponed, however, possibly to avoid a public disturbance, for April 6 was a day of expansive patriotic sentiment, marked by the arrival in Tokyo of the emperor of Manchukuo, a showpiece of the Kwantung army. On Sunday, April 7, attended by his son, Minobe was escorted by a plainclothes policeman to the premises of the Tokyo district procurator's office, where he spent several hours in "conference" with officials assigned to his case. Chief procurator, Iwamura Michiya, presided; chief of the thought bureau, Tozawa Shigeo, a former student of both Uesugi and Minobe conducted the questioning. The interview started early in the day and lasted into the evening; according to some accounts it extended more than fourteen hours.[88]

Lacking an official record of what transpired in that meeting, we must rely on the account given by Ozaki, who consulted most of the persons involved.[89] During the morning Tozawa tried to extract from Minobe an admission that his assertion of the permissibility of criticizing imperial rescripts was in error. Would Minobe not concede that even if rescripts on political, economic, and military matters were subject to criticism on the responsibility of ministers of state, still rescripts dealing with matters of public morality (e.g., the rescript on education) could not be criticized by subjects? Minobe at first admitted that most legal authorities held this to be true and he opened the afternoon session by volunteering that he had erred in not making the distinction which Tozawa had pointed out.[90] He then launched into a long defense of his whole state-personality theory with all its corollary propositions, ignoring Tozawa's efforts to confine the discussion to the question of criticism of rescripts.

Iwamura apparently thought Minobe had made a saving concession. He told reporters that there was no basis for prosecution for lese-majesty, nor, since Minobe had undertaken to revise his interpretation, were there any grounds for charges under the Publications Law. He said that the whole matter could be settled by an order from the home ministry banning the publication of various books of Minobe.[91] On the following day the censorship bureau ordered the aforementioned ban. Although represented as an independent action, it seemed to demonstrate close coöperation between Goto and Ohara.

Any hope that this would end the matter had already been dashed, for when Minobe spoke to the reporters immediately after his interrogation, he explained that he could not discuss details of the examination, "as the Procurator has asked me not to reveal its nature. The examination ended in the morning, but the writing of its record took time. . . . Regarding my books, I have long intended to revise their terms and expressions, but it seems there is still a gap between the Government's wish and my scientific ideas."[92] The next day the newsmen got to him again and found him bristling with resentment at the home ministry's order:

I bow to the penalty arising from an application of the law. But *Kempō Seigi* is in its twelfth edition and *Kempō Satsuyō* is in its fifth. How is it that though both have been in publication many years it has now become necessary to take administrative action against them? If these works conflict with the law, then all the successive home ministers up to now are properly responsible for overlooking this fact. And, of course, if there are punishable aspects of my theory, then the successive university presidents and ministers of education who took no action all the long while that I lectured on the constitution as a university professor are likewise responsible. How has this come about? That is something that can not be explained by this action. . . .[93]

He said further that he had no intention of resigning his emeritus status at To-Dai, his membership in the imperial academy, or his seat in the house of peers, albeit noting that he was "somewhat weary of lecturing and if they want me to stop that I shall not be sorry to do so."[94]

Spokesmen for various anti-organ theory, pro-clarification groups expressed at once their dissatisfaction with the action taken by the gov-

ernment. Citing Minobe's recalcitrant language, they insisted that positive steps be taken to remove him and other alleged proponents of the
organ theory from their official positions immediately, and to issue an
official and unequivocal definition of national polity. General Hayashi
was for the moment content to confine his public remarks to the comment: "I will decide later, depending on the possible effects of the
[censorship bureau] order, whether it will be necessary for me to give
the Premier further advice."[95] The succeeding few weeks were, however,
relatively quiet on the surface. The army and navy, the home ministry,
and the education ministry carried forth the clarification policy adopted
by the cabinet at the end of March. Late in April the army press issued
Dai Nihon Teikoku Kempō no Kaishaku in Kansuru Kenkai (*Views
Concerning the Interpretation of the Constitution of the Great Empire
of Japan*), a pamphlet urging that the only acceptable basis for interpretation of the constitution was the spirit of Japan's own peculiar national
polity.[96] On May 10 Hayashi met with Okada to advise him of the
army's continuing apprehension of the dangerous consequences of the
government's failure to establish such an interpretation officially and to
wipe out the organ theory.[97] The right-wing press continued to pour out
incendiary literature with an urgent note imparted through a revival of
the excitement evoked by Araki Sadao's sensational designation of 1936
as the year of crisis for Japan.[98] Nevertheless, there was a considerable
lull in the organ-theory clamor during May and June, accounted for in
part by the fact that the minister of war—in the absence of the diet
the primary source of direct clarification pressure on the government
—had absented himself to Manchukuo, leaving his subordinates to deal
with the problem posed by the fractious Imperial Way Faction.

But the surcease of pressure upon the government was only an illusion. The internal crisis in the army was bound to result in a more
rather than a less insistent demand for action on clarification. Indeed,
Hayashi and the Control Faction were in danger of losing control of
the army to the Imperial Way leaders, who were beginning once more
to rally the young officers under the anti-organ-theory banner. To strike
at the young zealots and their senior protectors, Nagata adopted a two-
fold strategy. On the one hand, Hayashi continued to push the Okada
Cabinet on the organ-theory and clarification issues, action which would
not only serve the larger interests of the army but would help to stem
revolutionary hysteria among the young officers and reservists. Thus

Hayashi's repeated insistence that the government make a definite official pronouncement on the correct meaning of national polity had urgent practical relevance to the army situation.[99] To government pressure on the service ministries to cut off the political activism of regular and reserve military personnel Hayashi could reply with effective counter-pressure: the government might expect more rather than less rebelliousness from the military radicals unless it gave explicit satisfaction on the national polity issue. Thus Hayashi was for the moment the agent by which the military power seekers pressed upon the civil government the fateful compromise with naked force which intruded at every juncture down to the establishment of the Tojo Cabinet.[100]

On the other hand, Nagata, with Hayashi's support, carried forward a great purge within the army, involving the transfer of hundreds of officers. Beginning with some of the most suspect of the young officers in April and May, it brought the removal of Mazaki in July and further mass transfers of disaffected units in August. All through this period Hayashi could not afford to take a soft attitude publicly on the national polity issue, for to do so would have given credit to the accusations of military radicals and their civilian allies that he was punishing officers who had attacked the organ theory and shown the most fervent devotion to the true national polity. The general public, of course, knew almost nothing of this struggle within the army until it was exposed by the assassination of General Nagata in August.[101]

OKADA BETWEEN THE SEIYUKAI AND THE ARMY

At the end of June the clarification forces resumed direct and overt pressure upon the government; in August they forced another capitulation. The continued recess of the diet denied the Seiyukai the opportunities and spared the government the pains of a return to that forum. The Seiyukai leadership was nevertheless active in anticipation of the next session.[102] On June 21 the Seiyukai directors announced the party's major objectives in the immediate future. To no one's surprise this declaration confirmed the decision taken in the preceding diet that the cry for clarification of national polity and the expunging of the organ theory was now the Seiyukai's best hope of harrying the Okada Cabinet from office. The Seiyukai also demanded a return to responsible government—meaning, of course, to a Seiyukai Cabinet.[103] It was reported that President Suzuki had supported a resolution advanced by Kuhara at the policy meeting that the *jūshin* should be "impeached" should they obstruct realization of the party's program.[104]

In the first week of July delegations from the Seiyukai "clarification committee" called on Home Minister Goto, Justice Minister Ohara, and Premier Okada to heckle and scold them for their footdragging attitude. The committee made clear its view that specific condemnation of the organ theory and retirement of all persons associated with it constituted the necessary first step toward clarification. Nor did they leave any doubt about the ultimate Seiyukai aim of destroying Saionji, Ichiki, Makino, and the others of the court clique who blocked the path to power. They seem to have ignored (or suppressed reference to) the real obstacle to their ambitions, the army.[105]

The government of Admiral Okada, resting as it did on the support of the Minseito minority and the good will of the *jūshin*, in lieu of any real political foundations of its own, could not shrug off the Seiyukai threat. However impotent to grasp the reins of government, the Seiyukai was quite capable of making the government's position unbearable, largely by blocking its legislative program. The Seiyukai was building up a situation in which it might benefit from provoking a dissolution and an election. Should it be returned to its majority its demands for the cabinet commission would be all the more difficult to deny, regardless of military opposition. At very least, a favorable election outcome would completely destroy the government's effectiveness. The return of a Minseito majority might be hardly less disastrous to the government, for that party might prove equally unwilling to support a transcendental cabinet. Aside from this, the Seiyukai pursuit of the organ-theory question, supplementing the hysterical campaign of right-wing patriots and the reservists, was seriously jeopardizing the reputation of the "liberal" *jūshin* before the public and was undercutting their position *vis-à-vis* the ambitions of the military.

Playing on the army's known antipathy for party government, Okada and the court officials attempted to persuade Hayashi to moderate his own demands for the vindication of national polity, pointing out that the Seiyukai was exploiting the issue for partisan purposes. Statements by Hayashi and Osumi early in July showed some concession to this plea. Hayashi, again under pressure from the supreme war council, conferred with Okada on July 5 urging positive steps toward clarification of national polity. His statement to the press following that meeting indicated, however, that he would settle for limited immediate objectives: "A solution may not be immediately possible. But with our eyes fixed steadily on our objectives, we may have to strive for four or five years."[106]

Four days later Navy Minister Osumi personally conveyed to Okada the navy's views on the constitutional question. Having kept more or less on the sidelines up to this point, Osumi now seconded Hayashi: the government should clearly define national polity, although it was necessary to move cautiously against the deeply entrenched organ theory. The continued forebearance of the navy, he warned, was conditional upon immediate government moves toward clarification. He assured that the navy was determined not to let its stand be exploited to the political purposes of the Seiyukai.[107]

On July 13 Premier Okada advised court circles through Grand Chamberlain Admiral Suzuki Kentaro that the government was bowing to the pressure, that as soon as the cabinet could agree on an official statement it would be issued. All questions of national polity would be settled. And the question of what to do about Minobe would be dealt with, but separately.[108]

The separation of Minobe from the broader clarification issue here was an act of deference to the solicitude of the palace for Minobe's fate. It also raised a major hazard in the course navigated by Admiral Okada. An important part of his mission—perhaps the principal part of it—was to keep his cabinet alive and thus to forestall the perils that would attend raising a new government. The chief threats to the survival of the Okada Government lay in the possibility of withdrawal of army participation and the possibility of parliamentary obstruction by the Seiyukai. Okada made the best of the game of playing off the army against the Seiyukai. But the affairs of the Seiyukai encouraged its leaders to seek exactly the cabinet crisis that Okada sought to avoid; moreover, powerful and aggressive elements within or connected with the army shared this purpose. Both these adversaries had, as we have seen, made the organ theory-clarification issue a prime weapon in their respective arsenals. It would seem that Okada might best have disarmed these forces—or at least defused their ammunition—by sacrificing Minobe.

But the court circles to whom Okada owed his commission denied him this solution. During the first six months of the crisis, the palace exerted heavy pressure on the Okada Cabinet to save Minobe.

Many passages in the Harada-Saionji diary testify to the preoccupation of the *genrō* and other court officials with Minobe's troubles. The emperor's remarks, as reported to Harada by Grand Chamberlain Suzuki in April, are especially noteworthy:

> If there is to be an argument whether sovereignty resides in the monarch or in the state, I can understand it, but it is quite absurd to argue whether the organ theory is good or bad. In my opinion the state-sovereignty theory is preferable to the monarchical-sovereignty theory, but what difference does it make after all in a country such as Japan in which there is an identity of monarch and state? Monarchical sovereignty easily falls into despotism. Now if there arise in the universities two contending theories, the monarchical sovereignty theory and the monarch-as-organ theory, is that not to be admired as a restraint on the despotic tendencies of the monarchical sovereignty theory? They talk about Minobe, but I think Minobe could never be disloyal. Is there really anyone his equal in Japan today? To consign such a one to oblivion would be lamentable. . . . Minobe may have gone too far in some respects, but I can never think ill of him.

Similarly the emperor is reported to have said to his aide, General Honjo:

> It is all right in the pamphlets to cite theories of various schools of thought, but it is quite improper to interject the names of Ichiki or other individuals. Along with the emperor-organ theory question comes the heaping of abuse on Ichiki personally, does it not? The military are determined to put the blame on Ichiki, but Ichiki is a loyal subject. Ichiki's spirit is pure and he should never be subjected to public censure. . . . Is it not a great contradiction that the military should proceed to attack the organ theory in opposition to my views?[109]

The court's concern stemmed from several causes, including the emperor's personal interest in Minobe and the desire to preserve his value as an anti-militaristic symbol. But, most importantly, everyone involved recognized from the first that if Minobe were to fall on the basis of his constitutional theory this would be just the first step toward what must then rapidly ensue: the fall of Ichiki, Makino, and Kanamori, the men on whom Saionji had pinned his hope for the survival of "liberal" influence around the throne. Thus Okada had to find a formula to meet Hayashi's requirements and yet somehow leave Minobe un-scathed—or at least one that would not go beyond Minobe. Minobe's stubbornness hardly simplified the problem.

And a related problem confronted Saionji meanwhile: Ichiki was seriously pressing to be released from the presidency of the privy council. His departure would throw the problem of Hiranuma into Saionji's lap again and, because it would appear to be a retirement under fire, would seem an acknowledgment of culpability on the organ-theory issue, thus serving the same end as Minobe's conviction. Moreover, if Ichiki went he would doubtless take Makino and Kanamori with him.[110]

THE GOVERNMENT ATTEMPTS APPEASEMENT

The Okada Cabinet was consumed for the balance of July trying to reach an agreement on the promised statement. Okada's antagonists soon disabused him of any hope he may have had of avoiding explicit denunciation of the organ theory. By the end of July the premier felt that the deliberations had advanced far enough to permit turning over the task of drafting the clarification statement to the cabinet secretariat. It was reported to the press, however, that Hayashi and Osumi were threatening to withhold their endorsements, chiefly on the grounds that the proposed declaration made no mention of Minobe or the organ theory.[111] Hayashi, sensitive to the ominous reaction to the recent trans-fer of General Mazaki and regularly exposed to the nagging advice of the supreme war council, had to have at least a token concession from the cabinet. Indeed, on July 26 Hayashi delivered to Okada a draft declaration prepared in the ministry of war.[112] He apparently succeeded in communicating the urgency of his requirements to Okada for, on July 30, the premier told newsmen that much of the army's views had in fact been woven into the contents of the declaration being prepared.[113] Hayashi's efforts were noisily assisted by the Seiyukai. A "mass rally" convened by the party at Hibiya Park on July 31 "passed" a resolution castigating the government for its insincerity in handling the organ-theory matter. Further adjustments in the statement were made on August 1 and on that day the navy indicated that it had approved the government's declaration.[114]

On August 3, the government's National Polity Clarification Declaration was published.[115] It was not to be the last such pronouncement.

The declaration affirmed—on the authority of Amaterasu, the Promulgation Edict, and Article I of the Imperial Constitution—that sovereignty resided in the emperor: Theories holding "that the Emperor is to be regarded as an organ for the purpose of exercising this power. . . . are absolutely counter to the fundamental principles of national polity." The government "regretted that academic theories in connection with the basic principles of national polity have come to be argued." Moreover, the government placed "emphasis on clarification of national polity," looking forward to the enhancement of the national glory. The circumlocution regarding Minobe clearly intimated the government's reservations. Okada's separate statement specifically defending Ichiki and Kanamori made them still more explicit. Hayashi concurred in Okada's assertion that the national polity question did not involve Ichiki, but he referred to the declaration as "merely the first step" toward the desired end.[116] Clearly the government had not succeeded in settling anything. It could be said, in fact, that Okada by his public exoneration of Ichiki and Kanamori had tied the life of his cabinet to the capacity of those two to survive the clarification onslaught.[117] The Seiyukai, the Meirinkai, and even the venerable reactionary Count Kaneko Kentaro were quick to protest the inadequacy of the government's efforts.[118] The patriotic hosts had acquired an overwhelming thirst for Ichiki's blood, which they could have only if Minobe's was let first.

Thus the cry of the right extremists for the punishment of defilers of national polity and their powerful protectors continued to rise. The clamor was hardly interrupted by the assassination of General Nagata on August 12. True, this event caused a brief suspension of direct military pressure on the government, for General Hayashi, possibly to save his own skin in the aftermath of the Nagata murder, moved over to the supreme war council and was replaced as war minister by a pliant nonentity, General Kawashima Yoshiyuki.[119] The Nagata incident was eventually to bear fruit in the form of a sensational trial of the assassin, Colonel Aizawa, a trial which, during the opening weeks of 1936—until it was superseded by the February 26 rising—was to provide a new focus for rightist passions. But before that trial opened in January the government had been forced once more publicly and formally to submit to the renovationist pressures for clarification.

In public statements leading up to the August 3 declaration, Okada had anticipated subsequent objections by announcing that action regarding Minobe would be for the ministry of justice to decide. This tactic turned the burden back upon Ohara during the ensuing weeks. There was no doubt that in the view of procurators concerned with the case Minobe's writing concerning the criticism of imperial rescripts was punishable under the Publication Law. There was, however, a question of whether to prosecute. Following the examination of Minobe on April 7 the decision—in view of Minobe's admission of error, the home ministry's banning of the offending works, and the fact that most of the offense had originated many years previously—had been against prosecution.[120] Minobe's angry words to the press on April 10 might have led to an immediate reversal of this decision, but reluctance to proceed against Minobe formally without the approval of the throne and a desire to avoid the appearance of giving in to outside pressure prevailed against precipitate action.[121] And when Chief Procurator Iwamura was transferred shortly thereafter to become head of the criminal division of the ministry, Inomata Jiroku, who came in from Fukuoka to take charge of the Minobe case, was advised by Ohara to proceed slowly and carefully, and to be especially diligent in preserving the integrity of the judicial department against military interference.[122]

The Minobe issue had, however, become the very heart of the extremist attack on the government. The flood of anti-government literature grew. The service ministers, backed by demonstrations and proclamations of the reservist organizations, made repeated ultimatums. Under its banner more and more arrogant gangs of toughs baited the police in Tokyo and elsewhere. As the summer wore on, the government found it increasingly difficult to hold to its policy of inaction.[123]

RESUMPTION OF ATTACK ON MINOBE

It was becoming especially difficult for the procuratorial officials, who tended to think that Minobe ought to be prosecuted, to resist the continuous clamor for action. By the end of July the fact that Procurator General Hayashi and Justice Minister Ohara were at odds on the question had ceased to be a secret.[124] Eto Genkuro complained that "though authorities mete out severe punishment to patriots who happen to break the law, they seem unable to act with celerity in cases involving recalcitrant men and dangerous scholars."[125] The government might shrug off this grousing, but it could not ignore the metropolitan police bureau's claim that failure to prosecute Minobe was stimulating terroristic activities. Moreover, the home ministry criminal affairs bureau report on the Nagata assassination pointed to the rumor current among rightists that the displacement of Inspector General Mazaki was due to the influence of the *genrō-jūshin*, for whom Nagata had been a puppet. Nagata was said to have represented a major sedition to promote the organ theory, destroy national polity, disrupt the army, and prevent the Showa Restoration; the transfer of Mazaki was seen as a design to weaken the attack on the organ theory.[126]

When General Kawashima entered the Okada Cabinet, he did so only on the understanding that immediate unequivocal action on the clarification problem would be forthcoming. Thus an additional threat now hung over the government: that failure to meet Kawashima's demands would result in his resignation and the fall of the cabinet.[127] Like Hayashi, Kawashima made the most of the peril posed by the military radicals and their civilian auxiliaries, who were exploiting the arrest of Colonel Aizawa in undisguised preparation for a *coup d'état*. If these overzealous patriots were to be kept under discipline, the good faith of the government must be positively demonstrated.[128] With the government thus charged by the army with responsibility for any future breach of military discipline, Ohara could no longer stand pat on the Minobe question. But he could and did attempt to manage the business in such a way as to spare sensitivities in court circles.

Again Minobe's failure to play out the role of the abject penitent jeopardized Ohara's attempts to effect a quiet settlement. When it was reported early in September that the procurators were preparing to prosecute Minobe under the Publication Law unless he should recant his heresy, diligent reporters sought him out to hear and report his reactions. He obliged with a calmly defiant statement. His writings, he observed, were "all based on conviction resulting from research. If I am to become a criminal because of them, I can only bow my head and serve my sentence. I have advocated no theory, however, that interprets the Emperor as a mere organ of the state. I still believe my theory to be correct and I cannot imagine that it constitutes a crime. . . . [Resignation from the house of peers] would amount to an admission that I am wrong in this. If I receive a prison sentence I shall be deprived of my seat."[129]

On September 14 Minobe was brought again to the premises of the Tokyo district procurator's office and subjected to a six-hour reëxamination by Tozawa. The proceedings were severely formal. Minobe was asked to write out and sign his replies to critical questions. That evening he wrote to Ohara advising him of his intention of resigning from the house of peers.[130]

Minobe Ryokichi's narrative of these events seems to support the view that the elder Minobe's equivocation in his relation to the procurators was simply the result of the impossibility of resolving the dilemma between self-respect and prudence.[131] Minobe *fils* tells us that as the government strove to pursue a course between the right-wing attacks on the one side and the emperor's wishes on the other, his father "passed each unhappy day surrounded by guards with no assurance that even his life would be spared. Nevertheless there was no sign of a change in his firm attitude." He proffers a letter, discovered only after his father's death, which does not indicate his least intention of resigning his public posts at that time:

Upon mature reflection . . . I am now of the certain opinion that . . . to resign voluntarily would only be taken as an admission of wrong-doing and as a public apology for error. To throw away my scholarly career and leave behind the memory of disgrace would be for me unbearably painful. Of course, if by chance the courts should find me guilty, I would naturally lose my posts, and if the house of peers votes to expel me then I will suffer that too. But for me by my own action to [seem to] acknowledge my own guilt would be for me an unbearably painful, unforgettable thing. . . . When you reflect on the past few years you find the currents that would destroy constitutional government have grown stronger and stronger, and the voices raised for the destruction of liberal thought have risen sharply. But liberalism means constitutionalism; indeed it is the first fundamental of constitutional government. In spite of the fact that this is declared in the very Imperial Edict promulgating our octroi constitution and is inscribed in every article in Chapter II of the constitution, there is a public clamor for the extirpation of liberty. There can be no doubt that this is an outstanding manifestation of the tide that runs to the destruction of constitutional government. From the beginning it has been my constant endeavor to oppose this trend. Even thought I have not had the strength to repulse it, I firmly believe that it is against my duty, as one who has devoted his life to the study of the constitution, to bow to this current and to retire out of consideration for my personal security. I have resolved without regret to give myself to my humble best to the defense of the constitution, even at the sacrifice of my person. . . .

This firm resolve did not meet the approval of his counselors, for, as his son observes, it was clear that if he did not resign he would be put to trial for violation of the press law. Thus, "our circle . . . thought it would be prudent, even though he had not intended to, [for him] to resign his public positions in order to avoid prosecution, and we urged this on father. He was warmly pressed to do so by his close friend Matsumoto Joji. Father was finally persuaded and he informed the Ministry of Justice of his decision to resign all his public posts. . . ."

On the afternoon of September 17 the office of the procurator general announced that, in view of Minobe's admission of error in his writing and his undertaking to correct that error in the future, the charges against him would be dropped. There would be no leniency in the future, however. Minobe's reply to Ohara was reported in the papers at that time. Neither that reply nor the procurator's statement indicated that the intention of resigning from the house of peers had been a consideration in the decision to quash the indictment.[132]

Minobe sought to dispel any doubts on that score. In a provocative statement to reporters as he left the house of peers on September 18 after handing his resignation to Konoye, he clearly implied that he had deliberately delayed his resignation until it could not be construed as a retreat on his principles or as a condition of his release from prosecution:

I have resigned from the House of Peers, but that is not because of the question of changing my theory of recognizing mistakes in my books; I have resigned because I found it difficult to fulfill my duties as a member of the House of Peers in the present atmosphere of that House.

I have long been determined to resign at a proper time. Whether my theory is right or wrong is another question. Disregarding that question . . . I have deemed it appropriate to withdraw from the House for the sake of discipline there. The speech I made there in the last session incurred the intense enmity of some members of the House and the House has shown no disposition to oppose such an attitude upon the part of the members. If I remain in the House I may disturb its atmosphere, and for the maintenance of order in the House of Peers I believe it is proper for me to resign.

Some public criticism has been directed against my theory and when it first came to be regarded seriously there were opinions expressed that I should be indicted. This, I thought, would be a serious blow to my theory, which I regard above anything else in the world. . . . The time has come, however, for me to resign formally, now that the judicial authorities have come to a decision yesterday not to prosecute me.[133]

With these words it appeared that Ohara's hopes of having settled the matter had vanished.[134]

That Minobe would not be brought to the bar was by no means assured. The announcement of the suspension of the prosecution and his unrepentant explanation of his resignation brought angry remonstrances from the service ministers, the reservist groups, and the Seiyukai. The extremist press unleashed anew its venomous clamor.[135] Kawashima and Osumi, under pressure from the supreme war council, accused Okada of reneging on the declaration of August 3.[136] They asserted that Minobe's demonstrated lack of contrition was intolerable. Kawashima told Okada that even if he were personally prepared to accept the government's action on Minobe, he could not do so publicly because of the attitude in the army and among the reservists.[137] The clarification extremists in the army were highly suspicious of the senior military officers who were in contact with the civil branches of the government, and who had the habit of "reversing themselves completely" under the influence of a conversation with Saionji or with other important personalities close to the throne.[137] The Seiyukai, represented by Yamamoto Teijiro, informed Okada that nothing less than the conviction of Minobe, Kanamori, and Ichiki would still that party's demands. Eto Genkuro filed new criminal charges against Minobe under the Publication Law, citing the newly published Hō no Honshitsu (July, 1935) as destructive of the existing form of government and as subversive of the constitution. The procurator general's office let it be known that it was reconsidering Minobe's case and that only "a prudent statement" from him could forestall an indictment.[138]

For a week it was expected daily that the cabinet might be toppled by the withdrawal of Kawashima and Osumi.[139] The government's position was saved only with difficulty even after Minobe made a further capitulation in the form of a letter sent to Ohara on September 20, which Ohara submitted to the press as part of his statement explaining the decision to drop the prosecution. According to Ohara's release, Minobe's letter had expressed great "regret that reports printed in newspapers on September 18 as a statement made by me caused fresh public discussion. My attitude, however, has not changed from what I stated to the Procurator and also in my previous letter to the Minister of Justice. As the newspaper report does not fully represent my true meaning, I wish to withdraw it."[140] In a cabinet meeting on September 25, Kawashima and Osumi forced the agreement to disclose the full truth concerning the correspondence between Minobe and Ohara. Presumably they wanted Minobe's letter of September 14 to be published along with identification of the various parties who were supposed to have advised him to write the several letters. They hoped, perhaps to show intervention in the judicial process by members of the imperial court.

Ozaki states that Minobe had been induced to write the second letter by the urgent counsel of a number of his friends. They had warned him of great personal danger should he persist in his self-vindication. They had pointed out to him the very difficult position in which he had put the ministry of justice. Ozaki claims that Minobe retracted his statement of September 18 because he did not want to see the ministry of justice thrown into the vortex of a political commotion.[141] Matsumoto Joji was mentioned in the papers as Minobe's adviser on this occasion and in connection with his resignation. Matsumoto, a personal friend and a professional colleague of Minobe, was further described as a go-between on behalf of Ohara.[142]

In spite of the cabinet decision on September 25, Ohara gave only limited satisfaction to the military demand. On September 27 he offered only this brief explanation:

At the second examination of Dr. Minobe by the procurators on September 14, he expressed sincere regret that his books had caused public disturbance, and stated that since March of this year he had been refusing to lecture at school or to write for newspapers or magazines. He also stated that he had been on good behavior since then, not even going out of his house except on urgent necessity, and he expressed the intention of devoting himself to his studies in the future, promising at the same time not to give lectures on the constitution, and also his determination to resign from the House of Peers at an opportune time.[143]

Ohara said that the letters from Minobe had been in Minobe's own hand and had been delivered by Minobe's son. He concluded with the assertion that "the Ministry of Justice will not make public anything more than the above explanation, to anyone, under whatever circumstances," and cited sections of the Criminal Code to justify his refusal to publish the correspondence.

THE SECOND CLARIFICATION

At the cabinet meeting of September 25 Kawashima and Osumi demanded that the government make unmistakably clear by a further official statement that it held the same view of national polity as that held by the military. They contended that the dilatory and equivocal handling of the Minobe case had thrown grave doubts on the sincerity of the August 3 declaration. Osumi went so far as to ask the cabinet to endorse the resolution on national polity adopted by the Congress of the Imperial Reservist Association on August 27. The pair also insisted that the government not only declare openly what measures toward clarification it intended to take but disclose fully just what had been done to date. They complained that much of the clarification policy of the home and education ministries had been executed so quietly that the public did not know that it was going on and were consequently confused as to the government's attitude and policy on the organ-theory problem.[144]

One of these demands was met when the government on October 1 issued a report on the education and home ministries' moves to eradicate the organ theory and to reaffirm the true national polity.[145] This was followed on November 4 by cabinet approval of the army's proposal to establish a "council for the renovation of thought." This body, consisting of a number of political, academic, military, business, and social personalities, was assigned the task of elaborating plans for the development of the Japanese spirit and the instruction of the people in the true principles of national polity.[146]

The fortnight beginning October 1 was consumed in the attempt of the government and the military to reach an agreement concerning the text of a second declaration on national polity meeting the third of the conditions laid down by Kawashima and Osumi on September 25.[147] The problem of bringing Okada and the military of the cabinet onto common ground (perhaps it would be more accurate to say common language covering their disparate grounds) was exceedingly difficult. A cabinet crisis threatened once again. The crux of the matter was the question of Ichiki's and Kanamori's retirement. Kawashima and Osumi had agreed to make no further specific references to these two gentlemen, but they seemed, albeit indirectly, still to be seeking their removal. They wanted an unequivocal affirmation of the supreme power of the emperor as well as specific outlawing of any theory holding the state to be the subject of sovereignty. The government was equally determined to avoid an attack on Ichiki and Kanamori, whether directly or obliquely. It sought therefore to limit the declaration to a denunciation of the organ theory, with no names mentioned.[148]

On October 15 the Second Declaration of Clarification of National Polity was promulgated by the government:

By expressing its conviction of the proper meaning of the national polity, the Government recently made clear the path to be followed by the nation, in the hope that its glory might be further exalted.

To begin with, the fact that the Emperor is the subject of sovereignty is a fundamental principle of Japan's national polity; it is the firm faith of all subjects of the Emperor, a conviction absolutely unshakable. The Government believes that herein lies the meaning of the Promulgation Edict and the articles of the Constitution.

Any theory which, merely on the basis of foreign examples, holds that the subject of sovereignty is not the Emperor but the state, and that the Emperor is an organ of the state—such as the so-called organ theory—must be strictly eradicated, for they run counter to our divine national polity and do great harm to its true conception. . . .[149]

Justice Minister Ohara, speaking to the press on the day it was published, emphasized that this declaration was not intended to give any particular interpretation to the constitution but to clarify fundamentals of national polity.[150]

The government's statement of October 15 constituted a clear victory of the military-renovationist forces over the remnants of the liberal constitutional regime. Through seven months of ruthless political bushwhacking and extortion, the army leaders had, not without peril to themselves, ridden the pseudo-constitutional issue of clarification and exploited the irrational passions of the headless and multiform fascist movement. They had weakened the civilian regime and finally forced from it official endorsement of the military-renovationist "correct" view of constitutional order.

But the significance of the victory was not explicit even in the Second Declaration of Clarification of National Polity, which was a prodigy of obscurity. It cried: *clarification of national polity!* But national polity was beyond rational explanation and analysis. To be sure, the declaration put an end to the government's long and tortuous retreat since the diet resolutions in March. To be sure, it demonstrated the futility of devious evasions and procrastinations. But the progeny was hardly less tortured than the labor, hardly less devious than its lineage. And indeed, no heredity, no gestative term could have produced a clarification of national polity beyond the ritual recitation of an article of faith, such as the government finally issued. The conception itself was an anomaly.

The brains behind the campaign for clarification were not ignorant of this difficulty. The anonymous general staff officer who wrote the army's pamphlet on interpretation of the constitution conceded that the concept of national polity was not scientifically grounded and exhorted scholars to correct that weakness. Moreover, the campaign for clarification was not, in the 1935 phase, a campaign to substitute a concrete alternative for the existing form of government. Ignoring occasional romantic references to such things as a return to the *Dajōkan* system, the cry was for the elimination of various more or less vaguely identified evils, all of which were linked to the institutions and politics of parliamentary party government.

It was easy to expose sacrilegious implications in Minobe's organ theory, the source of the only remaining respectable and authoritative intellectual defense of normal constitutional government. What was left when that view of the constitutional system had been discredited and suppressed was only some vague notion that the Imperial Constitution was simply a translation into modern legal form of the "ancient principle" of Japanese polity: "rule by the throne with the assistance of the people." And that was a formula that could mean anything or nothing. Minobe had not hesitated to expose it as a mask—historically a mask for oligarchic despotism. That he found it perfectly compatible with his idea of responsible, representative, civilian government simply demonstrated the vacuity of the formula.

What the military accomplished concretely by the declarations of August 3 and October 15 was, then, to establish that henceforth on all matters of defense the throne would rely exclusively upon the assistance of the general staffs, to affirm (or reaffirm, as the clarificators would insist) as constitutional doctrine (already for four years a fact) that the military determined the employment of the military power of the state, and that the government had only to back up the military initiative fiscally, economically, and diplomatically.[151]

But there was another dimension to the military's victory. Sweeping

away the corruption of constitutional liberalism and reëstablishing the
pure principles of the state's foundation in the public conscience
cleared the way for imposition of a new ultranationalistic authoritarian
order in Japan. While this aspect of the victory need not have fallen
to the military, the circumstances of the empire at this time ensured
that they would call the turns. More particularly those who emerged as
masters, were that element of the military whose leading part was known
as the Control Faction. The so-called "Second Purge of Ansei," culminating in Mazaki's previously mentioned removal, was a key move in
this regard. It represented a positive commitment to a continuing policy
of continental expansion and away from the plebeian radicalism to
which the Imperial Way Faction had catered. With their violent renovationist drive the young officers, reservists, and civilian counterparts had
supplied a club with which the army had browbeaten the government,
but the radicals knew that the October declaration was no victory for
them.[152] In the months ahead they diverted their energies into the agitation surrounding the Aizawa trial, until in the aftermath of the February
émeute their leaders were suppressed and the Control Faction assumed
unchallenged hegemony in the army which moved then to fasten its
despotism on the state.[153] The national polity theme continued large
in the view of the army even after the liquidation of the young officer-
Imperial Way threat. This was indicated by Kawashima's successor,
General Terauchi, who advised the cabinet in November, 1936: "(1)
That we should push forward in the development of our own peculiar
constitutionalism, acting as far as possible in accordance with the true
principles of our national polity and the essence of our Imperial Constitution. (2) That the Imperial Diet be properly restricted in its actions
to the scope of authority established for it by the constitution."[154]

CLEANSING THE ACADEMIC STABLE

One aspect of the Minobe Affair deserves further notice here—the extension of the purge of the organ theory throughout the higher school
system. As the preceding chronicle has indicated, much of the burden
of administrative implementation of the government's clarification policy, beginning with the decision of the cabinet on March 30, fell upon
the ministry of education. There is nothing surprising in this, for the
universities—the natural and almost exclusive habitat of the offensive

theory—along with the rest of the state educational system were recognized as an important instrument for the inculcation of the authoritarian, nationalistic tenets of a militarized society.

The problem of exorcizing the organ theory fell within the competence of the thought bureau (*shisō kyoku*), which had been established in the ministry of education in June, 1934. In spite of the complaints from the right concerning the government's inaction, the fact is that a thorough purging of the academic field was going on between March and November, 1935. Thirty-two textbook titles by sixteen authors (not including Minobe), all recent or current authorities in the field of public law, were ordered suppressed.[155] But clearing the library and bookshop shelves of the condemned literature was only part of the story. It was also necessary to police the form and content of public-law classrooms against the deliberate or unconscious intrusion of the proscribed doctrines. This was a more ticklish task requiring continuing vigilance. It was carried out by the thought bureau systematically and thoroughly, with a mixture of crudity and subtlety. Administrative orders and instructions to academic administrators piled up. Repeated demands for reports accounting for the progress made in their institutions kept the administrators on their toes. Professors' and students' lecture notes were reviewed. Observers attended lectures unannounced.

The desired result was achieved without dismissal of personnel.[156] There were, to be sure, some instances, mostly involving more prominent professors, when indefinite suspension from teaching constitutional law was ordered, notably in the cases of Watanabe Sotaro at Kyushu Imperial University[157] and Sasaki Sōichi at the Kobe University of Commerce.[158] Among those who were temporarily suspended from teaching constitutional law were Tabata Shinobu at Doshisha; Nakajima Shige at Kansai Gaku-in; Nomura Junji, Nakano Tomio, and Nakamura Yasaji at Waseda; Asai Kyoshi at Keio; Kawamura Matakai at Kyushu Imperial; and Miyazawa Toshiyoshi at To-Dai.[159] Miyazawa was in the particularly difficult position of being a prominent student of Minobe and his direct successor at To-Dai. Two of his books were on the proscription list; he had already been displaced on the higher civil service examination board.[160] In most cases suspensions were lifted upon evidence of compliance with ministry instructions, which usually involved correction of the lecture syllabus, assignment of new textbooks, and specific adjuration of the organ theory or of "radical democratic ideas."

It is said that Miyazawa's lectures on the constitution after 1935 "skipped" the section on sovereignty.[161]

The thought bureau papers present an unbroken record of "voluntary" (or at any rate passive) conformance with the ministry's clarification policy. One of the notable features of this process was the celerity and thoroughness and silence with which the academic world went about the business of purging itself of all offense to the government. Nakamura Akira has given this impression, reflecting his own experiences, of the atmosphere which prevailed from that time:

At Tokyo Imperial University I heard Dr. Minobe's lectures before he retired. When I graduated the Manchurian Incident had already occurred. When I began teaching on the constitution at Taihoku (Taipeh) Imperial University, Dr. Minobe had already been persecuted by the militarists for his emperor-organ theory. . . . Freedom of discussion ended at that time. . . . My lectures fell under control and political supervision, both tangible and intangible. For almost ten years from 1937 the life of the lecture platform was very trying. There was a rash of interpretations to deal with the many unclear points of the Meiji Constitution. They were not treated as academic issues but were disposed of by political authority. . . .[162]

Hasegawa Masayasu says that 1935 was the beginning of a period of general drying up of scholarly inquiry, that the only important or lasting development in constitutional theory after the clarification campaign was the introduction of the doctrines of Carl Schmidt.[163]

Perhaps this sweeping and apparently unresisted overturning of prevailing academic doctrine needs no explanation beyond recalling the atmosphere of the time and the defenseless position of the universities in respect to governmental interference. Certainly it cannot be assumed that all university professors were indifferent to what was happening. But the battle for intellectual freedom for the teacher and for institutional autonomy of the universities had already been lost. Indeed academic freedom had never been strong. Even during 1920–1928, when freedom of thought was officially affirmed for the higher schools, socialists and democrats were driven from the faculties of the public universities. By 1928 hardly a progressive of the Yoshino Sakuzo stamp was left in the universities. They had been removed by administrative process or driven to resignation by official policies of repression and by social, professional, and political harassment. When Hatoyama pushed through the ouster of Professor Takikawa in 1933, the pretense of university autonomy was discarded. Sasaki and a few others resigned in protest, but they did not save Takikawa or move university faculties elsewhere to do any more than voice sympathy and register protest.

There was no doubt additional embarrassment for professors of public law in 1935. If they would resist the purge, the issue upon which they would have to stand was the organ-theory question. While there was considerable endorsement of Minobe's interpretation of the Meiji Constitution and widespread if superficial acceptance of the state personality—organ theory basis of it, many academic authorities had serious reservations concerning the organ theory *per se*. Some had rejected it, in some cases on grounds of the Kelsenian critique, more commonly on the ground that its state-centered character was basically hostile to true democratic development. But neither of these reasons for rejecting the organ theory could be urged to any avail in 1935. Miyazawa has said in regard to this problem:

it is very clear that [the organ theory issue of 1935] was a purely political question. It was not a question of the theoretical validity . . . the question was whether that theory was contrary to national polity, and whether those who asserted it were subversive. There were, however, many at that time who challenged the theoretical soundness of the emperor-organ theory and many who understood that Anglo-Saxon theory completely refuted the necessity of the concept of state personality. I myself discerned at an early date that the organ theory was vulnerable to theoretical criticism, and at that time I was actually thinking of writing a criticism of it. But this affair arose and the organ theory was strongly attacked as being contrary to national polity, and so I changed my plans. A regrettable thing about that affair was that it made the organ theory contrary to national polity, and that was the issue that had to be argued. . . .[164]

This is a statement made long after the events, and in the context of a different dispute, but it may be assumed that it fairly describes a difficulty experienced by others at the time.

The Aftermath

The government's declaration of October 15 ended the first phase of the clarification movement; it also ended the Minobe Affair. The few scattered incidents of the succeeding five months traceable back to the Minobe controversy were anticlimactic. Their significance was overshadowed by the matters of greater interest then afoot.

Minobe's resignation from the house of peers, under the cloud of a charitably suspended indictment, made the surrender of their offices by a number of other bureaucratic personages inevitable. That they did not leave their posts immediately was due simply to the desire of the inner court circles to avoid the appearance of duress.[165] Makino was the first to go, giving up the position of lord privy seal to Saito late in December on grounds of ill health.[166] On January 7 Kanamori left the cabinet legislative bureau.[167] Ichiki resigned the presidency of the privy council in March, at the time of the formation of the Hirota Cabinet. It was at that time, too, that Ohara paid the price for his stout services on the firing line, for General Terauchi made it one of the conditions of his entering the new cabinet that Ohara be excluded.[168]

Minobe ceased to be "news" after mid-October, but he did not escape the attention of the bullies and censors of the extremist groups. The closing weeks of 1935 must have been harrowing for him. Ozaki's story gives this impression of his circumstances: Minobe remained under police protection at his residence, which he transferred in November from Takehayacho to suburban Kichijoji. Uniformed police patrolled the street before his house constantly, a precaution induced by abusive and threatening letters addressed to him daily. His regular companions were his wife and son; most of his old social acquaintances had seen little of him since April. Even Mochizuki Keisuke, who remained close to Minobe through the summer, found it necessary to avoid open contact with him after he became Okada's minister of communications in October.[169]

The atmosphere in Tokyo at the new year was explosive. The violence of the renovationist attack on the "military-bureaucratic-capitalist clique" mounted to a new pitch under the stimulus of the Aizawa trial. Simultaneously, civil and military police carried out ruthless extralegal suppression of all forms of agitation and extreme expression. The metropolis' garrison division, known by the police to be a hotbed of renovationist sentiment, was restive under orders for transfer to the continent. Meanwhile the nation experienced the excitement of a general election, the Sixty-eighth Diet having been dissolved on January 21 as a result of a Seiyukai resolution of nonconfidence, which cited the failure of the government's clarification program as a major cause of dissatisfaction. On February 20 eleven million voters went to the polls.[170]

On February 21 the morning papers carried the news of the surprising defeat of the Seiyukai. A substantial plurality of the voters had thrown their support behind the Okada Government and thus to the Minseito.[171] On that morning Minobe was assaulted in his home by a young man who gained entrance in the guise of a former student, shot Minobe in the leg, and subsequently wounded one of the police guards before he was captured. Minobe's wound was not serious but he was confined for some days at the Imperial University Hospital, where, as a precaution against further molestation, he was secretly quartered in the children's ward. The press was not informed of his whereabouts. Only his wife and son and a few intimate friends visited him there. In that asylum he was undisturbed by the commotion on February 26.[172] The bungled attempt on Minobe's life was doubtless a direct consequence of the flood of abusive and incendiary references to him in the literature of the right, although no evidence brought out at the culprit's trial linked his action to any organized conspiracy. It was, apparently, the self-planned and self-executed gesture of an unstable and insecure person inspired by the railings of the pamphleteers.

So far as the leaders of the renovation movement were concerned, further attack on Minobe was hardly necessary. The *kaminagara* madness had more or less accomplished its goals when the government conceded to the clarification program. The substance if not the form of the demand for Minobe's crucifixion had been realized when his theory was specifically and officially denounced and when he had been forced to resign all his official and professional dignities. In the course of the ten years following 1935 Minobe lived out his enforced retirement in the seclusion of his study at home. The surcease of notoriety was interrupted only slightly and incidentally as a consequence of his son's troubles with the political police. True to his pledges to Ohara, he directed his writing away from politically controversial subjects. There was, of course, no call for his presence on the academic or public rostrum. His removal from public life was total. The clarification forces, and perhaps he himself, must have thought it was also permanent.

VIII

Postscript: Minobe and the New Constitution

The last three years of Minobe's life coincided with the opening years of the period of important constitutional change in Japan following World War II. Viewed as an effort to span the constitutional void of the era of fascistic military despotism, his brief but active postwar career appears quite unimpressive—it was indeed quite barren of the fruits of doctrinal vindication. Within six months of the war's end, the whirlwind of the Occupation had destroyed not merely the flesh but the very frame of the old order. The gulf which Minobe sought to bridge proved to be one of such dimensions that his devices and formulas were hardly operative. The leap of events seemed to have left him in a peculiar limbo of anachronistic good intentions. The old champion of relatively advanced liberal constitutionalism found the promise of realization shattered by the postwar explosion of radical, legal and institutional reform. The new forces moved by different paths and far outdistanced the bounds of his earlier thinking.

But the inutility of outdated views did not necessarily imply that their erstwhile champion, too, was beyond the pale. As a matter of fact, Minobe was not content to accept the role of relic. He neither passively surrendered the field nor retreated from it in indignation, but came to affirm positively the revolutionary character of the new era. Once the die was cast, he attempted to apply to the new constitution his rigorous interpretive analysis. To be sure, there were still serious limitations on the significance of his efforts, which were in any case quite short-lived. But, quite independent of Minobe's own activities, echoes of his constitutional theory were manifestly influential in the postwar attitude of the Japanese government and of the major political parties in the making of the new constitution, in its interpretation, and in respect to the later issue of its revision. Indeed, Minobe has come to enjoy posthumously a renewed, somewhat equivocal appreciation in the literature of constitutional theory since 1955.

This postscript consists first of a brief narration of the conspicuous and meaningful events of Minobe's life between capitulation of Japan in August, 1945, and his death in May, 1948. There follows an assessment of his relationship to the revision of the Imperial Constitution and an evaluation based on consideration of selected issues in that revision.[1] It is possible to advance in closing only a sketchy and tentative response to the indicated line of inquiry into the influence of Minobe's ideas in the post-Occupation debate on constitutional revision.

Minobe Returns to Action

Release from professional and civil disability came swiftly for Minobe in October, 1945. Under pressure from headquarters (SCAP), the Japanese government repealed by ordinance the statutes and ordinances restricting speech, press, assembly, and association, and set in motion the restoration to the educational system of the academic purgees of the preceding decade and a half. On October 10 the minister of education announced a new liberal educational policy which would permit, among other things, the investigation of various constitutional theories not inconsistent with Article I of the still operative Meiji Constitution. He stated that his ministry disowned the "narrowminded view" that the organ theory of the state was contrary to national polity and promised a speedy displacement of pro-militarists from the educational system.[2]

Minobe reëntered the arena of constitutional debate with alacrity, "bursting forth in scholarly activity as water from a broken dam."[3] Before the year was out he had arranged with his publishers for the reissuing of three of his prewar books, notably the celebrated *Kempō Satsuyō*.[4] It was not, however, until the last quarter of 1946 that his pen resumed its erstwhile feverish pace, for he was chiefly concerned

with public affairs and official duties during the closing months of 1945
and through the summer of 1946.

Within three weeks of the end of the war, Minobe's name was publicly associated with the abortive effort of Hatoyama Ichiro to establish a new, anti-militarist, constitutionally liberal, politically and economically conservative party cutting across prewar party lines. Minobe
and Miyazawa were among a group of journalists, academicians, and
businessmen, hitherto unattached to and critical of the old parties, who
participated in the organizational phases of this movement as advisors.[5]
How active a part Minobe played in the councils of this group is not
disclosed by the sources cited here. In any case, there is no evidence
that he maintained connections with Hatoyama when in October,
1945, the latter's efforts turned to the narrower goal of establishing the
Liberal Party as successor to elements of the prewar Seiyukai. By then
Minobe had been called to the first of his several official appointments,
none of which appear to have involved partisan commitment. On constitutional questions there was, however, considerable compatibility
between Minobe's views and those of the Liberals at that time. With
some overlapping of tenure, he moved from the cabinet committee
for investigating constitutional problems, to the privy council, to the
prime minister's screening (political purge) committee.

On October 24, 1945, Minobe was appointed advisor to the cabinet
committee for the investigation of constitutional questions (Naikaku
Kempō Mondai Chōsa I-inkai) established by the Shidehara Cabinet
on that date.[6] Existing solely on the basis of a cabinet understanding
without formal authority, this committee was commonly known by
the name of its chairman, Minister of State Matsumoto Joji, who himself selected the original membership. Although Matsumoto continued
in his post as minister of state through the life of the Shidehara Cabinet, the committee dissolved without notice following its meeting on
February 2, 1946.[7] The record presented by Satō Tatsuo shows that
Minobe participated actively in the plenary sessions of the Matsumoto
committee.[8] One week prior to the final session of that committee the
cabinet nominated Minobe to the privy council.[9] His willingness to
participate in the affairs of this bureaucratic agency, which he had once

so sharply criticized, is probably to be understood in terms of his interest in personal vindication and his sense of obligation to service. Moreover, he had a professional interest in the reform or extinction of the council. We may assume that he was not immune to the appeal of a chance to continue his connection with the momentous and decisive constitutional action now clearly in prospect. The only other channel through which he might have satisfied this interest, the house of peers, was presumably closed to him by considerations of face.[10]

Since the proceedings of the council were not normally published, Minobe's role in its business (His appointment lasted until the extinction of the council with the expiration of the Imperial Constitution in May, 1947.) is not known in detail. His active attendance upon privy council business probably was limited to his service on the council's committee to investigate the draft revision of the Imperial Constitution, which functioned between mid-April and early June and again in October, 1946. Of that committee's proceedings and of the council's plenary sessions acting on its reports we do have an official record.[11] From these, it appears that Minobe was an articulate member of the committee, that he harassed Matsumoto and Shidehara with questions and critical comments regarding the government's draft revision, that he voted alone against approval of the draft in committee, and that he abstained alone in the plenary session of the council which approved the draft for presentation to the diet. It shows also that he took no part in the proceedings when the diet-amended draft revision was brought back to the council in October before submission for imperial sanction and promulgation.

On July 1, 1946, Minobe took up his duties as chairman of the public officials suitability screening committee (*Kōshoku Tekihi Shinsa I-inkai*) newly created in the office of the prime minister. This committee operated for six months until it was superseded by new screening machinery in January, 1947. During this period it reviewed the qualifications of nearly 9,000 higher officials. This review was part of the procedure for removing or barring from public office persons who fell under the terms of the SCAP directive in January 1946 to eradicate militarist and ultranationalist influence from the governmental and political arenas. The bulk of this work was completed early in August, 1946, and cannot have imposed a serious burden upon Minobe in the last quarter of the year.[12]

Minobe's service on the screening committee constituted a bridge between the first and second phases of his postwar career. With the clearance of the government's draft revision through the privy council in June, 1946, he was faced with the fact that Japan was to have a new and radically different constitution and that public-law commentary and argument in the future would be based upon a fundamental law entirely different from that which had constituted the basis of his life's work. By early autumn he was totally engrossed in the tremendous effort to rewrite his major public law commentaries on the basis of the new constitution, a grand project with which he had only barely come to grips when illness and death intervened.

In the twelve-month period to April, 1948, Minobe published four books on the new constitution.[13] He apparently conceived of these works as being the successor to his major commentaries on the Imperial Constitution.[14] But they were successors only in a formal sense, for these postwar volumes are thin copies of their prototypes (except in the case of *Nihonkoku Kempō Genron*, which is a fair remaking of *Kempō Satsuyō*). The rather disappointing result is easily enough explained: the gamut of his interests was too diverse, the span of his days was too brief. He could not begin writing on the new constitution until the autumn of 1946 and early in 1948 he fell ill. His illness imposed increasing limits on his capacity until the end. Even had he been well and single purposed in this period, he could hardly have surmounted the shallowness of experience, the lack of precedents, that plagued all attempts to explain or interpret the still unfleshed skeleton of new constitutional order in Japan. Minobe himself was well aware of these limitations.[15] But he seems not to have felt it in the least incongruous to apply the method and viewpoint of the *Staatsrechtslehre* to the new constitution. In any case, all of these volumes except the *Nihonkoku Kempō Genron* soon passed out of currency, having been shortly superseded by a stream of more substantial and up-to-date commentaries.[16]

In the hectic, groping days of 1947–1948, however, these "stop-gap" publications by Minobe compared favorably with all that were being produced. They undoubtedly performed an important service in providing initial orientation of scholars and officials who had to come to terms with this new charter of obscure origin, unclear principles, strange language, and peculiar structure. At the same time and by the same token, Minobe's works helped to ensure that the theoretic and analytic view of the new constitutional system among officials and academicians would proceed from the familiar juristic premises of the passing order.[17] Ikeda Masaaki observes that immediately following the making of the constitution and up until the reawakening of interest in methodological issues (around 1955), "there was need for explanation and interpretation of its text and for clarification of fundamental theory based on such interpretation. In this first, interpretative period, the superior work of Minobe and Sasaki cannot be ignored. In spite of the 180-degree turn which the making of the new constitution meant, they were able to construct an interpretive democratic theory with many points of reference for the instruction of later students. But these works had limits which were soon transcended in the publications of succeeding scholars."[18] Nakamura Akira, whose approach to constitutional interpretation is closely related to Minobe's, directs his approbation to the political quality of Minobe's postwar commentaries: "Being systematic expositions, they were above the level of the mass of pamphlet-type commentaries. Their strength among all these lay in the positively democratic affirmation which characterized his exposition."[19]

Takayanagi Kenzō, writing in 1949, was rather more reserved in his commendation:

I do not, of course deny the value of the analytic or deductive method in the interpretation of law. It adequately serves to meet the requirement of a logical, straightforward ordering and executive of the new constitution and related new laws. In the interpretation of the new constitution normative similarities and differences between it and the Meiji Constitution are often indicated. This, indeed, makes sense. I am one who greatly admires the speed with which the great Meiji constitutional authority, Minobe Tatsukichi, after the war hastened to publish his *Nihonkoku Kempō Genron*. We should be thankful for his contribution to the understanding of the new constitution and how it differs from the old which jurists gain from it. But even Minobe Tatsukichi had no time to consider at length the Anglo-American background of the new constitution. He has employed the traditional way of thinking under the Meiji Constitution and has simply recited an analysis of the provisions of the new constitution with a tendency to distort its meaning. . . .[20]

This passage is cited at length because it points up an aspect of the criticism of the interpretive juristic method then current but later more or less to disappear, at least in explicit terms, namely, the designation of British and American legal and political theory and experience as the source of real insight into the philosophy of the new order.

As a matter of fact, Minobe's postwar writing did extend to the publication of an introduction to the American constitution in May, 1947.[21] In the preface to this book he said that its publication was a response to the fact that "with the establishment and putting into operation of our new constitution, democracy has been newly made the basis of our constitution and the public [has] become accordingly very much interested in the Constitution of the United States, which stands in the vanguard of democratic states." But the book was not a very helpful contribution to the need which he defined, for it was a very thin work physically and intellectually.

In the spring of 1948 Minobe completed the manuscript of an exposition of the electoral law, which was published posthumously.[22] He continued, moreover, his earlier practice of writing for the journals and newspapers, notably with articles in October, 1945, and in May, 1946, on the question of constitutional revision, a matter with which he was at the time officially engaged.[23] And following the diet's affirmative action on the draft revision of the constitution, Minobe wrote a number of articles dealing with problems of constitutional and administrative law. The last of these, an article on administrative appeals, had first been drafted as a chapter of a never-completed revision of his principal textbook on administrative law.[24]

Minobe died at his home on May 23, 1948, engaged in writing almost to the last minute. A requiem ceremony was conducted by the law faculty at Tokyo University (the former Tokyo Imperial University) on May 29.[25] His passing was the occasion for the appearance of eulogistic notices and commemorative essays in various academic and professional journals.

In Defense of the Imperial Constitution

Circumstantially and on the basis of his published views, Minobe is identified with the effort made in the early period of the Occupation to preserve the Meiji Constitution. The first notice he gave of how he stood on the question of constitutional revision came in an interview reported by the Associated Press correspondent, Charles Spencer, on October 13, 1945.

It has always been my belief that since the Japanese Constitution is quite laconic, if it were properly executed it would present no obstacle to democratic government. Accordingly I do not believe that revision of the constitution is now necessary. It is only a matter of interpretation and good intentions. The only difficulty would be from certain forces that try to make of it a mystical thing. If it comes to amendments, then I think care must be taken to avoid its degenerating into an unscholarly, vulgar debate. For this reason I have seen no purpose in my intervening. . . . If the decision is made to amend the constitution then we can only get on with it, giving it our best. . . .[26]

A few days later, on the eve of the announcement of his appointment to the Matsumoto committee, he elaborated on this argument in an article running in a metropolitan daily:[27] Revision of the constitution is not necessary, he declared, for democratization can be achieved by amending the laws and ordinances governing the diet, the house of peers, elections, the administrative departments, local government, and so on. The validity of this assertion is evident, he went on, to anyone who keeps in mind the distinction that ought to be made regarding the term "constitution," between its *real* sense and its *formal* sense, likewise between the *formal* (legal) and the *real* (political) sense of the term "democracy." A constitution in the real sense is not necessarily in agreement with what is actually provided in the formal constitution. He told his readers that many things which are part of the real constitution are not described in the formal; on the other hand much of the real constitution is based on laws, ordinances and actual political practice. As for democracy, in its formal sense it is absolutely incompatible with monarchy, but politically it can be fully realized under monarchy, as, for example in England. It ought to be understood that when there is talk of democratizing the constitution what is meant is the real constitution and political democracy. Emphasis is not on legal formalities but on the actual ordering of government. Democracy in this sense requires no change in the formal constitution.

Of course, Minobe went on, Japan's real constitution for the past several years had been undemocratic and unliberal. It was only natural that aliens not familiar with the Japanese constitutional system should assume that the Imperial Constitution was at fault, when in fact the evils of these years were the result of bad government, bad laws, and perversion of the true spirit of the Imperial Constitution. Indeed, the chief difficulties of the past could be summed up under four headings: (1) militarism in government and politics, (2) the diet's loss of influence, (3) the suppression of popular liberties, and (4) the prevalence of a narrow and mystical concept of national polity.

The militaristic perversions were traceable, Minobe observed, in part to extraconstitutional ordinances, but chiefly to extralegal military interference in politics and the employment of military force against the opponents of militarism. The diet lost its power directly as a result of the use of terror against its members and of the corruption of the electoral process. It was true, to be sure, that the diet had "more or less restricted powers in comparison with the parliaments of other states. But these restrictions are not serious, and ... it will not be difficult to correct their consequences by developing proper political habits in respect to their application." From this bland piety he went on to the patent recognition that "It will of course be necessary to eradicate those erroneous interpretations of the past which have supported autocratic, despotic government under the color of the assertion of a paramount and unlimited imperial prerogative, and especially those which have asserted that the diet can have no part in the exercise of the prerogative." For the restoration of the liberties of the people, Minobe felt that there should be, in addition to the abolition of such obnoxious legislation as the Peace Preservation Law, a general reform of administrative and judicial procedures aimed at abatement of the prevailing officialism (*kankenshugi*). The diet should participate in the deliberations on this reform. Finally, there being no basis in the constitution for the mystical concept of national polity, freedom of expression and of honest academic inquiry would surely sound the death knell of this troublesome doctrine.

Even if it should be deemed desirable to amend the Meiji Constitution in order to ensure its democratization, this was not the time for such action, Minobe maintained. The unsettled conditions of late 1945 were not at all suitable to the serious business of constitution-making. The future of the nation should not be staked upon the sort of hasty and passionate decisions which these conditions would elicit. Therefore, he advised, the question of revision should be postponed until order has been restored in Japan.

Judging from these statements, the government can have had few qualms about the recruitment of Minobe to the service of the Matsumoto committee. The congeniality of his views to them was quite evident. Indeed, the Occupation authorities came to believe that Matsumoto's reliance upon Minobe was close.[28] It appears from the record of the Matsumoto committee that this suspicion was not altogether unwarranted. In the first plenary session of the committee, when the question of the scope of the investigation was under consideration, Minobe took a position fundamentally at odds with that of councilor Nomura, a position which he incorporated in a memorandum which he submitted to the committee on November 8.[29]

The issue between them was this: Nomura felt that compliance with the Potsdam terms would require immediate adjustment of the constitution to the demilitarization of the state and the democratization of the government, and that an effort to deal with these particular points rather than a general revision should be the committee's purpose. Minobe, on the other hand, seconded Matsumoto's view that the committee should not limit itself to satisfying the Potsdam terms but should study each article with hitherto arising doubts and questions in mind. It would be foolish to engage in hasty or ill-considered change to meet condition, such as demilitarization, of a purely temporary nature, said Minobe. It could only give rise to some such fatuity as making Article I to read: "The Empire of Japan is ruled by an Emperor who is under the direction of the Allied Powers." If the committee were to proceed under political pressure for undue speed then he would want to resign. He agreed with Matsumoto that since the Potsdam Declaration left it to the freely expressed will of the Japanese people there was no need to tamper with Articles I–IV (the *kokutai* articles) "for the Japanese people were as firm as mountains in their absolute support of the emperor system." In his memorandum to the committee, Minobe wrote: "In order to establish a new Japan and reform the sentiments of the people should we not rather set about a total revision?" This would mean careful study of each article not to be undertaken carelessly or precipitately.

Matsumoto indicated that he hoped to find a middle way between the "extremes" represented by Minobe and Nomura. It is uncertain what important influence Minobe's ideas may have had on the draft which Matsumoto subsequently reported to the cabinet for approval

and which was viewed by MacArthur and his aides as being so unprogressive as to require SCAP's direct intervention in drafting a new
revision.[30] The Matsumoto draft was certainly different in detail, and,
if anything, rather more inclined to cleave to the received constitution
than were the proposals made to the committee by Minobe. Both were
notably conservative in the sense that changes, when proposed, were
aimed at meeting old problems and not at the development of the
revolutionary potentials of the present moment.[31]

MINOBE AND THE CONSTITUTIONAL LOYALISTS

Judgment as to the meaning of Minobe's adherence to the constitutional loyalist cause in the October-March period must depend on the
meaning assigned to that cause. There can be little doubt that the
government's approach to constitutional reform was dilatory and evasive between early October, when the subject was first broached by
the supreme commander, and mid-February when the Japanese "jeep-
way" to revision was rudely discarded in favor of the direct and rapid
"airway" approach of the Americans.[32] The procrastination of the Shidehara Cabinet was doubtlessly due in part to the government's—and
the diet's—lack of a political mandate prior to the general elections of
April, 1946. The imperial commissions ostentatiously displayed by Higashikuni and Shidehara hardly constituted adequate basis for political
initiative. Moreover, from December, 1945, both the cabinet and the
diet were wracked by the SCAP-directed purges. Public opinion on the
constitutional issue was very narrowly based and was being activated
very slowly. Demobilization and rehabilitation problems were greatly
preoccupying; it was simple for the public to "put rice before the constitution, never thinking to find rice through the constitution."[33] And
Occupation officials, until February, 1946, held closely to the directive
of the American government that democratization was to be supported
and encouraged but not imposed. Even after General MacArthur ordered rejection of the Matsumoto draft on February 1, the urgency
of revision and the reasons for the urgency were communicated only
quite ambiguously to the Japanese government and not at all to the
Japanese public.[34]

These factors tend to be overlooked or to be treated lightly in the
emphasis often given to the government's effort to preserve the im-

perial institution as enshrined in the opening articles of the Meiji Constitution, a purpose signaled in the penultimate free decision of the imperial regime, its decision to offer acceptance of the terms of the Potsdam Declaration, "with the understanding that the said Declaration does not comprise any demand which prejudices the prerogatives of His Majesty as Sovereign Ruler."[35] The desire to preserve the social fabric of Japan—believed to be tied inextricably to the imperial system —against the revolutionary spectre of bolshevism had provided a primary impulse to surrender without an ultimate test of arms. To be sure, the social order which the government wished to save reserved great power and privilege to its members and the traditional ruling class generally. The triangular relationship between their interest, the threat to that interest, and the protective aegis of the throne was stated by Hatoyama Iichiro at the organization session of the Liberal Party in November, 1945: "We must do our utmost to preserve the emperor system, attack proletarian dictatorship, and support the system of private property."[36]

This continued, if slightly reformulated dedication to the national polity theme burdened the political mentality of government leaders well into the opening months of the Occupation. Many seem to have construed it as their chief purpose to keep the performance of the Potsdam obligations within the pattern of the Meiji Constitution, going only so far and only in such form as was consistent with it. They seem to have thought that by resuming their prewar image as lovers of things English and American they would be able to retain exclusive control over carrying out the Potsdam terms.[37]

But it would be a mistake to read into their common service to the cause of national polity a unity of view as to how and to what purpose they should proceed. As the rapidly shifting teams of custodians fumbled toward adjustment to the revolutionary realities of the post-surrender period, the national polity theme shifted variously. Assertions in its behalf were subdued; it was disguised under progressively more strained and subtle definition. This transformation came about under pressure of forces external to the government and persisted through successive changes in the political balance within the government. But whatever those alterations, the banner of national polity did continue to be honored in some measure by virtually every political camp in the country. It remained, in whatever variant, in whatever disguise, the *sine qua non* of political aspiration. There was a wide gulf in general political outlook and purpose between the regimes of Suzuki and Higashikuni on the one hand and that of Yoshida Shigeru on the other, and a still wider gulf between those and the aspirations of the Social Democrats. But all were committed in one degree or another to the preservation of the throne as the keystone of national ideology.

When all due allowance has been made for the catholicity of the appeal of the Meiji monarchy, there still stands against the Japanese government under Prince Higashikuni and Baron Shidehara the charge made by Occupation authorities, and by some Japanese writers then and since, that its approach to political reform was thoroughly reactionary. Some have seen in the enduring unprogressive attitude of the government a pervasive anti-democratic political bias. Most darkly, the approach to reform was condemned as mere camouflage for a temporarily submerged authoritarian right which sought to hold intact the constitutional basis for eventual revival of oligarchic dictatorship. Alternatively, it was believed that the government, if not actually motivated by reactionary political objectives, at least represented privileged elements in Japanese society who recognized as the greatest threat to their interests the social radicalism of the left and who now, as in the past, were more willing to risk the hazards of the authoritarian right than those of radical democratic social politics. In the least unsympathetic terms, the government was seen as aspiring to a kind of Victorian, middle-class, liberal parliamentary order and believing its realization possible under the Meiji Constitution. Others, looking more narrowly at the composition of the Matsumoto committee and the Shidehara Cabinet, have seen in the stubborn conservatism of these men the psychology and interest of academic and bureaucratic legalists, who were by instinct and indoctrination disposed to appreciation of the bureaucratic monarchy, to resentment and suspicion of democratic encroachments on areas of high policy, and to serious myopia regarding the actual political forces at work behind the struggles over constitutional theory.[38]

In any case, it is clear enough that the ruling strata were unable to approach constitutional reform positively. Even under prodding by General MacArthur they were content to try "to patch things up with the antique and obscure Matsumoto draft," which SCAP officials described as even more conservative than the most conservative of the unofficial revision proposals.[39]

If these three broad categories of motivation are accepted as adequate, it appears that Minobe cannot be identified with any of them except to some degree, perhaps, with the last. In any case, it is not necessary to look for remote or complex causes for there is sufficient explanation of his behavior in the subjective factors of personal and professional commitment. Minobe had always held the historical constitution, the imperial monarchy, in the highest esteem. He undoubtedly had a sentimental attachment to the Imperial Constitution.[40] The very essence of Minobeism was its attempt to accommodate the traditional monarchical institution with the logic of its marriage to modern western constitutionalism. If there was a suspicion of hypocrisy in the *jushin*'s recourse to "normal constitutional government" in 1945, there could be no such suspicions of Minobe's sentiments.

Indeed, Minobe anticipated in the return to regular civil government the vindication of his own constitutional position.[41] Minobe had staked —and sacrificed—his whole career upon a liberal interpretation of the Meiji Constitution. He had now witnessed the utter dispersal of the forces which had prevailed against "normal constitutional government" and against himself. Why should he now anticipate that fulfillment of Japan's surrender would require renunciation of the Meiji charter? There was every reason to suppose the interpretation he had placed on that constitution now had good prospects of flourishing. As he saw it, satisfaction of every requirement laid down by the Potsdam Declaration could be accomplished within that interpretation. Thus, he was hardly disposed to see the necessity or desirability of shifting the basis of constitutional development to new and unknown ground. The suggestion that amendment was necessary was a challenge to his lifelong contention that a constitutional parliamentary democracy was entirely possible on the basis of the existing constitution. All this considered, it is not necessary—indeed it would be a mistake—to see in Minobe's resistance to revision a demonstration of reactionary or antidemocratic political purpose.[42]

What, then, of the notion that, however much Minobe deserved his prewar reputation as a liberal, his stand on his old position was, in the revolutionary context of 1945–1946, objectively retrogressive, that his arguments in defense of his position gave aid and comfort to essentially anti-democratic forces, and that his narrowly legalistic view of the constitutional problem exposed an essentially undemocratic, bureaucratic preference?

As we have seen, he had been able even before 1935 to advance his progressive interpretation of the Meiji Constitution only by finding in it a greater affinity for liberalism and democracy than other competent authorities would admit was there to find. Friends of democracy might then have counted his reifying powers a valuable aid to their cause, but can it be reckoned so in the face of the revolutionary opportunities of 1946? If all that was required was reaffirmation of the "Taisho Revolution" and the spirit of "normal constitutional government," then one might indeed ask, why revise the constitution? But had it not now become the role of the truly enlightened liberal to seek constitutional affirmation of the legitimacy of popular sovereignty and the reconstitution of the monarchy in the spirit of the New Year Rescript?

His statements against revision of the Imperial Constitution and his association with the Matsumoto committee have earned for Minobe classification as one of "those representatives of the prewar, so-called liberal school whose postwar activities symbolize their political limitations."[43] SCAP believed him to be the source of the constitutional doctrines espoused by the government, most of them quite obstructive of the Occupation's purposes concerning constitutional reform.[44] Professor Hasegawa has taken Minobe's statement of October 20 and several articles written by Kanamori before he became minister of state to represent the "true disposition of the Shidehara Cabinet." At the same time Hasegawa has recognized that Minobe's reluctant admission that revision might yet be thought necessary contained the seeds of the divergence between Minobe and the government that within a relatively short time led Minobe to abandon to the government, to Kanamori in particular, the "Minobe school's" attitude of negation and resistance.[45]

While the existence of some connection between Minobe's ideas and those of the government prior to April, 1946, seems relatively evident, albeit not entirely clear, the extent and nature of influence of his ideas outside government circles are rather less substantiable. It appears that he took no personal interest in the efforts of various nongovernmental groups to develop positions on the issues of constitutional reform. It is interesting, however, that both the Liberal Party and the Socialist Party, both already emerging as the effective poles of electoral and parliamentary politics, published proposals for constitutional revision explicitly based on the doctrine of state sovereignty and retaining some degree of governmental prerogative for the emperor.[46] Some writers have cited this circumstance as showing both the essentially reactionary character of the state sovereignty doctrine (its acceptability to the Liberals) and the immaturity of the Socialists (for being chained to the old tabu against popular sovereignty).[47] It may also be taken to suggest that the cautious and timid expectation, which Minobe shared with the government, of what the nation would tolerate in respect to constitutional reform was shared also by those who were immediately concerned with electoral calculations.

The Constitutional Revolution

However much his constitutional views had served and might continue to serve the purposes of the Japanese government, Minobe himself moved after March, 1946, toward an adjustment to the emerging new order. He came at last to accept tacitly that the absolutism of the Meiji monarchy was altogether hostile to the development of democracy, that nothing less than a general revision of the constitution would permit the realization of democracy in Japan. The transformation was incomplete and many concessions remained unvoiced; he did not apologize for or explain his own initial opposition to revision. And he retained for the new as for the old sovereignty the keystone of his constitutional theory, the state sovereignty concept.

Despite his official connection with the Matsumoto committee, Minobe was apparently completely surprised by the publication of the government draft revision on March 6.[48] On March 12 he conceded to reporters that the draft did "provide Japan with the basis for the establishment of democratic government" as required by the terms of surrender. But he criticized the draft on three particular grounds: (1) it went too far in the curtailment of the imperial prerogative; (2) it put Japan in an intolerably weak position in respect to hostile foreign power; and (3) it failed to establish a separation of powers and thus created the danger of parliamentary excess. He warned moreover, that adoption of the draft might provoke popular disturbances.[49] These remarks echoed the objections Matsumoto had raised in vain during the period of "negotiation" between receipt of the MacArthur draft on February 13 and cabinet acceptance of it on February 22.[50] On first consideration they seem to be the logical antecedent to the captious spirit with which he greeted the government draft in the privy council. His badgering of the government spokesmen before the council, however, cannot be explained simply as a result of his adherence to an anti-revisionist position which the government had perforce abandoned. The questions and objections put by him in the early stages of the privy council's deliberations raised a challenge to the legitimacy of the draft revision in terms of its own pretended democratic origin, character, and purpose, and indicated that he had gone beyond the government in his acceptance of the revolution.

BOMBSHELL IN THE PRIVY COUNCIL

Consultation of the privy council in the matter of the projected revision was little more than a gesture, made necessary by the decision to adhere as closely as possible to the amendment process prescribed by the Meiji Constitution. The exercise before the council gave the government what amounted to a rehearsal of its forthcoming task of advocacy before the diet; it also afforded the government an interval between the general election and the opening of the diet during which to protract its "refinement" of the draft in liaison with SCAP.[51] In any case, the privy council was not intended or permitted to effect any real modification of the government's draft.[52]

The council operated in this case through a twelve-man investigating committee, whose deliberations covered some forty hours in all. Minobe's part in the proceedings of this committee falls into two distinct phases. In the first and more interesting phase he held a singular position, sharply out of step with the general tenor of the proceedings; later, he joined other members in making critical comments and inquiries about particular passages of the text as they came before the committee.

Minobe held his peace through the opening session when sovereignty, prerogative, and national polity were the subject of lengthy and quarrelsome questions and pronouncements.

It may be thought ironic that, when Councillor Hayashi Raisaburo, the same who as procurator general in 1935 had favored the prosecution of Minobe, probed the weaknesses in the government's defense of the draft revision, Matsumoto met his attack doggedly but ineptly with the rhetoric of Minobe's old defense of his constitutional the-

ories.[53] That Minobe's silence at that time was not the silence of approval was hinted when he interrupted Hayashi's quiz of Matsumoto
to exact a vote on whether the deliberations were to proceed chapter
by chapter and article by article or to begin with a consideration of
the draft as a whole.[54] It may be inferred that he was not pleased with
the decision to proceed topically, for the only business he had to discuss was unrelated to the particular content of the draft revision. When
his turn came toward the end of the first session, he posed his "bombshell" question to "the consternation of every one present":

I have grave doubts concerning the submission of this draft to the privy
council:
a. In my humble opinion, the provisions of Article LXXIII of the present
   constitution must be understood to have been invalidated by the reply to
   our acceptance of the Potsdam Declaration and the Surrender. What is
   the government's view on this?
b. Is it not incomprehensible that this draft should be submitted to the privy
   council and then in the diet to the house of peers, both of which bodies
   are by this very draft to be abolished as unworthy of perpetuation?
c. Although it says in the preamble of the draft, 'We the Japanese people
   . . . do ordain and establish this constitution," in spite of these fine words,
   the initiative of the revision was made by imperial command, and the
   original draft itself, which must have the greatest weight in the diet's
   deliberations, was produced by the government. Moreover, when it has
   received the concurrence of the diet, which has the power to amend only
   within very narrow limits, it will receive imperial sanction and be promulgated. Is it possible to say after all this that it is done in accordance with
   the freely expressed will of the people? Or is this simply a fraudulent
   declaration?
In view of these doubts, I believe that the government should now withdraw this draft. Since the invalidation of Article LXXIII . . . leaves us now
in a condition of having no effective provision for constitutional amendment,
[the revision question] should be introduced in and decided by a special
constituent diet in accordance with a procedure to be determined by the next
regular diet. . . . I think the final decision should be made by a popular
referendum. The present way of going about it is fraudulent. Will the nation
not be shamed at having such a lie displayed in the very masthead of the
constitution?[55]

Minobe moved the adoption of his proposal to terminate the proceedings before the privy council, but no one supported the motion.
Matsumoto attempted to answer Minobe by raising counterobjections:

It would be impossible for the diet to prescribe a novel method of constitutional amendment without a formal amendment of Article LXXIII—a long and uncertain project. Irie Toshio came rather more to the point in his later response to Minobe.[56] Irie denied that acceptance of the Potsdam Declaration in any way affected the validity of Article LXXIII; he said that there was more than one way to elicit the freely expressed will of the people; and he argued that since the constitution would be promulgated only after it had been approved by the diet, which had power to amend the draft freely, the formalities of imperial initiative and promulgation in no way would vitiate its character as an expression of the people's will.[57] But Irie, who was then chief of the cabinet legislative bureau, was only half sincere when he represented the government as having rejected the "Potsdam Revolution" idea.

Minobe's challenge to the democratic legitimacy of the draft revision may have been simply a somewhat devious tactical move to frustrate any attempt to undertake a real revision of the Meiji Constitution. The opinion then current that a popularly elected diet would be politically incapable of producing a radical revision of the Imperial Constitution was indeed hinted by Minobe in his statement of March 12. In an article published on May 1 he predicted that a popular referendum would approve a revised constitution only if the emperor system was kept intact.[58] While the government itself had urged this view during February in dealing with SCAP, it was not now willing to run the risk of provoking SCAP's threat to publish the MacArthur draft unless the Japanese government produced a comparable draft under its own sponsorship.[59] The conservative anticipation of popular opposition and diet obstruction failed completely to materialize in the event. In any case this was not necessarily the reasoning behind Minobe's attack in the privy council.

It is impossible to be sure what his purpose was, however, for his "bombshell," it appears, marked the divide between the phase of resistance and the phase of affirmation in the development of his attitude toward constitutional revision. Indeed, it may be that he took the rejection of his motion as the cue for reconciliation to a new constitutional era, and it is altogether consistent with his habits of thought that, having done so, he should be eager to eradicate the patent contradictions in the procedure and form of its realization. There can be no doubt that his refusal to vote for approval of the draft was due to objections to the undemocratic process by which it was being brought into effect.[60] His lone abstention in the plenary session of the council, with the emperor present, was a mark of characteristic fortitude and conviction. In the last stages of the committee's deliberations he had criticized various particular provisions of the draft, but taken all together these were not of such weight as to warrant his conspicuous refusal to approve the draft.[61]

Regardless of its uncertain purpose and however obstructive its effect, Minobe's stand in the privy council was far more progressive than the general line of criticism there; it was more advanced apparently than that expressed in the house of peers by Sasaki Soichi, who spoke and voted against the revision bill because it changed the basic political character of Japan and because it pretended to do it on the basis of a nonexistent popular will.[62] That Minobe's attack on the procedural issue was not capricious is indicated by his repetition of his objections to the "disgusting dishonesty" of the preamble of the new constitution in his *Shin Kempō Gairon*.[63] He notes there that:

if the demands in the Allied reply were inconsistent with the provisions of Article LXXIII . . . and . . . were absolutely binding on Japan, then the provisions of Article LXXIII which are thereby contradicted must be deemed to have lost their validity. Therefore, I believe that the proper way to have revised the constitution would have been to have enacted a special law called the "Constitutional Revision Procedure Law" to take the place of Article LXXIII. Such a law . . . might set up a special popular assembly for making a constitution, and this constituent assembly would be competent to initiate a revision and to enact it.

But he was by then done with casting votes against the revision. He was merely explaining the accomplished fact, not attacking its legitimacy. For he goes on to point out that his was not the view of the government because

they were content to assume that even though the revision was drafted by the government and introduced to the diet by imperial command, since it was freely decided in the diet, it could be regarded as having been determined by the freely expressed will of the people. The Supreme Commander for the Allied Powers accepted this, and even in the diet it was accepted without exception. Putting aside for the moment the theoretical issue and considering only the fact that it was legally confirmed that Article LXXIII of the constitution had retained its validity, it becomes necessary to construe it that the new constitution, which was made by this procedure, was validly made by a proper procedure.

This is the same position expressed somewhat less captiously in *Nihon-koku Kempō Genron*.[64]

THE "POTSDAM REVOLUTION" THESIS

In view of his recent utterances, Matsumoto and Irie must have been surprised that Minobe raised the procedural question in the privy council. Sensitive as they were to the difficulties surrounding the matter of procedure—a problem over which they felt themselves to have little control—they were embarrassed to the point of exasperation by his voicing the "Potsdam Revolution" or "August Revolution" thesis. Because of its significance in relation to subsequent revisionist thought and in Minobe's reputation among progressive defenders of the new constitution in recent years, this procedural problem warrants further consideration here.

Although the assumption of revolutionary constitutional discontinuity had arisen in some quarters toward the end of 1945, it was given its first effective public expression by Miyazawa Toshiyoshi in the May, 1946, issue of *Sekai Bunka*.[65] According to Miyazawa, the emperor system continued after August 15, 1945, and the Meiji Constitution remained in effect as before. But the basis of the emperor system was transferred from divine will to popular will and the basis of the Imperial Constitution was shifted from divine right to popular sovereignty. Miyazawa was preparing his article for publication at about the same time that Minobe was raising Matsumoto's hackles in the privy council. What they may have owed to one another's views on this is not clear nor of critical importance—but there was a significant difference in their purposes. Minobe proposed in the privy council to abandon procedure under Article LXXIII in favor of the establishment of a democratically representative constituent assembly, a course altogether unserviceable to the government.[66] On the other hand, Miyazawa was seeking to justify a very liberal interpretation of the role of the diet in proceeding under Article LXXIII, and to justify the view that the presumptive restrictions on the right of the emperor to propose a change in *kokutai* had been relaxed. For this he thought a theory of constitutional mutation was indispensable.[67]

The possible inaccuracy of Irie's assertion to Minobe that the government believed that the terms of surrender had not invalidated Article LXXIII has already been mentioned. The basis for doubting Irie is that while the government did indeed deny the August Revolution idea as stated by Minobe in the privy council and by Miyazawa in the house of peers, it tacitly accepted the benefits of Miyazawa's argument. It followed a procedure logically predicated on a revolutionary interpretation of the meaning of Article LXXIII, a procedure transforming it from a cardinal indicia of the authoritarian character of the Meiji system to a vehicle for the realization of what purported to be democratic revolution. While constantly citing the terms of surrender as the motivating force behind the drive for speedy revision, the government steadfastly refused to admit the idea of a quasi-revolution and it turned aside the "August Revolution" proposition when it came up in the diet using the same denial that it had made to Minobe in the privy council.[68] Miyazawa's argument that Article LXXIII, as authoritatively interpreted prior to August, 1945, did not permit amendment changing national polity was met by the straightforward denial that the draft revision embodied or entailed any change in national polity. Members of the diet were for the most part content to accept the government's view on the legality of the revision procedure.[69]

As the quotation from the *Shin Kempō Gairon* (page 273) shows, Minobe came to accept the *de jure* validity of the revision. His final words on the subject are to be found in *Nihonkoku Kempō Genron* where the following passages testify to his final affirmation of the democratic basis of the new constitution:

By our acceptance of the Potsdam Declaration we fell under the firm obligation to make a new constitution according to the freely expressed will of the people, but among the terms of surrender there was no provision for the method by which the freely expressed will of the people might be made known. Since it would take time to proceed by electing a popular assembly to draft and deliberate on a new constitution, and since there was no assurance that the draft of a new constitution thus produced would . . . gain the approval of SCAP, GHQ, it was deemed that such a method was really inappropriate to the existing conditions at home and abroad. There was no

alternative but to dissolve the house of representatives and to bring forth a
new imperial Diet on the basis of a general election in which the making of
a new constitution was at issue, making it the representative organ through
which the will of the people should be manifested, and to establish the new
constitution on the basis of the free deliberation of that diet. . . .

The important thing is that even though the new constitution was formally decided by the procedure laid down in Article LXXIII of the old
constitution, that does not mean that the validity of the new constitution
is based on the former constitution. The fact that the old constitution completely fails to recognize that the people have such power is in itself enough
to make clear that the new constitution was not made on the basis of the old
. . . but on the basis of the acceptance of the Potsdam Declaration [whereby]
the people are newly invested with the character of supreme authority of
the state (*kuni no saikō-kensha*) [and thus] with the power to make a new
constitution. In other words, we must assert that acceptance of the Potsdam
Declaration was a revolutionary act which in this particular subverted the old
constitution. If we designate an act by which a constitution is destroyed by
means not provided in that constitution as "revolution," then acceptance of
the Potsdam Declaration was nothing but a revolutionary course of action.
The people did not acquire sovereignty first from the new constitution; by
the surrender they had already acquired sovereignty, and the new constitution
was established on the basis of this already existing popular sovereignty.[70]

Although these paragraphs show a characteristically formalistic view
of the events, they are significant as an assertion of the legitimacy
of the new constitution against subsequent attempts to effect a reversion to the old system. Indeed, taken as the complement of his
stand in the privy council, they ensure Minobe special credit in the
eyes of some of the latter-day friends of the Showa Constitution.[71]
Not only did he affirm the legitimacy of the new constitution—an important point in the view of the subsequent (post-1952) constitutional
defense movement—but he did so in terms which distinguished him
from those who, like Kanamori, adhered to a bureaucratic version of
kensei jōdō liberalism with arguments smothered in traditional obscurities. That this affirmation was made only after Minobe had openly
denounced the false colors under which the government had presented its draft revision, and after he had challenged the government
to accept the logical imperatives of its nominal commitment to popular sovereignty and parliamentary supremacy, has earned him high
marks in the latter-day constitution defense camp.

Minobe's participation in the privy council's transactions was quite passive after the middle of May. His solitary vote against approval of the government's draft revision in the council plenum on June 8 was the final act in his personal connection with the making of the new constitution.[72] His disengagement from public connection with the debate in the summer and autumn enabled him to prepare his contribution to the spate of commentaries with which scholars and publicists celebrated the promulgation of the Constitution of Japan on November 3, 1946. The first installment of *Shin Kempō Chikujō Kaisetsu* appeared that month in *Hōritsu Jihō*. The stop-gap *Shin Kempō* series was superseded in April, 1948, by the *Nihonkoku Kempō Genron*, the final, fullest and most mature of his new commentaries.

The New Sovereignty

The draft revision published by the government on March 6 was in many particulars and in general philosophy far more radical than anyone had expected. It has been said that the general public was pleasantly surprised—although some were incredulous and some were shocked. Contradiction and equivocation were widely evident in efforts to come to grips intellectually with the change.

Certainly shock and confusion were evident enough in Minobe's response. He simply had not conceived that such far-reaching consequences would flow from the surrender. He had not thought it possible nor, once the possibility presented itself, desirable that such a drastic metamorphosis should occur. Yet his shock was not that of the realization of ultimate fears. He had viewed the surrender not in the spirit of paradise lost but of paradise regained—a return to the spirit of Taisho constitutional liberalism under a purified understanding of the imperial constitutional system.

Three types of responses to the revision bill in the diet have been identified.[73] One was vehement objection because the revision did violence to national polity and to traditional social values. Minobe's actions after May 1—his vote in the privy council and his appreciative interpretation of the new constitution—preclude identifying him in any way with this diehard position. Nor, by the same measure, can he be placed among those who shared the sentiments of the first group but who were persuaded, out of fear of "losing the bigger game," to retreat to the line of the SCAP-inspired draft revision accepting it with resigned cynicism. Most of the articulate members of the diet as well as the government officials concerned fell into this second group. For Minobe, however, neither the preservation of the *kaminagara* mystique of the nationalists nor the power concerns of the bureaucratic—capitalistic "ruling class" were at issue. He regretted the Meiji Constitution, but he was no laggard in recognizing the virtues of the new one as in guaranteeing the constitutional principles he had long championed, and, in a sense, he falls closest to the third type of response, which was acceptance and approval of the government's proposed revision. The Socialist members of the Ninetieth Diet almost exclusively displayed this reaction.[74] One would not want to draw a very close parallel between Minobe's overall constitutional views and those of the Socialists, but there was at that time an objective harmony in their respective affirmations of the fundamental political structure of the Showa Constitution. Minobe's simultaneously arguing the Potsdam Revolution thesis and seeking the preservation of the Meiji monarchy (as in "Kempō Kaisei no Kihon Mondai" was certainly of the same cloth as the assertion by Katayama Tetsu, Socialist leader in the house of representatives, that retention of the monarchy was not incompatible with democratizing the constitutional order.[75]

The mode and form of Minobe's attempted adjustment are best shown in his treatment of the problem of sovereignty in *Nihonkoku Kempō Genron*. The *Genron* opens with a 75-page section on general concepts of law, the state, and the constitution, in which are condensed the corporate theory of the state, the doctrine of the legal personality of the state, the concept of state organs, the doctrine of state sovereignty, and the concept of constitutionalism. As in a corresponding section of *Kempō Satsuyō*, the corporate theory of the state presented in the *Genron* takes on political significance primarily in relation to the constitutional assignment of sovereignty. Thus, in his discussion of popular sovereignty (*kokumin shuken*)—which together with perpetual peace, respect for human rights, and the centrality of parliament make the four fundamental principles of the Showa Constitution—Minobe brings that constitution under the logic of the corporate state-state personality theories, culminating in the doctrine of state sovereignty:

The former constitution employed the term *tōchiken* instead of the term *shuken*; the new constitution, on the contrary, uses the term *shuken* rather than *tōchiken*. But these terms are practically synonymous; both of them mean the competence or authority to rule [*tōchi no kennō*]. When it is said that *tōchiken* belongs to the emperor, or when it is said that it belongs to the people, we do not mean that either the emperor or the people is the subject of the right to govern, for the right to govern is vested always in the state itself. But the competence to exercise the governmental authority of the state, that is to say, the power to put in motion the governmental authority of the state, as an original direct organ of the state, was vested by the former constitution in the emperor, and by the new in the people. . . .

The ideological foundation of the new constitution differs radically from that of the old. Under the Meiji Constitution the governmental prerogative was transmitted through an immutable line of monarchs from the founding of the state. The authority to govern was thus assigned on the basis of national historical tradition. It is assigned in the new constitution to the people. . . . [In either case] this accounts only for the ideological foundation, it is only a manner of thinking, for it does not tell by which organ governmental power is actually exercised. . . . The so-called popular-sovereignty principle does not mean that the people themselves directly perform the superintendence of governmental authority. . . .[76]

Minobe's adherence to the state-sovereignty theory in this context was in a sense, regrettable. It represented a highly personal view, singularly lacking in rapport with the progressive psychology of the newer academic generation and hardly buoyant in the new current of democratic ideology. Its usefulness to the post-1948 academic world was therefore quite limited. And from the political point of view, the doctrine, which had served a noble purpose when invoked to tame the absolutism of the imperial system, now, with liberal democratic formulas and institutional arrangements expressly and unequivocally established, was an embarrassment. That conservative opponents of the new system now found virtue in the once abhorrent doctrine did nothing to enhance its credit.

Actually, as employed in the *Genron*, the state-sovereignty theory was not a serious impediment to Minobe's own appreciation of the Constitution of 1947. As before, he sought to explain away the apparent conflict between his juristic theory of the constitution and the prevailing constitutional forms and practices, but he was not attempting to attack the juridic foundations of popular sovereignty. The substance of the issue had evaporated. He accepted the ideological burden of popular sovereignty with little reservation. The people to whom the sovereign role is assigned is no longer the abstract community of the historical nation; it is the collectivity of existing politically competent individuals. The people is no mere logical construct hovering behind active agencies of government reputed to be its responsible representatives; it is an electorate exercising its sovereign role directly in the constitutional referendum.

Minobe's treatment of the national polity problem in his new constitutional commentaries is barely perfunctory. What makes it a matter of some interest is the contrast between his own reticence on the subject and the high currency of theories traceable to him in the government's pronouncements concerning national polity. Matsumoto, Kanamori, and Irie expended great energy in protracted, obscure, ludicrously futile, and not clearly necessary efforts to maintain before the incredulous privy council and diet that the government's draft revision did not entail any change in national polity.[77] This effort ran concurrently with and to the embarrassment of an equally pressing but less conspicuous campaign to convince the supreme commander that the government fully appreciated the scope of the constitutional reform required under the terms of surrender.

The government, having foresworn open acknowledgment of the corporate theory of the state and the state personality-state sovereignty idea, was not free to argue the distinction between a mutable state form and an immutabe national polity derived from it, though it was quite content to let others satisfy themselves on that basis. The government itself held rather to the distinction between a legalistic definition of national polity, which equated it with the absolute properties of monarchy as set forth in Articles I to IV of the Imperial Constitution, and an ethical-cultural definition, which equated it with the people's awareness at all times of the emperor as the center of the nation's devotion. This distinction made it possible for the government to insist that the constitutional revision in no way changed national polity and at the same time to admit that it did indeed bring about a real change in national polity.

Kanamori's summation of his position on the national polity issue in the Ninetieth Diet is laced with pure vintage Minobe:[78] The term *kokutai* had no political or legal meaning or usage until the Meiji era. It acquired a political significance in Hozumi's use of it to mean the perpetually immutable sociological fact which is distinctive for each particular state, the extinction of which means the extinction of the state. In Japan this fact was the emperor's sovereignty, according to

Hozumi. *Kokutai* appeared in the positive law for the first time in the Peace Preservation Law of 1925, meaning there the imperial sovereignty affirmed in Articles I through IV of the Meiji Constitution. The first establishment of this novel and mistaken equivalence in the public mind caused the subsequent confusion in the diet debates and in the popular opinion. Dispassionate consideration, Kanamori thought, showed that imperial sovereignty had never been the fundamental characteristic of the Japanese state: thus, in the sense of the fundamental characteristic of the state there has been no change in national polity; only the pseudo-national polity of the Peace Preservation Law has been altered. The distinctive characteristic of the Japanese state throughout history and in the most common understanding of it currently is that in Japan there is an emperor and he is the focus of the nation's sentiment. This is the substance of Kanamori's notion of *kokutai*; this is what he meant when he said in the diet that *kokutai* means the close unity of the emperor and the people, deeply sensed in the heart of the people, and that the emperor is the center of the nation's devotion (*kokumin no akogare no chūshin dearu*).[79]

Kanamori did not evoke Minobe's authority in the diet, but in spite of official inhibitions against utterance of state-sovereignty theory the paternity of the government's defense of its "no change in national polity" line was clear. He always managed to imply somehow that those who opposed him in this were akin to the historical foes of the organ theory.[80] Compare what Minobe wrote in *Nihonkoku Kempō Genron*:

Formerly it was generally thought that the distinctive character of Japan's national polity had as its central element the fact that the country was ruled by an eternally unbroken line of emperors. But there is only one instance of the statutory use of the term *kokutai* and that is in the provisions of the Peace Preservation Law . . . upon which the supreme court (May 31, 1929) put this construction: "The term *kokutai* in the Peace Preservation Law is to be construed as meaning that the Japanese Empire is reigned over by Emperors of an eternally unbroken line and they are the superintendents of governmental power." . . . and it is national polity in just this sense that the Japanese government sought to preserve in its conditional acceptance of the terms of the Potsdam Declaration. . . .

There can be no doubt that the new constitution has affected a revolution in national polity in this sense . . . our reservation to the Potsdam terms notwithstanding. . . . But there is another sense in which the term "national polity" is used. Sometimes it is the spiritual or moral connotation rather than the juristic one which is emphasized, to point up the unparalleled depth of the Japanese people's reverence for the emperor as the heart of the nation. . . . If it is national polity in this sense that we are talking about, then the new constitution provides it in making the emperor the symbol of the state. Even though his governmental prerogative is diminished the emperor retains his position as the center of the state. Thus, in this sense we can say that the new constitution makes no revolution in national polity.[81]

This is Minobe's exposition of an official explanation which in turn was based on Minobe's own arguments. But the issue was no longer of vital interest to him. It was no longer an essential part of his constitutional theory. Neither did it pose any obstacles to a progressive view of the new constitutional order.

Uncertain Fame

The fates seem to have conspired to consign Minobe to oblivion once again. He had returned to public life and had accepted the call to engage in the great business of constitutional reform. Putting aside his disappointment in the aborted return to "normal constitutional government," he awkwardly embraced the new constitutional order and diligently adapted his textbook rubrics to it. After 1948, however, Minobe's writing ceased to be a significant source of insight into the new constitutional system. By 1950, except for a few polite or sentimental references or citation on some particular point of law, Minobe had faded from constitutional literature, leaving behind an impression of untimely conservatism.

Although it is hardly likely that Minobe's postwar writing will soon or far, achieve new stature or meaning, it is premature to relegate him to the dust bin of history. In fact, there has been a notable revival of interest in him, chiefly in his role in the historical development of modern Japanese constitutional theory. This revival seems to have been a by-product of the debate over constitutional revision that began with the end of the Occupation and continues into the 1960's. More particularly, it is an interest arising from the needs and concerns of the anti-revisionist writers and publicists, that is, of those who have opposed revision of the Constitution of 1947.[82]

The renewal of interest in Minobe was, to be sure, but a facet of a renaissance of general constitutional theory. Like the more inclusive category, it displays an uneasy dualism between method and ideology. It is a significant fact that to the extent that it looks to alien precept and inspiration, Japanese constitutional scholarship was reverted to primary reliance on continental European—chiefly German—example and authority. American and British writers generally have attracted sharply diminished attention. To be sure, various social-psychological forces have worked against demonstrations of Americanism in Japan since 1950. The irony has often been noted that the heart of the movement to defend the "MacArthur constitution" has been the political and intellectual left, which is otherwise suspicious and critical of the United States and the west, while the forces most eager to scrap the Occupation and its works are, in political program, pro-American although not necessarily enthusiastic about American culture. This is, however, a superficial and, at most, ancillary explanation of the reversion to Europe. More important is that in searching for a systematic, sophisticated, theoretical rationale, the anti-revisionist forces have found very little satisfaction in the relatively more empirical and pragmatic concerns of American and British thinkers, whose views of general constitutional theory are, moreover, only rarely congenial to the Marxian-oriented thinking of the anti-revisionists.

The impressive upsurge of interest in Anglo-American law beginning in 1947 proved to be short-lived, except among some part of the practicing bar and judiciary. The return to Europe is hardly surprising in view of the already deeply rooted intellectual and psychological connection of Japanese juristic thought to that of the European continent. The impetus to the study of British and American theory—in the social sciences as well as in law—was apparently not strong enough seriously to change the orientation of the Japanese academic intellect. *Kempō-gaku* tends to remain, as it was in Minobe's student days, *Staatsrechts-lehre*. The German juristic tradition is not, of course, ideologically or methodologically monolithic and today's generation of scholars has its own purposes and its own insights.[83]

Minobe's significance in this new scene derives from his having been the best known carrier in Japan of the line of constitutional theory founded in the legal philosophy of Georg Jellinek. He could hardly have been overlooked by students of *kempōgaku* even if their interest had been only historical. But combined with the revival of interest in the history of Japanese constitutional theory has come a revitalized concern in comparative constitutional theory and the methodology of constitutional science—a combination providing the philosophical and rhetorical basis of the intellectual resistance to threatening conservative moves toward revision of the Showa Constitution.

In this connection the pioneering work of Suzuki Yasuzo has been notaby fruitful. His models have recently been widely emulated in studies attempting to combine careful historical research with an understanding of the development and institutionalization of ideas, studies striving at the same time to keep the conceptual view anchored in sophisticated awareness of empirical social movement. Inevitably such examinations into Japanese constitutional thought since the Meiji era have been drawn, chiefly by ideological attraction to Minobe. His conspicuous academic and official influence, his vital role in the universalization of Japanese constitutional thought, his salience (by the norms of Marxist analysis) as epitome of bourgeois liberal constitutionalism— all make him a major pole in the compass of these studies.

The field of constitutional science in Japan today is occupied by three schools distinguished by differences of method and ideology, and each directly related to one of the prewar schools. One of these, the socialist school, boasts its scientific grasp of total social and economic reality. In spite of the self-assurance of its representatives and the prominence of their writing, this group of historical materialists is numerically weak; very few leading academic authorities are among its members, notably Suzuki Yasuzo, Hasegawa Masayasu, and Kuroda Ryoichi. Marxist thought has a high, if intellectually superficial, popularity and seminal influence in the universities. However, since 1945 the dominant position in *kempōgaku* has remained with the survivors of the prewar contest between the orthodox and the liberal schools of constitutional interpretation. The supernationalistic, feudalistic, authoritarian national polity school was all but obliterated by the destruction of the power system with which it was associated—whether permanently is uncertain, however, for it undoubtedly reflected some basic predilection and emotions which have probably not been fully expunged from Japanese society. In any case, whether as heirs by default of the authoritarian line or, as they would prefer to think, because of the virtues of their science, the cosmopolitan, bourgeois, parliamentary, democratic school came into all but complete command of the arena of academic constitutional theory by 1946.

One result of this unchallenged ascendency has been to throw into relief a long existing difference within the liberal school, a difference rooted in issues of interpretive methodology rather than in the political character of the constitutional system. This difference provides the major distinction between schools designated variously as (1) the school of formal, conceptual, or logical interpretation (the *keishikiron-teki, gainenteki, ronrihōgakuha*), the school which aspires to authoritative, purely juristic, apolitical, nonsubjective interpretation; and (2) the teleological school of interpretation (the *mokutekironteki kai-shaku hōgakuha*), the liberal school properly speaking, the school which concerns itself with free interpretation, giving meaning and value to the law. The first is also known as the Kyoto or Kansai school. It is identified with Sasaki Soichi. Its more notable postwar adherents include Tabata Shinobu, Oishi Yoshio, Yamamoto Kozo, Watanabe Munetaro, and Hitomaro Kazuoku. The second school, known as the Tokyo school, is identified with Minobe. Names prominently associated with this school since his death have been Miyazawa Toshiyoshi, Ukai Nobushige, Nakamura Akira, Kiyomiya Shiro, Arigura Ryokichi, Tagami Joji, Sato Isao, Ashibe Nobuki, Wada Hideo, and Sakuma Tadao. The stature of Minobe and others of this group has been enhanced in historical perspective as well as on the contemporary scene by their connection with the political, administrative, and academic centers of the country in Tokyo.

The confusion which arose as a result of failure to distinguish between the methodological and ideological characteristics of these schools involves also a significant inversion of their relationship to the constitutional problems of the day.[84] During the Taisho and early Showa periods, Minobe and Sasaki had been thrown together in the harmony of their ideological opposition to the *kaminagara*, bureaucratic views of Hozumi and Uesugi. In methodological terms, however, there was a gulf between Minobe, who drifted from the balanced Jellinekian dualism to the open search for value after the manner of Heinrich Triepel, and Sasaki, who moved along an opposite tangent toward the strict logical positivism of Laband and Anschütz. Miyazawa and Ukai have pointed out that the Uesugi-Minobe quarrel was more a political conflict than an argument over theory. Methodologically speaking, there was more in common between Minobe and Hozumi than between Minobe, who positively affirmed the political nature of law and sought by reference to the normative force of social conscience "to impart by interpretation an entirely new meaning" to it, and Sasaki, who approached a purely scientific, juristic attitude, shunning every subjective bias, and was unable to escape from the restriction of the positive law of the Meiji constitutional system.

Thus it was Minobe who came to epitomize the "liberal school" properly speaking, and to represent for postwar students of Japanese constitutional theory the arch-protagonist of middle-class liberalism and parliamentary democracy. Moreover, when purged of its "nostalgic reservations," Minobe's constitutional theory was acknowledged by progressive critics to have provided, as in the case of Nakamura Akira, the point of departure for a positively democratic interpretation of the new constitution to make it the instrument of transition to popular democracy.[85]

But despite the generous appreciation of its historical value, recent treatises on constitutional theory have brought the Tokyo school under sharp criticism on general methodological as well as ideological grounds. The assault comes in the form of the no-longer-to-be-slain-by-silence, vigorously pressed criticism leveled by sociologically oriented philosophies by law, Marxian and other. This criticism holds that the schools of liberal interpretation (the Kyoto school as well as that of Minobe) represent merely interpretive techniques, are limited to juristic methods, and have the state not only as an interpretive device but as a conditioning value. It alleges, conversely, that pragmatic efforts to comprehend political forces and to employ comparative legal analysis, even at the cost of indulging in an excess of dogmatic "objectivity," have not overcome their shortcomings. Basic among these, according to this criticism, is that they have denied or ignored the possibility of treating *kempōgaku* as a theoretical science embracing the total social order and have thus largely denied to themselves means of achieving a scientifically sophisticated comprehension of the constitution.

But the state science-state law science (*kokkagaku-kokuhōgaku*) basis of interpretive constitutional theory draws criticism not only on methodological grounds. The interdependence of method and ideology in the minds of these critics is nowhere more plainly made explicit than in the never allayed suspicion with which they regard the "democratic" results proceeding from interpretive constitutional science. In their view, now that the way is open to pursue a constitutional science which would comprehend the political and social foundation of the constitution, which would serve not the state and its bureaucracy but the interests of the people, the capacity of the interpretive schools to meet these new needs is doubtful—the more so because its practitioners had survived the military-fascist period only by the most damaging compromises. These critics see the liberal school of constitutional interpretation as "a two-edged sword," capable of progressive but also of reactionary movement, likely to be capricious and halfhearted in the service of the revolutionary cause of perfecting democracy. And the tendency of *kempōgaku* scholars on the left to doubt the value of attempting to regenerate the virtues of the liberal school in the era of the Showa Constitution finds concrete validation in connection with the problem of constitutional change.

Many of those who have opposed revision of the Constitution of 1947 have not been opposed to revision under acceptable auspices, which is to say, under "popular" or socialist guidance.[86] To be sure their resistance is not based on a belief that the Showa Constitution is ideal— what they describe as an expression of pure Lockeianism, as a model of bourgeois parliamentary democracy, as having only in lesser measure than its predecessor the quality of *Scheinkonstitutionalismus,* can hardly be their paragon. Nevertheless, they have defended its legitimacy against all attacks by the conservative pro-revisionists. They have denied that the conditions of its making violated international law. In order to deny the charge that the Showa Constitution was imposed (*oshi-tsukerareta*), they have performed ironical feats of sophistry in justifying the policies and even the purposes of the Occupation. They have argued that, even if it had been imposed, the real test of its legitimacy is whether it satisfies the requirements of democracy, whether it meets the historical necessities of the current objective stage of development. They have argued that whatever the subjective and objective imperfections of the new constitution at its inception, it is being gradually purged of those faults as the mass of the people by their participation transform it from a national (*kokuminteki*) to a popular (*jinminteki*) constitution. And finally, they have asserted that the alleged public support for revision is in fact an artificial phenomenon, real enough in commanding political and economic circles, perhaps, and made to seem quite widespread as a result of the big play given to it in news media, but untrue of popular opinion, where the mood is said to be against revision, not for it.[87]

That the Constitution of 1947 has not been subjected to general or piecemeal revision is due not to the potency of the anti-revisionist arguments but to the failure of the conservatives to muster the required special majority in the diet, and to a lack of uniform determination among the conservatives.[88] And the successful evasion of Article IX by interpretation doubtless contributes to the conservative government's lack of drive for formal revision. For, as Matsumoto Sannosuke points out, it "knows that as long as the constitution remains intact, the people will not go to extremes in opposing the government policy" in respect to rearmament.[89]

The pliability of the constitution under the pressures of conservative governmental requirements and initiatives has dismayed the opposition. The circumstance of constitutional "change by interpretation has been the cause of some disenchantment with Minobe among progressive constitutional theorists. At issue is the Jellinekian doctrine of constitutional change—a theory which Minobe had made well known in Japan.[90] There are two problems posed for the anti-revisionists in the Jellinek-Minobe doctrine. First, it sets no limits on what parts, or how much, of a constitution can be altered by formal amendment or revision (*Verfassungsänderung: kempō kaisei*). This position was now embraced by the government parties and by other revisionists, including many of the same conservatives who had opposed general revision in 1946. The counter to the Jellinekian doctrine by conservative anti-revisionists in 1946 and by the radical anti-revisionists a decade later was found in Carl Schmidt's theory of the graded structure of constitutions, according to which certain provisions of a constitution express the key constituent political decisions of the sovereign (people) and can be changed only by revolution. The conservatives in 1946 had taken his position in asserting that the national polity sections of the Meiji Constitution could not be changed by the formal amendment process—this indeed was the idea with which Miyazawa's August Revolution thesis was designed to deal. In the 1950's, anti-revisionists have claimed the same preferred status for the popular sovereignty, fundamental rights, and anti-war provisions of the Showa Constitution.

The second problem posed by Jellinek's theory came from his assertion that constitutional change (*Verfassungswandlung; kempō henkō*) might occur, in the absence of a will to change the constitution formally, by interpretation, as a result of political necessity, through usage, through disuse, or by filling in gaps. This theory was for Minobe, as it had been for Jellinek under the German Imperial Constitution, an indispensable release from the discouraging rigidity of the positive law. It was an important corollary of the general assertion of the normative force of political facts and of social will. Denied by Socialist strength in the diet the possibility of affecting formal constitutional change, the conservative governments since 1950 have, on the basis of "political necessity," interpreted into existence a number of changes, for example, evading the prohibition against rearmament. According to the Opposition they also interpreted away a number of constitutional guarantees of individual liberty. The anti-revisionists are unable to prevent the "unconstitutional" behavior of the government; the diet and the courts have sustained the government. They are left with nothing to do but to register protests. Their counterarguments do not absolutely deny the *henkōsetsu*, but they do deny its applicability in an open democratic political order such as now presumably prevails in Japan.

The anti-revisionists repeatedly protest that what might have been quite appropriate in Bismarck's Germany or in Imperial Japan is not at all suitable in contemporary Japan. In confronting this problem, they find more comfort in the strict, logical positivism of the Kyoto school of Sasaki than in the teleological approach of Minobe. When the problem of the day was to breathe liberal parliamentary democracy into the Imperial Constitution, the virtues of Minobe's Jellinekian free interpretation were of high value. Now that the problem is to prevent a drifting away from the democracy positively established in the terms of the Showa Constitution, strict constructionism has a great attraction.

Whether this most recent note of minor irony is to be the last to mark the irony-ridden course of Minobe's part in the constitutional history of Japan remains to be seen. The judgment of his surviving peers and his chief successors indicates, in any case, that his position in that history is not likely to be substantially changed hereafter. By any standard he was an important figure in his era. By the standard of constitutional liberalism his role was almost entirely salutary.

Notes

NOTES TO CHAPTER I

1. In addition to other works to which subsequent particular reference is made, the following standard works have contributed to this introduction: Hugh Borton, *Japan's Modern Century*; Chitoshi Yanaga, *Japan Since Perry*; Osatake Takeshi, *Nihon Kempō Seitei Shiyō*; and Miki Kiyoshi, editor, *Gendai Tetsugaku Jiten*.

2. Excellent analyses of the Liberty and Popular Rights Movement, based on authoritative Japanese sources, are E. Herbert Norman, *Japan's Emergence as a Modern State*, Chapter 4; Robert A. Scalapino, *Democracy and the Party Movement in Pre-war Japan*, Chapters 2 and 3; and Nobutaka Ike, *The Beginnings of Political Democracy in Japan*.

3. In Sansom's view, "if it comes to a judgment as to the origins of the political thought that most influenced Japanese public opinion [in early Meiji], one is bound to conclude that English, French and American ideas had the greatest effect. Nevertheless, what guided the government was not public opinion but the convictions of its leaders, which were those of all autocratic statesmen East and West." George B. Sansom, *The Western World and Japan*, pp. 494–495.

4. Sansom warns against overstating the German influence. *Ibid.*, pp. 314, 350, 375 and *passim*. The Osaka writer Nakase Juichi argues that its home in the imperial university provided only a superficial and narrow base for the German influence. He emphasizes the vigor of British theory at Waseda and in the opposition parties. "Meiji Kempō ni okeru Tennō Kikan Setsu no Keisei," *Hōritsu Jihō*, 34 (April, 1961), 44–71.

5. The purposefully restrained tone of the oligarchs' concession to constitutional government is indicated by the words of Yamagata Aritomo and Ito Hirobumi. In a memorial of 1879 the former asserted: "It is not unique for statesmen to direct popular sentiment to lie with the government. To attain this objective they must appropriately put into practice the demands of the common people. That is, they must establish a constitution. . . . Now that we have come this far, we may perhaps advance to the point of establishing a popular assembly . . . [as] the basic element of the nation's constitutional system. . . . If the assembly has extensive powers, we must be careful not to establish it too quickly. How-

ever, we need not be wise men to know that it will have to be done sooner or later." In the following year Ito recorded similar views: "it is easy to change the conditions of a country, but it is difficult to alter world-wide trends. . . . European concepts of revolution have gradually spread to various nations. By combining and complementing each other they have become a general trend. Sooner or later every nation will undergo change as a result. . . . Elsewhere enlightened rulers, with the help of wise ministers, led and controlled these changes, thus solidifying their nations. . . . At present, it is the responsibility of the government to follow a conciliatory policy and accommodate itself to these tendencies, so that we may control but not intensify the situation and relax our hold over the government but not yield it. . . ." Quotations are from George M. Beckmann's translations in *The Making of the Meiji Constitution*, pp. 128–129, 131–132.

6. "National polity" is the most commonly employed translation of *kokutai*. The vagueness of the translation is true to the ambiguity of the term in its use in Japan, in spite of canonical efforts to define it. Its connotations are as rich and disparate as those of "the American way of life." Indeed, the disagreement among the Japanese as to the content of the concept represented by *kokutai* is, as will be seen, significant. It is always construed to include the emperor system in some form.

7. Oddly, neither Ito nor his assistants were students of German. Inoue's references to German materials were through French translations. And when Ito Miyoji, as private secretary to Ito Hirobumi, kept notes on the lectures of Gneist and Stein he wrote them in English, translating from the Japanese of the interpreter. Professor Tabata says of these men that they "digested the German constitution on the basis of Confucian training to which English studies had been added." Tabata Shinobu, "Meiji Kempō Sōan Kisōsha to Sono Kokka Shisō," *Dōshisha Hōgaku*, 5 (July, 1950), 26.

8. Imperial Ordinance of March, 1882, given in full by Kaneko Kentaro, "Teikoku Kempō Seitei no Yurai" ("The Origins of the Establishment of the Imperial Constitution"), in Kokka Gakkai, *Meiji Kensei Keizai Shiron*, 62–64. To this general charge were subtended thirty specific questions, two of which concerned the law of the imperial household, fourteen, the organization of parliament, two, the judicial organs, and twelve, administration.

9. Rupert Emerson, *State and Sovereignty in Modern Germany*, pp. 18 f.

10. Gneist served in both the Prussian and Imperial parliaments, and in both was a member of the liberal opposition to the Bismarckian regime. *Der Grosse Brockhaus*, Vol. IX, p. 399. Gneist was not, however, an advocate of party government. He considered partisan control of administration to be an obstacle to the achievement of the *Rechtsstaat*. Emerson, *op. cit.*, pp. 37, 38.

11. Cited *ibid.*, p. 35. Gneist contributed substantially to this phase of the constitutional movement by his studies in English administrative law and procedures. *Ibid.*, p. 38.

12. *Ibid.*, pp. 59–62.

13. Nakamura Akira, *Kokuhōgaku no Shiteki Kenkyū*, pp. 107–112, 122.

14. Gerhard Anschütz asserted the universal validity of the juristic concept of the state thus: "it is the theory of the personality of the state which alone on a purely juristic basis offers a non-contradictory explanation of the state in agreement with modern political thinking. . . . The requirements of modern political

thinking which this theory satisfies are: (1) A unity of the state transcending the changing relations between governors and the governed. (2) The quality of the state as a unity endowed with power and will, capable of action, the subject of rights and duties. (3) The character of the state as a social unit . . . a commonwealth, the nature of the state's will as a common will, the nature of sovereignty as a corporate competence or power. (4) The inclusion in the state corporation of the rulers, one or many . . . in such a way that the ruler is not placed outside or above the corporation, but is included as its principal servant. . . ." Elsewhere he wrote: "The principle of the sovereignty of the state . . . is valid everywhere for every state, regardless of its constitutional structure. . . ." Cited by Johannes Mattern, *Principles of Constitutional Jurisprudence of the German National Republic*, pp. 99, 115.

15. Jellinek, in criticism aimed principally at Otto Gierke, rejected the organic theory of the state and, indeed, denied the validity of any conception of the state as a personality except from the juristic point of view. His so-called *Zwei-Seiten Theorie* was later the point of departure from which, by reference to Kantian principles, Hans Kelsen arrived at his pure theory of law.

16. Emerson, *op. cit.*, pp. 49–55.

17. See statement by Rōyama Masamichi in Maruyama *et al.*, "Nihon ni okeru Seijigaku no Kako to Shōrai—Tōron," *Seijigaku*, Vol. I, No. 1 (1950), 45. See also Matsumoto Sannosuke, "Nihon Kempōgaku ni okeru Kokkaron no Tenkai: Sono Keiseiki ni okeru Hō to Kenryoku no Mondai wo Chushin ni" in Fukuda Kanichi *et al.*, *Seiji Shisō ni okeru Seiō to Nihon: Nambara Shigeru Sensei Koki Kinen*, Vol. II, pp. 172–173; Nakamura, *op. cit.*, p. 109.

18. Rōyama, *loc. cit.*, 45, suggests that Jellinek's moderate liberalism and his reputation as an "international scholar," much influenced by British, French, and American thought, enhanced his appeal to Japanese of progressive constitutional views in late Meiji and early Taisho.

19. A commonly used abbreviation of *Tōkyō Teikoku Daigaku* (Tokyo Imperial University), this short form will be used frequently throughout this discussion.

20. Rōyama Masamichi, *Nihon ni okeru Kindai Seijigaku no Hattatsu*, pp. 11–36, 59–62.

21. Out of this critical tradition there emerged a positivist school (*jisshōgakuha*) of political science which struggled with little success throughout the history of the Imperial Constitution to escape the bonds of interpretive state science. *Ibid.*, p. 62.

22. Rōyama finds in the promulgation of the constitution the close of the first "epoch" of active political thought in modern Japan and the beginning of a long period of stability, in which thinking was dominated by one line of reasoning and political science adhered to the dominant methodology (the reasoning and method of *Staatslehre* and *Staatsrechtslehre*). It was not until the period of World War I that this static situation was challenged. See exchange between Rōyama and Maruyama Masao in Maruyama *et al.*, "Nihon ni okeru Seijigaku . . . ," *loc. cit.*, 36–38.

23. Stein contributed to the development in Germany of a sociological basis for the science of administration. His influence was to modify the extreme *logische* method of the positivist school represented by Otto Mayer. But the reception of Stein in Japan was superficial, resting on an appreciation not of his sociological method but of the conservative administrative concepts of his late years. The

rule of "formalized 'administration by law' out of keeping with actual conditions," as epitomized in the works of Mayer, was introduced and perpetuated in Japan by Minobe and others. See remarks of Tsuji Kiyoaka and Hirano Yoshitaro in Suehiro Iwataro, *et al.*, "Nihon Hōgaku no Kaiko to Tembō-Zadankai," *Hōritsu Jihō*, 20 (December, 1948), 33–35.

24. Rōyama, *Nihon ni okeru Kindai Seijigaku no Hattatsu*, p. 82. Also Suzuki Yasuzō, *Nihon Kempō Shi Kenkyū*, pp. 290–312.

25. Imperial Ordinance No. 3 (March 1, 1886). For a full exposition of this ordinance see Fukube Unoyoshi, editor, *Tōkyō Teikoku Daigaku Goju Nen Shi*, Vol. I, pp. 932–937. (This work will be cited hereafter as *Daigaku Goju Nen Shi.*) The name of the university was changed in 1897 to Tokyo Imperial University in order to distinguish it from Kyoto Imperial University, founded at that time. Subsequently imperial universities were established at Fukuoka, Sendai, Sapporo, Nagoya, Taihoku (Taipeh), and Keijo (Seoul), but none of these substantially challenged the position of To-Dai as the center of bureaucratic training and capstone of the state school system.

26. Imperial Ordinance No. 36 (July, 1887). Rōyama Masamichi, *Seiji Shi*, pp. 246–250, 290.

27. Itani Zenichi, *Meiji Ishin Keizai Shi*, pp. 234–235.

28. Even after the constitution went into effect legislation concerning education was enacted by ordinance rather than by diet action. The educational system was a part of the administrative structure of the state and as such was within the imperial prerogative (Article X of the constitution). The diet's influence was further limited by its ineffective budgetary powers and by the Yamagata ordinance of 1899 which required privy-council approval of changes in basic educational ordinances.

29. Ōtsu Junichiro, *Dai Nihon Kensei Shi*, Vol. III, pp. 486–487, 491–493; Okamoto Niji, *Meiji Taishō Shisō Shi*, p. 56; *Daigaku Goju Nen Shi*, Vol. I, pp. 348–351, 454–458, 512.

30. Kada Tetsuji, *Nihon Kokka Shakai Shugi Hihan*, pp. 206–208.

31. Nobutaka Ike, *Japanese Politics*, p. 247.

32. Sansom, *op. cit.*, p. 426.

33. Masaaki Kosaka (David Abosch, trans.), *Japanese Thought in the Meiji Era*, p. 364.

34. Kanamori Tokujiro, *Kempō Igen*, p. 2.

35. Procurators Examination Ordinance (Ministry of Justice Ord. No. 3 of 1891), Articles VIII and XVI; the Attorneys Law (Law No. 7 of 1893), Article IV; the Foreign Service and Consular Officers Examination Ordinance (Imp. Ord. No. 23 of 1893 and Imp. Ord. No. 187 of 1893). Naikaku Kiroku Ka, *Genkō Hōrei Shuran* (1907), Vol. V, pp. 4, 51, 58, 59; Vol. X, p. 45. The Higher Civil Service Examination Board operated directly under the prime minister. It consisted of a chairman and a number of standing and provisional members. The chief of the Cabinet Legislative Bureau was customarily (after 1918 by law) chairman. Imp. Ord. No. 54 of 1893, *Genkō Hōrei Shuran* (1912), Vol. III, p. 6; Imp. Ord. No. 9 of 1918. Sterling T. Takeuchi's English translation, in Leonard D. White, editor, *The Civil Service in the Modern State*, pp. 535–539.

36. See remarks of Suehiro Iwataro, chief of the To-Dai law faculty in "Nihon Hōgaku no Kaiko . . . ," *op. cit.*, 11.

37. Rōyama, *Seiji Shi*, pp. 290–291; and Ōtsu, *op. cit.*, Vol. III, pp. 485–494.

38. Rōyama: "Indeed the major task in modern Japanese political history is to see how the Japanese administrative system exercised its power, broadly in politics and in the narrower constitutional sense." *Seiji Shi*, pp. 287 ff. Also, Suzuki Yasuzō, *op. cit.*, pp. 114–118. Rōyama has elsewhere clearly assigned to the bureaucracy an important role in frustrating the development of a legally and politically responsible government in prewar Japan: "Sekinin Seifu to Kanryō Seido" ("Responsible Government and the Bureaucratic System") in Rōyama Masamichi, *et al.*, *Kanshi Seido no Kenkyū*, pp. 5–44.

39. These generalized remarks do not imply that there was a complete harmony of purpose and view among the bureaucrats. From the beginning there were major conflicts not only of personality and method but of purpose, as for instance between Ito and Yamagata. It was partly on the basis of these differences that the parliamentary parties were able to establish, however imperfectly and transitorily, their claim to a share in the government of the empire. The solidarity of the civil bureaucracy was seriously weakened under the influence of the swelling forces of capitalism in Japanese politics, especially after 1914. The resurgence of the bureaucrats in the 1930's occurred under less auspicious circumstances, for by then the ideology of Japanese fascism had made its mark on them, and the councils of state came increasingly under the sway of military exigencies and thus of military men. On the relationship between the bureaucracy and the parties see Scalapino, *op. cit.*, chaps. 5 and 6.

40. Imperial Ordinance No. 97 of 1893 laid down basic rules of the civil-service examination system which were not significantly changed until 1929. Article XIV prescribed for the general administrative examination (judicial and foreign-service examinations were separately administrated) constitutional law, criminal law, civil law, administrative law, economics, and international law as compulsory subjects for examination. The examinee was permitted, in addition, to elect for examination either commercial law, the law of criminal procedure, or the law of civil procedure. Naikaku Kiroku Ka, *Genkō Hōrei Shuran* (1907), Vol. I, p. 241. This manifestation of "legal omnipotence" was continued under the revision of 1918 (Imp. Ord. No. 7), under which the administration of the general, judicial, and foreign-service examinations was consolidated. The only change in the general administrative examination was the addition of public finance to the list of optional examination subjects. Only the foreign-service examination admitted subjects outside the fields of law and economics. *Genkō Hōrei Shuran* (1922), Vol. I, pp. 373–374. The policy of legal emphasis was broken in 1929. Imperial Ordinance No. 15 of that year reduced the number of compulsory examination subjects in the general administrative examination to four (constitutional law, administrative law, civil law, and economics) and gave the examinee three electives out of a list of twenty subjects including philosophy, psychology, sociology, political science, literature, natural history, political history, economics, commercial policy, and various fields of law. An English translation of the 1929 ordinance is given by Takeuchi in White, *op. cit.*, pp. 535–539. A survey of the course requirements at To-Dai between 1893 and 1925 for students seeking degrees in law and political science shows a close parallel with the one-sided legal bent of the civil-service examinations during that period. There was particular emphasis on public-law studies in the political-science curricula. *Daigaku Goju Nen Shi*, Vol. I, pp. 1106–1112; Vol. II, pp. 171–178, 713–714.

41. In that year the functions of the law school of the ministry of justice were transferred to To-Dai. In 1886 the president of To-Dai (until 1893 ex-officio chief of the To-Dai law faculty) was given supervisory powers over the curricula and standards of the five major private law schools in Tokyo.

42. *Daigaku Goju Nen Shi,* Vol. I, p. 583.

43. Takayanagi Kenzō, "Kempō Kaishaku no Kihon Mondai," *Hōritsu Taimuzu,* 21 (July, 1949), 5 ff. He likens the relationship between Japanese and German law to that between American and English law.

44. A survey of university regulations and curricula shows that English and French law dominated Japanese official law training up to 1887. After 1872 French law gained the ascendency and played a major role in the developing of the first modern criminal law in Japan (1880). The option of specialization in German law was introduced in 1877. From 1900 until after World War I, German law specialists were in the majority. While there was a steady development of instruction in Japanese law from 1878 and a gradual escape from dependence on foreign instructors, foreign-law specialization was a requirement for all law graduates down to 1922. *Daigaku Goju Nen Shi,* Vol. I, pp. 186 ff., 313 ff., 582 ff., 1116 ff.; Vol. II, p. 688; and Suehiro Iwataro *et. al.,* "Nihon Hōgaku no Kaiko . . . ," *op. cit.,* 15 ff.

45. See comment by Hirano Yoshitaro, *ibid.,* 16.

NOTES TO CHAPTER II

1. The diligent scholarship of Nakase Juichi has produced interesting data on the Minobe family up to 1870 and on the intellectual and social atmosphere of Minobe Tatsukichi's native Takasago, but he adduces virtually no new data on Minobe Tatsukichi himself, going little beyond the account given of his father by Minobe Ryōkichi. Minobe Ryōkichi, *Kumon Suru Demokurashii,* pp. 36–37, 61–68; Nakase Juichi, "Minobe Tatsukichi no Shisō Keisei no Zentei," *Keizaigaku Zasshi,* 45 (July, 1961), 74–103. Nakase's interest in Minobe stems from his concern with political ideas of the Meiji-Taisho period. His particular virtue is in the careful development of the social context and the interpersonal influences behind the political ideas. The various articles of his authorship cited in this study constitute, in substance, chapters of his book, *Kindai ni Okeru Tenno Kan,* published in 1963. Ienaga Saburo's *Minobe Tatsukichi no Shisō Shiteki Kenkyū* published in 1964, limits itself to a close analysis of the writings of Minobe and of his preceptors from the time of his entrance at the imperial university.

2. Nakase Juichi, "Minobe Tatsukichi no Shisō Keisei no Zentei," *loc. cit.,* 13.

3. Chitoshi Yanaga, *Japan Since Perry,* pp. 520, 533; T. A. Bisson, *Japan's War Economy,* pp. 46–47. Yanaga lists Minobe Yoji as one of the members of a group of young bureaucrats whose careers were greatly advanced by their collaboration with the military in the planning board. *Op. cit.,* p. 521, note 5. It is recorded that Minobe Yoji accompanied Admiral Okada, "for the sake of a casual appearance," when Okada visited Arima Yoriyasu in September, 1944, to discuss ways and means of forcing Premier Tojo out of office. Okada Keisuke, *Okada Keisuke Kaikōroku,* p. 209. After the war he continued to write on problems of economic planning.

4. Suzuki Yasuzō, *Kempō no Rekishiteki Kenkyū,* p. 429. Also Sugiyama Hirosuke,

"Jiyūshugi Kyōju Ron," *Kaizō*, 17 (April, 1935), 216. Sugiyama refers to Minobe as a "bourgeois gentleman" and as a "typical gentleman of the newly risen capitalism."

General biographical data on Minobe and others in this and succeeding paragraphs is based for the most part on standard biographical dictionaries including: Iseki Kuro, editor, *Dai Nihon Hakushi Roku*, Vol. I; *Hakushi Meigan*; Sakuma Akira, editor, *Nihon Kankai Meigan* (1942); and Ino Saburo, editor, *Taishū Jinji Roku*, (12th edition).

5. Minobe Tatsukichi, "Taikan Zappitsu," *Kaizō*, 16 (April, 1934), 151. This brief article is the only substantial bit of autobiographical writing done by Minobe. It covers the period from 1896 to 1934. This article was reprinted in *Gikai Seiji no Kentō* along with two other brief notes of biographical interest: "Daigaku wo Saru ni Nozomite" ("On the Eve of Retirement from the University"), a sentimental reflection on the occasion, and "Shiken Jigoku" ("Examination Misery") (1929), a humorous report on the burden of grading law school (civil-service) examinations during the summer recess.

6. "Taikan Zappitsu," *loc. cit.*, 152. He points out that the postgraduate careers of the other twelve members of his class were divided equally between civil service, diplomacy, business, and academic work.

7. "Taikan Zappitsu," *loc. cit.*, 152 ff.

8. Ichiki Kitokuro (1867–1944), studied under Rathgen, graduated from To-Dai in 1887, studied in Germany, was appointed professor of state law at To-Dai in 1894. For thirteen years he was active both as a university professor and a high-ranking officer in the home ministry secretariat, a paragon of the then current professor-bureaucrat in his continual coming and going between lecture hall and ministry. He subsequently became a member of the house of peers, chief of the cabinet legislative bureau, minister of education and home minister (in the Okuma Cabinet of 1914), member of the privy council, imperial household minister (1933), and president of the privy council (1934). He remained a bureaucrat to the end, declining to follow other official colleagues into the party ranks. But he came to be known as a "lesser Saionji" and in the early 1930's he ranked as one of the "powerful figures close to the throne." After 1932 he was under attack from the right wing of the bureaucracy, particularly by his personal rival, Hiranuma Kiichiro, and his followers. His public career ended in 1936 under the cloud of his association with the liberal school of constitutional interpretation. Sugiyama Hirosuke, "Ichiki Kitokuro," *Kaizō*, 17 (June, 1935), 243–250; Baba Tsunego, "Fuasshiyo to Seitō," *Kaizō*, 17 (May, 1935), 274 ff.; Nakase Juichi, "Meiji Kempō ni okeru Tennō Kikan Setsu no Keisei," *Hōritsu Jihō*, 34 (April, 1962), 69–70; Itō Yuro, editor, *Tennō Kikan Setsu no Bokumetsu Sen*, pp. 2, 8.

9. "Taikan Zappitsu," *loc. cit.*, 154.

10. Hozumi Yatsuka (1860–1912), younger brother of the eminent civil-law authority, Hozumi Nobushige, graduated from To-Dai in 1883 and became professor of constitutional law and state law at that school in 1889, after studying in Germany. He served also as a member of the house of peers and as an imperial household councilor. He began teaching at the time of the promulgation of the constitution and devoted himself to the formulation and dissemination of the "orthodox" interpretation of the imperial constitutional system. As a contributing editor to the semi-official newspaper *Nichi Nichi*, he did yeoman

service for the government during 1889–1890 in asserting the monarchical-sovereignty theory against the interpretations put forth by popular-rights journalists. For a useful analysis of Hozumi's contribution to Japanese constitutional theory see Matsumoto Sannosuke, "Nihon Kempōgaku ni okeru Kokka Ron no Tenkai: Sono Keiseiki ni okeru Hō to Kenryoku no Mondai wo Chūshin ni" in Fukuda Kanichi, et al., Seiji Shisō ni okeru Seiō to Nihon: Nambara Shigeru Sensei Koki Kinen, pp. 177–190.

11. "Taikan Zappitsu," loc. cit.

12. Kōsaka Masaaki (David Abosch, trans.), Japanese Thought in the Meiji Era, pp. 378–379.

13. Akagi Kazuhiko, "Gendai Kempō Kyōju Sōhyō," Kaizō, 17 (June, 1935), 258. The division of labor between constitutional law and state law was formalized by the creation of separate chairs for these subjects in 1901. Fukube Unoyoshi, editor, Tōkyō Teikoku Daigaku Goju Nen Shi, Vol. II, pp. 181, 198. Thus Hozumi and Ichiki monopolized the public-law field at To-Dai until Ichiki, in pursuit of his bureaucratic career, gave up the chair of state law to Nomura Junji in 1906 and his chair of administrative law to Minobe in 1908. Hozumi served as chief of the law faculty from 1897 to 1911.

14. Tanaka Jiro and Ukai Nobushige, "Kokuhō-gaku or Comparative Constitutional Law," Japan Science Review: Law and Politics, No. 1 (Tokyo: 1950), 39–40.

15. Uesugi Shinkichi (1878–1929) graduated from To-Dai and was appointed assistant professor there in 1903. He studied in Europe from 1906 to 1909, succeeding his patron, Hozumi, upon his return to Japan. He taught constitutional law at To-Dai until his death, but his academic fortune and prestige declined with the rise of the liberal school after 1914. As standard bearer of the orthodox school he brought to it an even deeper emphasis on the so-called spiritual aspects of Hozumi's constitutional doctrine. He was active in conservative political movements on and off campus. For a brief but thorough exposition of Uesugi's constitutional theory, see Matsumoto, op. cit., pp. 192–206. Akagi, loc. cit., and Sugimura Shosaburo, "Hyōgi-in Hōgaku Hakushi Uesugi Shinkichi Shi no Kōryo," Kokka Gakkai Zasshi, 43 (May, 1929), 155–156. Kokka Gakkai Zasshi (Journal of the Political and Social Science Society) is published at Tokyo. It is cited hereafter as KGZ.

16. Actually Minobe had written at least one article earlier: "Kempō no Kaishaku ni kansuru Gigi Sūzoku," KGZ, 13 (January, 1899), 34–36.

17. Minobe, "Kunshu no Kokuhōjō no Chi-i," Hōgaku Shirin, 50 (November, 1903), 1–6.

18. It was against such cosmopolitanism as this that Hozumi Yatsuka aimed his shafts: "Hitherto there has been a kind of heresy in our academic circles which subscribes to the erroneous notion that theory knows no national limits. Some scholars of constitutional law think in terms of a universalization of domestic and alien jurisprudence. I stand in direct opposition to this point of view, refusing to be controlled by foreign examples and theories. . . . I believe in a particularized interpretation of a country's constitution." Kempō Teiyō, Vol. I, preface, pp. 2 f.

19. For a somewhat different view of Uesugi's classroom personality, see Dan Kurzman, Kishi and Japan: The Search for the Sun, pp. 91–92. His biographer relates that Nobusuke Kishi was personally attracted to Uesugi while a student at To-Dai, and that at one time Uesugi had proposed to Kishi that he groom himself as Uesugi's successor at the university. Ibid., pp. 98–99.

20. Suzuki Yasuzō refers to Uesugi's conversion about 1909 from warm devotion to the state-sovereignty theory to advocacy of the theory of the emperor as the subject of sovereignty. He cites Uesugi's own references to the period of "disordered thinking" between graduation and his return from Europe, during which time he had attacked the doctrines of his teacher, Hozumi. *Nihon Kempō Shi Kenkyū*, pp. 295, 308. Also Matsumoto, *op. cit.*, p. 194. Minobe himself implies that Uesugi had suddenly changed his position. "Taikan Zappitsu," *loc. cit.*, 156. The point has been made that Uesugi's doctrinal position was primarily the result of his acceptance of Hozumi's protection and the attendant obligation of strict personal loyalty. Ozaki Shiro, *Tennō Kikan Setsu*, pp. 14 ff. Nakase Juichi shows that, while Uesugi originally held to the state sovereignty theory, he at no time derived liberal constitutional principles from it. "Meiji Demokurashii no Nashiyonarizumu e no Tenkan," *Dōshisha Hōgaku*, 78 (March, 1963), 189–191.

21. Minobe's pupil, Miyazawa Toshiyoshi, has referred to a letter (no date given) from Hozumi to the venerable Kato Hiroyuki in which he wrote: "Your excellency's refutation of the emperor-organ theory has greatly inspired us. In Japanese academic circles there are many who have faithfully copied the West with such theories as that which holds the emperor to be an organ, and this has been harmful. Chief among these is Professor Minobe at Tokyo Imperial University. At the present time about the only one besides myself who subscribes to the theory that the emperor is the subject of governmental power is Professor Uesugi Shinkichi. Since he is writing a book, it is his desire that it be presented to your excellency with the hope that you will read it." Miyazawa calls this a disgraceful example of carrying tales to the palace. In Maruyama *et al.*, "Nihon ni okeru Seijigaku no Kako to Shōrai," *Seijigaku*, Vol. I, No. 1 (1950), 24. Matsumoto suggests that it was Minobe's 1908 essay on Jellinek's *Verfassungsänderung und Verfassungswandlung* that first struck sparks from Uesugi. *Op. cit.*, pp. 193–194.

22. Itō Yuro, *Tennō Kikan Setsu . . .*, p. 2.

23. Akagi, *op. cit.*, p. 259.

24. *Ibid.*, pp. 258 ff. Ozaki, *Tennō Kikan Setsu*, pp. 18–20.

25. Miyazawa Toshiyoshi appears hard put, in view of Minobe's relations with his students, to explain his success as a teacher: "People often ask me how it was that so many public-law scholars appeared as pupils of Minobe. I reply that Minobe's method of guiding his disciples was of all methods the best, the simplest, and most difficult. That method requires that the teacher himself be consumed by a burning zeal for scholarship, that he pursue zealously without rest his precious labors that they may be made public. This it was more than anything else that taught and inspired us, and that is why nothing more in the way of method was needed. That is why there are by no means few who have been taught by him, who indeed may be considered to be his pupils, even though they had no opportunity for direct contact with him individually. . . . Minobe as an individual was somehow an unsociable person, difficult to approach, and young men felt ill at ease before him. Nevertheless many young scholars competed in the queue before his door. . . . Behind his uninviting exterior lurked an unlimited paternal affection for his pupils and this was the basis of their reciprocal affection for him." "Minobe Sensei no Gyōseki," *KGZ*, 62 (July, 1948), 14.

26. In a brief autobiographical note published in 1934, Minobe recalled his rather

unsuccessful experiences as a member of a literary association of Japanese
students in Berlin (1900). The chief interest of the group was in producing
haiku poetry. Minobe encountered great difficulty "in harmonizing reason and
poetry." "Daigaku wo Saru ni Nozomite," in *Gikai Seiji no Kentō*, p. 397.
27. "Taikan Zappitsu," *loc. cit.*, 156 ff.
28. Suzuki, *Nihon Kempō Shi Kenkyū*, p. 308. One academic critic describes the
change in Uesugi's position as the resolution of conflicting Jellinekian and
Hegelian influences in favor of an almost purely Hegelian position. Nakajima
Shige, "Tagenronteki Kokka Gakusetsu to Ronrigakujō no Jiga Jitsugen Setsu,"
Dōshisha Ronsō, 11 (May 25, 1923), 8–9, note 8. While espousing the strict
positivism of Laband against the more tolerant position of Jellinek, Uesugi in his
earliest major writing, *Teikoku Kempō*, 1910, still adhered to a corporate theory
of the state. Progressively through subsequent publications he purged his writing
of this embarrassment, coming around fully to an organic theory of the state.
Matsumoto, *op. cit.*, pp. 201–205.
29. Sixteen articles written by Minobe, Uesugi, and others, constituting the critical
portion of the literature of the 1912 debate, were published by Hoshijima Jiro
as *Saikin Kempō Ron*. First published in 1913, this work is cited here from its
seventh edition, 1927. Hoshijima was an ardent Minobe "fan" among the
student observers of the quarrel. For valuable comment on this debate by two
of Minobe's pupils see Miyazawa Toshiyoshi, "Kikan Setsu Jiken to Minobe
Tatsukichi Sensei," *Hōritsu Jihō*, 20 (August, 1948), 42 ff.; also his "Minobe
Sensei no Gyōseki," *loc. cit.*, 10 ff.; and Ukai Nobushige, "Minobe Hakushi no
Shisō to Gakusetsu—sono Rekishi no Igi," *Hōritsu Jihō*, 20 (August, 1948), 45.
30. Hoshijima, *op. cit.*, pp. 13, 34–36, 63 ff., 168–173. Minobe's *Kempō Kowa* was
the edited and enlarged publication of lectures delivered by Minobe in the
summer of 1911, under the auspices of the ministry of education, before a study
conference of middle-school teachers. Uesugi himself had lectured in the summer of 1911 at the invitation of the Prefectural Education Association. Before
that, from 1898 through 1910, Hozumi had annually engaged in the summer
instruction of secondary teachers on the subject of the constitution and national
ethics, emphasizing the familial-state theme. Kōsaka (Abosch), *op. cit.*, pp.
385–388; and Ishida Takeshi, *Kindai Nihon Seiji Kōzō no Kenkyū*, pp. 22–24.
31. The constitutional text referred to reads thus:
    Art. I. The Empire of Japan shall be reigned over and governed by a line of
    Emperors unbroken for ages eternal.
    Art. IV. The Emperor is the head of the Empire, combining in Himself the
    rights of sovereignty, and exercises them according to the provisions of the
    present Constitutions.
    Text as in Harold S. Quigley, *Japanese Government and Politics*, p. 336.
32. Hoshijima, *op. cit.*, pp. 21–24. The Japanese term *minshu* is a contraction of
kokumin shuken (popular sovereignty). In other forms—for example, *minshu-
teki* or *minshushugi*—it means "democratic" or "democracy." Because of the
political connotation of popular sovereignty, use of *minshu* in the sense of
"democratic" was apt to be construed as being contrary to the constitution. On
the other hand the legalistic connotation of the term made it inadequate as an
equivalent of the richer and more flexible "democracy" as used in the west. Okamoto Niji, *Meiji Taishō Shisō Shi*, p. 335. Professor Oda Yoradzu in one of his
contributions to the debate suggested: "Since it belies actual conditions to

make democracy mean government by the people, I think much error can be avoided by using the term *minsei* [the most common usage of this term is as the equivalent of civil government]. In this sense of democracy, but not in Aristotle's sense, our national polity is compatible with democracy, indeed it must be democratic. . . ." Hoshijima, *op. cit.*, pp. 189–190. The problem of finding a suitable equivalent for *"demokurashii"* continued into the post-World War II period. See note 60 below, for discussion of Yoshino Sakuzō's *mimponshugi*.

33. *Ibid.*, pp. 14, 28 ff.
34. *Ibid.*, p. 34. In the course of a later quarrel with Yoshino Sakuzō, Uesugi said: "I think that the attitude of newspapers and magazines toward scholars in recent times is offensive. I feel that the managers of these publications seek to benefit themselves by the influence of wide popular applause that comes when they publish the expositions of liberal scholars and then induce other scholars to prepare refutations. While there have been exceptional men among our scholars from the beginning, there have been some who have advanced beyond their merits. These men have gone abroad to school at an early age and have returned . . . to enter directly into important institutions." "Waga Kensei no Kompongi," *Chūō Kōron* (March, 1916), 45. On the role of editorial enterprise in promoting and exploiting public controversy between academic persons in Japan, see Nobutaka Ike, *Japanese Politics*, pp. 241–242.
35. Hoshijima, *op. cit.*, pp. 3–7. Minobe reminded his opponents that these theories were not new with him in Japan, but had been introduced on the eminent professional authority of Ichiki. Minobe asserted that Hozumi, Uesugi, and others had all relied on some form of the corporate or organic theory of the state in explaining the constitution; that they were merely quibbling when they objected to the term "organ." See Nakase Juichi, "Meiji Kempō ni okeru Tennō Kikansetsu no Keisei," *Hōritsu Jihō* (April, 1962), 26–28.
36. *Ibid.*, pp. 10, 45–49, 53, 56, 205 ff.
37. Matsumoto, *op. cit.*, p. 169.
38. *Ibid.*, pp. 13–15, 79, 86–90, 146–151. Minobe, too, had recourse to the pages of *Taiyō* and to the newspaper *Yomiuri Shimbun*. "Taikan Zappitsu," *loc. cit.*, 156.
39. Hoshijima, *op. cit.*, p. 148.
40. *Kempō Teiyō*, Vol. I, preface, p. 4; and Hoshijima, *op. cit.*, pp. 92 ff., 151–158, 280 ff.
41. *Ibid.*, pp. 205 ff., 306–315.
42. *Ibid.*, pp. 10, 221–238.
43. *Ibid.*, pp. 1–3. See also a similar contemporary statement by Minobe cited in Ishida, *op. cit.*, p. 27.
44. Preface, pp. 6, 8. Also his "Kokutai no Seika wo Hakki suru no Aki," *Chūō Kōron*, 34 (January, 1918), 91–104. In this article Uesugi set forth his belief that Japan's national polity—an unbreakable union of people and emperor in a relationship of filial and paternal regard—was Japan's only source of strength in the competition of the Powers in the Pacific. Echoing the words of Hozumi, he wrote: "Having this inherently and naturally firm authority, we are equipped with the most important condition of social progress; it constitutes our first weapon in the battlefield of world struggle." In yet another article Uesugi said: "It is clear from whatever position one views it, the spirit of our constitution excludes parliamentary government. . . . It is therefore regrettable that so many have taken parliamentary government to be the ultimate virtue of constitutional

government." He asserted that popularism in itself was too narrow and too base a concept to be taken as the essence of constitutional government, which is in truth nothing but good government. He found in Japanese history clear demonstration of the fact that the emperor was the true custodian of popular welfare, and that the people never suffered such grinding misery as when the emperor-centric polity was ignored or perverted. "Waga Kensei no Kompongi," loc. cit., 19, 30, 40. Both of these articles were directed not against Minobe but against Yoshino Sakuzō's democratic journalism of the World War I period. It was in the course of this encounter with Yoshino that Uesugi made connections which were to endure for some years with Takabatake Motoyuki, a pioneer of the national socialist movement in Japan. Kinoshita Hanji, Nihon Fuashizumu Shi, Vol. I, pp. 38–39, 56–57, 82–84.

45. Hasegawa Masayasu, Kempōgaku no Hōhō, p. 6. See also Ukai, "Minobe Hakushi no Shisō to Gakusetsu," op. cit., 45 ff., and Nakamura Akira, Nihonkoku Kempō no Kōzō, p. 65.

46. Ito, op. cit., p. 8. Aizawa Hiroshi, Nihon Kyōiku Hyakunen Shidan, pp. 308–315.

47. Miyazawa, "Kikan Setsu Jiken to Minobe Tatsukichi Sensei," op. cit., 43; Hasegawa, op. cit., pp. 5–6.

48. Akagi, op. cit., pp. 258 ff. Uesugi, "Kokutai no Seika wo Hakki suru no Aki," loc. cit., 95.

49. Miyazawa, "Kikan Setsu Jiken to Minobe Tatsukichi Sensei," 43. Minobe himself records: "Fortunately, with few exceptions, my theory was accepted, and my defense met with approval in the ministry of education and in other official circles. There was no need of my retiring. But I was never again given a ministry of education commission in connection with middle-school examinations in legislation, nor in the preparation of legislation text books for the middle schools." "Taikan Zappitsu," loc. cit., 157.

50. Miyazawa, "Kikan Setsu Jiken to Minobe Tatsukichi Sensei," loc. cit. In the 1918 edition of Kempō Kōwa, Minobe dropped the provocative preface of the first edition. In his "Taikan Zappitsu" (p. 156) he expressed regret that the record of the 1912 dispute had been kept before the public in successive editions of Hoshijima's work.

51. Rōyama Masamichi, Seiji Shi, p. 390.

52. For a succinct statement of what was meant by "the influence of the elder statesmen," see Robert K. Reischauer, Japan: Government and Politics, pp. 108–109.

53. Kenneth W. Colegrove, Militarism in Japan, pp. 18–23.

54. Rōyama, op. cit., p. 392.

55. Satō Isao, Nihonkoku Kempō Ju-ni Kō, pp. 199–203; Rōyama, op. cit., pp. 391–395.

56. Suzuki Yasuzō, Nihon Kempō Shi Kenkyū, p. 117.

57. Rōyama, op. cit., pp. 389 ff., 395.

58. Ibid., p. 398.

59. Rōyama Masamichi, Nihon ni okeru Kindai Seijigaku no Hattatsu, pp. 103, 138, 158 ff.

60. Mimponshugi may be translated as "democracy," although it was conceived to avoid some of the ideological implications of the more common minshushugi (see note 32 above). Okamoto expands it to jinmin honi no kokutai (national

polity based on the people). *Op. cit.*, pp. 332–334. The term has been described as a prudent falsification which failed, however, to pacify the guardians of national polity. Sakisaka Itsuro *et. al., Arashi no naka Hyakunen*, p. 14. By the use of this term Yoshino sought to emphasize the importance of processes and objectives in government. For him, the aim of constitutional government is the realization of complete democracy in government. See his "Mimponshugi no Igi wo Toite Futatabi Kensei Yūshū no Bi wo Motorasu no Michi wo Ronzu," *Chūō Kōron*, 33 (June, 1918), 96–135. In expounding the concept of *mimponshugi* he sought to establish the basis upon which to advance practical, functional democracy without alienating himself from the imperial institution, the central ideological symbol of the Japanese nation. Not only did *mimponshugi* fail to appease the right, it was belittled from the left as "cadet democracy." See Murofusa Takanobu, "Gendai no Seinen wo Ugokashizutsuaru Seironka Shisōka," *Chūō Kōron*, 34 (January, 1919), 123. In later writing Yoshino abandoned the use of this term.

61. Rōyama, *Nihon ni okeru Kindai . . .*, pp. 103–106. Ishida, *op. cit.*, pp. 29–30.
62. Comments by Maruyama Masao *et al.* in "Nihon ni okeru Seijigaku no Kako to Shōrai," *op. cit.*, 38, 47.
63. The chair was created by the ministry of education on the recommendation of the academic council of the university, on which Minobe himself served as one of the two elected representatives of the law departmment from April, 1919. *Daigaku Goju Nen Shi*, Vol. II, pp. 564, 1847.
64. The law faculty (*hōka daigaku*) became the law department (*hōgaku bu*) under the revision of the university ordinances in April, 1919. The chiefs of departments (*buchō*) were appointed by the minister of education from among the professors of the department. *Ibid.*, Vol. II, p. 682.
65. Naikaku Insatsu Kyoku, *Kampō* No. 8265 (December 12, 1911), p. 156.
66. Naikaku . . . , *Kampō* No. 1151 (January 16, 1932), p. 367; *Tōkyō Asahi Shimbun* (January 16, 1932), p. 2.
67. His appointment was made by the Inukai (Seiyukai) Cabinet, under Art. I, sec. 4 of the House of Peers Ordinance, which provides for appointment for outstanding service to the state or for scholarly distinction. Naikaku . . . , *Kampō* No. 1606 (May 11, 1932), p. 266.
68. Miyazawa, "Minobe Sensei no Gyōseki," *op. cit.*, 330.
69. See note 23, chap. 1.
70. See Tanaka and Ukai, *op. cit.*, p. 43.
71. *Erinekku no Jinken Sengen Ron.* Included in this volume were three additional translations of excerpts from Jellinek's *Allgemeine Staatslehre*. Minobe credited the original translations to various other Japanese students at Heidelberg. This volume was republished by Nihon Hyōron Sha in 1946.
72. On minority rights (Jellinek) in *KGZ*, September and November, 1904; on the sources of English constitutional law (Hatschek, *Englische Staatsrecht*, Chapter 3) in *KGZ*, June and October, 1906; on constitutional change (Jellinek,*Verfassungsänderung und Verfassungswandlung*) in *Hōgaku Kyōkai Zasshi*, June and August, 1908; on Jellinek's *Staatsform* theory in *KGZ* in October, 1909.
73. This work, cited here from the edition of 1947, was the published version of a series of special lectures he delivered at To-Dai early in 1918, celebrating the establishment of a chair of American constitution, history, and diplomacy which

was endowed by A. B. Hepburn of the Chase National Bank of New York. Robert S. Schwantes, *Japanese and Americans: A Century of Cultural Relations*, p. 100.

74. *Jiji Kempō Mondai Hihan, Gendai Kensei Hyōron, Gikai Seiji no Kentō, Nihon Kempō no Kihon Shugi.*

NOTES TO CHAPTER III

1. References to *Kempō Satsuyō* hereafter are to the fourth (1931) edition unless otherwise indicated. Minobe's books and articles are cited hereafter by title only, unless special identification is in order.

2. Minobe represented one of two methodologically distinct positions within the interpretive-analytic (liberal or constitutional) school. One of these was known as the liberal (*jiyuteki*) school, the other as the "logical positivist" (*ronriteki-jisshōteki*) school. It was with the first of these that Minobe's name was identified. Sasaki Soichi was the writer most commonly associated with the second. Once the dualism between the interpretive-analytic school and the historical orthodox school had ended with the post-World War II liquidation of the orthodox position, the differences within the interpretive-analytic school gave rise to a new dualism now designated by the headings "teleological" (*mokutekironteki*) (Minobe and others of the Tokyo School) and "formal" (*keishikiteki*) (Sasaki and others of the Kyoto School). See Kobayashi Takasuke, *Kempōgaku no Honshitsu*. A product of the great burst of interest in problems of methodology in constitutional studies in the mid-1950's, this book, written under a grant of the ministry of education, presents a very useful compendious taxonomy of German and Japanese constitutional theory.

3. This aspect of Minobe's position is discussed by Hisata Eisei in his essay "Sengo Nihon Shi ni okeru Kempōgaku no Kadai to Tembō," in Kobayashi Takasuke, *et al.*, *Nihonkoku Kempō Shikō: Sengo no Kempō Seiji*, pp. 332–333.

4. Hasegawa Masayasu, *Kempōgaku no Hōhō*, pp. 3–5. Until 1945, according to Hasegawa, Japanese constitutional science was anti-popular, nothing but a technique of interpretation of the Imperial Constitution the better to serve the purposes of the bureaucrat's craft and the inculcation of civic morality—of no use or meaning to non-official interests. Jurisprudence tended to be official jurisprudence, especially in the case of constitutional science. Constitutional science had from the first a political purpose. So long as this was not challenged, there was little stimulus—indeed, just the opposite—for a real inquiry into methodology. *Ibid.*, p. 12.

5. Kuroda Ryōichi, "Kempō Kaishaku no Ikkōsatsu," in Suzuki Yasuzō, editor, *Kempōgaku no Kadai*, 33–79. Kuroda's essay is of great value as an analytic and critical survey of the problem of methodology in Japanese constitutional science. In it he carries on in the vein of Suzuki Yasuzō's pioneer work in the development of an historical materialistic critique of academic constitutional theory in Japan. Kuroda focuses chiefly on the liberal schools of Sasaki and Minobe, offering a rather appreciative evaluation of Minobe and his disciples.

   For helpful comments on Minobe's methodology see also Ukai Nobushige, "Minobe Sensei no Hikakuhōteki Kenkyū," *Kokka Gakkai Zasshi* (KGZ hereafter), 62 (July, 1948), 34–39, and "Minobe Hakushi no Shisō to Gakusetsu—

sono Rekishi no Igi," *Hōritsu Jihō*, 20 (August, 1948), 45–49; Suzuki Yasuzō, *Kempō no Rekishiteki Kenkyū*, Book III, Chapter 1 ("The Historical Transformations of Constitutional Concepts"), pp. 392–437; and Tanaka Jiro, "Nihon Kempō ni Kansuru Saikin Ni-san no Choso," *KGZ*, 46 (April, 1932), 112–131.

6. (3d edition; 1923), p. 107. Italics added. This note is a paraphrase of Jellinek's statements in *Allgemeine Staatslehre*, pp. 50–52, 130 f., and in *System der subjektiven öffentlichen Rechte*, pp. 13–15.

7. *Nihon Kempō*, p. 108. Italics added.

8. "Keruzen Kyōju no Kokka oyobi Kokusaihō Riron no Hihyō," III, *KGZ* 44 (October, 1930), 1532, 1541 ff.

9. Matsumoto Sannosuke, "Nihon Kempōgaku ni okeru Kokka Ron no Tenkai: Sono Keiseiki ni okeru Hō to Kenryoku no Mondai wo Chūshin ni," in Fukuda Kanichi, *et al.*, *Seiji Shisō ni okeru Seiō to Nihon: Nambara Shigeru Sensei Koki Kinen*, pp. 207–208.

10. *Nihon Kempō*, p. 70, where he deals with limitations to the efficacy of legal concepts and fictions in the explanation of law. Also *ibid.*, pp. 536–539, where he states his criticism of Laband's juristic method, of which more later.

11. Hans Kelsen, *Hauptprobleme der Staatsrechtslehre: entwickelt aus der Lehre von Rechtsätze*, pp. 85 ff. Minobe complained of misinterpretation of the *Zwei-Seiten Theorie* in Jellinek's methodological theory, as for instance by Hans Kelsen in *Der sociologische und der juristische Staatsbegriff*, pp. 114 f. Cf. Otto Mayer, "Die juristische Person und Ihre Verwertbarkeit im öffentlichen Recht," in Paul Siebeck, editor, *Staatsrechtliche Abhandlungen: Festgabe für Paul Laband*, p. 3.

12. Cf. Jellinek: "Es ist unmöglich, wissenschaftlich haltbare juristische Resultate zu gewinnen, wenn man den Inhalt der Lebensverhältnisse gänzlich ignoriert." Without this perception of "the content of life relationships" there is only "a world of concept without reality, of form without content, of results without significance." Quoted by Kelsen, *Hauptprobleme . . .*, *op. cit.*, pp. 93–94.

13. The political party was, for instance, a shoal upon which his constitutional theory was ever about to founder. In the introduction to his *Gikai Seido Ron* (1930), a 450-page work devoted to "a survey of the parliamentary systems presently operating" in England, America, France, and Germany, he said: "Such questions as how do the parliamentary systems of these states actually work from a political point of view, what are the personal qualifications of the individual members of these parliaments, and what is the role and the trend of the influence of political parties in these parliaments, are quite essential to a real political knowledge of the parliamentary system, but this work concerns itself with such matters hardly at all."

14. Ukai, "Minobe Sensei no Hikakuhōteki Kenkyū," *loc. cit.*, 357 ff. The original reference is to *Die Erklärung der Menschen und Burgerrechte*, p. 31 (p. 6 of the 1946 edition of Minobe's translation of this work: *Jinken Sengen Ron*). Jellinek said: "Die Literatür für sich ist niemals produktiv, wenn sie nicht in dem historische und sozialen Boden findet. Wenn man der literarische Ursprung einer Idee aufweist, hat man damit keineswegs auch die Geschichte ihrer praktischen Bedeutung erkannt. Die Geschichte der Politik ist heute noch viel zu viel Literatürgeschichte, viel zu wenig Geschichte der Institutionen selbst. . . ."

15. *Kempō no Rekishiteki Kenkyū*, *op. cit.*, p. 425. Suzuki's criticism is aimed par-

ticularly at Minobe's failure to "grasp concretely the real historical and political significance of the constitution" as a production of post-Restoration social and political forces.

16. The question arises whether Minobe may have found in his European studies not the origin but merely the confirmation of his political views. It can be said only that there is nothing in his own writing or in that of his critics, friendly or hostile, to suggest a native origin of his liberalism. Whether Ichiki's influence was liberal or not, it was in any case really a European influence. Nakase advances the idea that Minobe elected the liberal course in his early career because "in the era of the Meiji '30's Japanese conditions urgently demanded it of him." Nakase depicts the progressive and radical political developments of that era and relates Minobe's work to them. Nakase Juichi, "Tennō Kikan Setsu Kakuritsu Katei ni Okeru Minobe Riron no Tokushitsu," *Dōshisha Hōgaku*, 72 (June, 1962), 155–195.

17. See pages 40–41 above.

18. There were, however, a few comparative studies at later dates, such as his work on the American Constitution (1918), some articles on the Weimar Constitution, and his *Gikai Seido Ron* (1935).

19. Possibly in this also he reflected the teachings of Jellinek, who wrote in *Allgemeine Staatslehre*, pp. 42 ff.: "Institutions are forever changing, but every change is not a development. Development is only such change as leads from creation to completion.... Certainly it is not for us to discount the value of historical research ... but [such research] serves above all for an understanding of the past and not of the present. For the present it suffices that we quite understand simply the development of an institution."

20. Minobe's criticism of Kelsen appears in its most complete form in his "Keruzen Kyōju ...," *op. cit.*, 1177–1212, 1375–1406, 1532–1550. In this article Minobe displayed a degree of professional censoriousness rare for him. He recounted that his doubts about Kelsen, arising from his reading of *Hauptprobleme der Staatsrechtslehre* (1911), were confirmed by his reading of *Probleme der Souveränität* (1920) and *Der soziologische und der juristische Staatsbegriff* (1922): "I was firmly convinced that this way of thinking was altogether bad for jurisprudence ... that he [Kelsen] misunderstood the nature of jurisprudence" and indulged in conceptual play "almost completely worthless, scientifically speaking." Minobe declared that he could not "condone the currency of this way of thinking among young [Japanese] scholars," and had therefore set himself the task of refuting Kelsen's basic doctrines. The substantial reason for Minobe's concern about the influence of Kelsenian theories in Japan is indicated by his catalogue of charges (*ibid.*, 1375 ff.): "Having eliminated from his conceptual structure all reference to social and psychological factors," he ended up by: (1) denying the corporate nature of the state, (2) denying state sovereignty and the exercise of legislative power by the state, (3) denying that the state imposes duties on itself, (4) denying the *Zwei-Seiten Theorie*, and (5) by asserting that what we call the state is the whole body of state law, in other words, that the concept of state is the same as the concept of law.

21. "Keruzen Kyōju ...," I, *loc. cit.*, 1180–1186; III, 1532 ff. See Imanaka Tsugimaro, "Seijigaku," in Miki Kiyoshi, editor, *Gendai Tetsugaku Jiten*, p. 297.

22. "Keruzen Kyōju ...," I, *loc. cit.*, 1191–1193.

23. *Ibid.*, 1193 ff. Minobe referred to the *volonté générale* of Rousseau, the *Rechts-*

uberzeugung of the historical school, the *Anerkennungs-theorie* of Bierling, and the *Behauptungstheorie* of Berolzheimer as expressions of the idea that the essence of law lies in its recognition in the social conscience of society. *Ibid.*, 1197. He was critical of Kelsen's rejection of Durkheim's theory of social psychology. *Ibid.*, II, 1380.

24. *Ibid.*, I, 1200 ff.; and *Kōhō to Shihō*, p. 11.
25. *Kempō Seigi*, pp. 3 ff.
26. *Nihon Kempō*, pp. 61–72.
27. *Ibid.*, pp. 536–537. Minobe describes Laband's method thus: (1) A complete separation between constitutional science and political science: "The dogmatic academic duty of jurisprudence is to bring each law under a general concept, and it is from these general concepts that the effects of a law are to be drawn. This is a purely logical mental process. To fulfill this duty there is absolutely no other method than logic." [Laband] (2) Constitutional law concerns nothing but the established law of a particular state. It is separate from *allgemeine Staatsrecht* and from natural law studies. The positive constitutional law of a state is a unified whole without gaps.
28. *Ibid.*, pp. 66, 538 ff. Cf. Georg Jellinek, *Verfassungsänderung und Verfassungswandlung*, pp. 8–34. Ishida Takeshi has pointed out the limited consequences of this Jellinekian doctrine in Japan, where constitutional amendment was impossible and where constitutional change by interpretation was frustrated by the domination of the political structure of government by antiprogressive social interests. *Kindai Nihon Seiji Kōzō no Kenkyū*, pp. 299 f. Cf. Kobayashi, *op. cit.*, pp. 132–142, for a statement on the importance of the *Verfassungswandlung* doctrine in Minobe's theory.
29. The discourse of this paragraph is based principally upon Kuroda, *op. cit.*, pp. 60–69. The teleological element in Minobe's method comes to full fruit in the work of his follower, Nakamura Akira: "Simply to render a logical translation of the text of a given constitution taking it as a completed system is not the duty of constitutional science as a branch of social science. Considering the development of Japan's cultural wealth and perceiving the direction of world history, the bourgeois democratic revolution is thought to be the theme of the times and the first rule of constitutional interpretation is to give effect to it." *Shin Kempō Nōtō*, p. 138.
30. Quotations from the fifth edition of *Kempō Satsuyō* are taken from Tanaka Jiro, *op. cit.* The fifth edition followed by a year Minobe's "Keruzen Kyōju. . . ." The preface and various reorganizations of and additions to the text testify to Minobe's concern at that time with the inroads of Kelsenian doctrine.
31. Miyazawa Toshiyoshi, "Minobe Sensei no Gyōseki," *KGZ*, 62 (July, 1948), 9.
32. "Minobe Sensei no Hikakuhōteki Kenkyū," *loc. cit.*, 44. In this article Ukai offers an interesting comment on the difference between Minobe and Laband, attempting to explain how these two positivists arrived at completely opposite conclusions: Minobe in support of parliamentary liberalism, Laband in support of bureaucratic monarchy. According to Ukai, what distinguished and redeemed Minobe was his historical vision and his emphasis on the significance of ethics and custom in law. *Ibid.*, pp. 41, 48.
33. Cf. Tanaka, *op. cit.*, p. 584. Also Suzuki, *Kempō no Rekishiteki Kenkyū*, p. 418, where he says: "Minobe's theory reminds me of the pure bourgeois legal concept of natural law. . . ." It seems to this writer that a more approximate analogy

is to be found in the effort by American legal philosophers to find a pragmatic standard in lieu of natural law by reference to an intersubjectively established norm based on the communal mind. See Samuel I. Shuman, *Legal Positivism: Its Scope and Limitations,* p. 99.

34. *Nihon Kempō,* p. 34; and *Kempō Satsuyō,* p. 1.

35. *Nihon Kempō,* p. 66.

36. *Kempō Satsuyō,* pp. 121–123. Italics added.

37. *Ibid.* Italics added.

38. Yanase Yoshimiki, "Minobe Sensei to Shin Kempō," KGZ, 62 (July, 1948), 32.

39. The main source for this section is *Nihon Kempō,* the substance of which is condensed in the first 84 pages of *Kempō Satsuyō.*

40. *Nihon Kempō,* pp. 531–535. Minobe divided public law into judicial law (criminal law, law of criminal procedure, and law of civil procedure), and public law in the strict sense (constitutional law, administrative law, and the law of public corporations). Constitutional law, as the fundamental law of the state, is the basis of all public law. The distinctiveness of these six categories is not sharp; nor, for that matter, is the distinction between public law (in the broad sense) and private law. Minobe was critical of Kelsen's failure to recognize that relations between state and subject differ in quality from those between subject and subject by virtue of the coercive authority attributed to the state. On the other hand, he denied the validity of the position taken by most Japanese administrative law authorities that the distinction between public law and private law is absolute, and that private law concepts and methods cannot be applied to public law problems. *Ibid.,* pp. 526–531; and *Kōhō to Shihō,* pp. 7–13.

41. He accepted Ihering's assertion that "purpose is the creator of all law," but he rejected Ihering's identification of that purpose with *Sozialutilitarismus.*

42. *Nihon Kempō,* pp. 3–34; and *Kempō Satsuyō,* pp. 1–6. In the definition of law the term "will" (*ishi*) may also be read "purpose." In his postwar (1948) *Nihonkoku Kempō Genron* (p. 2), he explains: "In its original sense the term *ishi* means the psychological process of the motivation of human behavior to some particular end. But the external manifestation of *ishi* is behavior. Thus when we say that law is a rule of human will [or purpose], we mean tht it is a rule of human behavior."

43. *Nihon Kempō,* pp. 61–72, where he discusses the uses and abuses of legal concepts.

44. *Ibid.,* pp. 80 ff.

45. Minobe knew that he was out of step with most authorities in describing the relationship between a corporation and its organs as one of agency. He would not accept, however, the alternative suggested by Gierke, and endorsed by some Japanese legal scholars, that the relationship should be understood as *Darstellen.* The important thing was that the will of the person constituting the organ be directed to the ends of the corporation. *Ibid.,* pp. 85–87.

46. *Ibid.,* pp. 93–95.

47. *Ibid.,* pp. 97–107; Jellinek, *System der subjektiven öffentlichen Rechte,* pp. 26–27, and *Allgemeine Staatslehre,* pp. 137 ff.

48. "Die Staat ist die mit ursprunglichen Herrschermacht ausgerustete Verbandsseinheit sesshafter Menschen." *Ibid.,* p. 181. The term *tōchi* equates with *Herrscher* or *herschen; dantai* means corporation.

49. Here he concluded that so far as the organic theory posited the state as being

made up of many individuals but constituting a life entity distinct from that of its individual components, and as having its own will and the power to maintain its own existence, it was correct. But "organic" is a natural science term and its use in social science gives rise to misconceptions. For instance, a natural organism is naturally endowed with a unity of purpose, but a social organism achieves unity of purpose only through law. He cited Leon Duguit's attack on the organic theory. He found that Gierke's exposition of the organic theory confused the juristic concept of personality with the sociological concept of corporation, an error perceived and corrected by Jellinek. *Kempō Kōwa*, pp. 6 ff.; *Nihon Kempō*, pp. 112–129; *Kempō Satsuyō*, pp. 9–12.

50. *Kempō Kōwa*, pp. 2–8; *Nihon Kempō*, pp. 127–140; and *Kempō Satsuyō*, pp. 13–15. Cf. Jellinek's reference to the state as a "purposive unity." *Zweckeinheit*, cited by Imanaka Tsugimaro in his essay "Kokka no Honshitsu" ("The Nature of the State"), in Rōyama Masamichi, editor, *Seiji oyobi Seijishi Kenkyū: Yoshino Sakuzō Sensei Tsuitō Kinen*, p. 106.

51. Hozumi Yatsuka, *Kempō Teiyō*, Vol. I, p. 113.

52. *Ibid.*, p. 1, *Nihon Kempō*, p. 130.

53. *Ibid.*, pp. 141–147; *Kempō Kōwa*, pp. 8–12; *Kempō Satsuyō*, pp. 17–19.

54. Lest this discourse be written off as overly rarefied conceptualization, we are well reminded by Matsumoto Sannosuke's study that the propositions concerning the law consciousness of society, on the basis of which governmental power acquires validity as the right of a corporate legal personality, goes to the heart of Minobe's attempt to escape from the Austinian absolutism of Hozumi without going over to the Hegelian absolutism of Uesugi. *loc. cit.*, pp. 207–218.

55. *Nihon Kempō*, pp. 148–173; and *Kempō Satsuyō*, pp. 7–9.

56. *Nihon Kempō*, pp. 174–180, 189; *Kempō Satsuyō*, p. 22.

57. *Nihon Kempō*, p. 177; *Kempō Kōwa*, pp. 15–22.

58. Hozumi, *op. cit.*, pp. 41–48.

59. *Ibid.*, pp. 200, 213.

60. *Nihon Kempō*, pp. 181 ff.; 192 ff.

61. *Ibid.*, pp. 185–197.

62. *Ibid.*, pp. 215–274; also *Kempō Satsuyō*, pp. 30–42.

63. Minobe denied that there is a conflict between the idea of the indivisibility of sovereignty and the separation of powers as an element in constitutional government. The objections to the separation of powers put forth by Rousseau, Kant, Duguit, Laband, Hozumi, and others was the result of their failure to recognize that the indivisibility of *kokken* means only the indivisibility of state will, and not that it must be expressed through a single organ. All that is required is a method of harmonizing the expressions of the various organs. *Nihon Kempō*, pp. 227 ff.

64. Minobe concluded against the use of the term *shuken* (sovereignty, from which comes the term *shukensha*, the sovereign). He felt that this term had acquired historically such diverse political connotations as to be scientifically useless. While the concept of sovereignty (monarchical or popular) had been very potent politically, such political values were irrelevant to the problem of the juristic nature of the state. Where *shuken* has been used in legal context, more precision would have resulted from the use of *kokken* or *tōchiken*, he said. *Ibid.*, pp. 256–274; *Kempō Kōwa*, pp. 19–21.

65. *Nihon Kempō*, pp. 294–298; *Kempō Satsuyō*, pp. 43–45.

66. *Nihon Kempō*, pp. 287–293.
67. Following Jellinek, *Allgemeine Staatslehre*, pp. 544 ff.
68. *Nihon Kempo*, pp. 300–307; *Kempō Satsuyō*, p. 48.
69. *Nihon Kempo*, pp. 308–310; *Kempō Satsuyō*, pp. 49 f.
70. *Nihon Kempō*, pp. 310–321.
71. *Ibid.*, pp. 329–333; *Kempō Satsuyō*, pp. 46 f., 58 ff.
72. *Nihon Kempō*, pp. 321, 348; *Kempō Satsuyō*, p. 61.
73. *Kempō Kōwa*, p. 36. It is not likely that Hozumi or Uesugi could quarrel with Minobe's use of the term *kunmin dōchi*. This was indeed the term employed by the arch-Tory Okubo Toshimichi to convey the essential meaning of constitutional monarchy. Not the term itself but the meaning read into it was the point of issue. See Okubo's memorial of 1873, given in George Beckmann, *The Making of the Meiji Constitution: The Oligarchs and the Constitutional Development of Japan, 1868–1891*, p. 113. See also Ishida, *op. cit.*, pp. 292–294.
74. *Nihon Kempō*, pp. 318–328; *Kempō Satsuyō*, pp. 56–58.
75. *Nihon Kempō*, pp. 300 ff. A useful attempt to clarify Minobe's use of *seitai* as distinct from *kokutai*, and of *tōchiken* as distinct from *shuken*, has been made by Nakamura Akira in his *Nihonkoku Kempo no Kōzō*, pp. 19–25.
76. Minobe cited Hozumi, Uesugi, Shimizu, Fukushima, Kakehi, and Ichimura as subscribing to this view of *kokutai*. *Nihon Kempō*, pp. 340–345. The authority of Ito Hirobumi apeared to lie with those who held this view. Ito had written that the constitution asserted no "newly settled opinion," but rather merely confirmed "more strongly than ever" the original and immutable national polity. Cited from Beckmann, *op. cit.*, p. 84.
77. *Nihon Kempō*, p. 329; *Kempō Kōwa*, pp. 44–45.
78. "Mombusho no Kokugo Kana Tsukai Kaikaku-an wo Nanzu" ("Criticism of the Ministry of Education's Proposed Reform of the *Kana* System"), in *Jiji Shimpō* (July 28–31, 1931), cited here from *Gikai Seiji no Kentō*, pp. 522 ff. The term *kokutai* is said to be of native origin, not an imported word. Matsumoto Shigetoshi, *Tōchiken Ron*, p. 179. Still, Japanese scholars have sought to find its equivalent in western languages and thought. Ogushi Toyo suggests that it be translated *Staatsgestalt*, meaning state form in an ethical rather than a legal sense. "Die Entwicklung des japanischen Konstitutionalismus seit dem Weltkriege," *Jahrbuch des öffentlichen Rechte*, 19 (1931), 369. Tanaka Tsugimaro finds a parallel for it in a combination between what Bodin called "the eternally immutable law peculiar to the nations" (the Salic law in the case of the French monarchy) and Hegel's *Volksethik*. *Seijigaku Tsūron*, pp. 70–73.
79. See reference to the work of Tsurumi Shunsuke in I. I. Morris, *Nationalism and the Right Wing in Japan: A Study of Post-War Trends*, pp. 427–428.
80. *Nihon Kempō*, p. 386. His analysis of the ideas of popular self-government and liberty and their institutional expression was preceded by a forty-page survey of constitutional development in Europe.
81. *Ibid.*, pp. 387–391; *Kempō Satsuyō*, pp. 61 f.
82. *Nihon Kempō*, pp. 392–398, 413–416; *Kempō Satsuyō*, pp. 62–64.
83. *Nihon Kempō*, pp. 398–409.
84. *Ibid.*, pp. 410–412.
85. *Ibid.*, p. 427.
86. *Kempō Satsuyō*, pp. 65 f.

87. *Nihon Kempō*, pp. 456–458.
88. *Kempō Satsuyō*, pp. 66 f.
89. *Ibid.*, p. 68.
90. *Nihon Kempō*, pp. 432–442. The description of Jellinek's position given above is based on Alfred Voigt, *Geschichte der Grundrechte*, pp. 114–118.
91. *Ibid.*, pp. 67 f.; *Nihon Kempō*, pp. 442–451; Hozumi, *Kempō Teiyō*, I, pp. 103–113.

NOTES TO CHAPTER IV

1. Rōyama Masamichi, *Nihon ni okeru Kindai Seijigaku no Hattatsu*, p. 14; Ukai Nobushige, "Minobe Hakushi no Shisōto Gakusetsu—sono Rekishi no Igi," *Hōritsu Jihō*, 20 (August, 1948,) 46.
2. Ukai Nobushige, "Minobe Sensei no Hikakuhōteki Kenkyu," *Kokka Gakkai Zasshi*, 62 (July, 1948), 39 ff. *Kokka Gakkai Zasshi* appears hereafter as *KGZ*.
3. Ishida Takeshi, *Kindai Nihon Seiji Kōzō no Kenkyū*, p. 294.
4. *Kempō Satsuyō* (5th ed.), preface, p. 5.
5. That those speaking from the front lines of the struggle for party government were not necessarily favorably impressed with the worth of academic constitutional theory is suggested by the following passage from a journal article. Although the article does not mention Minobe, he may well have been one of those in the author's mind as he wrote: "Publication of Ito's commentaries opened the way for [those of] others, some of which were different from his. Indeed there was much criticism of Ito's interpretation. The burden of systematic commentary, however, fell on university professors who were under the influence chiefly of German thought, and who were willing to follow the lead of the *genrō* and their likes. ... Even those who strove for party cabinets would not quarrel with the so-called bureaucrats in interpreting the constitution. They maintained a defeatist attitude in the debate. ... Not only were the parties without any prominent constitutional interpreters, but when they came into power, either because they were apprehensive of the displeasure of the *genrō* or because it was simpler to coöperate with the bureaucrats, they sought to avoid offending the inviolable gods ... they did not want to struggle with experts trained in the universities of the German Empire, and they thought it better not to attract derision for clumsiness. This was the attitude in the house of representatives; in the house of peers there were many who aspired to out-German the Germans. ... Miyake Setsurei, "Kempō Happu-go Tadashini San-ju Nen," *Chūō Kōron*, 34 (February, 1919), 77–79.
6. One of the liberated souls who early made the flight from the *Staatslehre* to political positivism, Yoshino Sakuzō was a more radical and aggressive revisionist than was Minobe. Paradoxically, Yoshino shared Uesugi's belief that Minobe's state-sovereignty theory was objectionable because of its close connection with the "un-Japanese" idea of popular sovereignty. See his "Ware no Kensei Ron no Hihyō wo Yomu," *Chūō Kōron*, 31 (April, 1916), 103–123. His own *mimponshugi* (see note 60, chap. 2) gave expression to the spirit of constitutionalism without the taint of popular sovereignty, reflecting his belief that constitutionalism was not an exclusively alien thing, without any basis in Japanese experience, that it was rather, in a sense, "truly our own."
7. *Kempō Satsuyō* (4th edition), pp. 103–124. The body of laws that made up

the constitutional law of the Japanese state included: the Imperial Constitution and its Preamble; the Imperial House Law; various laws, ordinances, and treaties, such as the Diet Law, the House of Peers Ordinance, the Cabinet Ordinance, the Law of the Organization of the Courts of Law, the Electoral Law, and treaties defining territorial limits, extraterritorial rights, etc.; customary law, such as the precedents of diet procedure; constitutional convention, such as the political parties and the *genrō*. Similarly in *Chikujō Kempō Seigi* (cited hereafter as *Kempō Seigi*), pp. 31–35.

8. *Kempō Satsuyō* (5th edition), preface, p. 5.
9. *Kempō Satsuyō* (4th edition), p. 118. Hereafter, this edition (1930) is cited unless otherwise noted.
10. *Kempō oyobi Kempō Shi Kenkyū*, pp. 325 ff.; Kobayashi Takasuke, *Kempōgaku no Honshitsu*, pp. 137–142.
11. Cf., *Kempō Kōwa*, pp. 49–63; and *Kempō Satsuyō*, pp. 85–101.
12. *Kempō Teiyō*, Vol. 1, pp. 136–144, 156 f. Elsewhere he wrote: "To understand the constitution one must be read in the history of the Meiji Restoration. The Restoration was the recognition of national polity. It added nothing to national polity. It originated in a debate over national polity, and its great task was to establish a constitution which provided a form of government faithful to national polity." "Kempō Seitei no Yurai," in *Meiji Bunka Zenshū*, Vol. IV, 419.
13. Suzuki Yasuzō, *Kempō no Rekishiteki Kenkyū*, pp. 399, 422, 426 f.; Suzuki Yasuzō, *Nihon Kempō Seiritsu Shi*, pp. 7–9.
14. Suzuki, *Kempō no Rekishiteki Kenkyū*, pp. 405–414.
15. Sasaki Sōichi, born 1878, graduate of Kyoto University, professor of constitutional law and administrative law at that university from 1913 to 1933, and subsequently at the Ritsumeikan (Kobe). Sasaki ranked with Minobe among the "liberal" constitutional scholars. The political interpretation which he put on the origin of the constitution at this early date is not easily reconciled with the legal positivism with which he was subsequently prominently identified.
16. Similarly, the noted constitutional historian Osatake Takeshi challenged the validity of efforts made by some to equate with constitutionalism the traditional notion that there had been a complete harmony between the imperial will and the spirit of the people from the beginning of the empire: "I deny that this is constitutional thought, for it does not embrace the idea of popular representative participation in government." *Nihon Kensei Shi*, Vol. 1, p. 3.
17. *Nihon Kempō Seritsu Shi*, *op. cit.*, p. 6. The paragraphs immediately above owe much to Suzuki's comments on the problem, including the citation from Sasaki's essay "Rikken Hi-rikken." That essay has been included in a collection of articles republished under the same title in 1950.
18. *Kempō Satsuyō*, p. 73. It consists of three elements: (1) the structure of the state; (2) the organization of the central government of the state; and (3) the basic law of the administrative and judicial power of the state. Cf., *Kempō Seigi*, pp. 6 f.
19. *Ibid.*, p. 7.
20. *Kempō Satsuyō*, pp. 85–88.
21. Although Minobe's distinction between the essential and the formal has important consequences for the problem of constitutional change, it does not go beyond the pale of the positive law. Its purpose is not that of political

criticism such as is implicit in the idea of *Scheinkonstitutionalismus* (pretended constitutionalism), deriving from Ferdinand Lassalle's famous distincton between written and real constitution, that is, between the written constitution and the actually existing relations of power in the state. Ishida, *op. cit.*, p. 290; and Kobayashi, *op. cit.*, pp. 10, 38.

22. *Kempō Satsuyō*, pp. 89, 93.
23. *Ibid.*, pp. 89–101.
24. "Nihon Kempō no Tokuiro," *KGZ*, 40 (March, 1926), 336 f.; *Kempō Seigi*, pp. 5 f.; *Jiji Kempō Mondai Hihan*, p. 45.
25. *Kempō Seigi*, preface, pp. 5 f.; "Nihon Kempō no Tokuiro," 337.
26. *Kempō Seigi*, pp. 16–23. In *Kempō Satsuyō*, pp. 121–124, discussion of the Japanese form of government is brought under three headings: monarchy, constitutionalism, and centralization.
27. *Kempō Seigi*, p. 19; *Kempō Satsuyō*, pp. 125–217; "Nihon Kempō no Tokuiro," *loc. cit.*, 164–186.
28. *Kempō Seigi*, pp. 20–23.
29. *Kempō Kōwa*, pp. 65 ff. In *Kempō Satsuyō* he did not use the expression "state organ" in relation to the emperor, but he returned to it in *Kempō Seigi* and in "Nihon Kempō no Tokuiro." The connection was implied, if not expressed, in all his interpretive works on the Imperial Constitution.
30. *Kempō Seigi*, pp. 16–18.
31. "Nihon Kempō no Tokuiro," *loc. cit.*, 8–16.
32. *Kempō Seigi*, pp. 65–78; "Nihon Kempō no Tokuiro," *loc. cit.*, 18.
33. *Tōchiken*, rendered in the authoritative English text as "the rights of sovereignty," is used throughout this study to mean governmental rights and authority, in keeping with Minobe's efforts to emphasize its finite content and to avoid the absolute connotations of the concept of sovereignty. The English texts of the Preamble and Articles I and IV and of subsequently cited articles of the Constitution are as given in Harold S. Quigley, *Japanese Government and Politics*, pp. 335 ff.
34. *Kempō Seigi*, pp. 121–134; *Kempō Satsuyō*, pp. 210 ff.
35. *Ibid.*, p. 127.
36. "Nihon Kempō no Tokuiro," *loc. cit.*, 185–187; *Kempō Satsuyō*, pp. 125 ff.; *Kempō Seigi*, p. 18. The quoted passage may be likened to the "mainspring" simile used by writers in the English constitution tradition. For example, J. A. Corry: "the executive is the mainspring of government. It makes the wheels go round . . . nation-states can continue in some fashion without a functioning legislature or judiciary of significant independence. But when the executive breaks down, the central government collapses." *Elements of Democratic Government*, p. 75. The concept, the "government" (*seifu*), closely approximates that of British usage; it includes the cabinet plus certain of its adjunctive and coördinate bureaucratic organs.
37. *Kempō Kōwa*, p. 88; *Kempō Seigi*, pp. 162 ff.; *Kempō Satsuyō*, pp. 210 ff.; 217–231. Other distinguishable aspects of the imperial prerogative were the imperial household prerogative exercised by the emperor as head of the imperial family on the advice of the imperial household minister (not a member of the cabinet), the rewarding of merit and service by the emperor as the fountainhead of honor in the Japanese state, and the performance of the principal Shinto rites by the emperor as chief celebrant of the empire.

38. The Japanese use the term *gyōsei* where we would use "executive" in discussing the three-power theory of government. *Gyōsei* means "administration" (*Verwaltung*). Minobe defined it as "the process by which the state achieves all of its purposes except those civil and criminal matters which are governed by legislation," in other words, all state activity which is not legislative or judicial in nature. *Kempō Satsuyō*, p. 519; *Gyōsei Hō Satsuyō*, Vol. I, p. 7. This residual or deductive theory of administration was of European derivation and was advanced in Japan chiefly by Minobe and Sasaki Sōichi; it was not approved by all Japanese authorities, however. Cf., Nomura Jiichi, "Gyōseihōgaku ni okeru Gyōsei Gainen," *Hōgaku Ronsō*, 38 (July, 1932), 103–108; and Rōyama Masamichi, "Gyōsei no Gainen Kōsei ni okeru 'Tōchi' no Igi" ("The Meaning of 'Tochi' in the Conceptual Structure of Administration"), in his *Seiji oyobi Seijishi Kenkyū—Yoshino Sakuzō Sensei Tsuitō Kinen*, 173–176.

39. Hozumi, *Kempō Teiyō, op. cit.*, Vol. II, pp. 657 ff.; Sasaki Sōichi, *Nihon Kempō Yōron*, pp. 333 ff.; Satō Ushijiro, *Teikoku Kempō Kōgi*, pp. 48 f.

40. The contents of these articles may be summarized as follows:
Art. VI. Veto.
Art. VII. Convocation, prorogation and closing of the diet, dissolution of the house of representatives.
Art. VIII. Emergency ordinance power.
Art. IX. Police ordinance power.
Art. X. Civil and military offices, salaries, appointments and dismissals.
Art. XI. Military command.
Art. XII. Military administration.
Art. XIII. Declaration of war, conclusion of peace, making treaties.
Art. XIV. Declaration of state of siege.
Art. XV. Granting titles and honors.
Art. XVI. Amnesty and pardon.

41. There is evidence that this was the intention of the drafters of the constitution. Cf. Suzuki Yasuzō, *Nihon Kempō Shi Kenkyū*, pp. 152 ff.

42. *Kempō Kōwa*, pp. 89–92; *Kempō Satsuyō*, pp. 152–154; "Nihon Kempō no Tokuiro," *loc. cit.*, 190.

43. This position derived from his understanding of Anschütz's doctrine of "the general reservation of statutes" (*Allgemeinevorbehalt des Gesetzes*), to which Ichiki, Sasaki, and others also subscribed. According to this principle, statutes (general legislated norms) are superior to ordinances and, in the last analysis, every administrative and judicial act of the state is subordinate to the legislative (statute-making) acts of the state. See Tagami Joji, "Public Law," *Japan Science Review: Law and Politics*, Vol. IV (1953), 35–36.

44. *Kempō Seigi*, pp. 163–168. I have not held strictly to his arrangement of this material.

45. "Nihon Kempō no Tokuiro," *loc. cit.*, 187 ff.

46. The word "law" (*hōritsu; loi, Gesetz*, statute), as in "the Diet Law," indicated an expression of state will enacted with the consent of the diet and promulgated as a *hōritsu*. Laws in this formal sense were alterable or revokable only with the diet's consent. *Kempō Seigi*, pp. 168, 225.

47. "Nihon Kempō no Tokuiro," *loc. cit.*, 189 f.

48. *Kempō Satsuyō*, pp. 213 f. According to Article IX, "the Emperor issues or causes to be issued orders necessary to the execution of law. . . ." Minobe's point

was simply that the phrase "causes to be" could be read into each of the prerogative items.

49. "Nihon Kempō no Tokuiro," *loc. cit.*, 188 f.; *ibid.*, pp. 237 f.; *Kempō Seigi*, pp. 115 f.

50. A comprehensive survey of this problem has long been available to American students in Tomio Nakano's *The Ordinance Power of the Japanese Emperor.*

51. *Kempō Satsuyō*, pp. 442 f.

52. *Ibid.*, p. 442.

53. *Ibid.*, pp. 431–440; *Kempō Seigi*, pp. 198–223. Closely related to this general emergency ordinance power was the power of the government under Article LXX to issue emergency financial orders in case of urgent necessity when the diet was not in session. *Kempō Satsuyō*, pp. 556–558; *Kempō Seigi*, pp. 701–706.

54. The verb used in Article VIII was *shōdaku* (consent in the sense of acquiescence); that used in Article V was *kyōsan* (consent in the sense of approval). The difference in the action of the diet in the two cases seems to have been rather a matter of convention than the consequence of a clear distinction in meaning in the constitutional text. Minobe used the term *dō-i* (which he equated with *Zustimmung*) to designate the mode in which the diet exercised its substantive competence in legislative, fiscal and self-regulative matters. *Kempō Satsuyō*, p. 349.

55. *Kempō Seigi*, pp. 227–233; *Kempō Satsuyō*, p. 444.

56. Law No. 84 of 1890 (concerning penalties applicable in cases of violation of ordinances) fixed the penalty at ¥200 and one year imprisonment. *Kempō Seigi*, pp. 232–237; *Kempō Satsuyō*, pp. 445–447.

57. *Kempō Satsuyō*, pp. 448 f.; *Kempō Seigi*, pp. 238–249.

58. *Kempō Satsuyō*, pp. 464–471; *Kempō Seigi*, pp. 263–269.

59. In his exercise of the military prerogatives, the emperor was "generalissimo" of the empire (*daigensui*) and his powers as such were collectively designated "the supreme command" (*tōsuiken* or *i-aku taiken*).

60. *Kempō Satsuyō*, pp. 563–565.

61. *Kempō Kōwa*, pp. 93–97; *Kempō Satsuyō*, pp. 237 f.; *Kempō Seigi*, p. 115.

62. *Kempō Kōwa*, pp. 129 f.; *Kempō Seigi*, pp. 115 f.

63. *Kempō Kōwa*, pp. 134–138; *Kempō Seigi*, pp. 510 ff.

64. Hirobumi Ito, *Commentaries on the Constitution of the Empire of Japan*, pp. 92 ff.

65. *Kempō Teiyō, op. cit.*, II, p. 530; and Hoshijima Jiro, ed., *Saikin Kempō Ron*, p. 29.

66. *Kempō Satsuyō*, p. 270; *Kempō Seigi*, p. 512. The term *hohitsu* was accepted by all commentators as the equivalent of the English constitutional term "advice." Minobe used it interchangeably with the phrase *shingen to yokusan* (advice and assistance). *Kempō Satsuyō*, p. 285.

67. *Ibid.*, p. 271.

68. Yale E. Maxon, *Control of Japanese Foreign Policy: a Study in Civil-Military Rivalry: 1930–1945*, pp. 8–10; Robert Butow, *Tojo and the Coming of the War*, pp. 170–177. Both of these rely on the Harada-Saionji Diaries and on the records of the Tokyo War Crimes Tribunal, especially the testimony of Kido Kōichi.

69. *Kempō Seigi*, p. 512.

70. *Kempō Satsuyō*, pp. 301–315; "Nihon Kempō no Tokuiro," *loc. cit.*, 164–173.

71. *Gendai Kensei Hyōron*, pp. 181 ff.; and *Gikai Seiji no Kentō*, p. 25.

72. In addition to the staff organs of the army and navy, which were charged with advising and executing military command policy, an ordinance of 1887 had created the supreme war council and another in 1898 established the board of marshals and fleet admirals. Important defense policy decisions were submitted to one or both before imperial sanction was given. Neither the council nor the board had executive responsibilities. Minobe found in them an analogy with the privy council and the *genrō* respectively, classifying them as "consultative" organs (*komon kikan*) rather than as assisting or "advising" (*hohitsu*) organs. The board of marshals and fleet admirals consisted of a small number of the most senior officers of the army and navy. The supreme war council was composed of the members of the board, the minister of war, the minister of navy, chief of the army general staff, chief of the navy staff, and, at times, other officers of either service.

73. The war ministry and navy ministry ordinances were amended in 1900 by the *genrō* Yamagata to make only general officers and admirals on active duty eligible to serve as minister. In 1914 the Yamamoto Cabinet pushed through the privy council an amendment to those ordinances making reserve officers eligible. This was the rule throughout the period here concerned. In May, 1936, the ordinances were again amended to restore the 1900 limitation.

74. I have relied chiefly upon Nakano Tomio, *Tōsuiken no Dokuritsu* as well as the indicated sections of Minobe's works for the formal and legal aspects of this problem. Yale E. Maxon's previously cited monograph, *Control of Japanese Foreign Policy*, presents a valuable political analysis focused on foreign policy issues in the post-Mukden era. The problem of military-civil relations is so basic to political and constitutional history of prewar Japan that in postwar literature of history and political analysis almost every substantial work has something to contribute to our understanding. It appears, however, that there has been as yet no single comprehensive, systematic analysis of prewar civil-military politics in Japan.

75. Reference here to the German development is based on Gordon A. Craig, *The Politics of the Prussian Army: 1654–1945*, pp. 226 ff.

76. Nakano, *Tōsuiken no Dokuritsu, op. cit.*, pp. 495–498.

77. *Kempō Satsuyō*, p. 224.

78. "Waga Kokuhō ni okeru Gumbu to Seifu to no Kankei" ("Relations Between the Military and the Government in Japanese State Law"), *Kaizō* (June, 1930), cited here from *Gikai Seiji no Kentō*, pp. 125 ff.

79. *Kempō Satsuyō*, pp. 563–567; *Kempō Seigi*, pp. 258–260.

80. In this respect the Japanese departed from the German model, according to which the "responsible" minister of war was not a member of the military command structure.

81. *Kempō Satsuyō*, pp. 568–572; *Kempō Seigi*, p. 261.

82. Abe Isoo and Miyake Yujiro, eds., *Shōwa Go Nen Shi*, pp. 65–70.

83. The previously cited "Waga Kokuhō ni okeru Gumbu to Seifu to no Kankei" was a product of the naval treaty controversy. Its publication in the magazine *Kaizō* in June, 1930, was preceded by "Kaigun Jōyaku no Seiritsu to Tōsuiken no Genkai" ("The Making of the Naval Treaty and the Sphere of the Supreme Command"), *Asahi Shimbun* (May 2–4, 1930). The latter article owns the distinction of being the only work of Minobe published in English translation.

It was reprinted under the title "Cabinet and Camp" in *Japan Chronicle* (May 15, 1930). He placed three articles on the treaty question in *Teikoku Daigaku Shimbun* (Tokyo Imperial University daily newspaper) between April and October, 1930. All of the above are reproduced in *Gikai Seiji no Kentō*, pp. 99–142.

84. *Ibid.*, pp. 105 ff.

85. *Ibid.*

86. Harada Kumao, comp., *Saionji Kō to Seikyoku*, Vol. I, pp. 41–42, 145–149.

87. See his "Ankoku Seiji Jidai" ("The Age of Political Darkness") written in 1928, cited here from *Gendai Kensei Hyōron*, pp. 252–255.

88. *Gikai Seiji no Kentō*, p. 122. His fears coincided with those of Saionji as reported by Harada. Harada, *op. cit.*, Vol. I, pp. 145, 210.

89. *Gikai Seiji no Kentō*, pp. 118 ff.

90. Harada, *op. cit.*, Vol. I, p. 42.

91. Maxon, *op. cit.*, pp. 75–78, and p. 46, where he cites from Marquis Kido's diary a statement made in the early 1930's by the then Colonel Nagata Tetsuzan giving these reasons for military concern with domestic politics: the necessity for protecting the military position in an age of disarmament and unfavorable public opinion, for protecting the rights of supreme command which had been jeopardized as a result of the London naval agreement, and for protecting military salaries from reduction.

92. Minobe was alarmed at the intemperance of the Seiyukai. He blamed that party for giving currency to the charge that the Minseitō were guilty of violation of the imperial prerogative of supreme command, which was tantamount to a charge of treason. He gave it as his opinion that the Seiyukai had no better excuse for voicing such an inflamatory accusation than the difficulty of exciting popular emotion by reference to the one allegation that might have been sustained by the facts: namely, that the cabinet had trespassed on the competence of the chief of the navy staff. "Iwayuru Tōsuiken Kamban" ("The So-called Violation of the Supreme Command"), *Teikoku Daigaku Shimbun* (October 16, 1930), cited here from *Gikai Seiji no Kentō*, pp. 139–142.

93. See Mori Shōzō, *Sempū Ni-ju Nen*, pp. 44 f.; Tsunego Baba, "Parliamentary Revival," *Contemporary Japan*, 3 (June, 1934), 15. A "retired naval officer," speaking on behalf of "patriotic ex-servicemen" against Minobe in 1935 said: "Understanding . . . calls for an examination of the attitude of the ex-servicemen toward the disputed interpretation which is less manifest in the haze which jurists have thrown around it than in recent political developments. One must go back to the conclusion of the London Naval Agreement of 1930. . . ." "On Japan's National Polity," *Contemporary Japan*, 4 (December, 1936), 336 f. In 1930, for the first time since 1913, Minobe's constitutional theory was discussed in the diet, when Nakamura Keijue criticized his position on the naval treaty question in the house of representatives. *Kampō Gōgai* (*Official Gazette Extra*) (March 26, 1930), House of Representatives, pp. 50–51.

94. *Kempō Seigi*, p. 257. Also "Gun-min Rikan to Gunjin Seiji Kanyo" ("Military-Civilian Discord and the Participation of Military Men in Government"), *Gikai Seiji no Kentō*, pp. 330–332. This article was published in Tokyo Nichi-nichi Shimbun on February 5, 1934. In it Minobe commented on the debate in the Sixty-fifth Diet concerning the political activities of military personnel and the publication by the army and navy ministries, in December, 1933, of a

Manifesto Against the Movement to Alienate Civilians from the Military (*Gun-min Rikan Undō ni taisuru Seimeishō*).

95. *Kempō Seigi*, p. 536.
96. "Rikushō Dairi no Setchi to Muninsho daijin no Shinrei" ("New Precedents Concerning Ministers Without Portfolio and the Establishment of an Acting Minister of War") published originally in *Teikoku Daigaku Shimbun* (June 23, 1930), cited here from *Gikai Seiji no Kentō*, pp. 158 ff.
97. *Kempō Seigi*, pp. 256 f.; *Kempō Satsuyō*, pp. 308–310.
98. *Kempō Seigi*, p. 255; cf., *ibid.*, p. 727 where Minobe cited the possibility of such a change as an example of the possibility of liberalizing the constitution through the process of *Verfassungswandlung*.
99. Articles LVII–LIX.
100. The primary sources for the following discussion of the cabinet are *Kempō Kōwa*, pp. 129–144; *Kempō Satsuyō* pp. 271–284; and *Kempō Seigi*, pp. 506–535.
101. *Naikaku Kansei*, Imperial Ordinance No. 135 (December 26, 1889), Article I: "The Cabinet is composed of the various Ministers of State." Text as given by Quigley, op. cit., pp. 359 f.
102. Article V of the Cabinet Ordinance required cabinet deliberation on (1) projects of law and budget; (2) treaties and international affairs; (3) imperial ordinances; (4) inter-ministerial disputes; (5) popular petitions submitted via the imperial household ministry or the diet; (6) extra-budgetary expenditures; and (7) appointment and dismissal of superior officials. Article VI permitted any minister to bring any matter of his responsibility before the cabinet via the prime minister. The *kōshikirei* required countersignature by the full cabinet on several types of laws, imperial ordinances, and rescripts.
103. *Sūmitsu-in*. This title was a direct translation of the English "privy council," but there was never any illusion that the similarity between the Japanese article and its English counterpart, at least in its contemporary form, was any more than superficial. The best English language study of this institution is Kenneth W. Colegrove, "The Japanese Privy Council," *American Political Science Review*, 25 (October, 1931), 881–905.
104. Article LVI. "The Privy Councillors shall, in accordance with the provisions for the organization of the Privy Council, deliberate on important matters of State, when they have been consulted by the Emperor."
105. The privy council shared with the imperial household ministry the function of counseling the imperial family council in regard to such important matters as the establishment of a regency and the succession to imperial family property, under the terms of the Imperial Household Law. The president of the privy council was *ex officio* a member of the imperial family council. It is further indication of the relation of the privy council to the throne that it was by no means infrequently that the emperor attended meetings of the privy council.
106. The central task of the privy council was set forth in Article VI of the Privy Council Ordinance (text as in Quigley, *op. cit.*, p. 354):

The Privy Council shall hold deliberations and present its opinions to the Emperor for his decision on the under-mentioned matters:

1. Differences of opinion as to the interpretation of the Constitution, or of the laws appertaining thereto, and questions relating to the budget and other financial matters.

2. Drafts of amendments of the Constitution or of laws appertaining thereto.

3. Important Imperial ordinances.

4. Drafts for new laws and drafts for abolition of existing laws; treaties with foreign countries; and the planning of administrative organizations.

5. Any other matters whatever, besides those mentioned above, touching important administrative or financial measures upon which the opinion of the Privy Council has been specially required by order of the Emperor; and matters upon which the opinion of the Privy Council has to be taken, by reason of some special provision of law or ordinance.

107. Typically the council consisted of superannuated members of the civil and military services, former members of the house of peers, a few former ministers of state (rarely, an ex-prime minister), and a few conservative academicians. Appointments to the council were made on the nomination of the prime minister subject to the veto of the imperial household minister and the president of the privy council. Colegrove, *op. cit.*, 897–900.

108. *Kempō Satsuyō*, pp. 296–300; *Kempō Seigi*, pp. 553–664. The brief and relatively noncontentious treatment of the privy council in these texts must be supplemented by reference to his "Sūmitsu-in Ron" ("The Privy Council Question"), KGZ (August, 1927), cited here from *Gendai Kensei Hyōron*, pp. 68–128; and to his "Sūmitsu-in Seijiteki Taido" ("The Political Posture of the Privy Council"), *Teikoku Daigaku Shimbun* (July 1, 1929), cited here from *Gikai Seiji no Kentō*, pp. 227–230. See Harada, op. cit., Vol. I, pp. 145–146 for Minobe's advice that Hamaguchi was not bound to heed the decisions of the privy council in respect to ratification of the London Naval Treaty.

109. Article III of the supplementary regulations to the Privy Council Ordinance provided: "The Privy Council shall have official connections with the Cabinet and with the Ministers of State only, and officially shall not communicate with or have any connection whatever with any of His Majesty's private subjects."

110. "Sūmitsu-in no Seijiteki Taido," *loc. cit.*, p. 227.

111. "Kinkyū Chokurei ni taisuru Sūmitsu-in no Taido" ("The Attitude of the Privy Council in Respect to Emergency Ordinances"), *Teikoku Daigaku Shimbun* (July 4, 1928), cited here from *Gendai Kensei Hyōron*, pp. 263 ff.

112. "Sūmitsu-in Ron," *loc. cit.*, p. 128.

NOTES TO CHAPTER V

1. The quotation is from a 1930 article on electoral reform published in *Chūō Kōron*, cited here from *Gikai Seiji no Kentō*, pp. 390 ff.

2. The expression sometimes applied was "a parliament-centered interpretation." Cf., Tanaka Jiro, "Nihon Kempō ni Kansuru Saikin Ni-san no Chosho," *Kokka Gakkai Zasshi* (hereafter KGZ), 46 (April, 1932), 117–119. Tanaka drew significance from Minobe's organization of his material in *Kempō Satsuyō*. The fifth edition of that work consisted of five parts: (1) basic concepts, (2) general theory, (3) the emperor, (4) the imperial diet, and (5) state processes (judicial, administrative, budgetary, and military). Other writers did not set the diet apart and on a level with the monarchical institution in this fashion, the common practice being rather to lump it together with the courts, the administrative organs, etc.

3. "Kokutai Shisō ni Motozuku Kempō Ronsō" ("Constitutional Polemics Based

on National Polity Notions"), published originally in *Teikoku Daigaku Shimbun* (December 17, 1928), cited here from *Gendai Kensei Hyōron*, pp. 287–292.

4. Minobe crossed the line between legal and political writing consciously and with apologies for venturing outside the limits of his professional competence. Introducing a controversial article in *Chūō Kōron* in 1934, he said: "This writer, as a mere lawyer versed in the study of public law, with no practical political experience at all, and even a very poor background in political science, is not at all qualified to discuss this matter. . . ." *Gikai Seiji no Kentō*, p. 42.

5. *Kempō Seigi*, p. 424.

6. *Ibid.*, p. 179.

7. *Ibid.*, p. 179; *Kempō Satsuyō*, pp. 313, 317.

8. *Kempō Kōwa*, pp. 35 f.; *Kempō Seigi*, p. 421; *Kempō Satsuyō*, p. 316.

9. *Kempō Seigi*, pp. 422 ff.; *Kempō Satsuyō*, pp. 314–316.

10. *Ibid.*, p. 320; *Kempō Seigi*, p. 423.

11. *Ibid.*, pp. 447 ff.; and "Kizoku-in Ron" ("The House of Peers Question") published originally in *Kaizō* (August, 1924), cited here from *Gendai Kensei Hyōron*, pp. 133 ff.

12. *Ibid.*, p. 136.

13. Article XXXIV of the constitution decreed that the house of peers be composed of members of the imperial family, the orders of nobility, and imperial appointees in accordance with the provision of the House of Peers Ordinance.

14. *Kempō Satsuyō*, pp. 522–527; "Kizoku-in Ron," *op. cit.*, pp. 141, 152.

15. *Ibid.*, pp. 147–148. This article appeared first in 1924, shortly after the Kenkyukai faction of the house of peers had so far asserted its power as to bring about the establishment of a government based on the house of peers and headed by one of its own members, Kiyoura.

16. *Kempō Satsuyō*, pp. 322 f. The electoral laws of the house of representatives, on the other hand, were subject to veto by the peers. Efforts of the successors of the Kiyoura Government to amend the House of Peers Ordinance were defeated by the house of peers. Minobe attributed that defeat to poor tactics on the part of the government and not to adamant opposition to reform in the house of peers. "Kizoku-in Ron," *op. cit.*, pp. 154 ff.

17. *Ibid.*, pp. 159 f.

18. *Ibid.*, pp. 157 f. It will be recalled that Minobe became a member of the house of peers by imperial appointment in 1932. His behavior in that chamber could not by any means be considered as favorable to the partisan interests of the Seiyukai, under whose auspices he was nominated.

19. In *Kempō Kōwa* (pp. 62 f.) Article XXXV of the constitution provided: "The House of Representatives shall be composed of members elected by the people, according to the provisions of the Law of Elections." Minobe's commentary on this article and on the electoral law in *Kempō Satsuyō*, (pp. 327–341) and *Kempō Seigi* (pp. 447–454) was limited to straightforward analytic description of the existing electoral system with a brief criticism of the combination of the single vote with the multi-member district. It may suffice to note that he viewed the electoral franchise, in the juristic sense, not as a personal right but as a right vested in the electors as organs of the state: the electoral law merely determined who constituted the electoral organ of the state (*sanseiken*). *Kempō Satsuyō*, pp. 327–330.

20. Universal male suffrage was established by a revision of the electoral law in 1925, and was first put into effect in the election of 1928. Wrting after that date Minobe spoke of women's suffrage as something "not yet" adopted in Japan. He deplored the blank ballot system since its effect was to create a high literacy qualification. *Ibid.*, pp. 330–332.

21. See "Senkyo Kakusei Ron" ("On Electoral Reform"), *Gendai Kensei Hyōron*, pp. 3–59, based on articles published originally in 1928–1929; also the section on electoral reform in *Gikai Seiji no Kentō*, pp. 351–464, based on articles published first in the period 1931–1934.

22. *Gendai Kensei Hyōron*, pp. 4, 7. He cited the restrictive electoral law and other policies of the kingdom of Prussia, aimed at repression of the Socialist Party, as important causes of the collapse of the monarchical regime in Germany: "I believe that these events testify to the fact that the restriction of popular rights and the suppression of democratic elements by coercive authority never preserves the stability of monarchy." "Weimar Kempō no Tokuiro" ("Characteristics of the Weimar Constitution"), an address delivered before a To-Dai student group in June, 1929, cited here from *Kempō to Seitō*, p. 147.

23. *Gendai Kensei Hyōron*, pp. 8 f.

24. *Ibid.*, pp. 16–18; *Gikai Seiji no Kentō*, pp. 410–414.

25. For his criticism of these proposals see his discussion of electoral policy in *Gendai Kensei Hyōron*, pp. 26–29, and *Gikai Seiji no Kentō*, pp. 399–407, 459–464; of indoctrination of civics and public ethics in *Gikai Seiji no Kentō*, pp. 381–399; of public management of electoral campaigns in *Gendai Kensei Hyōron*, pp. 30–34, and *Gikai Seiji no Kentō*, pp. 374–380.

26. *Gendai Kensei Hyōron*, pp. 19–27; *Gikai Seiji no Kentō*, pp. 356–366.

27. *Gendai Kensei Hyōron*, pp. 35–59; *Gikai Seiji no Kentō*, pp. 367–372,, 421–426.

28. *Gendai Kensei Hyōron*, pp. 46–57, 148, 439–443.

29. *Ibid.*, p. 59.

30. The following provisions of the constitution are particularly important in the ensuing discussion:

Article V. The Emperor exercises the legislative power with the consent of the Imperial Diet.

Article VIII. The Emperor, in consequence of an urgent necessity to maintain public safety or to avert public calamities, issues, when the Imperial Diet is not sitting, Imperial Ordinances in the place of law.

Such Imperial Ordinances are to be laid before the Imperial Diet at its next session, and when the Diet does not approve the said Ordinances, the Government shall declare them to be invalid for the future.

Article XXXVII. Every law requires the consent of the Imperial Diet.

Article XXXVIII. Both Houses shall vote upon projects of law submitted by the Government, and may respectively initiate projects of law.

Article XL. Both Houses may make representations to the Government, as to laws or upon any other subject. . . .

Article LIV. The Ministers of State . . . may, at any time, take seats and speak in either House.

Article LV. The respective Ministers of State shall give their advice to the Emperor, and be responsible for it. . . .

Article LVII. The judicature shall be exercised by the Courts of Law according to law, in the name of the Emperor.

Article LXII.   The imposition of a new tax or the modification of the rates [of an existing one] shall be determined by law. . . .

Article LXIV.   The expenditure and revenue of the State require the consent of the Imperial Diet by means of an annual Budget. . . .

Article LXX.   (Emergency Imperial Financial Ordinances)

Article LXXI.   When the Imperial Diet has not voted on the Budget, or when the Budget has not been brought into actual existence, the Government shall carry out the Budget of the preceding year.

Article LXXIII.   When it has become necessary in future to amend the provisions of the present Constitution, a project to the effect shall be submitted to the Imperial Diet by Imperial Order. . . . No amendment can be passed unless a majority of not less than two-thirds of the Members present is obtained.

Article LXXIV.   No modification of the Imperial House Law shall be required to be submitted to the deliberation of the Imperial Diet. . . .

31. The power of interpellation, for instance, was based on Chapter X of the Law of the Houses of the Diet.

32. *Kempō Satsuyō*, p. 348; *Kempō Seigi*, pp. 422 ff.

33. Cf. *supra*, pp. 86–89.

34. Tomio Nakano, *The Ordinance Power of the Japanese Emperor*, pp. 66–68.

35. *Kempō Satsuyō*, pp. 213, 349–364.

36. *Kempō oyobi Kempō Shi Kenkyū*, pp. 15–65. Cf. Miyazawa Toshiyoshi, "Rippō Gyōsei Ryo Kikan no aida no Kengen Bumpai no Genri," Part V, KGZ, 46 (November, 1932), 54–63. Miyazawa presents an interesting survey of the development of the debate concerning the legislative power. He traces the emergence of the liberal position from Ito through Ichiki to Ichimura, Sasaki and Minobe. The opposing view, resting on a strict formal separation of powers and the absolute exclusiveness of the imperial ordinance power, was advanced by Hozumi and followed by Uesugi and Shimizu. Miyazawa himself subscribed to Minobe's position.

The positions of the parliamentary and bureaucratic schools of interpretation had become exactly "reversed" on this issue. The idea of a harmonization of powers under the all-embracing imperial prerogative had been advanced by the drafters of the constitution to confound the anticipated pretentions of the diet. When in due course the cabinets were forced to come to terms with the diet, bureaucratic authorities began to insist that the constitution provided for a strict separation of powers. They sought thereby to create the basis for a claim that the diet and the party cabinets were encroaching upon the emperor's prerogative.

37. *Kempō Satsuyō*, pp. 413–416.

38. *Ibid.*, pp. 394–406; *Kempō Seigi*, pp. 135–148, 456 f. The "legislative items" idea was the counterpart of the "prerogative items" idea advanced by Hozumi and others of the orthodox school (see chap. 4) in their concern for the defense of the imperial prerogative against encroachment by parliament. It paralleled their insistence on absolute separation of powers and their rejection of the "democratic" modifications of that doctrine in German theories which influenced Ichiki and Minobe. Cf. Miyazawa, "Rippō . . ." *op. cit.*, pp. 51–63.

39. *Kempō Satsuyō*, pp. 425 ff.

40. *Ibid.*, pp. 418–423.

41. *Kempō Seigi*, pp. 428 ff.

42. *Ibid.*, pp. 21 ff.

43. See pp. 95–96.

44. *Kempō Satsuyō*, pp. 129 f.; Hirobumi Ito, *Commentaries on the Constitution of the Empire of Japan*, p. 93.

45. This characterization of the German Imperial-Prussian monarchical system is that of Bismarck's biographer Erich Eyck in his *History of the Weimar Republic*, pp. 17–18. Compare the words of Ito and Bismarck on the matter of ministerial responsibility. Speaking before the Prussian house of deputies in 1886, Bismarck declaimed his philosophy thus: "One who is not a minister may permit himself the luxury of representing publicly and officially a party opinion; in a ministerial position, as a leading minister, I cannot accept a party view permanently." Before the Reichstag in 1879, the chancellor said: "A leading minister always needs the help of parties but he can never subject himself to the rule of a party." Cited from Fritz-Konrad Krüger, *Government and Politics of the German Empire*, pp. 39–40.

Ito found it expedient to organize partisan support in the diet but nonetheless clung closely to the Bismarckian line when he addressed the founding session of the Rikken Seiyukai in 1900: "[the sovereign] retains absolute freedom to select his advisors from whatever quarter he deems proper; be it from among political parties or from circles outside those parties. When ministers have been appointed and invested with their respective official functions, it is not under any circumstances whatever for their fellow party men or their other political friends to interfere in any manner with their discharge of their duties." Cited from Alfred Stead (ed.), *Japan by the Japanese*, pp. 72 ff.

46. The permanently damaging consequences for the parties of the conditions, under which the accommodation between the bureaucratic and party leaders was actually worked out, are fully delineated and analyzed by Robert A. Scalapino, *Democracy and the Party Movement in Pre-war Japan*, Chapter 5.

47. A transcendental government (*chōetsu naikaku*), or, as sometimes called, a national harmony cabinet (*kyokoku itchi naikaku*) was composed entirely, or chiefly, of nonparty men and of civil and military bureaucratic leaders and technicians. A reversion to this type of cabinet occurred in 1932 with the Saito and succeeding cabinets. *Kempō Seigi*, pp. 539 f.; Charles B. Fahs, *Government in Japan: Recent Trends in Its Scope and Operation*, pp. 71 f.

48. *Kempō Kōwa*, p. 144; *Kempō Satsuyō*, pp, 287 ff.; *Kempō Seigi*, pp. 341 ff.

49. *Kempō Kōwa*, p. 146.

50. *Kempō Satsuyō*, pp. 290 f.

51. *Ibid.*, pp. 283 f.; *Kempō Kōwa*, p. 145.

52. *Kempō Seigi*, p. 535; *Kempō Kōwa*, pp. 145–152; *Kempō Satsuyō*, pp. 129 f., 291 f.

53. Page 155. It will be recalled that this work was produced on the eve of the First Constitutional Defense Movement (1911) and was criticized by Uesugi for partisanship on the side of the Saionji faction against Katsura. See pp. 32–36 above.

54. *Kempō Satsuyō*, pp. 179 f.

55. *Kempō Seigi*, pp. 536, 539 f.

56. *Kempō oyobi Kempō Shi Kenkyū*, pp. 252–256. Also various journal and newspaper articles reprinted in the second and sixth chapter of *Jiji Kempō Mondai Hihan*.

57. Representative of this interest was his *Kempō to Seitō*.

58. Fahs, *op. cit.*, pp. 66 ff.
59. "Seitō Seiji ni okeru Kanryō" ("Government Officials under Party Government"), *Chūō Kōron* (July, 1931), cited here from *Gikai Seiji no Kentō*, pp. 76–96.
60. *Ibid.*, pp. 80–83.
61. The failure of liberalism and democracy in the prewar years has prompted energetic efforts to identify and trace out the roots of the failure. Notable among these is Scalapino's previously cited *Democracy and the Party Movement in Pre-war Japan*. Particularly pertinent to this phase of the study of Minobe are Scalapino's observations on the causes and consequences of the nonemergence in Japan of the practical and philosophical bases of a free society. On the same point from a different angle see Marion J. Levy, Jr., "Some Aspects of 'Individualism' and the Problem of Modernization in China and Japan," *Economic Development and Cultural Change*, 10 (April, 1962), 225–240. Also of value in this respect are chapters of Ishida Takeshi's *Kindai Nihon Seiji Kōzō no Kenkyū* dealing with "The Structure of the So-called Party System" and "The Character of Bureaucratic Control in the Fascist Period."
62. Robert E. Ward, "Political Modernization and Political Culture in Japan," *World Politics*, 15 (July, 1963), 593.
63. Nakamura Akira, *Shin Kempō Nōto*, pp. 81 f.
64. "Taikan Zappitsu," *Kaizō*, 16 (April, 1934), 158 f.; *Nihon Kempō*, p. 451.
65. Ōmori Yoshitaro, "Gendai ni okeru Jiyūshugi no Kōyō to Genkai," *Kaizō*, 17 (May, 1935), 1–4.
66. Ishida, *op. cit.*, pp. 30, 162 ff. Ienaga Saburo makes a major contribution to our understanding of Minobe by his exposition of Minobe's thought on individual rights in relation to state power. He develops his analysis from Minobe's writings on administrative law and judicial precedents, most of which have not been consulted in this study. Ienaga concludes that: ". . . in spite of partial defects, Minobe's positive attitude on liberty and rights, seen as a whole, was hardly equaled among legal scholars under the Meiji constitution." *Minobe Tatsukichi no Shisō Shiteki Kenkyū*, pp. 169–238; the quoted passage is on p. 235.
67. *Kempō Seigi*, pp. 22–23; similarly *Kempō Satsuyō*, p. 171.
68. Contrast Uesugi Shinkichi, *Kempō Jutsugi*, p. 278: "Each individual belonging to the state is able to develop his personality fully through subordination to sovereignty. Absolute submission to sovereignty develops human personality and is the sole requirement for the attainment of the highest ethic . . . it is only as subjects that men achieve the proper qualities of men. If men are to attain natural freedom, they can do so without grief only by living in the character of subjects making up the state and submitting to its sovereignty."
69. *Kempō Seigi*, p. 328.
70. *Kempō Satsuyō*, pp. 168–191; *Kempō Seigi*, pp. 330–413.
71. *Kempō Satsuyō*, pp. 169–172.
72. We need not concern ourselves with the other two categories he identified and discussed: beneficial rights, e.g., the right of civil suit; and rights of participation, e.g., the right to serve as an elector. *Ibid.*, pp. 186–191.
73. Cf. Paul Laband (*Staatsrecht des deutschen Reiches*, Vol. I, p. 142) on the subject of popular rights: "Die Freiheits-oder Grundrechte sind Normen für die Staatsgewalt, welche dieselbe sich selbst giebt, sie bilden Schranken für die Machtbefugnisse der Behörden, sichern dem Einzelnen seine natürliche

Handlungsfreiheit in bestimmten Umfange; aber sie sind keine nicht subjektive Rechte der Staatsbürger, sie sind keine Rechte, denn sie haben kein Objekt." Cited from Kobayashi Takejiro, *De japanische Verfassung, vergleichen mit ihren europäischen Vorbildern*, pp. 36–37.

74. *Kempō Satsuyō*, pp. 172–174.
75. *Ibid.*, pp. 173, 176–182.
76. *Ibid.*, pp. 183–184; Kempō Seigi, p. 328.
77. *Ibid.*, pp. 330–332; *Kempō Satsuyō*, p. 182. The position of the bureaucratic school, which Minobe attacked, was represented by Uesugi (*op. cit.*, pp. 282–283), who insisted that individual rights were strictly limited by the enumeration in the constitution. The enumeration was a definition, not merely a summary of important items to be elaborated by the diet. On this point Uesugi was joined not only by Satō Ushijiro, *Teikoku Kempō Kōgi*, pp. 105, 119–124, but by Sasaki Sōichi, *Nihon Kempō Yōron*, pp. 217–228, 245–246. Cf. Ukai Nobushige, "Minobe Hakushi no Shisō to Gakusetsu," *Hōritsu Jihō*, 20 (August, 1948), 48; and Tanaka, *op. cit.*, pp. 126–127.
78. *Kempō Seigi*, p. 333.
79. *Ibid.*, p. 334; *Kempō Satsuyō*, pp. 176, 184. Two other constitutional provisions also limited the guarantees of freedom: Article XXXII deprived members of the armed forces of their protection; and Article XXXI permitted restriction of popular rights though the operation of the military command prerogative in time of military crisis.
80. *Kempō Seigi*, pp. 383–385; *Kempō Satsuyō*, pp. 179 f. For a summary of the position of leading Japanese authorities on the question of property rights under the constitution and laws of Japan, see Ōishi Yoshio, *Teikoku Kempō to Zaisan Sei*, pp. 67–82.
81. *Ibid.*, pp. 105–120.
82. "Chian Iji Hō Hihan" ("Critique of the Peace Preservation Law"), *Teikoku Daigaku Shimbun* (October, 1926), cited here from *Gendai Kensei Hyōron*, pp. 211–213. Article I of the law declared its purpose to be the preservation of national polity. Article X provided; "Persons who associate or organize with the object of denying the system of private property, persons who knowingly form such an association, or persons who act to carry out the purposes of such an association, shall be punished by ten years or less of penal servitude and imprisonment." After the law was amended in 1928 it distinguished between national polity and the property system. Criticism of or attacks upon the former were absolutely forbidden, while criticism of the economic order was permitted as long as it was not associated with action aimed at the socialization or nationalization of property. The penalties applied in the former case were more severe than those applied in the latter. Minobe, "Chian Iji Hō Kaisei no Kinkyū Chokurei" ("The Emergency Imperial Ordinance Amending the Peace Preservation Law"), *Keizi Ōrai* (August, 1928), cited here from *Gendai Kensei Hyōron*, pp. 267 ff. Cf. Ōishi, *op. cit.*, pp. 112–120 for reference to judicial interpretations of the law.
83. It was alleged by one contemporary commentator that Minobe's intervention in this matter was at the solicitation of his friend, Matsumoto Joji. Imanaka Tsugimaro, "Nihon Fuasshizumu no Gen Dankai," *Kaizō*, 17 (May, 1935), 265. Matsumoto was a career bureaucrat who had once served as chief of the legislative bureau and most recently as minister of commerce and industry in

the last five months of the Saito Government. His official career was interrupted in 1936 as a result of his association with Minobe's heresy.

84. Tokyo *Asahi Shimbun*, January 22–24, 1935. The story was given page-one coverage, with photographs and caricatures. See also *Japan Advertizer* (Tokyo), January 24 and 31, 1935.

85. Sugiyama Hirosuke, "Jiyūshugi Kyōju Ron," *Kaizō*, 17 (April, 1935), 214 f. The editors of *Asahi Shimbun* viewed it as a very salutary intervention by disinterested authority in defense of the law. "Dr. Minobe is not affiliated with any group in the upper house; he is independent. Moreover, he is not connected even remotely with the Imperial Rayon scandal. For a man of his position to talk of the scandal from the standpoint of a legal expert is for the good of the country." January 24, 1935, p. 3. To be sure, not everyone reacted with approval. At least one writer recorded that Minobe's action constituted an unwarranted and unworthy defense of capitalist rascals who had gotten no worse than they deserved. Sasa Hiroo, "Minobe Tatsukichi Ron," *Chūō Kōron*, 5, (March, 1935), 287–289. Itō Yuro wrote that Minobe's defense of human rights was really only a defense of plutocracy. *Tennō Kikan Setsu no Bokumetsu Sen*, pp. 167 f.
    The content of the interpellation consisted, in brief, of an exposition of the meaning of the constitutional guarantees of personal freedom and judicial process; a description of the function of the ministry of justice, to which Minobe ascribed a special obligation to cherish and preserve those guarantees; and a review of the evidence that the procurators had been guilty of violating the rights of the prisoners. He concluded by demanding of the minister (Ohara Naoshi) whether the prisoners had not been illegally detained and whether the procurators had not used improper methods interrogating the prisoners. Tokyo *Asahi Shimbun*, January 24, 1935, p. 1. The stenographic record of the interpellation is given in *Kampō Gōgai*, January 24, 1935, House of Peers, Sixty-seventh Diet, pp. 14–19.

86. Ukai, *op. cit.*, p. 49. See also colloquy between Ukai and Tsuji Seimei, in Suehiro Iwataro, *et al.*, "Nihon Hōgaku no Kaiko to Tembō," *Hōritsu Jihō*, 20 (December, 1948), 13–16, 33–40.

87. Article XXIII. No Japanese subject shall be arrested, detained, tried or punished, unless according to law.
    Article XXIV. No Japanese subject shall be deprived of his right of being tried by the judges determined by law.

88. *Kempō Satsuyō*, pp. 176–178; *Kempō Seigi*, pp. 358–375.

89. "Keisatsu Kensoku no Genkai," published in *Teikoku Daigaku Shimbun*, December 21, 1927, cited here from *Gendai Kensei Hyōron*, pp. 227–230.

90. "Jōjin no Hanzai to Gunjin no Hanzai" ("The Crime of the Common Man and the Crime of the Soldier"), *Hanzaigaku Kenkyū* (Studies in Criminology), March, 1934, cited here from *Gikai Seiji no Kentō*, pp. 561–574.

91. *Hanran* was the offense under military law corresponding to the criminal offense of *nairan* (insurrection or rebellion); it consisted of attempts by force to overthrow the government, seize territory, or subvert the military authority of the state or the constitution.

92. *Kempō Satsuyō*, p. 181. He disposed of the article with a bare three lines of comment.

93. "Shimbunkami Hō Kaisei Mondai," *Chūō Kōron*, March, 1919, 41–50.

94. "Chian Iji Hō Hihan," *op. cit.*, in *Gendai Kensei Hyōron*, pp. 208–213. On the legislative history of the Peace Preservation Law, see Miyake Shōtaro, "Chian Iji Hō," *Iwanami Hōritsugaku Jiten.*
95. "Chian Iji Hō Hihan," *op. cit.*, in *Gendai Kensei Hyōron*, pp. 208–213. Presumably from this same period comes Mori Shōzō's undocumented quotation of Minobe: "There is truth in the Communist Party. . . . Whether right or wrong Marxist principles are firmly held beliefs rooted deep in the heart, and ought not to be suppressed by authority and force." *Fusetsu no Hi*, p. 234.
96. "Chian Iji Hō Kaisei no Mondai" ("On the Question of Revising the Peace Preservation Law"), published in *Teikoku Daigaku Shimbun*, June 4, 1928, cited here from *Gendai Kensei Hyōron*, pp. 259 ff.; and "Chian Iji Hō Kaisei no Kinkyū no Chokurei," *op. cit.*, in *Gendai Kensei Hyōron*, p. 279.
97. Major police roundups of Communist Party members took place in 1928, more than 1,500 arrests being made in that year. In the general election of February, 1928, the Worker-Peasant Party (Rōdō Nomintō) polled 180,000 votes, about a quarter of the total proletarian votes cast in that election which resulted in the return of eight left-wing party men in a total of 466 seats. The Worker-Peasant Party was dissolved by police order in April 1928 on grounds of alleged Communist connections.
98. "Kyōsantō Jihen ni tsuite no Kansō" ("Reflections on the Communist Party Affair"), *Teikoku Daigaku Shimbun*, November 18, 25, December 2, 1929, cited here from *Gendai Kensei Hyōron*, pp. 417–433.
99. "Rondon Jōyaku wo Mawaru Ronsō" ("The Arguments Concerning the London Treaty"), published in *Teikogu Daigaku Shimbun*, September 8, 1930, cited here from *Gikai Seiji no Kentō*, p. 121.
100. "Kyōsantō Jihen ni tsuite no Kansō," *op. cit.*, in *Gendai Kensei Hyōron*, pp. 432–433.
101. "Gikai Seido no Kiki" ("The Parliamentary System in Peril"), published in *Chūō Kōron*, March, 1931, cited here from *Gikai Seiji no Kentō*, pp. 16–17. When a prominent Proletarian Party member of the diet was assassinated in 1929, Minobe wrote: "I do not say that the Government is directly responsible for this crime, but if the official attitude toward opposition thought were magnanimous, probably such outrages as these would not occur." "Yamamoto Daigishi no Ōshi wo Itamu" ("Regrets on the Assassination of Diet Member Yamamoto"), published in *Teikoku Daigaku Shimbun* (March 11, 1929), cited here from *Gendai Kensei Hyōron*, p. 315.
102. "Kyōsantō Jihen ni tsuite no Kansō," *op. cit.*, in *Gendai Kensei Hyōron*, pp. 428–430; Chian Iji Hō Hihan," *op. cit.*, in *ibid.*, pp. 206–207; and "Gakusei no Shisō Seikatsu" ("The Intellectual Life of Students"), published in *Teikoku Daigaku Shimbun*, April 17, 1933, cited here from *Gikai Seiji no Kentō*, p. 532. On the "bolshevization" of the university faculties see Kada Tetsuji, *Nihon Kokka Shakai Shugi: Nihon Fuasshizumu Ron*, pp. 215–227.
103. "Chian Iji Hō Hihan," *op. cit.*, in *Gendai Kensei Hyōron*, pp. 213–215.
104. "Gakusei no Shisō Seikatsu," *op. cit.*, in *Gikai Seiji no Kentō*, pp. 533–534.
105. Takikawa was restored to his post in 1946 and became president of Kyoto University until his death in 1963. It is reliably reported that Hatoyama Ichiro, the minister of education in 1933, was rebuffed when, in 1954, he solicited Takikawa's participation as minister of education in the cabinet which Hatoyama was then forming. See Isono Seiichi in Sakisaka Itsuro *et al.*, *Arashi*

no naka Hyakunen, pp. 97–112, and Minobe Ryōkichi, *Kumon Suru Demoku-rashii,* pp. 35–60.

106. On the dismissal and imprisonment of Professor Morito Tatsuo in 1920, and the resignations of professors Yoshino Sakuzo (1924), Inoue Tatsujiro (1926), and Kawakami Hajime (1928), see Sakisaka, *op. cit.,* pp. 155–176; Kikugawa Tadao, *Gakusei Shakai Undō Shi,* pp. 118–120; and Okamoto Niji, *Meiji Tai-shō Shisō Shi,* pp. 342 f.

107. "Takikawa Kyōju no Mondai" ("On the Question of Professor Takikawa"), and "Futatabi Kyōtō Daigaku on Mondai ni Tsuite" ("More on the Kyoto University Question"), published in *Teikoku Daigaku Shimbun,* May 20 and June 12, 1933, cited here from *Gikai Seiji no Kentō,* pp. 534–545.

108. Minobe's version of the academic relation to the government was possible only by a very strained reading of the autocratic context and authoritarian language of the imperial ordinances. Whatever operational "understandings" were es-tablished, they were not reflected in the law. It must have been, at least in part, with the hope that this embarrassment might be abated that Minobe took the position that any future reform of the educational system should be made the occasion for putting that system under statutory definition. "Mom-bushō no Gakusei Kaikaku-an" ("The Ministry of Education's Proposed Re-form of the School System"), published in *Teikoku Daigaku Shimbun,* Sep-tember 14, 1931, cited here from *Gikai Seiji no Kentō,* p. 480.

109. "Kyōdai Hōgakubu Kaimetsu no Kiki" ("The Impending Destruction of the Kyo-Dai Law Faculty"), published in *Chūō Kōron,* August, 1933, cited here from *Gikai Seiji no Kentō,* pp. 545–552. It has been recorded that Sasaki and others whose resignations were accepted had counseled the junior members of the department to withdraw their resignations and to continue the fight for academic freedom at Kyoto. Mori, *op. cit.,* pp. 219–224.

110. "Kyōdai Hōgakubu Kaimetsu no Kiki," *op. cit.,* in *Gikai Seiji no Kentō,* p. 549. The Seiyukai interpellation in the house of representatives, in response to which Hatoyama committed himself to Takikawa's dismissal, attacked the "Red professors" at Kyoto and Tokyo. Mori's chronicle of this period relates that the Takikawa affair was incited by one of the groups led by Professor Minoda Kyōki of Keio University, whom he describes as successor in the right-wing tradition of Uesugi Shinkichi. *Op. cit.,* p. 221. According to Okamoto and Kikugawa, Uesugi and his student followers in the Kōkoku Dōshikai had taken the lead in forcing the ousting of Professor Morito in 1920. The suc-cessful attack on the "Reds" at Kyoto permitted Minoda and his associates to concentrate their fire on those they so designated at To-Dai, among whom Suehiro Iwataro and Minobe were the chief targets. Takamiya Tahei, *Tennō Heika,* p. 237.

111. "Kokutai Shisō ni Motozuka Kempō Ron," *op. cit.,* in *Gendai Kensei Hyōron,* pp. 287–301.

112. Article I of the treaty stated: "The High Contracting Parties solemnly declare in the names of their respective peoples. . . ." Ratification was finally approved by the privy council (July, 1929) on condition that there be attached a declara-tion of reservation to the effect that the offensive phrase was understood not to be applicable to Japan, Seiji Hishida, *Japan Among the Powers,* pp. 275–276.

113. Minobe assigned the fault to a too literal translation by the foreign ministry. The term "people" should have been rendered *kokka* (state of country) rather

than as *jimmin* (people), which was poor Japanese, was not true to the sense of the term "people" in legal usage, and was inconsistent with the translation of "High Contracting Parties" as *teiyaku koku* (contracting states). Neither in state law nor in international law do states conclude treaties on behalf of the people; chiefs of state conclude treaties as representatives of states. Minobe showed some vindictiveness in recalling that he had made his advice on terminology available to the government in the *Jiji Shimpō* at an earlier date. "Fusen Jōyaku no Jiku Futabi Ron" ("Further Discourse on the Text of the Anti-war Pact") (previously unpublished), in *Gendai Kensei Hyōron*, pp. 302–310.

114. "Kokutai Shisō ni Motozuku Kempō Ron," *op. cit.*, in *Gendai Kensei Hyōron*, pp. 296–301.

115. "Inoue Junnosuke Kun no Sōnan" ("The Loss of Mr. Inoue Junnosuke"), published in *Chūō Kōron*, March, 1932, cited here from *Gikai Seiji no Kentō*, 289–295. Inoue was known as the "wizard" of the Minseito's hard money financial policy. He had direct family connections with the Mitsubishi.

116. *Ibid.*, pp. 291–292.

117. "Ankoku Seiji no Jidai" ("The Age of Political Darkness"), published in *Teikoku Daigaku Shimbun*, April 30, 1928, cited here from *Gendai Kensei Hyōron*, pp. 253–254.

118. "Waga Gikai Seido no Zento" ("The Future of Our Parliamentary System"), published in *Chūō Kōron*, March, 1932, cited here from *Gikai Seiji no Kentō*, pp. 46–47.

NOTES TO CHAPTER VI

1. In I. I. Morris, *Nationalism and the Right Wing in Japan: A Study of Post-War Trends*, Intoduction, p. xviii.

2. Richard Storry, *A History of Modern Japan*, p. 182.

3. "Gendai Seiyoku no Tembō," Tokyo *Asahi Shimbun*, January 3, 1935, p. 5; "Hijōji Nihon no Seiji Kikō" ("The Political Structure of Japan in Crisis"), published in *Chūō Kōron*, January, 1933, cited here from *Gikai Seiji no Kentō*, pp. 30–34; and "Waga Gikai Seido no Zento" ("The Future of Our Parliamentary System"), published in *Chūō Kōron*, January, 1934, cited here from *ibid.*, pp. 43–48.

4. The best analytic treatment of the general situation summarized here is given by Scalapino, *Democracy and the Party Movement in Pre-war Japan*, pp. 365–392.

5. Cited *ibid.*, p. 242.

6. "Saitō Naikaku no Seiritsu to Seitō Seiji no Gyōei" ("The Establishment of the Saito Cabinet and the Maintenance of Party Government"), published in *Teikoku Daigaku Shimbun*, June 27 and July 4, 1932, cited here from *Gikai Seiji no Kentō*, p. 305.

7. "Waga Gikai Seido no Zento," *op. cit.*, in *Gikai Seiji no Kentō*, p. 48; "Seitō Seiji no Shōrai" ("The Future of Party Government"), published in Tokyo *Asahi Shimbun*, January 18–22, 1934, cited here from *Gikai Seiji no Kentō*, p. 74.

8. "Hijōji Nihon no Seiji Kikō," *op. cit.*, in *Gikai Seiji no Kentō*, p. 37.

9. "Kyokoku Itchi Naikaku no Seiritsu" ("Establishment of a National Unity

Cabinet"), published in *Chūō Kōron*, September, 1932, cited here from *Gikai Seiji no Kentō*, pp. 313, 314. Not everyone at the time nor since has given the *genro* such high marks on this decision of state. Most recently Robert Butow has seconded Konoye's contemporary judgment that Saionji had seriously over-estimated the strength of the anti-parliamentary forces. *Tojo and the Coming of the War*, p. 70.

10. "Kyokoku Itchi...," *loc. cit.*; and "Terorizumu Okō to Seikyoku no Zento" ("Terrorism Rampant and the Future of Politics"), published in *Teikoku Daigaku Shimbun*, May 23, 1932, cited here from *Gikai Seiji no Kentō*, pp. 296–298.

Hiranuma Kiichiro was a career bureaucrat, who, as an active leader of conservative ultranationalism, had close contacts with nationalist elements in military, party, bureaucratic, and business circles. As a senior privy councilor he had long been a thorn in the side of party governments. More particularly he had been a bane to Saionji and other moderates within the inner court oligarchy. Kinoshita Hanji describes him as "the very model of a Fascist." *Nihon Fuashizumu Shi*, Vol. I, p. 154. Harada is replete with references to the struggle of the *genrō* and his collaborators to frustrate Hiranuma's ambitions. Harada Kumao, comp., *Saionji Kō to Seikyoku*, Vol. IV. See pp. 208–209.

11. Various previously cited articles as given in *Gikai Seiji no Kentō*, pp. 3–7, 46–47, 60–64, 304–308.

12. "Terorizumo Okō...," *op. cit.*, in *Gikai Seiji no Kentō*, pp. 298–299.

13. "Kyokoku Itchi...," *op. cit.*, in *Gikai Seiji no Kentō*, pp. 112, 114–115.

14. *Ibid.*, p. 116.

15. This section on the political role of the military is based chiefly on Yale C. Maxon, *Control of Japanese Foreign Policy: a Study of Civil-Military Rivalry: 1930–1945*, Chapters 2–4; Richard Storry, *The Double Patriots*, Chapters 3–5; Chitoshi Yanaga, *Japan Since Perry*, Chapters 32, 33; Scalapino, *op. cit.*, Chapter 9; and Masao Maruyama's introduction to Morris, *op. cit.*, pp. xii–xxvii.

16. See the very lucid clarification of army faction complexities made in James B. Crowley, "Japanese Army Factionalism in the Early 1930's," *Journal of Asian Studies*, 21 (May, 1962), 309–326.

17. Use of the terms "fascist" and "fascism" here and elsewhere in this study requires perhaps some comment. To speak of fascism in prewar Japan immediately raises a challenge, since some of the basic indices of fascism as it is known in the west were absent from the right-wing movement in Japan duirng the 1930's. Notably lacking was the leadership principle; there was no fascist party or fascist military force; nor did any of the rightist regimes achieve the level of totalitarian control expected of a fascist state. On the other hand, there was a distinctive fascist movement in Japan, with significant and active groups espousing a fascist concept of the organization of the state and society: elitism, the organic harmonization of interests, statism, extreme ethnocentric nationalism, and aggressive advancement of empire. Under the ascendancy of the military, however, Japanese fascists were absorbed into a larger movement too eclectic in ideology, too factionalized in makeup, and too conservative in tradition to be encompassed adequately in the category, fascism. The authoritarian regimes of the 1930's and 1940's were no doubt fascistic in complexion but they had best be called militarist.

Maruyama Masao, who writes with authority on the subject, speaks of

"Japanese fascism" which he carefully distinguishes from the European models. According to his analysis this phenomenon matured in the period 1931–1936. He describes the phase 1936–1945 as the period of perfected fascism in which the military "openly controlled from the top" a ruling structure based on an uneasy alliance of semi-feudalistic bureaucratic power and the power of monopoly capitalism and bourgeois parties. *Gendai Seiji no Shisō to Kōdō*, Vol. I, pp. 28, 36–58.

18. "Gikai Seido no Kiki" ("The Parliamentary System in Peril"), in *Gikai Seiji no Kentō*, pp. 14–18.

19. "Inoue Junnosuke Kun no Sōnan" ("On the Loss of Mr. Inoue Junnosuke"), published in *Chūō Kōron*, March, 1932, cited here from *Gikai Seiji no Kentō*, pp. 293–295. A. Morgan Young has suggested that one of Minobe's major offenses in the eyes of the military was his constant reference to their administrative and economic incompetence, obvious slaps at the economic control policies of the army in Manchuria and at home. Under the circumstances they were bound to be construed also as criticism of the Seiyukai Party, which was more or less committed to implementing the military program. *Imperial Japan: 1926–1938*, p. 271.

20. "Terorizumu Okō . . . ," *op. cit.*, in *Gikai Seiji no Kentō*, pp. 299 f.; and "Saitō Naikaku . . . ," *op. cit.*, in *ibid.*, pp. 307 f.

21. "Naikaku Seido no Shuju Sō" ("Various Aspects of the Cabinet System"), published in *Keizai Ōrai*, October, 1932, cited here from *Gikai Seiji no Kentō*, pp 2–3; "Seitō Seiji no Shōrai," *op. cit.*, in *ibid.*, pp. 66–72; and "Gendai Seikyoku no Tembō," *loc. cit.*

22. "Waga Gikai . . . ," *op. cit.*, in *Gikai Seiji no Kentō*, pp. 43–45.

23. Yanaga, *op. cit.*, p. 511. The war minister discounted the consternation which met this direct appeal to the nation: "From the point of view of national defense the present system has its weak points. The purpose is to stimulate study of the present system by those having knowledge of the facts. It is in no sense a call to action." Harada, *op. cit.*, Vol. IV, p. 91. Crowley describes it as an attempt to marshal public opinion behind the army's program and convince the leaders of the political parties that national economic planning would meet with public approval. *Op. cit.*, p. 318.

24. "Gendai Seikyoku no Tembō," *loc. cit.* The passage from *Keizai Ōrai* is cited from an extract of Minobe's "Critical Review of the Okada Cabinet's Proposal to Establish a National Policy Council," *Japan Weekly Chronicle*, February 21, 1935, 224–225.

25. "Gendai Seikyoku no Tembō," *loc. cit.*

26. "Naikaku Seido . . . ," *op. cit.*, in *Gikai Seiji no Kentō*, pp. 19–20 .

27. "Saitō Naikaku . . . , *op. cit.*, in *Gikai Seiji no Kentō*, p. 309; and "Waga Gikai . . . ," *op. cit.*, in *ibid.*, pp. 50–53.

28. "Saitō Naikaku . . . ," *op. cit.*, in *Gikai Seiji no Kentō*, pp. 302–303, 308; and "Seitō Seiji no Shōrai," *op. cit.*, in *ibid.*, pp. 58–64.

29. "Hijōji Nihon . . . ," *op. cit.*, in *Gikai Seiji no Kentō*, p. 37; "Gendai Seikyoku no Tembō," *loc. cit.*

30. Various articles as given in *Gikai Seiji no Kentō*, pp. 37, 50, 72–74, 304–305.

31. "Saitō Naikaku . . . ," *op. cit.*, in *ibid.*, pp. 309–310.

32. "Waga Gikai . . . ," *op. cit.*, in *ibid.*, p. 57.

33. The first actual step toward the creation of an expert policy-making agency

was taken in May, 1935. The cabinet investigation bureau established at that time was of purely bureaucratic composition. By successive steps its competence was expanded and it came under military domination. Known as the "planning board" after October, 1937, it became the principal mechanism by which the military, in combination with sundry bureaucrats, extended their influence over every phase of state policy. Yanaga, *op. cit.*, pp. 518–521, 533; Charles F. Fahs, *Government in Japan: Recent Trends in Its Scope and Operation*, pp. 68–70.

34. "Gendai Seikyoku no Tembō," *loc. cit.* He spoke of functional representation and corporatism in this connection. At another time he called for a roundtable conference of leaders, including representatives of political as well as economic interests. "Hijōji Nihon . . . ," *op. cit.*, in *Gikai Seiji no Kentō*, p. 38.

35. "Waga Gikai . . . ," *op. cit.*, in *Gikai Seiji no Kentō*, pp. 54–57; "Seitō Seiji no Shōrai," *op. cit.*, in *ibid.*, pp. 74–75.

36. Matsumoto Sannosuke, "Nihon Kempōgaku ni okeru Kokka Ron no Tenkai," in Fukuda Kanichi, *et al.*, *Seiji Shisō ni okeru Seiō to Nihon: Nambara Shigeru Sensei Koki Kinen*, pp. 207, 218.

NOTES TO CHAPTER VII

1. Arase Yutaka and Kakegawa Tomiko, "Tennō 'Kikan Setsu' to Genron no 'Jiyū—Nihon Fuashizumu Keiseiki ni okeru Masu Medeia Tōsei (san)," *Shisō*, 458 (August, 1962), 66, 74.

2. Maruyama Masao, *Gendai Seiji no Shisō to Kōdō*, Vol. I, pp. 61–62.

3. Hugh Byas, *Government by Assassination*, p. 271.

4. Miyazawa, "Kikan Setsu Jiken to Minobe Tatsukichi Sensei," *Hōritsu Jihō*, 20 (August, 1948), 42.

5. See quotation from Miyazawa Toshiyoshi on page 251. Suzuki Yasuzō quotes from a number of "those formerly known as liberals or as standing close to the liberals" who in 1935 attacked the organ theory and the state-personality theory on grounds other than those advanced by the orthodox school—usually because of its identification with individualistic liberalism or its formalistic methodology. Among those whom he cites as registering such criticism were the political scientists, Nakano Tomio of Waseda and Imanaka Tsugimaro of Kyushu Imperial. *Nihon Kempō Shi Kenkyū*, pp. 331–332.

6. Miyazawa, *op. cit.*, p. 43.

7. There were no important representatives of *tennō shutai setsu* at To-Dai in 1935 (not since Uesugi's death in 1929) nor at the Kansai University or the Kansai Academy (both private institutions). The *tennō kikan* school was not effectively represented at Tohoku Imperial, Taihoku Imperial (Formosa), nor at the private universities Chuo, Hosei, and Ritsumeikan. On the other hand there were men of both schools at Kyoto Imperial and Kyushu Imperial, and in private institutions such as Keio, Waseda, Meiji, Doshisha, and the Kokugaku-in. Ministry of Education (Thought Bureau), Papers, especially Document 26. See Bibliographical Note I for a full citation and description of this source.

8. Notably in his *Ko-shintō Taigi* (*Great Principles of Ancient Shinto*) (1915) and *Kokka no Kenkyū* (*Study of the State*) (1913). Suzuki Yasuzō describes Kakehi's position as "pantheistic, polytheistic theocracy." "Tennō Kikansetsu Ronsō no Kei-i," *Kaizō*, 17 (April, 1935), 261.

9. This line of opposition is well represented in Hashimoto Bunju, *Shintō no Gendaiteki Kenkyū*, pp. 114–115, 410–418; Satō Kiyokatsu, *Dai Nihon Seiji-*

gaku, pp. 104–154, and *Minobe Nihon Kempō Ron Hihan, passim;* Satomi Kishio, *Tennō Kikan Setsu Kentō, passim.* Sato was a reserve general and co-founder with Kikuchi Takeo of one of the subsidiaries of Hiranuma's Koku-honsha. Satomi was president of an institute for the study of the science of national polity, which was also affiliated with the Kokuhonsha. Chitoshi Yanaga, *Japan Since Perry,* p. 494.

10. Otani Yoshitaka of Meiji University and Saji Kenjo of the Imperial Military Academy were leading examples of this line of criticism. See Ōtani Yoshitaka, *Kokutai Kempō Genri,* introduction; and Saji Kenjō, *Nihongaku toshite no Nihon Kokkagaku,* pp. 17–144. On the significance of Saji's position see Hisata Eisei, "Sengo Nihon Shi ni okeru Kempōgaku no Kadai to Tembo," in Kobayashi Takasuke, ed., *Nihonkoku Kempō Shikō: Sengo no Kempō Seiji,* p. 333.

11. Saji, *op. cit.,* pp. 33–35.

12. On Uesugi's association with Takabatake Motoyuki and other national socialists see Kinoshita Hanji, *Nihon Fuashizumu Shi,* Vol. I, pp. 38–39, 56; and Richard Storry, *The Double Patriots: a Study of Japanese Nationalism,* pp. 32–33.

13. Kinoshita, *op. cit.,* pp. 150–159.

14. *Ibid.,* pp. 57–58. Storry, *Double Patriots,* p. 36.

15. Yabe Sadaji, *Konoye Fumimaro,* Vol. I, p. 296, where it is written: "In the persecution of the liberal professors ... the man Minoda Kyoki, with his di-vinely inspired madness, played the part of the most infamous denunciator." Mori Shōzō refers to Minoda as a charlatan, a lacky scholar, a pseudo-scholar, and an academic hooligan, who, had he not died in 1946, would have made a fine class-A war criminal. *Fūsetsu no Hi,* pp. 221–222, 232.

16. Kinoshita, *op. cit.,* pp. 68–69, 167; Mori, *op. cit.,* pp. 230–232; and Yanaga, *op. cit.,* pp. 506–507.

17. Yabe, *op. cit.,* Vol. I, p. 296; and Takamiya Tahei, *Tennō Heika,* pp. 237–238.

18. Minobe was just one of the "influential group of democratic and communistic professors" at To-Dai who were severally and collectively indicted in the pages of this poisonous little volume. Others included: Miyazawa Toshiyoshi for ap-proving "popular sovereignty"; Kawai Eijiro for his Marxian criticism of na-tionalism; Yokota Kisaburo for denying national sovereignty in international law; and Suehiro Iwataro for his "incendiary ideas" concerning the rights of agrarian tenants.

19. See Home Ministry (Censorship Bureau), Papers, Document 4. This source is fully cited and briefly described in Bibliographical Note II. Also, Isono Seiichi, "Tōdai Hōgaku no 'Akakyōju'" ("The 'Red Professors' at the Tokyo Imperial Law Faculty"), in Sakisaka Itsuru, and others, *Arashi no naka Hyakunen,* pp. 94–97.

20. Minoda, *Minobe Hakushi . . . ,* pp. 46–48. In January, 1933, for example, when Minoda wrote to Minobe importuning him for a statement in response to one of Minoda's pamphlets criticizing Minobe, the latter replied:

"I have read your letter. And in accordance with your instructions I have at any rate looked over the pamphlet you enclosed. The substance is essentially the same as ... I have previously read elsewhere. In the future as in the past I have no intention and see no necessity whatever to refute such a line of argument. Those of sound common sense can readily understand whether it is reasonable or unreasonable, straight or distorted. Therefore I say it can be left to the judgment of the people.

Because you have taken great pains to send me instructions, I am at any rate answering you to this extent. Hereafter, should you write to me again, I probably will not reply."

Minoda wrote to Minobe again in January, 1934, this time a peremptory demand that he concede to arranging a public debate "to decide . . . the issues between us." To this Minobe replied curtly: "I have read your letter. Please understand that I have no intention whatever of being drawn into argument with you."

21. *Kampō Gōgai*, February 8, 1934, 65th Diet, House of Peers, No. 13, pp. 131–133. Baron Kikuchi was a member of the Kokuhonsha and of Okawa's Jimmukai.

22. Issue of February 12, 1934. Cited here from *Gikai Seiji no Kentō*, pp. 338–342.

23. He made also a defense of the specific criticism of his theory of constitutional modification through reinterpretation. *Ibid.*, p. 342.

24. Founded in 1932 in a not very successful effort to bring unity to the fragmentary ultranationalist-fascist movement, the Kokutai Yōgo Rengō Kai provided a kind of clearing house for such groups as the Genri Nihon Sha. Kinoshita, *Nihon Fuashizumu Shi*, Vol. II, pp. 277–278.

25. "Minobe Tatsukichi Hakushi, Suehiro Iwataro Hakushi Nado no Kokutai Bunran Shisō ni Tsuite." A copy of this paper is bound in with Minoda, *Minobe Hakushi no Taiken Jūrin*. It also appears as Document 12 in the Home Ministry (Censorship Bureau) papers described in Bibliographical Note II.

26. Minoda, *Minobe Hakushi* . . . , pp. 11–23.

27. "Pseudo-intelligentsia" is one of the terms used by Maruyama to indicate that part of the Japanese *petit bourgeoisie* (small manufacturing and commercial proprietors, landlords and landed peasants, factory foremen, contractors, school teachers, temple and shrine attendants, petty officials, etc.) which "made the *so-called* voice of the people" and provided the social basis for Japanese fascism. According to his analysis, even though students as a class belong in the true intelligentsia, which was not generally favorable to fascism, "many of the students who participated in the right-wing movement were, in terms of cultural consciousness, of the pseudo-intelligentsia." *Op. cit.*, pp. 58–60.

28. Hiranuma served successfully as vice-minister of justice (1911–1912), chief procurator, chief of the judicial police, president of the supreme court, and minister of justice (1923). He was awarded his title in 1926. Hiranuma became premier in 1939, and although his tenure in that office was brief he came by that road into the ranks of the *jūshin*, among whom he played an influential role. It has been reported that in the privy council and in the consultations of the *jūshin* he was a mint of legal opinions, taking much pride in his great knowledge of constitutional law and theory and in his self-appointed mission of defending national polity. Toshikazu Kase, *Journey to the Missouri*, pp. 112, 243. For somewhat different characterizations see Storry, *op. cit.*, p. 243 and I. I. Morris, *Nationalism and the Right Wing in Japan: A Study of Post-war Trends*, p. 258,

29. Kinoshita, *op. cit.*, Vol. I, pp. 151–154.

30. Harada Kumao, comp., *Saionji Kō to Seikyoku*, Vol. IV, pp. 204–210, 230–233, 277, 342. This is substantially confirmed in *Okada Keisuke Kaikoroku*, p. 127. See also the *Japan Weekly Chronicle*, March 28, 1935, 404.

31. The foremost example of new bureaucratic-military association after 1931 was the Kokuikai (Society for the Preservation of the State). The ideologue of this group was Yasuoka Masa-atsu, a defector from the movement of Okawa

Shumei. The aims of the Kokuikai were advancement of the interests of the state through the mobilization of professional talents, fostering the political education of the nation, development of industry and the economy, rectification of the fickle and dangerous thoughts of the people, and glorification of the national spirit. Kinoshita, *op. cit.*, Vol. I, pp. 155–160.

32. *Ibid.*, pp. 152, 157. Ironically one of the prominent members of the Kokuikai, Goto Fumio, having become home minister in 1934, found himself in the position of defending the Okada Cabinet against the charge that it had temporized on the question of the purging of Minobe. Justice Minister Ohara, long a member of the Kokuhonsha, was to be similarly embarrassed later in connection with his responsibility for the prosecution of the criminal charges against Minobe.

33. There was an "anti-treaty faction" among the naval officers, which coöperated successively with the Araki-Mazaki and the Nagata factions of the army in urging, among other things, a drive for clarification of national polity. See Yamamoto Katsunosuke and Ishihara Kanji, *Nihon wo Horoboshita Mono*, pp. 197–202. Longstanding interservice rivalry and current policy disagreements made close coöperation between the army and the navy difficult. For reasons of history and the peculiarities of social origin, the navy was less interested than the arrmy in radical renovation of the Japanese state and society; it was, of course, not enthusiastic at the prospect of an army-dominated military dictatorship. In 1930 senior navy officers had opted for discipline rather than for a fight to vindicate its claims against Hamaguchi. Recent Japanese historical scholarship has disclosed that it was not the chief of the naval general staff but the Seiyukai Party whch had made an issue of the alleged violation of the supreme command prerogative in 1930. See Akira Iriye, "Japanese Imperialism and Aggression: Reconsiderations, II," *Journal of Asian Studies*, 23 (November, 1963), 106.

34. Crowley, "Japanese Army Factionalism," *op. cit.*, pp. 311–312; Royal J. Wald, *The Young Officers Movement in Japan, ca. 1925–1937: Ideology and Actions*, pp. 73, 81–82; Yale C. Maxon, *Control of Japanese Foreign Policy: a Study of Civil-Military Rivalry: 1930–1945*, pp. 35–47, 98–105.

35. See pp. 178–179.

36. A double meaning is imparted by "control": internal control of the army and suppression of undisciplined political activities and external military control over the national economy for the purposes of war mobilization. The connection between the Control Faction and the Choshu tradition was nebulous enough to permit its leading members to deny that there was a connection, a denial which is borne out in Crowley's analysis. *Op. cit.*, pp. 316–317.

37. Yamamoto and Ishihara, *op. cit.*, p. 143.

38. The partisans of the young officers referred to this program as the Second Purge of Ansei, and cast Nagata in the role of the deputy sent by Ii Naosuke to purge the anti-*bakufu* elements (imperial loyalists) from the Imperial Court at Kyoto in 1858 (the fifth year of Ansei). *Ibid.*, p. 208.

39. According to Crowley there is no evidence linking senior Imperial Way officers (e.g., Mazaki) with members of the Kokutai Genri Ha (e.g., Aizawa Saburo) prior to the summer of 1935. *Op. cit.*, p. 312.

40. An interesting analysis of the Minobe Affair which stresses semantics of the attack on the organ theory is presented in Arase and Kakegawa, *op. cit.*, pp.

65–81. This article is concerned chiefly to criticize the press for its equivocal response to the attack.

41. Eto had been elected as an independent in 1932. Once in the house he had affiliated with the Seiyukai. But he had fallen out with that party in 1934, and his status was that of an independent when the sixty-seventh diet opened. On the exchange between Eto and Goto see *Japan Advertizer*, February 14, 1935, 3; *Japan Weekly Chronicle*, February 14, 1935, 203. The text is reported verbatim from the committee minutes in Itō Yuro, ed., *Tennō Kikan Setsu no Bokumetsu Sen*, pp. 14–21. On February 14 Minoda wrote in *Nihon Shimbun* an attack on *Asahi* and *Nichi Nichi* for their failure to report Eto's interpellation. (Hereafter, the *Japan Advertizer* will be cited as *JA*, the *Japan Weekly Chronicle* as *JWC*, and the *Japan Times and Mail* as *JTM*.)

42. Tokyo *Asahi Shimbun*, February 19, 1935, 1; *Kampō Gōgai*, February 19, 1925, 67th Diet, House of Peers, pp. 95–97. Kikuchi was seconded on this occasion by Baron Inoue Kiyozumi and Baron Mitsui Sanji. These men, together with Ida Iwakasu, all members of the Koseikai (a group of representative barons in the house of Peers), constituted the extreme faction in the house of peers on the organ-theory question.

43. *Kampō Gōgai*, February 26, 1935, 67th Diet, House of Peers, pp. 101–105. Tokyo *Asahi Shimbun*, February 26, 1935, 1. The government itself had replied to the interpellation through Home Minister Goto, Education Minister Matsuda Genji, and Justice Minister Ohara. The substance of their reply was that the writings of Minobe, Ichiki, Miyazawa, Suehiro and the others were expressions of academic theory. While the government did not subscribe to these theories, they found in them no seditious intention, Itō, *op. cit.*, pp. 33–37. Minobe's chiding references to the delinquence of the chair were aimed at Konoye Fumimaro, president of the house of peers since June, 1933. Konoye's biographer reports general approval in the papers of Konoye's handling of the Kikuchi-Minobe exchange. Yabe, *op. cit.*, Vol. I, p. 297.

44. Minobe Ryōkichi, "Tennō Kikan Setsu" ("The Emperor-Organ Theory"), in Sakisaka, *op. cit.*, pp. 119–120; *Takamiya, op. cit.*, p. 243; Kinoshita, *op. cit.*, Vol. II, p. 324; Okada, *op. cit.*, p. 110.

45. In Morris, *op. cit.*, p. xix.

46. Harada, *op. cit.*, Vol. IV, p. 352.

47. According to Matsumoto Joji's recollection, Kikuchi himself was heard to say from his seat during Minobe's address: "As you put it, it is entirely reasonable." This is from Minobe Ryōkichi, who observes wryly that "it was an age when reasonable things were not taken to be reasonable." "Tennō Kikan Setsu" in Sakisaka, *op. cit.*, p. 120.

48. *JA*, February 28, 1935, 3.

49. As summarized by Itō Yuro, Eto's information consisted of: (1) A quotation from Amaterasu O-mikami. (2) A statement of how this divine pronouncement constituted the basis of national polity. (3) A statement concerning the confirmation of national polity thus conceived by the Restoration. (4) A charge that Ichiki imported and Minobe propagated the heresy. (5) Citation of *Kempō Seigi* saying that emperor is the supreme organ of the state. (6) Quotations from various works setting forth the state-sovereignty theory. (7) Organ-theory passage from *Kempō Satsuyō*. (8) Quotation from *Kempō Seigi* on the problem of "mistakes" in the constitution. (9) Citation of Minobe's

criticism of imperial rescripts. (10) Minobe's affront to the diet in the Imperial Rayon Scandal matter. (11) Charging Okada with ignoring the authority of Hozumi and Uesugi. *Tennō Kikan Setsu no Bokumetsu Sen*, p. 281.

50. Japanese writers do not entirely agree about the role of the army. Kinoshita Hanji says, for instance, that the "second assault of the Army *kōdōha* was the movement for the extirpation of the emperor-organ theory and the related campaign for the clarification of national polity." This in itself does not necessarily mean that the Imperial Way Faction initiated the attack on Minobe, but that seems to be what Kinoshita means. It is clear that he posits a close liaison between the *kōdōha* and the civilian radicals. *Nihon Fuashizumu Shi*, *op. cit.*, Vol. II, pp. 324–325. Takamiya similarly gives prominent place to the *kōdōha*: "The Imperial Way Faction, in its struggle with the Control Faction, indulged in god-ridden thought and violent talk and the naive, illiterate young officers were its tools at that stage." But he qualifies this significantly by adding that the Seiyukai planned to seize power over the government through the Imperial Way Faction and to this end they exploited the vulnerability of the organ theory. *Op. cit.*, p. 238. This comes closer to the view expressed by Yabe: "the destruction of Minobe's theory complemented the aspirations of military-bureaucratic renovationists ... but the immediate attack arose not from the military but from the diet itself. It was launched by Seiyukai representative Reserve Major General Eto ... and in the house of peers, by Hiranuma's associate Kikuchi." *Op. cit.*, Vol. I, p. 297. Yabe makes too close an identification between Eto and the Seiyukai; so does Takamiya. Eto does not appear to have been acting as a Seiyukai man when he opened the attack on Minobe. Nor was Kikuchi, or any of his coädjutors of the February days, a member of the Kenkyukai, the peers faction usually identified with the Seiyukai.

51. This view of Hayashi's position helps to explain the "irony" of his moderating influence alluded to by Crowley, "Japanese Army Factionalism," *op. cit.*, p. 320, note 48. Crowley perhaps makes too much of Hayashi's initial calm defense of Minobe's writings. See pp. 223–224 and notes.

52. Crowley adduces no evidence to substantiate his plausible inference that contacts between Kuhara Fusanosuke of the Seiyukai and General Mazaki late in 1934 (according to Harada) and Kikuchi's attack on Minobe in February, 1935, were part of a single pattern of attack. *Ibid.*, pp. 319–320.

53. Okada, *op. cit.*, p. 109.

54. Kinoshita, *op. cit.*, Vol. I, pp. 135, 140–145, 148–149; Maruyama, *op. cit.*, p. 62. Speaking of Hayashi's position, Takamiya writes: "Actual power at the center was grasped by the *kōdōha* and the local reservists danced on the string from the center without asking questions." *Op. cit.*, p. 244.

55. Maruyama, in Morris, p. 109.

56. Itō, *op. cit.*, pp. 240–242.

57. JA, February 24, 1935, 1.

58. The army pamphlet series has been described as an expression of the views of the Araki group (Borton, *Japan's Modern Century*, p. 385), though some of the items in the series were published during Hayashi's tenure as minister of war. Their militaristic and renovationist tone is suggested by the titles of those appearing up to the end of 1934; *The Rift Between the Military and the People* (November, 1933), *Concerning the Regulation of Military Power in the Face of a Period of War* (January, 1934), *Concerning Restoration of*

Independent Action (January, 1934), *Thought War* (February, 1934), *The Dangerous Political Situation in Europe* (April, 1934), and *The Essence of National Defense and Proposals for Strengthening It* (October, 1934). Naikaku Insatsu Kyoku (Cabinet Printing Office), *Kanchō Kankō Tosho Mokuroku*, Vols. XXV–XXX (January, 1933–December, 1934).

59. Kinoshita, *op. cit.*, Vol. II, p. 325; Ozaki Shiro, *Tennō Kikan Setsu*, pp. 168 f. This fictionalized historical narrative was first published in the literary magazine *Bungei Shunjū* in 1951. It deals in its first half with the events of 1935 and their background. The emphasis is on personalities and atmosphere. Most of the extended dialogue is undocumented. In an explanatory note the author says that his account is based on notes he made in the course of several meetings late in 1950 with various persons having knowledge of the 1935 story. Among these were Ohara Naoshi, Kanamori Tokujiro, Ouchi Hoei, Miyazawa Toshiyoshi, Minobe Ryokichi, Tanaka Jiro, Tozawa Shigeo, and Baba Yoshitsugu, most of whom will appear in the present narration.

60. *JWC*, March 21, 1935, 373.

61. Itō, *op. cit.*, pp. 97 f.

62. Takamiya writes that Hayashi's statements of March 8 and 15 in the diet "led to great objections within the army. Thereafter he spoke on the subject only after consultation in the military affairs bureau, and even in cabinet meetings he spoke only from notes prepared by his secretary." *Op. cit.*, pp. 244 f. Later in the month it was reported that Hayashi had been admonished by the army members of the supreme war council to urge a more vigorous course of action on the cabinet. *JA*, April 1, 1935, 3. In mid-March Harada was already hearing of denials by Hayashi that he was engaged in a conspiracy to extort from the cabinet action against the organ theory. Harada, *op. cit.*, Vol. IV, p. 214; Okada, *op. cit.*, p. 118.

63. According to Kinoshita: "Army opposition to the organ theory was not a matter of difference between the Control Faction and the Imperial Way Faction, though Inspector General of Military Education Mazaki and Commander of the First Division Yanagigawa, who were the core of the Imperial Way Faction, were of course, judging from their assertions, rather deeply concerned in it. At first the Control Faction participated with the Imperial Way Faction in the attack on Minobe as a move toward the destruction of the Okada Cabinet." But he goes on to say that the Control Faction, "being very sensitive to the fact that public opinion and the upper political echelons were unhappy about it, relinquished the control of the movement to the Imperial Way Faction, as it were, letting the Imperial Way men use themselves up in the attack." *Op. cit.*, Vol. II, p. 326.

64. This account is substantially confirmed by Kabayama Tomoyoshi, who also claims Hayashi always believed that "thought questions" were equally with national defense questions within the proper sphere of military concern. *Hayashi Senjuro Den*, pp. 185, 190.

65. Abe Manosuke, writing in 1935, said that the Seiyukai's course in the sixty-seventh diet was suicidal and that the act of its president in introducing the clarification resolution of March 26 was an act of distinguished merit in the destruction of the political parties in Japan. "Minobe Mondai to Okada Naikaku," *Kaizō*, 17 (May, 1935), 284.

66. Two other groups within the party had close connections with the military-

rightist camp. One of these was led by Kuhara Fusanosuke, an industrialist who was among the first and most successful of the business community to follow Japanese arms onto the continent. In 1931 he had favored the party merger behind a strong economic and military program as proposed by Adachi Kenzo. Another group was that led by Mori Kaku, who, without Kuhara's financial interest, still manifested a close ideological affinity for the military and civilian expansionists. Robert A. Scalapino, *Democracy and the Party Movement in Pre-war Japan*, pp. 241–242, 368–379, 383–384.

67. Suzuki Bunshiro, "Gikai to sono Zento," *Chūō Kōron*, 50 (May, 1935), 355. Also Minobe Ryokichi, "Tennō Kikan Setsu," in Sakisaka, *op. cit.*, p. 122.

68. Kinoshita, *op. cit.*, Vol. II, p. 327. In his memoirs, Okada, a jaundiced witness, deals with Seiyukai's part in this matter under the heading: Party Men Who Dug Their Own Graves. He figuratively gnashed his teeth at the thought that his cabinet should be brought to a premature demise as a result of rascally opportunism on the part of the Seiyukai. *Op. cit.*, pp. 108, 112–113.

69. Kanamori was himself the author of a law textbook which eventually suffered suppression for its endorsement of the organ theory as "simply a matter of convenience" in thinking about the juristic character of the state. Itō, *op. cit.*, p. 263.

70. *JWC*, March 21, 1935, 372–373 and March 28, 1935, 402, 404.

71. Itō, *op. cit.*, pp. 113–116. Yamamoto closed with an emotional proposal that he expiate for his responsibility, as a member of the Seiyukai Cabinet which had advanced Minobe to the house of peers, by resigning his court rank. With some malice the editor of *Asahi* suggested that he resign instead from the house of representatives, setting an example for a number of his colleagues. Quoted in *JWC*, March 21, 1935, 373. It was understood by Harada that Yamamoto had been briefed for his attack on the organ theory by Count Kaneko Kentaro, who shared with another very old man, Ito Myoji, the prestige (greatly overrated in Saionji's view) of being the only surviving members of the group of young men who had assisted Ito Hirobumi draft the Meiji Constitution. Harada, *op. cit.*, Vol. IV, pp. 208, 213, 260, 269, 270.

72. *JWC*, March 28, 1935, 404.

73. In the house of peers the general terms of the resolution probably at least in part indicated hesitancy to pillory Minobe. Harada, *op. cit.*, Vol. IV, p. 212. Hijikata Yasuji, a personal friend of Minobe, although speaking for the resolution nevertheless defended Minobe's loyalty and asserted that the organ theory was juristically valid. Perhaps more typical of the prevailing opinion were the remarks of Mikami Sanji, who said Minobe was an innocent product of an educational system which did not adequately inculcate national history and Japanese and Chinese moral philosophy. *JWC*, March 28, 1935, 405. Suzuki Bunshiro, *op. cit.*, p. 351.

74. Yanaga, *op. cit.*, p. 491.

75. Maruyama, *op. cit.*, Vol. I, p. 62. See Arase and Kakegawa, *op. cit.*, pp. 69–70, for a perceptive discussion of effective propaganda of right-wing writers, notably Satomi Kishio, who persistently and mockingly questioned that anyone could in good faith apply to the emperor the term *kikan* (organ), which suggests "something cold" or a "lifeless and blasphemous vulgarity made of wood or metal."

76. Makino was a target because of his position as one of the important "palace

liberals." His vulnerability lay in an assertion he had made in the privy council "some thirty years earlier" in support of the organ theory. Kido told Harada that Hiranuma was probably responsible for public disclosure of the fact of that indiscretion. Harada, *op. cit.*, Vol. IV, pp. 217–218.

77. This group was founded on March 8 by Toyama Mitsuru ("his last public service"). Many prominent righists, including forty members of the diet, joined in the inauguration rally at Ueno Park on March 19, adopting a resolution demanding that all persons connected with the propagation of the organ theory be removed from public office. Itō, *op. cit.*, p. 226; Kinoshita, *op. cit.*, Vol. II, pp. 327–328; JWC, March 28, 1935, 404. In the course of 1935 the number of patriotic and ultranationalist and fascist-type groups rose to over two hundred. Many were united under the Kokutai Yōgo Rengō Kai. JTM, August 11, 1935, 1.

78. JA, April 1, 1935, 1.

79. Yabe, *op. cit.*, Vol. I, p. 297; Kinoshita, *op. cit.*, Vol. II, p. 326; Kampō, No. 2478 (April 10, 1935), p. 322.

80. Kampō, No. 2498 (May 4, 1935), 103–104.

81. JA, May 5, 1935, 5.

82. JWC, April 4, 1935, 439. Ozaki, *op. cit.*, p. 170; Okada, *op. cit.*, p. 120.

83. It will be recalled that Hiranuma and Suzuki Kisaburo had connections in the ministry of justice. Ozaki Shiro relates that there was a "hard group" of senior officials (Hayashi Raisaburo, for one) who had been students of Uesugi. *Op. cit.*, pp. 12–14.

84. JWC, April 4, 1935, 439.

85. During March Minobe's brother Shunkichi and his friend Matsumoto Joji were induced by members of the cabinet to reason with Minobe to this end, apparently without success. Harada, *op. cit.*, Vol. IV, pp. 215, 226; Okada, *op. cit.*, pp. 120–122.

86. JT, April 9, 1935, 1.

87. JA, April 9, 1935, 1, and April 19, 1935, 1; Minobe Ryōkichi, "Tennō Kikan Setsu" in Sakisaka, *op. cit*, pp. 125 f. For Ohara's explanation to the emperor why the Publication Law might be applied to Minobe, see Harada, *op. cit.*, Vol. IV, p. 229. Attention is called to documents 1, 2, 5, 6 and 11 of the censorship bureau folio *Minobe Hakushi no Chōsho ni Kansuru Tōben Shiryō* described in Bibliographical Note II. In these papers eight charges against Minobe's writings are taken up, documented, and evaluated. Only one of them is indicated as warranting further investigation under the Publication Law, namely: the charge (citing *Kempō Seigi*) that he elevated the diet to the level of the throne and denied that it derived its authority from the imperial prerogative. On the basis of internal evidence, these working papers (which were apparently compiled subsequent to the censorship order of April 9) are not conclusive as to the censorship bureau's official attitude toward Minobe. It may be noted that the charge which was most seriously pressed by the ministry of justice—that Minobe supported the legality and propriety of criticism of imperial rescripts—was not among the charges aired in these papers.

88. JA, April 8, 1935, 1; Ozaki, *op. cit.*, pp. 5–6, 16–26.

89. Ozaki purports to relate what happened in some detail. His style of presentation is quite impressionistic. *Ibid.*, pp. 26–36.

90. Ozaki makes a fanciful reconstruction of Minobe's thoughts as he waited in

the examination room for the interrogation to resume after the noon recess. He says that Minobe had been deeply affected by the morning session and that he had spent the noon hour in disturbed introspection: "It was not a concern for his name or status. Probably no criticism or persecution could have affected his feelings to the extent of penetrating his attitude as a scholar of jurisprudence. But his life-long experiences as a Japanese had their effect. Suddenly his heart was filled with the feeling that he did not want to end his days as a disloyal subject."

91. *JA*, April 8, 1935, 1.
92. *JA*, April 9, 1935, 1; *JTM*, April 8, 1935, 1.
93. *JA*, April 10, 1935, 1; Ozaki, *op. cit.*, p. 37.
94. In conversations with Ohara and Okada on April 8 and 10, Harada got first hand reports of the government's vexation at Minobe's lack of coöperation: at the failure to pin him down on what it was that he agreed to revise and at his resistance to the full application of the censorship bureau's order suppressing his offending works. Harada, *op. cit.*, Vol. IV, pp. 228–229.
95. *JA*, April 11, 1935, 1.
96. Suzuki Yasuzō, *op. cit.*, p. 328; Kabayama, *op. cit.*, p. 193.
97. *JA*, May 11, 1935, 1.
98. Storry, *op. cit.*, p. 168; Okada, *op. cit.*, pp. 119–122.
99. See Okada's account of the "pitiful" Hayashi's difficulties with the Imperial Way men and the reservists, *ibid.*, pp. 117–119.
100. As Robert Butow has pointed out, the *quid pro quo* was not merely renovation and clarification at home; it was always implied that if radical energies were to be bottled up at home they would have to be uncorked abroad. *Tojo and the Coming of the War*, pp. 70–71. The application of this argument within the inner court is demonstrated in conversations between the emperor and his chief military aide, General Honjo Shigeru, from whose diary (May 11–July 10) Ozaki reports thus: "Emperor: In its solicitude for itself the army has become extremely confused in respect to the spiritual and corporeal aspects of the throne. I want you to give serious thought lest the eradication of the organ theory result in immobilizing the army itself.... We hear the opinion expressed that the organ theory degrades the dignity of the imperial household, but actually it impairs the dignity of the imperial household to debate this matter. Honjo: May it please Your Majesty, in the army we say as a matter of faith that Your Majesty is a god-incarnate. The currency of the organ theory among the people makes it very difficult for military education and command.... Emperor: The army has been publishing everywhere, in the name of the reservists, pamphlets on the organ theory. This is not a proper function of the reservists, is it? Even while you are extirpating the organ theory in the army, cavalierly dealing with that which opposes your will, are you not treating me as an organ? Honjo: That would be improper indeed. But the great excitement in the country today over the organ theory is not the fault of the reservists; the fault must be laid to the weakness of the central authorities. If the reservists have transgressed propriety in raising the question, it is regrettable. I understand that the pamphlets have been issued on [the official army] index only to ensure that they be kept under view and not escape control.... Emperor: Just what is it that the ministers of the army and navy have proposed to the premier concerning the organ theory? Honjo: I understand that

the minister of war is apprehensive that the presently prevailing attitude of the government will never be able to placate the many organ-theory opponents who are now overrunning the country, and that he has urged the premier to go a step farther. Of course, the government takes it as something to be cautious of lest it be exploited to the use of politicians...." Ozaki, *op. cit.*, pp. 10–11, 38–42. The office of chief military aide to the emperor was not in this period that of confidential advisor and servant of the emperor. It was rather that of representative of the army general staff within the imperial palace. Maxon, *op. cit.*, p. 54.

101. Kabayama, *op. cit.*, pp. 191–193; Yamamoto, *op. cit.*, pp. 201–209.

102. *JTM*, May 24, 1935, 1.

103. *JWC*, June 27, 1935, 825. The other items of the program were standard Seiyukai planks: elimination of subservient foreign policy and increased financial aid in relief of the agrarian community.

104. *Ibid.*

105. *JA*, July 7, 1935, 1; *JWC*, July 11, 1935, 46.

106. *JA*, July 7, 1935, 4.

107. *JA*, July 10, 1935, 3; *JWC*, July 18, 1935, 78.

108. *JA*, July 14, 1935, 1.

109. Harada, *op. cit.*, Vol. IV, p. 238; Ozaki, *op. cit.*, pp. 38–42. Ozaki states that in November Mochizuke Keisuke, then minister of communications, relayed to Minobe Imperial Household Minister Yuasa's report that the emperor had expressed concern for the physical safety of Minobe and Kanamori. *Ibid.*, p. 63. See also Yabe, *op. cit.*, Vol. I, p. 299; Takamiya, *op. cit.*, pp. 248–251.

110. On the protracted labors of Saionji (through Harada), Imperial Household Minister Yuasa, Dr. Shimizu, and others to dissuade Ichiki, see Harada, *op. cit.*, Vol. IV, especially at pages 129–133, 306–307, 373–375, and 401. One gets the impression that Ichiki and some of the others involved did not feel so intensely as Saionji the vital importance of keeping Hiranuma from the privy council presidency.

111. *JA*, July 28, 1935, 1; July 29, 1935, 1; July 30, 1935, 3; and Okada, *op. cit.*, pp. 123–124.

112. Harada, *op. cit.*, Vol. IV, p. 300. Okada says that the army originally intended to demand cabinet adoption of its draft, but that Privy Councillor Shimizu Toru, whom they had consulted, withheld his approval, so the draft was suppressed. Shimizu was the principal legal expert consulted by the government on constitutional questions. Shimizu was also chief judge of the administrative tribunal. He was a moderate adherent of orthodox constitutional interpretation. He served as Okada's contact with Ichiki. Okada, *op. cit.*, p. 121; and Harada, *op. cit.*, Vol. IV, p. 306.

113. *JA*, July 31, 1935, 3. The cabinet understood, on the advice of the metropolitan police bureau, and presumably on the basis of Hayashi's representations to Okada, that General Mazaki and his adherents were maintaining the attack on the organ theory as a reaction to Mazaki's removal from the inspector generalship on July 16. Harada, *op. cit.*, Vol. IV, p. 303; and Storry, *op. cit.*, pp. 170–175.

114. *JA*, August 2, 1935, 1, 8.

115. *JA*, August 4, 1935, 1, 3.

116. *Ibid.*, and Kabayama, *op. cit.*, p. 193.

117. Yamaura Kanichi, *Hijōjikyoku to Jimbutsu*, p. 353; Minobe Ryōkichi, "Tennō Kikan Setsu," in Sakisaka, *op. cit.*, p. 125.
118. JA, August 5, 1935, 1, 3; Kinoshita, *op. cit.*, Vol. II, p. 329. Kaneko was enjoying a day in the sun. His ultraconservative views on constitutional questions were eagerly solicited and published by the right-wing press. And he was, indeed, one of the first beneficiaries of the education ministry's policy of engaging eminent conservative authorities to write and lecture under government auspices as part of the positive clarification campaign.
119. JTM, September 4 and 5, 1935; Takamiya, *op. cit.*, p. 247.
120. The applicable section of the statute dated from a 1934 amendment of the Publication Law and thus covered only his most recent publications.
121. The procurators did proceed with their work on the case by examining Minobe's publisher (Yuhikaku) and its printer. JTM, April 18, 1935, 1.
122. Ozaki, *op. cit.*, p. 36.
123. *Ibid.*, pp. 37–38.
124. JA, July 27, 1935, 1.
125. *Ibid.*
126. Harada, *op. cit.*, Vol. IV, pp. 287–288, 309, 318. This hysteria had its counterpart behind the scenes. Promoted for convenience to the supreme war council, Mazaki joined Araki there in imputing to Nagata a conspiratorial and seditious role. Crowley, "Japanese Army Factionalism," *op. cit.*, p. 321.
127. *Ibid.*, pp. 323–326.
128. Hayashi had spent the last weeks of his term as army minister attempting to quell the incipient uprising of the Imperial Way Faction and the young officers. On August 21 he had a long conference with General Araki, in which he urged Araki to exercise his influence in the interest of discipline. The war ministry convened late in August a series of conferences with garrison and divisional commanders, instructing them on the requirements of discipline, enjoining them to keep themselves and their subordinates out of politics, and ordering them to set an example of proper restraint. JTM, August 22, 1935, 1.
129. JA, September 8, 1935, 1.
130. JTM, September 15, 1935, 1; Ozaki, *op. cit.*, pp. 46 f.
131. "Tennō Kikan Setsu," *op. cit.*, pp. 126 f.
132. JA, September 18, 1935, 1. On the same day it was announced that similar charges against Kanamori Tokujiro had also been dropped. Kanamori did not resign his post as chief of the cabinet legislative bureau until the following January.
133. *Ibid.*, 1, 2; JTM, September 18, 1935, 1.
134. Minobe may have distressed the emperor as well as the cabinet, for it is reported that the emperor had expressed satisfaction at the news on September 18 that Minobe had resigned and that the prosecution had been dropped. Harada, *op. cit.*, Vol. IV, p. 336.
135. JA, September 19–23, 1935; JWC, September 20, 1935, 397–398.
136. JTM, September 19, 1935. 1.
137. Yamaura, *op. cit.*, p. 354. Ozaki, *op. cit.*, p. 47.
138. JTM, September 21, 1935, 1.
139. JTM, September 21–26, 1935; Harada, *op. cit.*, Vol. IV, pp. 336–337.
140. JA, September 21, 1935, 1; JTM, September 22, 1935, 1.
141. Ozaki, *op. cit.*, p. 47.

142. JA, September 18, 21, 1925. Matsumoto was a sometime academic legal authority (commerical law) and a bureaucrat. He served as minister of commerce and industry in the Saito Cabinet.
143. JTM, September 28, 1935, 1.
144. JTM, September 26, 1935, 1; Harada, op. cit., Vol. IV, p. 340.
145. JTM, October 2, 1935, 1–2. The report listed the following action:
    1) Measures concerning professors' lectures:
        a) Investigation into the theories of teachers on the constitution, by reviewing their books, lectures, and theses, and by personal examination.
        b) Instructions issued to public and private universities and colleges to give careful attention to selection of professors and lecturers and to revision of lectures.
    2) Measures concerning textbooks:
        Prohibition of use of textbooks found inappropriate for the clarification of national polity.
    3) Conferences of professors of law, economics, and ethics:
        a) On the use of the imperial rescripts and the Promulgation Edict as the basis of lectures on the constitution.
        b) Instructors to prepare themselves in national history and to inculcate its lessons in all students.
        c) Comparative studies to be used to demonstrate unique qualities of Japan.
        d) Moral studies to be emphasized.
    4) Special lectures on Japanese history, law and ethics to be given at all government higher schools.
    5) Ministry of education publication of Count Kaneko's lectures on the constitution and plans to publish officially approved books on the constitution by Dr. Kakehi and others.
    6) Measures concerning publications on the constitution:
        Censorship bureau prohibition of the sale and distribution, or orders for revision of all books purveying the organ theory or other subversive thoughts (more than thirty volumes on the law or the constitution already suppressed or voluntarily withdrawn). Violations of the Publication Law to be vigorously prosecuted.
146. JWC, October 31, November 7, 1935, 542, 573. Ozaki relates from personal experience as a sports reporter an incident at the National Sports Palace in November, 1935. The occasion was the opening of the sumo season. The premises were decorated with huge banners bearing slogans of the council for renovation of thought and with military pennants. Preliminary to the athletic events the president of the sumo society, an admiral, addressed the crowd in patriotic phrases. A demonstration of enthusiastic approval followed when General Hayashi and a retinue of staff officers arrived. At that point Minobe, who had ventured out to indulge his passion for the sport, got up and went home, whether in disgust or apprehension is not disclosed. Ozaki, op. cit., pp. 56–57.
147. JWC, October 17, 1935, 484–485; JTM, October 9–15, 1935.
148. On the struggle between Okada and Kawashima over "keeping personalities out of it," see Harada, op. cit., Vol. IV. pp. 337, 342, 346, 350, and 353. Ohara insisted on distinguishing Kanamori's position from Minobe's. Ichiki's writings had never been the subject of official investigation. JTM, September

12, 1925, 1. It was, ironically, Kanamori who, as chief of the cabinet legislative bureau, conducted the telephonic negotiations between the premier's office and the war ministry on October 13 and 14.

149. *JWC*, October 24, 1935, 542.

150. *JTM*, October 16, 1935, 1. In relating to Harada the details of the drafting of the second declaration, Okada reported that the cabinet had relied closely on Shimizu on the theoretical problem. He said that at the last minute (on the evening of October 14) Shimizu was summoned to the residence of the war minister to answer questions concerning the draft. Shimizu told them that if the state-personality theory were to be disestablished then state administrative activity would have to cease and in international law no treaty could be made between states. This was said to have surprised the army men and prompted their agreeing that the text of the declaration while asserting imperial sovereignty and denying the organ-theory should not deny the state-personality theory explicitly. Harada, *op. cit.*, Vol. IV, p. 351.

151. This point was well made by the Tokyo correspondent of the London *Times*, whose analysis of the organ-theory issue was reprinted in *JTM*, October 2, 1935, 8.

152. *JWC*, October 17, 24, 31, 1935, 485, 512, 514, 542; Wald, *op. cit.*, pp. 177–178. The Imperial Reservists Association was notably unhappy and on October 18 its complaints were conveyed to Kawashima by the association's president, General Suzuki. On October 19 and 21 Kawashima conferred directly with the general officers and branch chiefs of the association to urge patience and forebearance, possibly to remind them of their disciplinary obligations. In any case it was announced that the association would leave further measures to the service ministers. When the Army-Navy Officers Brotherhood League of Osaka held a public meeting on vindication of national polity and passed a resolution calling for the cabinet's resignation on October 21, the Fourth Army Headquarters reprimanded the officers involved for "dabbling in politics." *JWC*, October 17, 24, 31, 1935, 485, 512, 514, 542. The reservists took such injunctions lightly, however, and continued to agitate under renovationist and clarification slogans. Wald, *op. cit.*, pp. 177–178.

153. An official statement on the purposes of the February 26 rebels, issued by the army after their suppression, included the following passages, which point up the clarification motive: "to eliminate those perpetuating the destruction of national polity, such as the *genrō*, the statesmen close to the Throne, the financial magnates, the military clique, bureaucracy, and political parties ... in order to clarify great principles and to protect and make manifest the national polity. ..." *Ibid.*, p. 200.

154. For this and other formulations of later military renovationist objectives in the constitutional sphere, see Wada Hidekichi, *Ni-ni-roku Igo*, pp. 47, 55–56, 72–73.

155. Thought Bureau, Papers (see Bibliographical Note I), Document 8. Actually some of these titles were already out of print. The effect of the orders was to prohibit their use in the schools for any purpose.

156. Application of one or more of these measures is indicated in Thought Bureau, Papers, Documents 2–7, 21, 23, 28–34.

157. Thought Bureau, Papers, Document 25; Akagi Kazuhiko, "Gendai Kempō Kyōju Sōhyō," *Kaizo*, 17 (June, 1935), 259.

158. Thought Bureau, Papers, Documents 1 and 21; Suzuki Yasuzō, *op. cit.*, pp. 328–330. Sasaki continued to teach at the Ritsumeikan where he and his colleague, Ishigaki Tatsugoro, were subject to continuing scrutiny.

159. Thought Bureau, Papers, Document 24. These men suffered censorship of one or more of their publications. Nakano had the draft of his doctoral dissertation returned for revision of terminology. Documents 4 and 8.

160. Suzuki Yasuzō, *op. cit.*, p. 330.

161. Hasegawa Masayasu, *Kempōgaku no Hōhō*, p. 8. On the other hand, that simple negation of the organ theory was not always enough is indicated by the case of Kuroda Akira of Kyoto Imperial University. That gentleman had, according to a thought bureau investigator reporting in November, 1935, begun the year with misdirected caution. He had tried to divorce himself from the current dispute by asserting that both the organ theory and the theory of monarchical sovereignty were juristically inadequate, both being derivative of positions that had been demolished by Kelsen: "It is necessary to discard nonlegal theories such as these and to study the constitution from the point of view of pure law." The investigator was able to report, however, that the professor was now asserting in his lectures the healthier doctrine that "one must seek the basis of the constitution in the political character of the state. The explanation of the basis of our constitution is that it originated in the historical fact that the emperor is the core of unity of the entire state structure. Thus there exists an organic connection between the emperor and the state." Thought Bureau, Papers, Document 33.

162. In the preface to his *Shin Kempō Nōto*.

163. Hasegawa, *op. cit.*, p. 9. According to Hasegawa, Carl Schmidt, a critic of both Jellinek and Kelsen, survived the authoritarian auspices of his introduction in Japan to wield considerable influence in Japanese academic circles after World War II.

164. Suehiro *et al.*, "Nihon Hōgaku no Kaiko to Tembō," *loc. cit.*, pp. 24–25.

165. Yabe, *op. cit.*, Vol. I, pp. 308–310; also Harada, *op. cit.*, Vol. IV, pp. 385–390. From Yabe's account it appears that the delay was due in part to the difficulty of arranging the succession to the privy council presidency in such a way as to exclude Hiranuma once more, a purpose in which Saionji, Yuasa, Okada, and the emperor were balked by Konoye's refusal to be advanced over Hiranuma. Count Kiyoura also declined the post for the same reason.

166. *JTM*, December 27, 1935, 1. Both Makino and Saito were marked for assassination in February, 1936. Makino escaped; Saito perished.

167. *JA*, January 8, 1936, 1.

168. Yabe, *op. cit.*, Vol. I, p. 332. Maxon suggests somewhat different reasons for the army's rejection of Hirota's nominees, Ohara and Goto. *Op. cit.*, p. 111.

169. Ozaki, *op. cit.*, pp. 57–59. Mochizuki had been challenged by "bully representatives" in the diet and he feared that continued public association with Minobe would be made the subject of ministerial responsibility in the diet.

170. *JA*, January 3, 19, 1936; Robert K. Reischauer, *Japan: Government and Politics*, pp. 170–171; Scalapino, *op. cit.*, pp. 381–383.

171. *Ibid.*, p. 382.

172. Ozaki, *op. cit.*, pp. 61–62.

NOTES TO CHAPTER VIII

1. To the extent that the ensuing discussion is drawn into contact with the larger

problem of the origin and putting into operation of the Constitution of 1947, it relies upon sources that for the most part throw little light on Minobe's relationship to that problem. The earliest of these sources is Satō Isao's *Kempō Kaisei no Keika*, which appeared originally in the journal *Hōritsu Jihō* (April–December, 1946). Satō, then a member of the To-Dai law faculty, was employed as a technical assistant to the constitutional question investigating (Matsumoto) committee of the Shidehara Cabinet and immediately thereafter in the cabinet legislative bureau. Despite its author's inside position this book is useful chiefly for its systematic and analytic presentation of materials already reported in regular domestic and foreign news media.

The second principal source is the official terminal report of the government section, general headquarters, Supreme Commander for the Allied Powers (SCAP), *Political Reorientation of Japan, September 1945–September 1948* (cited hereafter as *Political Reorientation*) which consists of a volume of narration and a volume of related documents. The problem of constitutional revision is only one of its many concerns and is dealt with briefly, even somewhat cryptically.

The third source is Satō Tatsuo's "Nihonkoku Kempō Seiritsu Shi" which first appeared serially in the journal *Jurisuto* beginning in May, 1955. This is the main source of the Japanese side for Robert E. Ward's important essay, "Origins of the Present Japanese Constitution," *American Political Science Review*, 50 (December, 1956), 980–1010. Satō Tatsuo speaks with authority and with detailed documentation, having been chief of the first section, cabinet legislative bureau, during the critical first quarter of 1946. As such he was actively engaged in the drafting of the revision as an aide to Matsumoto and Kanamori. Fortunately for the purpose at hand, his history is being published in book form and in greater detail. The first volume, published in January, 1963, contains much data concerning the work of the Matsumoto committee not given in the earlier serialized version, *Nihonkoku Kempō Seiritsu Shi*, Vol. I, pp. 252–374. Citation of this source for matters falling later than December, 1945, will be to its appearance in *Jurisuto*.

Some of the important actors on the stage in 1946 have recorded personal accounts dealing in part with the making of the new constitution, notably, Matsumoto Joji, Irie Toshio, Kanamori Tokujiro and Yoshida Shigeru. These, supplemented by the personal depositions of the same and other persons having knowledge of the events, constitute the source materials upon which is based *Kempō Seitei no Keika ni Kansuru Sho I-in Kai Hōkokusho*, edited by Satō Isao and issued in 1961 by the constitution investigating (Takayanagi) committee (Kempō Chōsa Kai). (This volume will be cited hereafter as *Kempō Seitei Hōkokusho*.) Much of the data on the working of the Matsumoto committee given in this report is based on the testimony of Satō Tatsuo. A valuable critical review of these source materials is given in Satō Isao, "Kempō Chōsa Kai no Hōkoku Sho—Gaiyō to Mondai Ten," *Jurisuto*, 227 (June 1, 1961), 30.

2. SCAP, *Political Reorientation*, Vol. II, pp. 460–465; Tokyo *Asahi Shimbun*, October 11, 23, November 1, 1945, May 1, 1946; and Genji Okubo, *The Problems of the Emperor System in Postwar Japan*, pp. 21 f.

3. Miyazawa Toshiyoshi, "Minobe Sensei no Gyōseki," *Kokka Gakkai Zasshi*, 62 (July, 1948), 13. (*Kokka Gakkai Zasshi* is cited hereafter as KGZ.)

4. Published by Yūhikaku, this sixth edition of *Kempō Satsuyō* was essentially the

same as the fifth (1934) edition. See Associated Press interview with Minobe reported in Tokyo *Asahi Shimbun*, October 15, 1945. Also republished in 1946 was the much earlier (1906) collection of translations of Jellinek, the [*Erinekku no*] *Jinken Sengen Ron*. In December, 1946, Nihon Hyōron Sha republished his *Gikai Seido Ron*, which had appeared originally in 1930.

5. Kenneth E. Colton, "Pre-war Political Influences in Post-war Conservative Parties," *American Political Science Review*, 42 (October, 1948), 940 f.; Hatoyama Ichiro, "Watakushi was Kaku Shinzuru," *Bungei Shunju*, 29 (July, 1951), 64. Hatoyama's credentials are spotty. Entering the Seiyukai as a protege of Tanaka Giichi, he became a leading member of its Kuhara faction. As minister of education in the Saito Cabinet he was the antagonist of the universities in the Takikawa affair. He subsequently gained a reputation as a relatively constant and effective parliamentary opponent of the militarists in the diet from 1937 to 1942. He was purged by SCAP directive early in 1946, on the eve of assuming the premiership as leader of the Liberal Party. Hans H. Baerwald, *The Purge of Japanese Leaders Under the Occupation*, pp. 21–23. He was subsequently depurged and gained the premiership and the presidency of the Liberal Democratic Party (1955) as an outspoken advocate of revision of the Constitution of 1947.

6. Satō Tatsuo, *Nihonkoku Kempō no Seiritsu Shi*, I, pp. 252–253. SCAP, *Political Reorientation*, Vol. I, pp. 603 f; Tokyo *Asahi Shimbun*, October 26, 28, 1945.

7. Matsumoto's tenure in the cabinet was extended by SCAP dispensation early in March, 1946, after it had become clear that he fell under the terms of the purge. On March 26, with the end of his usefulness in view, Kanamori Tokujiro was brought into the cabinet to second him. When the Shidehara Cabinet gave way to the Yoshida Cabinet in May, Kanamori replaced Matsumoto as minister in charge of constitutional questions and in that role he managed the constitutional revision through the diet. Kanamori's blighted official career had been salvaged in the wake of the surrender and in February, 1946, he had been appointed to the house of peers. Tokyo *Asahi Shimbun*, February 2, 1946; Satō Tatsuo, *op. cit.*, *Jurisuto*, 110 (July 15, 1956), 22.

8. Satō Tatsuo, *Nihonkoku Kempō no Seiritsu Shi*, Vol. I, pp. 252–264, 280–284, 301–302, 310–313, 319–321, 366–372. All meetings, both plenary sessions (chairman and councillors attending) and investigating sessions, were held at the premier's official residence. Only an informal transcript was kept and after the first plenary session (October 22) all proceedings were secret. Minobe shared the role of councillor with Shimizu Toru, apparently a passive participant, and Professor Nomura Junji. Altogether there were seven plenary sessions; the proceedings of all but the final of these (February 2, 1946) are covered in the sources cited here. The working (investigating) committee of about a dozen academic and official persons was headed by Miyazawa Toshiyoshi and included other former students of Minobe, notably Kawamura Matakai (Kyushu Imperial University) and Kiyomiya Shiro (Tohoku Imperial University).

9. Tokyo *Asahi Shimbun*, January 27, 1946. The same newspaper had reported on the preceding October 20 "a persistent inclination in the government to push the appointment of Minobe to the privy council." He was not then appointed, however, allegedly because of Council President Baron Hiranuma's insistence that the existing vacancy was one reserved by custom to the bureauc-

racy of the ministry of education. If the obstacle had been the personal in-compatibility between Hiranuma and Minobe, that obstacle was removed in December when Hiranuma resigned, having been arrested as a war crimes sus-pect. Tokyo *Asahi Shimbun*, December 13, 1945.

10. The privy council itself took a tenaciously conservative attitude toward its own fate in the early months of the Occupation, and the draft revision which Mat-sumoto carried through the cabinet early in February, 1946, provided for the council's perpetuation, though in a sharply restricted role. The draft constitu-tional revision submitted to the privy council in April, 1946, made no provision for continuation of that body and no effort was made in the council to revive the issue. Morohashi Noburo, "Sūmitsu-in ni okeru Nihonkoku Kempō Shingi," *Jichi Kenkyū*, 31 (May, 1955), 35–37. Morohashi was chief of the privy council secretariat during 1946. See also Satō Isao, *Kempō Kaisei no Keika*, pp. 78–80.

11. The record is available in the form of three sets of United States Army Signal Corps photostats of journal records of the privy council covering committee and plenary sessions dealing with constitutional revision. These papers will be cited hereafter as Privy Council Records (photostatic). For fuller description of this source see Bibliographical Note III.

12. SCAP, *Political Reorientation*, Vol. I, pp. 28–33. The sources upon which this study is based do not reval what attitude Minobe carried into this work. Some of those whose records passed before him must have been identified in his mind with uphappy experiences in the past. But most of the prominent purge actions (resignations, dismissals, exclusions) had taken place prior to or immediately following the general election of April 10, 1946, and by the end of June the implementation of the January directive had been refined to the point where application to individual cases was hardly discretionary. It is proba-bly safe to assume that Minobe was not opposed to the purposes of the original directive nor to the method of its implementation. Baerwald feels that the screening committee failed to implement the purge directive fully because its bureaucratic composition was prejudicial to thorough action. He apparently classifies Minobe as a bureaucrat on the basis of his membership in the privy council. *Op. cit.*, p. 48.

13. *Shin Kempō Gairon; Shin Kempō Chikujō Kaisetsu; Shin Kempō no Kihon Genri; Nihonkoku Kempō Genron*. Parts of the first three of these volumes appeared initially as articles in various law journals.

14. Yanase Yoshimiki, "Minobe Sensei to Shin Kempō," KGZ, 62 (July, 1948), 17–19.

15. *Ibid.*, 19 f.; also Minobe in the introduction to *Shin Kempō Chikujō Kaisetsu*.

16. Revised editions of the *Nihonkoku Kempō Genron* and the *Shin Kempō Gairon*, edited by Miyazawa Toshiyoshi, were published in 1949 and 1950, respectively.

17. Yanase, *loc. cit.*

18. Kobayashi Naoki and Ikeda Masaaki, "Hōritsugaku Jugonen no Kaikō to Tembō —Kempō," *Jurisuto*, 217 (January 1, 1961), 39.

19. *Shin Kempō Nōto*, pp. 138–139.

20. "Kempō Kaishaku no Kihon Mondai," *Hōritsu Taimuzu*, 21 (July, 1949), 6–7.

21. *Beikoku Kempō Gairon*.

22. *Senkyo Hō Shōsetsu*. This volume was a by-product of his last public service. In January, 1948, he was appointed chairman of the national election manage-ment commission, established by action of the diet to function within the

office of the premier, taking over the electoral control functions of the defunct home ministry. SCAP, *Political Reorientation*, Vol. I, pp. 360 f., Vol. II, pp. 1040–1056. Minobe's analysis of the electoral law in this book was voided by the enactment of a completely revised electoral law in 1950.

23. "Kempō Kaisei Mondai," Tokyo *Asahi Shimbun*, October 1–3, 1945; and Kempō Kaisei no Kihon Mondai," *Hōritsu Shimpō*, 728 (May, 1946), 2–5.

24. "Gyōseijō no Sōshö," KGZ, 62 (July, 1948), 1–6. This posthumous publication carried with it a brief explanatory introduction by Tanaka Jiro, professor of administrative law at Tokyo University. In the same issue Tanaka published an article of his own, rejecting Minobe's position on the relation between administrative and judicial powers under the new constitution. "Minobe Sensei no Gyōsei Sōshō Ron," 50–64.

25. *Yomuri Shimbun*, May 25, 1948, 2.

26. Tokyo *Asahi Shimbun*, October 15, 1945.

27. Tokyo *Asahi Shimbun*, October 20–23, 1945. At the same time Miyazawa Toshiyoshi was writing that democratization of the constitution did not require significant formal revision. Tokyo *Mainichi Shimbun*, October 22, 1945.

28. Satō Tatsuo, "Nihonkoku Kempō no Seiritsu Shi," *Jurisuto*, 122 (January 15, 1957), 37.

29. Satō Tatsuo, *Nihonkoku Kempō Seiritsu Shi*, I, pp. 260–265, 280–282. This source clears up some of the ambiguity conveyed by the account in Kempō Chōsa Kai, *Kempō Seitei Hōkokusho*, pp. 201–209. It may be noted as a matter of minor interest that Minobe spoke pointedly in this session against Matsumoto's suggestion that Sasaki Soichi be made a councilor of the committee. Sasaki was then serving as an aide to Konoye Fumimaro who was engaged in an abortive attempt to prepare a draft revision of the constitution in the office of the lord keeper of the privy seal. Minobe protested that to appoint Sasaki to the cabinet's committee would give countenance to the altogether improper involvement of the lord keeper's office in the constitutional question. Minobe seems to have been "ahead" of Matsumoto on this point. The bizarre history of Konoye's project is given in *Ibid.*, pp. 133–165. The Matsumoto committee deliberately and, as it turned out, rather disastrously insulated itself from the SCAP-inspired views of constitutional reform which had guided the scuttled Konoye–Sasaki effort. Kempō Chōsa Kai, *Kempō Chōsa Kai Hōkokusho*, pp. 106–108; and Tabata Shinobu, "Sasaki Sōichi Hakushi no Teikoku Kempō Kaisei An ni Tsuite," *Dōshisha Hōgaku*, 81 (September, 1963), 1–33.

30. This so-called "A" draft was based on Matsumoto's personal ideas, worked up by Miyazawa and edited by Matsumoto. It was distinct from and substantially different in content from the so-called "B" draft, a composite of the ideas of the committee members. Kempō Chōsa Kai, *Kempō Seitei Hōkokusho*, p. 215.

31. Note may be taken here of some of the ideas advanced by Minobe in the committee: (1) Transfer to the constitution of the "constitutional items" in the Imperial House Law. (2) Abolition of the independent ordinance prerogative. (3) Giving treaties force of law from promulgation. (4) Abolition of prerogative to grant titles of nobility. (5) Reduction of the chapter on rights and duties to two general propositions: one, subjects are bound to perform all duties imposed by this constitution or by law; and two, the rights and liberties of subjects are inviolate except by provision of law. If some rights or liberties are to be put beyond legislative definition, separate enumeration in this chap-

ter. (6) If bicameral form is retained for the diet, constitution of the upper house on an elective basis. (7) Abolition of the privy council. (8) Establishment of an administrative appeals division in the supreme court to replace the existing separate court of administrative appeals. (9) Giving the cabinet exclusive power to advise the throne on the exercise of the prerogative. (10) Making the ministers of state individually and collectively responsible to the lower house of the diet. (11) Establishment of the right of the diet to initiate constitutional amendments.

32. The allusion is to the terms used by Vice-Minister Shirasu Jiro in describing to SCAP officers the shocked reaction of Matsumoto to the MacArthur draft. SCAP, *Political Reorientation*, Vol. II, p. 264.

33. Kobayashi Naoki, "Seiken Shi no Genriteki Kōsatsu," *Shisō*, 455 (May, 1962), 11; Satō Tatsuo, *op. cit.*, *Jurisuto*, 114 (September 15, 1956), 48.

34. Much is uncertain, due to lack of authentic records and contradiction of testimony, about what transpired between February 1 and February 26. The accounts given by Ward, *op. cit.*, *American Political Science Review*, 50 (December, 1956), 985–1001, and by Theodore McNelly "The Japanese Constitution: Child of the Cold War," *Political Science Quarterly*, 74 (June, 1959), 176–195, are quite useful but have been superceded in part by *Kempō Seitei Hōkokusho*, pp. 237–386.

35. The Potsdam Declaration provided in part: "The Japanese Government shall remove all obstacles to the revival and strengthening of democratic tendencies among the Japanese people.... The occupying forces of the Allies shall be withdrawn from Japan as soon as . . . there has been established in accordance with the freely expressed will of the Japanese people a peacefully inclined and responsible government...." SCAP, *Political Reorientation*, Vol. II, pp. 413–415. For divergent discussions of the constitutional significance of the acceptance of the Potsdam Declaration see, Satō Isao, *Kempō Kaisei no Keika*, pp. 2–4; Sasaki Sōichi, *Nihonkoku Kempō Ron*, pp. 105–112; and Hasegawa Masayasu, *Shōwa Kempō Shi*, pp. 203–212, 247–254.

36. Robert Butow, *Japan's Decision to Surrender*, pp. 13–18, 47–50, 112, 139–141, 160–179; Sakomizu Hisatsune, "Kōfukuji no Shinsō," Tokyo *Asahi Shimbun*, January 13–20, 1946; Hasegawa, *op. cit.*, pp. 205–208.

37. *Ibid.*, p. 209.

38. Note the innocent appearing academic-bureaucratic negativism witnessed by Miyazawa's reference to a committee established by the president of To-Dai immediately after the war to consider the problem of constitutional reform: "In retrospect it seems that none of the members of that committee then conceived that a revolution such as we see in the present constitution in respect to the emperor system could have been brought about. Consequently, even though there was talk about the emperor-system issue, setting aside our individual ideas, taking it as a practical matter, we thought in terms of something much closer to the Meiji constitutional model than to the present constitution." Miyazawa Toshiyoshi, *et al.*, "Shin Kempō no Ju Nen," *Jurisuto*, 129 (May 1, 1957), 3.

39. Kobayashi Naoki, *op. cit.*, *Shisō*, 455 (May, 1962), 2, 9; Hasegawa, *op. cit.*, p. 229.

40. Kobayashi Takasuke, *Kempōgaku no Honshitsu: Kempō oyobi Kempōgaku no Kenkyū*, p. 79.

41. The return to normal did not, however, result specifically in a vindication of the organ theory. The removal of the official ban on that theory in October, 1945, was not a sign of official endorsement of it. Throughout the period of constitutional revision the government consistently shied away from the particular language of the organ theory. The state-sovereignty idea, however, was explicit in the revision proposals of the Liberal Party and the Socialist Party, and, as we shall see, was implicit in the government's position. Even after the promulgation of the rescript on the renunciation of imperial divinity ("the ties between us and our people ... are not predicated upon the false conception that the Emperor is divine ...") on January 1, 1946, there was a notable failure in academic and official circles to embrace the long-proscribed formulas of the organ theory. While the New Year Rescript was undoubtedly of great importance in the liberation of scholarship and thought from the tabus of *kokutai* and *tennō*, Professor Yanaga probably overstated somewhat its intention and effect when he wrote that it "was tantamount to the revival of the organ theory ... and the vindication of Professor Minobe's constitutional views." Chitoshi Yanaga, *Japanese People and Politics*, p. 136. Cf. Hasegawa Masayasu, *Kempōgaku no Hōhō*, pp. 9–10.

42. Nakamura Akira, "Minobe Hakushi no Futatsu no Kempō Kaishaku Sho," *Hōritsu Jihō*, 19 (October, 1947), 54.

43. Hasegawa, *Kempōgaku no Hōhō*, p. 10; Kuroda Ryoichi, "Kempō Kaishaku ni Ikkōsatsu," in Suzuki Yasuzō, *et al.*, *Kempōgaku no Kadai*, p. 58.

44. In July, 1946, Col. Kades of government section, SCAP, GHQ, in an "unauthorized" statement to Kanamori, Irie, and Sato Tatsuo complained that they were treating the draft revision before the diet just as though it had the same meaning as the Matsumoto draft which had attempted to amend the Imperial Constitution in accordance with Minobe's theories and which General MacArthur had found entirely unacceptable. Satō Tatsuo, *op. cit.*, *Jurisuto*, 122 (January 1, 1957), 36.

45. Hasegawa, *Shōwa Kempō Shi*, pp. 223–224.

46. The Liberal Party published its proposals on constitutional revision on January 28, 1946. This document provided that the subject of sovereignty (*tōchiken*) is the Japanese state; the emperor is the superintendent of sovereignty. The Socialist Party's draft revision, published on February 22, 1946, provided: sovereignty (*shuken*) resides in the state ("the united body of the nation including the emperor"); sovereign power (*tōchiken*) is divided: the greater part is assigned to the diet, part is reserved to the Emperor. It is curious that of all the official and private proposals for constitutional reform, that of the Socialist Party was, on the central issue of sovereignty and democratic responsibility, most congruous with Minobe's constitutional views. Satō Isao, *Kempō Kaisei no Keika*, pp. 60–61, 88–89, 98, 278–281, 294–297.

47. Hasegawa, *Shōwa Kempō Shi*, pp. 221–222. According to Kobayashi Naoki's classification of important revision proposals published before April, 1946, only two—that of a progressive academic group known as the Kempō Kenkyū Kai and that of the Communist Party—stood to the left of the draft published as the government's on March 6. Moving from right to left, with the Meiji Constitution as the base of reference, Kobayashi classifies as reactionary (that is, proposing no real change) the Matsumoto draft, the Konoye-Sasaki draft, the Progressive Party's proposal, and the Liberal Party's proposal. He classifies as

conservative (explicit assertion of state sovereignty and of a popular share in the exercise of governmental power) the proposal of the Socialist Party. The cogency of Kobayashi's classification is relative to his use of it in arguing the overriding "historical necessity" of the democratization of the Japanese constitution following the war. "Seiken Shi no Genriteki Kōsatsu," *Shisō*, 455 (May, 1962), 8–10.

48. This according to Professor Ukai in a letter to the author. Compare the reaction of other academic personages as recorded in the recollection of one of them, Wagatsuma Sakae, "Shirarezaru Kempō Tōgi," *Sekai*, 205 (August, 1962), 63–67.

49. *New York Times*, March 13, 1946.

50. SCAP, *Political Reorientation*, Vol. I, pp. 106–107; Satō Tatsuo, *op. cit., Jurisuto*, 82 (May 15, 1955), 14; Kempō Chōsa Kai, *Kempō Seitei Hōkokusho*, pp. 359 ff.

51. Satō Isao, *Kempō Kaisei no Keika*, p. 93; *New York Times*, January 27, 1946.

52. Shidehara told the council that it would have to work under the same pressure of time as the cabinet was working under. Matsumoto told the committee that "since the draft had already been published in Japanese and English it would be politically impossible for the government to make any substantial changes in it." Morohashi Noburo, "Sūmitsu-in ni okeru Nihonkoku Kempō Shingi," *Jichi Kenkyū*, 31 (May 10, 1955), 39, 49; Satō Tatsuo, *op. cit., Jurisuto*, 103 (April 1, 1956), 35, 38.

53. Privy Council Records (photostatic), First Series, leaves 6–29.

54. *Ibid.*, leaves 11–12.

55. *Ibid.*, leaves 34–38, 59–60, 71. The "bombshell" epithet, a cliché of Japanese political reporting, is used by Morohashi, *op. cit., Jichi Kenkyū*, 31 (May 10, 1955), 49–51. See also Satō Tatsuo, *op. cit., Jurisuto*, 103 (April 1, 1956), 38–39.

56. Matsumoto had replied again when Minobe repeated his question at the end of the second session. When Minobe reiterated his vehement criticism in the third session Matsumoto in exasperation called on his aide, Irie Toshio, to reply. *Ibid.*, p. 39.

57. Privy Council Records (photostatic), First Series, leaves 71–72.

58. "Kempō Kaisei . . . ," *loc. cit.*, p. 3.

59. The nature and weight of the duress brought to bear upon Shidehara, Matsumoto, and Yoshida by American Occupation officials in February is a matter of dispute. There is no dispute about SCAP's threat to publish its draft if the Japanese did not publish a satisfactory substitute, but whether or not certain threats were made with regard to the emperor's fate is controversial; similarly controversial is whether SCAP's urgency was motivated by a desire to forestall an even more mischievous intervention by the Far Eastern Commission or whether it was simply concerned with advancing American interests at the expense of Japan. Satō Tatsuo, *op. cit., Jurisuto*, 82 (May 15, 1955), 91 (October 1, 1955), 12–14, 26–31; Ward, *op. cit., American Political Science Review*, 50 (December, 1956), 991–999; McNelly, *op. cit., Political Science Quarterly*, 74 (June, 1959), 186–189; Takayanagi Kenzō in Miyazawa Toshiyoshi, *et al.* "Kempō Kaisei Mondai to Kempō Chōsakai no Katsudō," *Jurisuto*, 241 (January 1, 1962), 20–22; and Kempō Chōsa Kai, *Kempō Seitei Hōkokusho*, pp. 226–373.

60. Morohashi, *op. cit., Jichi Kenkyū,* 31 (May, 1955), 51; Kanamori Tokujiro, *Kempō Igen,* p. 31.
61. Privy Council Records (photostatic), First Series, leaves 205–214, 250–260.
62. Satō Isao, *Kempō Kaisei no Keika,* pp. 245–247; Sasaki, *op. cit.,* pp. 96–103. But see Tabata Shinobu, "Kempō Kaisei Ron ni Okeru Sasaki Setsu to Minobe Setsu," *Dōshisha Hōgaku,* 64 (March, 1961), 27–43.
63. Pp. 10–11.
64. Pp. 117–118.
65. "Hachigatsu Kakumei to Kokumin Shuken Shugi" ("The August Revolution and the Principle of Popular Sovereignty"), cited here from Satō Isao, *Kempō Kaisei no Keika,* pp. 158–159. Miyazawa developed this thesis at length in his *Kempō Tai-i,* pp. 59–63. As stated there it is substantially identical to Minobe's treatment of the same problem in *Shin Kempō Gairon* and in *Nihonkoku Kempō Genron.*
66. He spelled out his brief privy council reference to the August Revolution basis of his thinking in the previously cited article, "Kempō Kaisei no Kihon Mondai," published on May 1.
67. On the opening day of the deliberations on the revision bill in the house of peers (August 26) Miyazawa restated his argument: "I think that the draft revision has as its premise the basic upheaval in our political structure brought by our acceptance of the Potsdam Declaration terms . . . that it is only on this basis that it can be thought to be constitutionally permissible. In other words the present constitutional revision is not simply an amendment under Article LXXIII; it is based on the supraconstitutional change which occurred at the end of the war. On this basis it is an amendment according to Article LXXIII and at the same time it transcends that Article." Cited here from Miyazawa Toshiyoshi, *Kokumin Shuken to Tennōsei,* pp. 93–94. See the Alfred C. Oppler memorandum on Miyazawa's position in SCAP, *Political Reorientation,* Vol. II, p. 663.
68. Kanamori has summed up retrospectively and reaffirmed the official position for which he had been the principal spokesman in 1946: "When we think about it coolly, the Potsdam Declaration imposed upon us an unconstitutional duty and we were therefore under an international obligation to discharge that duty somehow. But it mistakes the true nature of the case to think that this changed the constitution itself. All that was required of us was that we proceed according to Article LXXIII. We proceeded in such a way as to satisfy both the Potsdam requirement that the constitution be in accordance with the popular will and the constitutional requirement of imperial initiative and imperial sanction." *Kempō Igen,* pp. 32–35.
69. The government was supported in its no-revolution-in-August thesis by Sasaki Sōichi. Satō Isao, *Kempō Kaisei no Keika,* pp. 150–157, 175–177, 215–230; and Satō Tatsuo, *op. cit., Jurisuto,* 114 (September 15, 1956), 48. The Japanese government was not altogether free to accept advice from the privy council or the diet in the matter of revision procedure, for it operated under self-contradictory specifications set down by the Far Eastern Commission: (1) that complete legal continuity from the Constitution of 1889 to the new constitution should be assured; and (2) that the new constitution should be adopted in such a manner as to demonstrate that it affirmatively expressed the will of the Japanese people. SCAP, *Political Reorientation,* Vol. II, pp. 659–666.

70. Pp. 118–119.
71. Hasegawa, *Shōwa Kempō Shi*, pp. 247–254.
72. Privy Council Records (photostatic), First Series, leaves 289–314, Second Series, leaves 2–45; Morohashi, *op. cit.*, *Jichi Kenkyū*, 31 (July, 1955), 59–67, (August, 1955), 65–74. He is listed as absent in the records of the privy council's October sessions. Minobe apparently played no part in, or in relation to, the career of the revision bill in the diet. His status as privy councillor made him ineligible for inclusion in the sparkling group of academic and bureaucratic lawyers appointed to the house of peers before the opening of the Ninetieth Diet. Satō Tatsuo, *op. cit.*, *Jurisuto*, 110 (July 15, 1956), 22.
73. The classification and analysis are based on views expressed in the Ninetieth Imperial Diet. Kobayashi Naoki, *op. cit.*, *Shisō*, 455 (May, 1962), 4, 9, 12, 13.
74. Satō Isao observes that because of the progressive character of the draft revision, the government found itself at odds with its own diet supporters. "The Socialists were the ones who understood the intellectual base of the government draft and who supported it." *Kempō Kaisei no Keika*, pp. 172–174.
75. Satō Tatsuo, *op. cit.*, *Jurisuto*, 139 (October 1, 1957), 31. The Constitution of 1947 is formally styled The Constitution of Japan (Nihonkoku Kempō). It has been most commonly referred to as the new constitution, but since about 1958 the expression Showa Constitution has become fairly common.
76. Contrary to Minobe's assertion in this passage, *shuken* (the term always used in the sense of "sovereignty" in such phrases as "popular sovereignty") in the new constitution does not have the same meaning as the term *tōchiken* (governmental power) in the Imperial Constitution, although both are commonly translated as "sovereignty." Just as his interpretation of the Meiji Constitution depended on the use in Article IV of the term *tōchiken*, which he equated with *Regierungsgewalt* rather than with "sovereignty," so now his interpretation exploited the semantic ambiguities in the term *shuken* (*Souveranität*) in order to save his state sovereignty theory under the Showa Constitution.
77. See especially Privy Council Records (photostatic), First Series, leaves 6–48, Second Series, leaves 297–299; Satō Tatsuo, *op. cit.*, *Jurisuto*, 111–114, 122 (August 1, 15, September 1, 15, 1956, January 15, 1957); and Satō Isao, *Kempō Kaisei no Keika*, pp. 217–229.
78. *Kempō Igen*, pp. 23–29. This posthumously published work is a memoir dictated in 1952. The product of deliberate second thought, it benefits by comparison with the cluttered, fragmentary, hastily contrived and often self-contradictory course of his explanation before the diet.
79. Kanamori's *kokumin no akogare* definition of national polity was devised to permit the government to hold to its claim that there was no change in national polity under the new constitution, a claim in line, presumably, with fulfilling the legal and political requirements in proceeding under Article LXXIII. His use of it was one of the things that provoked the "informal" visit of Colonel Kades on July 17, which in turn gave rise to Kanamori's memorandum setting forth his six principles of constitutional revision. Point six in this statement provided: "But, in the moral and spiritual sphere, apart from the question of government structure, the emperor remains throughout, both before and after constitutional reform, the center of the nation's devotion." The statement that Japan's national character does not change refers to this point. Satō Tatsuo, *op. cit.*, *Jurisuto*, 122 (January 15, 1957), 39.

80. *Ibid.*, p. 37; and 114 (September 15, 1956), p. 53. Searching for a proper devil with which to identify his tormentors, Kanamori fell back on the old *bete noire*, Hozumi Yatsuka. Privy Council Records (photostatic), Second Series, leaves 297–299.

81. Pp. 121–123.

82. Among the works reflecting this development are: Miyazawa Toshiyoshi, *Kempō Kaisei*, especially Ashibe Nobuki, "Kempō Kaisei Mondai no Gaikan" ("Survey of the Constitution Revision Issue"), pp. 185–222; Suzuki Yasuzō, ed., *Kempō Kaisei no Kihon Mondai*, especially Kobayashi Takasuke, "Kempō no Kaisei to Henkō," pp. 209–231, and Wada Hideo, "Kempō Kaisei ni okeru Riron to Kachi" ("Theory and Value in Constitutional Revision"), pp. 155–208; Suzuki Yasuzō, *Kempō Kaisei to Kempō Yōgo*; Suzuki Yasuzō, ed., *Kempōgaku no Kadai*, especially Kuroda Ryōichi, "Kempō Kaishaku no Ikkōsatsu," *op. cit.*; Hasegawa Masayasu, *Kempōgaku no Hōhō*, and *Shōwa Kempō Shi*; Kobayashi Naoki, "Seiken Shi no Genriteki Kōsatsu," *op. cit.*; Kobayashi Naoki and Ikeda Masaaki, "Hōritsugaku Jugonen no Kaiten to Tembō—Kempō," *op. cit.*; Kuroda Ryōichi, "Kempō no Kaishaku," *op. cit.*; and Matsumoto Sannosuke, "Nihon Kempōgaku ni okeru Kokka Ron no Tenkai" in Fukuda Kanichi, and others, *Seiji Shisō ni okeru Seiō to Nihon: Nambara Shigeru Sensei Koki Kinen*, pp. 169–219; Watanabe Yōzō, *Seiji to Hō no Aida: Nihonkoku Kempō no Jugonen*, especially Part I, "Kempō to Hōchishugi" ("The Constitution and the Rule of Law"), pp. 3–20; Matsushita Keiichi, *Gendai Nihon no Seijiteki Kōsei*, especially Chapter 12, "Kempō Yōgo Undō no Rironteki Tembō" ("A Theoretical View of the Constitution Defense Movement"), pp. 256–274.

The bias of these references is almost wholly anti-revisionist. The pro-revisionist position, though manifest in the words and actions of the conservative parties and their representatives in parliament and in the tenor and weight of government policy, is poorly supported by academic and journalistic opinion. See, however, Ōishi Yoshio, *Kempō Kaisei no Hitsuyōsa*. The pro-revisionist position was well represented in the Kempō Chōsa Kai (1956–1964), the more conspicuously so by reason of the refusal of the Socialists to participate. Ikeda Masaaki, "Kempō Kaisei Mondai wo Meguru Ugoki," *Jurisuto*, 240 (December 15, 1961), 44–45. Even so, in the final stages of the committee's work, the firm revisionists failed in their desire to make the final draft a clear call for revision. The strong direction of chairman Takayanagi held the final report to a systematic exposition of all views presented. The pro-revision "majority" is clear enough, but the committee as such made no finding for or against revision. Satō Isao, *et al.*, "Kempō Chōsa Kai no Saishū Hōkoku wo Owarite," *Jurisuto*, 303 (August 1, 1964), 10–26; for a paraphrase translation of an earlier critical estimate of the committee's work by the same author, see *Journal of Social and Political Ideas in Japan*, Vol. I (August, 1963), 11–14. The socialist and academic opposition to revision has found expression through the Kempō Mondai Kenkyū Kai (Association for the Study of Constitutional Questions), which was founded in 1958 to conduct a watchdog and counterpropaganda effort in relation to the Takayanagi committee. For an illuminating exchange between Takayanagi and some of his critics on the Tokyo University law faculty, see Miyazawa, *et al.*, "Kempō Kaisei Mondai to Kempō Chōsakai no Katsudō," *Jurisuto*, 241 (January 1, 1962), 12–20.

83. Kobayashi Takasuke, *Kempōgaku no Honshitsu*, pp. 94–95; and Hasegawa,

Kempōgaku no Hōhō, pp. 183–189. In Minobe's own lifetime, the great names of the imperial period in Germany were being displaced by those of the Weimar generation, including Anschütz, Kelsen, Schmidt, and Triepel. Attention is directed today to new names: the Germans, Haug, Schindler, and Ehmke, the Swiss, Kägi, and the late French writer, Mirkine-Guetzevitch.

84. See Kuroda Ryōichi, "Kempō Kaishaku no Ikkōsatsu," *op. cit.*, pp. 56–74; and Kobayashi Takasuke, *Kempōgaku no Honshitsu*, pp. 61–86.

85. Kuroda Ryōichi, "Kempō Kaishaku no Ikkōsatsu," *op. cit.*, p. 65.

86. The disciplinary action taken by the Japan Socialist Party in June, 1963, against members of its editorial staff for openly asserting this point probably reflects tactical discretion rather than commitment to the contents of the "Peace Constitution."

87. Tsunetō Yasushi, "Kaiken Mūdo no Genjitsusa," *Sekai*, 198 (June, 1962), 67–71.

88. Takayanagi, who is no socialist and of whose chairmanship of the Kempō Chosa Kai the left was highly suspicious, has, throughout the committee's deliberations, declared his opposition to revision at this time. And he has specifically denied the desirability of changing the provisions concerning the status of the emperor and the renunciation of war. He asserted: "Now is not the time to revise the Constitution. The question of revision ought to be passed on to the next generation." News items in *New York Times* (September 8, 1963), *Washington Post* (November 26, 1963), and Tokyo *Asahi Shimbun* (July 4, 1964).

89. See his editorial note in *Journal of Social and Political Ideas in Japan*, Vol. I (August, 1963), 9–10.

90. The essay *Verfassungsänderung und Verfassungswandlung* was reproduced in translation as the last item in Minobe's *Kempō Oyobi Kempō Shi Kenkyū* in 1909.

Bibliography

BIBLIOGRAPHICAL NOTES

Three sources used for this study are in the form of manuscript documents.

I

A folio located in the Orientalia Division of the Library of Congress (321.1 M255) and inscribed with the legend: Mombushō Shisō Kyoku: Kaku Daigaku ni okeru Kempō Gakusetsu Chōsa ni Kansuru Bunsho (Chōsa no Seishitsujō Shibunsho) [Ministry of Education, Thought Bureau: Documents Concerning the Investigation of Constitutional Theory in the Various Universities (Private Papers on the Nature of the Investigation)]. The folio is stamped "secret." Its date of compilation and the authority under which it was compiled are not indicated. Its contents consist of various handwritten and typewritten papers, most of which are on ministry of education (Mombushō) stationery, and the latest date mentioned in any of the papers is September, 1936. The contents, which are not bound in a fixed sequence, are listed below following the order in which they were arranged at the time I examined them.

DOCUMENT 1. Typed on Mombushō paper (2 leaves): excerpts from the cabinet's declarations of August 3 and October 15, 1935, on clarification of national polity. Outline of policy laid down on October 1 to effect the execution of the cabinet's declaration (incomplete). Mimeographed versions of the declarations are attached.

DOCUMENT 2. Typed on Mombushō paper (3 leaves), dated August 10, 1935: notes on interviews with officials of the Kansai University and Doshisha University concerning respectively Nakajima Shige and Tabata Shinobu and the extent to which they have purged their lectures and publications.

DOCUMENT 3. Typed on Mombushō paper (2 leaves), dated August 19, 1935: notes on an interview with an official of Waseda University concerning Nomura Junji, Nakano Tomio, and Nakamura Yasaji.

DOCUMENT 4. Typed on Mombushō paper (2 leaves), undated: more comment on Nakajima, Tabata, Nakamura, Nakano, and Nomura.

DOCUMENT 5. Typed on Mombushō paper (2 leaves), dated October 5, 1935: notes on further interviews with Waseda officials concerning Nomura, Nakamura, and Nakano.

DOCUMENT 6. Typed on Mombushō paper (1 leaf), dated October 7, 1935: notes on interview with the head of Meiji University law faculty concerning Nomura Junji, Takeuchi Masao, and Nomura Nobushige, indicating that these men have purged themselves of error.

DOCUMENT 7. Typed on Mombushō paper (2 leaves), dated November 19, 1935: notes on oral report from chief of the bureau concerning the clarification measures at Tokyo Imperial University, with special attention to Miyazawa Toshiyoshi and Nomura Junji.

DOCUMENT 8. Typed table entitled "Publications on the Constitutional System Which Have Been Banned, Revised or Suspended"; lists 32 titles by 17 authors, three of which have been banned (Minobe's), two revised, and 33 suspended.

DOCUMENTS 9–11. Copies of various of the preceding documents.

DOCUMENTS 12–20. Handwritten notes, undeciphered.

DOCUMENT 21. Handwritten note, undated: speaks of the necessity of a close examination of the works of Sasaki Sōichi and Ishizaki Takugoro at the Ritsumeikan University.

DOCUMENT 22. Typed on Mombushō paper (1 leaf), dated July 29, 1935: from Thought Bureau to the head of the Matsumoto High School asking for copies of Kitagawa Junichiro's *Hōsei Gairon* (*Outline of Legislation*).

DOCUMENT 23. Typed on Mombushō paper (1 leaf), dated July 29, 1935: from Thought Bureau to Kansai University asking for copies of Yoshida Isshi's *Nihon Kempō Tokushitsu Ron* (*Discussion of the Special Characteristics of the Japanese Constitution*).

DOCUMENT 24. Handwritten on Mombushō paper (6 leaves), undated: a table listing twelve active teachers of constitutional law, the erroneous ideas attributed to them, and in some cases the steps taken by them to correct those errors.

DOCUMENT 25. Typed on Mombushō paper (2 leaves), undated: outline of action under three headings: (1) matters requiring urgent disposition (prohibition of publication or suspension from teaching) with regard to Nakajima Shige, Tabata Shinobu, Moriguchi Shigeji, Nomura Junji, Miyazawa Toshiyoshi, Asai Kiyoshi, and Nakano Tomio; (2) matters requiring strict attention (suspension and revision of publication, suspension from teaching) in regard to Sasaki Sōichi, Nomura Nobushige, Takeuchi Masao, Fujii Shinichi, Watanabe Sōtaro, Kawamura Matasuke, Yoshida Isshi, and Nakamura Susuma; (3) matters requiring attention (correction of terminology) in regard to Nishigawa Ichio, Shida Kotaro, and Tagami Jōji.

DOCUMENT 26. Mimeographed (1 leaf), undated: under the heading "Schools of Constitutional Theory," 34 professors are listed as belonging to the *Tennō shutai* or *Tennō kikan* school; some of those in the latter group are further classified as "materialists," "radical democrats," or proponents of pure jurisprudence.

DOCUMENT 27. Typewritten on Meiji University paper (4 leaves), undated: Takeuchi Masao's explanation of his *Kempō Genron* (*Principles of the Constitution*).

DOCUMENT 28. Handwritten on Mombushō paper (1 leaf), undated: Asai Kiyoshi's explanation of the revision of his lectures.

DOCUMENT 29. Handwritten on Mombushō paper (2 leaves), undated: a list of 27 higher educational institutions, public and private, showing who is teaching constitutional law, what schools of constitutional theory they belong to, and what corrections have been made in their lectures and writings.

DOCUMENT 30. Handwritten on Mombushō paper (2 leaves), undated: excerpts from an article published in November, 1935, by Nakamura Tsumiji on the subject of the Uesugi-Minobe debate.

DOCUMENT 31. Handwritten on Mombushō paper (11 leaves), undated: summary of Nomura Junji's 1936 lecture notes for the course in state law at Tokyo Imperial University.

DOCUMENT 32. Handwritten on Mombushō paper (19 leaves), undated: excerpts from Nakamura Tsumiji's Kempō Gyōsei Hō (Constitutional and Administrative Law).

DOCUMENT 33. Typewritten on Mombushō paper (4 leaves), undated: summary statement by head of the Kyoto Imperial University law department on the theories of Professor Kuroda Akira. Notes from a report by an investigator on Kuroda's lectures (in November, 1935?).

DOCUMENT 34. Handwritten on Kyushu Imperial University paper (27 leaves), undated: outline of Kawamura Matakai's lectures on the constitution.

II

A folio located in the Orientalia Division, Library of Congress (321 M194), and inscribed with the legend: Minobe Hakushi Chosho ni Kansuru Tōben Shiryō (Materials in Response to Questions Concerning the Works of Dr. Minobe). The date and authorship of the papers are not explicitly stated, but the folio consists of 12 documents totaling some 89 unbound and unnumbered handwritten, typewritten, and mimeographed sheets, most of them on home ministry (Naimushō) stationery; internal evidence indicates that these papers originated in the censorship bureau of the home ministry in 1935. The contents of the folio are listed below in the order of their arrangement as found.

DOCUMENT 1. (leaves 1–16). This document to be read with Document 6 (leaves 36–65). Both follow the same organization, Document 6 supplying detail not included in Document 1. Under each of 8 separate topics there are set forth: (a) passages from Minobe's writings which have been criticized, (b) gist of the complaints against those passages, (c) passages from Minobe's writings which serve to explain or refute the complaints, and (d) a summary statement of [the censorship bureau's] opinion. The eight topical headings are:

Concerning the responsibility of ministers of state (leaves 3–4, 38–40);
Concerning abolition of the privy council (leaves 5, 41);
Concerning the character of the diet in public law (leaves 6, 42–44);
Concerning the theory of the joint government by monarch and people (leaves 7–8, 45–47);
Concerning the independence of the judiciary and other powers (leaves 9, 48–50);
Concerning the independence of the supreme command (leaves 10, 51–52);
Concerning thought control (leaves 11–12, 55–62);
Concerning the legal origins of the constitution (leaves 13–15, 63–65).

DOCUMENT 2. Materials in response to questions concerning Dr. Minobe's Kempō Seigi. Brief statement of Minoda Kyoki's criticism of Minobe's assertion of the independence of the diet, followed by [the bureau's?] opinion (leaves 17–20).

DOCUMENT 3. Concerning the matter of dealing with Dr. Minobe's works. "Therefore it is thought that there will be no necessity of taking action with respect to these works under the Publication Law (as a thing disturbing public peace and order) or otherwise...." (leaves 22–24).

DOCUMENT 4. Concerning the matter of dealing with the works of Suehiro Iwataro. Recommendations of the bureau in respect to the works criticized by Minoda Kyoki. Recites the story of the banning of Suehiro's *Hōsō Mampitsu* in 1933 (leaves 25–29).

DOCUMENT 5. Concerning Minobe's criticism of the Peace Preservation Law. Excerpts from the article "Chian Iji Hō Hihan," and conclusions of the Bureau (leaves 31–34).

DOCUMENT 6. See Document 1.

DOCUMENT 7. Same as Document 2.

DOCUMENT 8. Table of Minobe's works which have been criticized (leaves 66–70).

DOCUMENT 9. Same as Document 3.

DOCUMENT 10. Same as Document 4.

DOCUMENT 11. An examination of Dr. Minobe's emperor-organ theory. It is not indicated whether the unfavorable interpretation set forth here is the bureau's or merely one reproduced from some other source.

DOCUMENT 12. A printed broadside entitled "Minobe Tatsukichi Hakushi Suehiro Iwataro Hakushi Nado no Kokken Bunran Shisō ni Tsuite" ("Concerning the Ideas of Dr. Minobe Tatsukichi, Dr. Suehiro Iwataro, and Others Which Are Destructive of the Constitution of the State), issued by the Kokutai Yōgo Rengō Kai, and subscribed to by 86 organizations.

III

This source consists of three sets of U.S. Army Signal Corps photostats deposited in the Orientalia Division of the Library of Congress.

FIRST SERIES. (321 S391 S1) Photostats of 314 leaves of Privy Council stationery upon which is inscribed in Japanese hand what purports to be a record of the proceedings before the privy council committee on the matter of the draft revision of Imperial Constitution to be Submitted to the Imperial Diet (Teikoku Kempō Kaisei-an wo Teikoku Gikai ni Fūsuru Ken—Sūmitsu-in Shinsa I-in Kai Hikki). These papers cover three series of meetings: eight meetings beginning on April 22 and ending on May 15, 1946 (leaves 1–260); three meetings beginning on May 29 and ending on June 3, 1946 (leaves 261–288); and two meetings on October 19 and 21, 1946 (leaves 293–314).

SECOND SERIES. (321 S391 S2) Photostats of 45 leaves of privy council stationery upon which is inscribed in Japanese hand what purports to be a record of the plenary sessions of the council (Sūmitsu-in Kaigi Hikki) on the subject of the draft revision on June 8, 1946 (leaves 1–20), and on October 29, 1946 (leaves 21–45).

THIRD SERIES. (321 S391 S2 English) Photostats of 26 leaves of privy council stationery upon which is inscribed a typewritten English translation of the preceding Second Series documents.

Morohashi Noboru, chief of the privy council secretariat throughout the period from March to November, 1946, has published an article describing the deliberations of the privy council on the draft revision of the constitution: "Sūmitsu-in ni okeru Nihonkoku Kempō Shingi" ("Deliberations of the Constitution of Japan in the

Privy Council"), in the journal *Jichi Kenkyū*, 31 (May, June, July, August, 1955). It appears to be a substantially accurate but not a literal account of the deliberations. Morohashi says (August, 1955) that his narration is based on his own memoranda except for the final plenary session of the council on October 29, 1946. In this instance he was given "the unprecedented liberty" of working from a photostat of the official record.

Official Publications and Documents

KEMPŌ CHŌSA KAI (Constitution Investigation Committee). *Kempō Chōsa Kai Hōkokusho (Report of the Constitution Investigation Committee)*. Tokyo: Ōkurashō Insatsu Kyoku, 1964.

KEMPŌ CHŌSA KAI JIMU KYOKU (Office of the Constitution Investigation Committee). Satō Isao, ed., *Kempō Seitei no Keika ni Kansuru Sho I-in Kai Hōkokusho (Report of the Subcommittee on the Process of Establishing the Constitution)*. Tokyo: Ōkurashō Insatsu Kyoku, 1961.

MOMBUSHŌ SHISŌ KYOKU (Thought Bureau of the Ministry of Education). *Kempō Gakusetsu Chōsa ni kansuru Bunsho (Documents Relating to the Investigation of Academic Constitutional Theory)*. See Bibliographical Note I above.

NAIKAKU INSATSU KYOKU (Cabinet Printing Office). *Kampō (Official Gazette)*, published daily and irregularly in Tokyo. Proceedings of the diet carried in extra editions: *Kampō Gōgai*.

————. *Kanchō Kankō Tosho Mokuroku (Index of the Library of Official Publications)*. Vols. 25–30 (January, 1933–December, 1934).

NAIKAKU KIROKU KA (Cabinet Archives). *Genkō Hōrei Shūran (Laws and Ordinances Presently in Effect)*. Tokyo: Yūhikaku, annual.

NAIMUSHŌ (Home Ministry). *Minobe Hakushi no Chōsho in kansuru Tōben Shiryō (Materials in Response to Questions Concerning the Works of Dr. Minobe)*. See Bibliographical Note II above.

SŪMITSU-IN (Privy Council). *Teikoku Kempō Kaisei-an wo Teikoku Gikai ni Fusuru Ken—Sūmitsu-in Shinsa I-in Kai Hikki (Various Documents of the Privy Council Sub-committee to Investigate the Draft Revision of the Imperial Constitution to be Submitted to the Imperial Diet)*. See Bibliographical Note III above.

SUPREME COMMANDER FOR THE ALLIED POWERS, General Headquarters, Government Section. *Political Reorientation of Japan: September 1945–September 1948*. Washington, D.C.: Government Printing Office, 1949. 2 vols.

Books and General Reference Works in Japanese

ABE ISOO AND MIYAKE YUJIRO, eds. *Shōwa Go Nen Shi (History of 1930)*. Tokyo: Nenshi Kankō Kai, 1936.

AIZAWA HIROSHI. *Nihon Kyōiku Hyakunen Shidan (History of a Century of Japanese Education)*. Tokyo: Gaku-in Tosho, 1952.

FUKUBE UNOYOSHI, ed. *Tōkyō Teikoku Daigaku Goju Nen Shi (History of Fifty Years of Tokyo Imperial University)*. Tokyo: Chūgai Insatsu, 1932. 2 vols.

FUKUDA KANICHI, and others. *Seiji Shisō ni okeru Seiō to Nihon: Nambara Shigeru Sensei Koki Kinen (Political Thought in Western Europe and Japan: in Celebration of Professor Shigeru Nambara's Seventieth Year)*. Tokyo: Tokyo Daigaku Shuppan Kai, 1961. 2 vols.

HAKUSHI MEIGAN (Index of Doctors). Tokyo: Who's Who in Japan Company, 1935.

HARADA KUMAO, comp. *Saionji Kō to Seikyoku* (*Prince Saionji and the Political Situation*). Tokyo: Iwanami Shoten, 1951–1952. 6 vols.

HASEGAWA MASAYASU. *Kempōgaku no Hōhō* (*The Method of Constitutional Science*). Tokyo: Nihon Hyōron Shinsha, 1957.

————. *Shōwa Kempō Shi* (*History of the Showa Constitution*). Tokyo: Iwanami Shoten, 1961.

HASHIMOTO BUNJU. *Shintō no Gendaiteki Kenkyū* (*Study of Shinto Today*). Tokyo: Hōbun Kanzō, 1925.

HIROTA NAOMORI. *Naikaku Kōtetsu Goju Nen Shi* (*The Cabinet Through Fifty Years*). Tokyo: Shunyōdō, 1930.

HOSHIJIMA JIRO, ed. *Saikin Kempō Ron* (*Recent Constitutional Theory*). 7th ed. Tokyo: Taiyōdō, 1927.

HOZUMI YATSUKA. *Kempō Teiyō* (*Elements of the Constitution*). Tokyo: Yūhikaku, 1910. 2 vols.

IENAGA SABURO. *Minobe Tatsukichi no Shisō Shiteki Kenkyū* (*Historical Study of the Thought of Minobe Tatsukichi*). Tokyo: Iwanami Shoten, 1964.

IMANAKA TSUGIMARO. *Seijigaku Tsūron* (*Introduction to Political Science*). Rev. ed. Tokyo: Taimeidō, 1951.

INO SABURO, ed. *Taishū Jinji Roku* (*Index of Popular Biography*). 12th ed. Tokyo: Kokusei Kyōkai, 1937.

ISEKI KURO, ed. *Dai Nihon Hakushi Roku* (*Index of Japanese Doctors*). Tokyo: Hatten Sha, 1921. Vol. I.

ISHIDA TAKESHI. *Kindai Nihon Seiji Kōzō no Kenkyū* (*Study of the Political Structure of Modern Japan*). Tokyo: Miraisha, 1956.

ITANI ZENICHI. *Meiji Ishin Keizai Shi* (*Economic History of the Meiji Restoration*). Tokyo: Kaizō Sha, 1928.

ITO HIROBUMI. *Teikoku Kempō Gikai*. See under English title: *Commentaries on the Constitution of the Empire of Japan*.

ITO YURO, ed. *Tennō Kikan Setsu no Bokumetsu Sen* (*The Struggle to Destroy the Emperor-Organ Theory*). Tokyo: Tōhō Shoin, 1935.

KABAYAMA TOMOYOSHI. *Hayashi Senjuro Den* (*Biography of Hayashi Senjuro*). Tokyo: Kitabakari Shobō, 1937.

KADA TETSUJI. *Nihon Kokka Shakai Shugi Hihan: Nihon Fuasshizumu Ron* (*Critique of Japanese State Socialism: Discourse on Japanese Fascism*). Tokyo: Shunjū Sha, 1932.

KANAMORI TOKUJIRO. *Kempō Igen* (*Testament of the Constitution*). Tokyo: Gakuyō Shobō, 1960.

KIKUGAWA TADAO. *Gakusei Shakai Undō Shi* (*History of the Student Socialist Movement*). Tokyo: Chūō Kōron Sha, 1931.

KINOSHITA HANJI. *Nihon Fuashizumu Shi* (*History of Japanese Fascism*). Tokyo: Iwasaki, 1950. 2 vols.

KOBAYASHI TAKASUKE. *Kempōgaku no Honshitsu: Kempō oyobi Kempōgaku no Kenkyū* (*The Essence of Constitutional Science: a Study of the Constitution and of Constitution Science*). Tokyo: Morikita, 1957.

KOBAYASHI TAKASUKE, and others. *Nihonkoku Kempō Shikō: Sengo no Kempō Seiji* (*Reflections on the Constitutional History of Japan: Postwar Constitutional Politics*). Tokyo: Hōritsu Bunka Sha, 1962.

KOKKA GAKKAI (The Political and Social Science Society). *Meiji Kensei Keizai Shiron*

(*The Constitutional and Economic History of Meiji*). Thirtieth year memorial publication. Tokyo: Yūhikaku, 1919.

MARUYAMA MASAO. *Gendai Seiji no Shisō to Kōdō* (*Thought and Action in Modern Politics*). Tokyo: Miraisha, 1956. 2 vols.

MATSUMOTO SHIGETOSHI. *Tōchiken Ron* (*On Sovereignty*). Tokyo: Chūgai Insatsu, 1917.

MATSUSHITA KEIICHI. *Gendai Nihon no Seijiteki Kōsei* (*The Political Structure of Present Day Japan*). Tokyo: Tōkyō Daigaku Shuppan Kai, 1962.

MIKI KIYOSHI, ed. *Gendai Tetsugaku Jiten* (*Dictionary of Modern Philosophy*). 2d ed. Tokyo: Hyōron Sha, 1947.

MINOBE RYŌKICHI. *Kumon Suru Demokurashii* (*The Agony of Democracy*). Tokyo: Bungei Shunju Sha, 1959.

MINOBE TATSUKICHI. *Beikoku Kempō Gairon* (*Introduction to the American Constitution*). 2d ed. Tokyo: Yūhikaku, 1949.

———. *Beikoku Kempō no Yurai oyobi Tokushitsu* (*The Origins and Special Characteristics of the American Constitution*). Tokyo: Yūhikaku, 1947

———. *Chikujō Kempō Seigi* (*Commentary on the Constitution Article by Article*). Tokyo: Yūhikaku, 1929.

———. *Erinekku no Jinken Sengen Ron* (*Jellinek's Declaration of the Rights of Man*). Tokyo: Yūhikaku, 1909. Republished by Nihon Hyōrōn Sha, 1946.

———. *Gendai Kensei Hyōron* (*Critique of Modern Constitutional Government*). Tokyo: Iwanami, 1930.

———. *Gikai Seido Ron* (*On the Parliamentary System*). Tokyo: Nihon Hyōron Sha, 1930. Rev. ed., 1948.

———. *Gikai Seiji no Kentō* (*Examination of Parliamentary Government.*) Tokyo: Nihon Hyōron Sha, 1934.

———. *Gyōsei Hō Satsuyō* (*Essentials of Administrative Law*). Tokyo: Yūhikaku, 1933. 2 vols.

———. *Hō no Honshitsu* (*The Nature of Law*). Tokyo: Nihon Hyōron Sha, 1930.

———. *Jiji Kempō Mondai Hihan* (*Critique of Current Constitutional Problems*). Tokyo: Hōsei Jihō Sha, 1921.

———. *Hyōshaku Kōhō Hanrei Taikei* (*Annotated Summary of Judicial Precedents in Public Law*). Tokyo: Yūhikaku, 1933, 1934. 2 vols.

———. *Kempō Kōwa* (*Lectures on the Constitution*). 4th ed. Tokyo: Yūhikaku, 1914.

———. *Kempō oyobi Kempō Shi Kenkyū* (*Studies on the Constitution and Constitutional History*). Tokyo: Yūhikaku, 1908.

———. *Kempō Satsuyō* (*Essentials of the Constitution*). Tokyo: Yūhikaku, 1923. Republished, 1946.

———. *Kempō to Seitō* (*Constitutions and Political Parties*). Tokyo: Nihon Hyōron Sha, 1934.

———. *Kōhō to Shihō* (*Public Law and Private Law*). Tokyo: Nihon Hyōron Sha, 1935.

———. *Nihon Gyōsei Hō* (*Japanese Administrative Law*). Tokyo: Yūhikaku, 1909. 2 vols.

———. *Nihon Kempō* (*The Japanese Constitution*). 3d ed. Tokyo: Yūhikaku, 1924.

———. *Nihon Kempō no Kihon Shugi* (*Basic Principles of the Japanese Constitution*). Tokyo: Nihon Hyōron Sha, 1934.

————. *Nihon Kokuhō Gaku (Japanese State Law)*. Tokyo: Yūhikaku, 1906.
————. *Nihonkoku Kempō Genron (Principles of the Japanese Constitution)*. Tokyo: Yūhikaku, 1948.
————. *Oshū Shokoku Sengo no Shin Kempō (New Constitutions of the European States since the War)*. Tokyo: Yūhikaku, 1922.
————. *Oshū Tairiku Shisei Ron* (tran. Albert Shaw, *Municipal Administration in Continental Europe*). Tokyo: Yūhikaku, 1899.
————. *Otto Maiya no Doitsu Gyōseihō (Otto Meyer's German Administrative Law)*. Tokyo: Yūhikaku, 1909.
————. *Senkyo Hō Shōsetsu (Election Law Explained in Detail)*. Tokyo: Nihon Hyōron Sha, 1948.
————. *Shin Kempō Chikujō Kaisetsu (Explanation of the New Constitution by Articles)*. Tokyo: Nihon Hyōron Sha, 1947.
————. *Shin Kempō Gairon (Introduction to the New Constitution)*. Tokyo: Yūhikaku, 1947.
————. *Shin Kempō no Kihon Genri (Basic Principles of the New Constitution)*. Tokyo: Kokuritsu Shoin, 1947.
MINODA KYOKI. *Minobe Hakushi no Taiken Jūrin: Taiken Jūrin, Kokusei Hakai, Nihon Mano no Ganshu Kakon (Dr. Minobe's Violation of the Prerogative: the Cancerous Roots of the Violation of the Prerogative, of the Destruction of the Government and of Japan's Manifold Ills)*. Tokyo: Genri Nihon Sha, 1935.
MIYAZAWA TOSHIYOSHI. *Kempō Kaisei (Constitutional Revision)*. Tokyo: Yūhikaku, 1956.
————. *Kempo Tai-i (Précis of the Constitution)*. Tokyo: Yūhikaku, 1949.
————. *Kokumin Shuken to Tennōsei (Popular Sovereignty and the Emperor System)*. Tokyo: Keisō Shobō, 1957.
MIYAZAWA TOSHIYOSHI, and others. *Kōhōgaku no Sho Mondai: Minobe Kyōju Kanreki Kinen (Problems in the Field of Public Law: in Celebration of Professor Minobe's Sixtieth Anniversary)*. Tokyo: Yūhikaku, 1934–1935. 2 vols.
MORI SHŌZŌ. *Fūsetsu no Hi (Tombstones in a Blizzard)*. Tokyo: Masu Shobō, 1946.
————. *Sempū Ni-ju Nen (The Twenty-year Whirlwind)*. Tokyo: Masu Shobō, 1945.
NAKAMURA AKIRA. *Kohuhōgaku no Shiteki Kenkyū (Historical Study of the Science of State Law)*. Tokyo: Nihon Hyōron Sha, 1949.
————. *Nihonkoku Kempō no Kōzō (The Structure of the Constitution of Japan)*. Tokyo: Ochanomizu Shobō, 1956.
————. *Shin Kempō Notō (Notes on the New Constitution)*. 3d ed. Tokyo: Kyōwa Shuppan Sha, 1949.
NAKANO TOMIO. *Tōsuiken no Dokuritsu (Independence of the Supreme Command)*. Tokyo: Yūhikaku, 1934.
NAKASE JUICHI. *Kindai ni Okeru Tennō Kan (Views of the Emperor in Recent Times)*. Tokyo: Sanichi Shobō, 1963.
ŌISHI YOSHIO. *Teikoku Kempō to Zaisan Sei (The Imperial Constitution and the Property System)*. Tokyo: Nihon Hyōron Sha, 1943.
————. *Kempō Kaisei no Hitsuyōsa: Kempō Kaisei no Shian Yōkō (The Necessity of Constitutional Revision: Gist of a Tentative Draft of a Revision of the Constitution)*. Tokyo: Yūshindo, 1962.

OKADA KEISUKE. *Okada Keisuke Kaikoroku* (*Memoirs of Okada Keisuke*). Tokyo: Mainichi Shimbun Sha, 1950.

OKAMOTO NIJI. *Meiji Taishō Shisō Shi* (*Intellectual History of Meiji and Taisho*). Tokyo: Monasu, 1929.

OSATAKE TAKESHI. *Nihon Kempō Seitei Shiyō* (*Essentials of the History of the Establishment of the Japanese Constitution*). Tokyo: Ikusei Sha, 1938.

——. *Nihon Kensei Shi* (*History of Japanese Constitutional Government*). Tokyo: Nihon Hyōron Sha, 1930. 2 vols.

ŌTANI YOSHITAKA. *Kokutai Kempō Genri* (*Principles of the National Polity Constitution*). Tokyo: Yūhikaku, 1935.

ŌTSU JUNICHIRO. *Dai Nihon Kensei Shi* (*Constitutional History of Japan*). Tokyo: Hōbunkan, 1927–1928. 10 vols.

OZAKI SHIRO. *Tennō Kikan Setsu* (*The Emperor-Organ Theory*). Tokyo: Kadokawa, 1955.

RŌYAMA MASAMICHI, and others. *Kanshi Seido no Kenkyū* (*Studies in the Official System*). Tokyo: Dōyu Sha, 1948.

——. *Nihon ni okeru Kindai Seijigaku no Hattatsu* (*The Development of Modern Political Science in Japan*). Tokyo: Jitsugyō no Nihon Sha, 1949.

——. *Seiji oyobi Seijishi Kenkyū—Yoshino Sakuzō Sensei Tsuitō Kinen* (*Studies in Politics and Political History—in Commemoration of the Late Professor Yoshino Sakuzō*). Tokyo: Iwanami, 1935.

——. *Seiji Shi* (*Political History*). Tokyo: Tōyō Keizai Shimpō Sha, 1940. Vol. II of *Gendai Nihon Bunmei Shi* (*History of Modern Japanese Civilization*).

SAJI KENJŌ. *Nihongaku toshite no Nihon Kokkagaku* (*Japanese State Science as a Japanese Science*). Tokyo: Dai-ichi Shobo, 1941.

SAKISAKA ITSURO, and others. *Arashi no naka Hyakunen* (*One Hundred Years in a Tempest*). Tokyo: Keisō Shobō, 1952.

SAKUMA AKIRA, ed. *Nihon Kankai Meigan* (*Index of Japanese Officialdom*). Tokyo: 5th ed. Nihon Kankai Jōhō Sha, 1942.

SASAKI SŌICHI. *Kempō Kaisei Dansō* (*Fragmentary Thoughts on Constitutional Revision*). Tokyo: Kōbundō, 1947.

——. *Nihon Kempō Yōron* (*Essentials of the Japanese Constitution*). Tokyo: Kinsaku Jikidō, 1933.

——. *Nihonkoku Kempō Ron* (*On the New Constitution of Japan*). Tokyo: Yūhikaku, 1949.

——. *Rikken Hi-rikken* (*Constitutional, Unconstitutional*). Tokyo: Asahi Shimbun Sha, 1950.

SATŌ ISAO. *Kempō Kaisei no Keika* (*The Process of Constitutional Revision*). Tokyo: 3d ed. Nihon Hyōron Sha, 1949.

——. *Nihonkoku Kempō Ju-ni Kō* (*Twelve Lectures on the Japanese Constitution*). Tokyo: Gakuyō Shobō, 1951.

SATŌ KIYOKATSU. *Dai Nihon Seijigaku* (*Japanese Political Science*). Tokyo: Heibun Sha, 1934.

——. *Minobe Nihon Kempō Ron Hihan* (*Critique of Minobe's Constitutional Theory*). Tokyo: Yūbunkaku, 1934.

SATŌ TATSUO. *Nihonkoku Kempō no Seiritsu Shi* (*History of the Establishment of the Constitution of Japan*). Vol. I. Tokyo: Yūhikaku, 1963.

SATŌ USHIJIRO. *Teikoku Kempō Kōgi* (*Lectures on the Imperial Constitution*). Tokyo: Yūhikaku, 1935.

SATOMI KISHIO. *Tennō Kikan Setsu Kentō* (*Critique of the Emperor-Organ Theory*). Tokyo: Nishōdō, 1935.

SUEKAWA HIROSHI. *Hōgaku Jiten* (*Dictionary of Law*). Tokyo: Nihon Hyōron Sha, 1951.

SUZUKI YASUZŌ. *Hikaku Kempō Shi* (*Comparative Constitutional History*). Tokyo: Keisō Shobō, 1951.

————, ed. *Kempōgaku no Kadai* (*Topics in Constitutional Science*). Tokyo: Keisō Shobō, 1954.

————. *Kempō Kaisei to Kempō Yōgo* (*Revision of the Constitution or Preservation of the Constitution*). Tokyo: Keisō Shobō, 1956.

————. *Kempō no Rekishiteki Kenkyū* (*Historical Studies on the Constitution*). Tokyo: Oda Shoten, 1933.

————. *Nihon Kempō Seiritsu Shi* (*History of the Establishment of the Constitution of Japan*). Tokyo: Gakusei Sha, 1938.

————. *Nihon Kempō Shi Kenkyū* (*Studies in the History of the Constitution of Japan*). Tokyo: Satsubunkaku, 1935.

SUZUKI YASUZŌ, and others. *Kempō Kaisei no Kihon Mondai* (*Key Issues in Constitutional Revision*). Tokyo: Keisō Shobō, 1956.

TAKAMIYA TAHEI. *Tennō Heika* (*His Majesty the Emperor*). Tokyo: Imaijin, 1951.

TANAKA RYŪKICHI. *Hai-i wo Tsuku—Gumbatsu Sen-ō no Jissō* (*Striking at the Roots of Defeat—True Picture of Military Despotism*). Tokyo: Sansui Sha, 1946.

TANAKA TSUGIMARO. *Seijigaku Tsūron* (*Introduction to Political Science*). Rev. ed. Tokyo: Taimeidō, 1951.

TANIGUCHI TOMOHEI, and others, *Hō Kaishaku no Riron: Tsunego Sensei Koki Shukuga Kinen* (*Theory of Legal Interpretation: in Celebration of Professor Tsunego's Seventieth Year*). Tokyo: Yūhikaku, 1960.

TOYAMA SHIGEKI AND ADACHI YOSHIKO. *Kindai Nihon Seiji Shi Hikkei* (*Manual on Recent Japanese Political History*). Tokyo: Iwanami, 1961.

TSUJI KIYO-AKI. *Nihon Kanryōsei no Kenkyū* (*Studies on the Japanese Bureaucratic System*). Tokyo: Kōbundō, 1952.

UESUGI SHINKICHI. *Kempō Jutsugi* (*The Constitution Truly Explained*). Rev. ed. Tokyo: Yūhikaku, 1924.

————. *Teikoku Kempō* (*The Imperial Constitution*). 2d ed. Tokyo: Yūhikaku, 1924.

WADA HIDEKICHI. *Ni-ni-roku Igo* (*Since Two-Twenty-Six*). Tokyo: Kaisei Sha, 1937.

WATANABE YŌZŌ. *Seiji to Hō no Aida: Nihonkoku Kempō no Jugonen* (*Between Politics and Law: Fifteen Years of the Constitution of Japan*). Tokyo: Tōkyō Daigaku Shuppan Kai, 1963.

WATSUJI TETSURO. *Kokumin Tōgō no Shōchō* (*Symbol of the People's Unity*). Tokyo: Keisō Shobō, 1948.

YABE SADAJI. *Konoye Fumimaro* (*Konoye Fumimaro*). Tokyo: Kōbundō, 1952. 2 vols.

YAMAMOTO KATSUNOSUKE with ISHIHARA KANJI. *Nihon wo Horoboshite Mono* (*That Which Has Destroyed Japan*). Tokyo: Shōkō Sho-in, 1949.

YAMAURA KANICHI. *Hijōjikoyku to Jinbutsu* (*Crisis and Personality*). Tokyo: Shinsei Sha, 1937.

YOSHINO SAKUZŌ. *Gendai Seiji Kōwa* (*Lectures on Modern Politics*). Tokyo: Bunka Seikatsu Kenkyū Kai, 1926.

————. *Nihon Musan Seitō Ron* (*On Japan's Proletarian Parties*). Tokyo: Ichigen, 1929.

Books in Western Languages

BAERWALD, HANS H. *The Purge of Japanese Leaders under the Occupation* (Vol. VIII, University of California Publications in Political Science). Berkeley: University of California Press, 1959.

BECKMANN, GEORGE M. *The Making of the Meiji Constitution: the Oligarchs and the Constitutional Development of Japan, 1868–1891*. Lawrence: University of Kansas Press, 1957.

BISSON, THOMAS A. *Japan's War Economy*. New York: Macmillan and the Institute of Pacific Relations, 1945.

BORTON, HUGH. *Japan's Modern Century*. New York: Ronald, 1955.

BUTOW, ROBERT. *Japan's Decision to Surrender*. Palo Alto: Stanford University Press, 1954.

——. *Tojo and the Coming of the War*. Princeton: Princeton University Press, 1961.

BYAS, HUGH. *Government by Assassination*. New York: Knopf, 1942.

COLEGROVE, KENNETH W. *Militarism in Japan*. Boston: World Peace Foundation, 1936.

CORRY, J. A. *Elements of Democratic Government*. New York: Oxford University Press, 1947.

CRAIG, GORDON A. *The Politics of the Prussian Army, 1640–1945*. Oxford: Clarendon Press, 1955.

EMERSON, RUPERT. *State and Sovereignty in Modern Germany*. New Haven: Yale University Press, 1928.

EYCK, ERICH (Harlan P. Hanson and Robert G. L. Waite, trans.). *A History of the Weimar Republic: 1915–1933*. Cambridge: Harvard University Press, 1962.

FAHS, CHARLES B. *Government in Japan: Recent Trends in Its Scope and Operation*. New York: Institute of Pacific Relations, 1940.

HISHIDA, SEIJI. *Japan Among the Powers*. New York: Longmans-Green, 1940.

IKE NOBUTAKA. *The Beginnings of Political Democracy in Japan*. Baltimore: Johns Hopkins University Press, 1950.

——. *Japanese Politics: an Introductory Survey*. New York: Knopf, 1957.

ITO, HIROBUMI (Baron Myoji Ito, trans.). *Commentaries on the Constitution of the Empire of Japan*. 2d ed. Tokyo: Chūō Daigaku, 1906.

JELLINEK, GEORG. *Allgemeine Staatslehre*. Berlin: Häring, 1905.

——. *Die Erklärung der Menschen und Burgerrechte*. Leipzig: Dunker und Humbold, 1895.

——. *System der subjektiven öffentlichen Rechte*. 2d ed. Tübingen: Mohr, 1905.

——. *Verfassungsänderung und Verfassungswandlung*. Berlin: Häring, 1906.

KASE, TOSHIKAZU. *Journey to the Missouri*. New Haven: Yale University Press, 1950.

KELSEN, HANS. *Hauptprobleme der Staatsrechtslehre: entwickelt aus der Lehre von Rechtsätze*. Tübingen: Mohr-Siebeck, 1911.

——. *Der sociologische und der juristische Staatsbegriff*. Tübingen: Mohr, 1928.

KOBAYASHI, TAKEJIRO. *Die japanische Verfassung, vergleichen mit ihren europäischen Vorbildern*. Rostock: Winterberg, 1902.

KOSAKA MASAAKI (David Abosch, trans.). *Japanese Thought in the Meiji Era*. Tokyo: Pan-Pacific Press, 1958.

KRÜGER, FRITZ-KONRAD. *Government and Politics of the German Empire*. Yonkers: World Book, 1915.

KURZMAN, DAN. *Kishi and Japan: the Search for the Sun*. New York: Oblensky, 1960.

MATTERN, JOHANNES. *Principles of Constitutional Jurisprudence of the German National Republic*. Baltimore: Johns Hopkins University Press, 1928.

MAXON, YALE C. *Control of Japanese Foreign Policy: a Study of Civil-Military Rivalry: 1930–1945* (Vol. V, University of California Publications in Political Science). Berkeley: University of California Press, 1957.

MORRIS, I. I. *Nationalism and the Right Wing in Japan: Study of Post-War Trends*. London: Oxford University Press, 1960.

NAKANO, TOMIO. *The Ordinance Power of the Japanese Emperor*. Baltimore: Johns Hopkins University Press, 1923.

NORMAN, E. HERBERT. *Japan's Emergence as a Modern State: Political and Economic Problems of the Meiji Period*. New York: Institute of Pacific Relations, 1940.

OKUBO, GENJI. *The Problems of The Emperor System in Postwar Japan: Surveyed from an Examination of Arguments on the Subject*. Tokyo: Japan Institute of Pacific Studies, 1948.

QUIGLEY, HAROLD S. *Japanese Government and Politics: An Introductory Study*. New York: Century, 1932.

REISCHAUER, ROBERT K. *Japan: Government and Politics*. New York: Thomas Nelson, 1939.

SANSOM, GEORGE B. *The Western World and Japan: A Study in the Interaction of European and Asiatic Cultures*. New York: Knopf, 1950.

SCALAPINO, ROBERT A. *Democracy and the Party Movement in Prewar Japan*. Berkeley: University of California Press, 1953.

SCHWANTES, ROBERT S. *Japanese and Americans: A Century of Cultural Relations*. New York: Harper Brothers, Council on Foreign Relations, 1955.

SHUMAN, SAMUEL I. *Legal Positivism: Its Scope and Limitations*. Detroit: Wayne State University Press, 1963.

SIEBECK, PAUL, ed. *Staatsrechtliche Abhandlungen: Festgabe für Paul Laband*. Tübingen: Mohr, 1908.

STEAD, ALFRED, ed. *Japan by the Japanese: A Survey by Its Highest Authorities*. New York: Dodd-Mead, 1904.

STORRY, RICHARD. *The Double Patriots: a Study of Japanese Nationalism*. Boston: Houghton-Mifflin Co., 1957.

———. *A History of Modern Japan*. London: Penguin Books, 1961.

TAKEKOSHI YOSABURO. *Prince Saionji*. Kyoto: Ritsumeikan, 1933.

VOIGT, ALFRED. *Geschichte der Grundrechte*. Stuttgart: Spemann, 1948.

WALD, ROYAL J. *The Young Officers Movement in Japan, ca. 1925–1937: Ideology and Actions*. Unpublished doctoral dissertation in history, University of California, Berkeley, 1950.

WHITE, LEONARD D., ed. *The Civil Service in the Modern State: A Collection of Documents*. Chicago: University of Chicago, 1930.

YANAGA, CHITOSHI. *Japan Since Perry*. New York: McGraw-Hill, 1949.

———. *Japanese People and Politics*. New York: Wiley, 1956.

YOUNG, A. MORGAN. *Imperial Japan: 1926–1938*. New York: Morrow, 1938.

Articles in Japanese

ABE MANOSUKE. "Minobe Mondai to Okada Naikaku" ("The Minobe Question and the Okada Cabinet"), *Kaizō*, 17 (May, 1935), 282–288.

AKAGI KAZUHIKO. "Gendai Kempō Kyōju Sōhyō" ("Critical Survey of Present Day Professors of Constitutional Law"), *Kaizō*, 17 (June, 1935), 258–266.

ARASE YUTAKA and KAKEGAWA TOMIKO. "Tenno 'Kikan Setsu' to Genron no 'Jiyū'— Nihon Fuashizumu Keiseiki ni okeru Masu Medeia Tōsei (San)" ("The Emperor 'Organ Theory' and 'Freedom' of Speech—Control of Mass Media in the Formative Period of Japanese Fascism (III)," *Shisō*, 458 (August, 1962), 65–81.

ASHIBE NOBUKI. "Kempō Kaisei Rongi" ("The Debate over Constitutional Revision"), *Jurisuto*, 131 (June 1, 1957), 80–85.

BABA TSUNEGO. "Fuasshiyo to Seitō" ("Fascism and the Political Parties"), *Kaizō*, 17 (May, 1935), 272–279.

HATOYAMA ICHIRO. "Watakushi wa Kaku Shinzuru" ("Thus I Believe"), *Bungei Shunjū*, 29 (July, 1951), 56–66.

HIRANO YOSHITARO. "Meiji Hōgakushi in okeru Ichi Gakuha" ("One School of Meiji Legal History"), *Hōritsu Jihō*, 5 (August, 1933), 9–14.

HISATA EISEI. "Sengo Nihon Shi ni okeru Kempōgaku no Kadai to Tembo" ("Theme and Development in Constitutional Studies in Postwar Japan"), in Kobayashi Takasuke, *et al., Nihonkoku Kempō Shikō: Sengo no Kempō Seiji (Reflections on Japan's Constitutional History: Postwar Constitutional Politics.* Kyoto: Hōritsu Bunka Sha. 1962, pp. 331–353.

HOZUMI YATSUKA. "Kempō Seitei no Yurai" ("The Origins of the Making of the Constitution"), in *Meiji Bunka Zenshū (Complete Meiji Civilization)*, Vol. IV. Tokyo: Nihon Hyōron Sha, 1937.

ICHIMURA MITSUKEI. "Rikkenkoku ni Tōchiken no Sōransha Ariya" ("Is There a Bearer of State Power in the Constitutional State?"), *Kyōtō Hōgakkai Zasshi*, 5 (March, 1910), 91–104.

IKEDA MASAAKI, "Kempō Kaisei Mondai wo Meguru Ugoki ("Activities Concerning the Issues of Constitutional Revision"), *Jurisuto*, 240 (December 15, 1961), 44–45.

IMANAKA TSUGIMARO. "Nihon Fuasshizumu no Gen Dankai" ("The Present Stage of Japanese Fascism"), *Kaizō*, 17 (May, 1935), 264–272.

KANAMORI TOKUJIRO. "Kempō no Dekita Michi no Omoide" ("Recollections on How the Constitution Came into Being"), *Nihon Rekishi*, 53 (October, 1952), 49–51.

KOBAYASHI NAOKI. "Seiken Shi no Genriteki Kōsatsu" ("Theoretical Reflections on the History of the Making of the Constitution"), *Shisō*, 455 (May, 1962), 1–18.

KOBAYASHI NAOKI and IKEDA MASAAKI. "Hōritsugaku Jugonen no Kaikō to Tembō— Kempō" ("Fifteen Years of Legal Scholarship in Retrospect and Prospect—the Constitution"), *Jurisuto*, 217 (January 1, 1961), 24–41.

KOBAYASHI TAKASUKE. "Kempō no Kaisei to Henkō—Toku ni Erinekku no 'Kempō Henkō Ron' e no Hihan" ("Constitutional Amendment and Constitutional Change—Particularly a Criticism of Jellinek's *Verfassungswandlungstheorie*"), in Suzuki Yasuzō, editor, *Kempō Kaisei no Kihon Mondai*, pp. 210–232.

KURODA RYŌICHI. "Kempō Kaishaku no Ikkōsatsu" ("Thoughts on Constitutional Interpretation") in Suzuki Yasuzō, *et al., Kempōgaku no Kadai*, pp. 33–79.

―――. "Kempō no Kaishaku" ("Interpretation of the Constitution") in Taniguchi Tomohei, *et al. Hō Kaishaku no Riron*, pp. 205–225.

MARUYAMA MASAO, and others. "Nihon ni okeru Seijigaku no Kako to Shōrai—Tōron" ("The Past and Future of Political Science in Japan—a Discussion"), *Seijigaku*, 1 (1950), 35–82.

MATSUMOTO SANNOSUKE. "Nihon Kempōgaku ni okeru Kokka Ron no Tenkai: Sono Keiseiki ni okeru Hō to Kenryoku no Mondai wo Chūshin ni" ("The Development of the Theory of the State in Japanese Constitutional Science: Focusing on the Questions of Law and Power in the Formative Period") in Fukuda Kanichi, *et al. Seiji Shisō ni okeru Seiō to Nihon: Nambara Shigeru Sensei Koki Kinen*, Vol. II, pp. 169–219.

MINOBE TATSUKICHI. "Erinekku Kyōju no Kokutai Ron" ("Professor Jellinek on National Polity"), *Kokka Gakkai Zasshi*, 23 (October, 1909), 1417–1448.

———. "Gendai Seikyoku no Tembō" ("The Present Political Outlook"), *Asahi Shimbun* (Tokyo), January 3, 1935.

———. "Gyōseijō no Sōshō" ("Administrative Appeals"), *Kokka Gakkai Zasshi*, 62 (July, 1948), 321–326.

———. "Kaisei Kempō to Naikaku Seido" ("The Revised Constitution and the Cabinet System"), *Hōritsu Shimpō*, 731 (October, 1946), 8–14.

———. "Kempō Kaisei no Kihon Mondai" ("Basic Questions Concerning Constitutional Revision), *Hōritsu Shimpō*, 728 (April–May, 1946), 2–5.

———. "Kempō Kaisei Mondai" ("The Question of Constitutional Revision"), *Asahi Shimbun* (Tokyo), October 1–3, 1945.

———. "Kempō no Kaishaku in kansuru Gigi Sūzoku" ("Doubts Concerning Constitutional Interpretation"), *Kokka Gakkai Zasshi*, 13 (January, 1899), 34–36.

———. "Keruzen Kyōju no Kokka oyobi Kokusaihō Riron no Hihyō" ("Criticism of Professor Kelsen's State Law and International Law Doctrines"), *Kokka Gakkai Zasshi*, 44 (August, September, October, 1930), 1177–1212, 1375–1406, 1532–1550.

———. "Kokkaihō Gaisetsu" ("Outline of the Diet Law"), *Hōritsu Shimpō*, 742 (January, February, 1948), 1–3, 5–8.

———. "Kunshu no Kokuhōjō no Chi-i" ("The Position of the Monarch in State Law"), *Hōgaku Shirin*, 50 (November 15, 1903), 1–6.

———. "Nihon Kempō no Tokuiro" ("Special Characteristics of the Japanese Constitution"), *Kokka Gakkai Zasshi*, 40 (January–August, 1926), 1–18, 164–190, 337–356.

———. "Rippō Gyōi no Seishitsu" ("The Nature of Legislation and Administration"), *Kokka Gakkai Zasshi*, 46 (April, June, July, 1932), 1–24, 18–31, 44–58.

———. "Shimbunkami Hō Kaisei Mondai" ("The Question of Revising the Press Law"), *Chūō Kōron*, 367 (March, 1919), 41–50.

———. "Shin Kempō ni okeru Gyōsei Sōshō" ("Administrative Suits Under the New Constitution"), *Hōritsu Taimuzu*, 2 (January, 1948), 11–14.

———. "Shin Kempō ni okeru Kempō Saiban Seido" ("The Constitutional Court System under the New Constitution"), *Hōritsu Shimpō*, 736 (July, 1947), 3–9.

———. "Taikan Zappitsu" ("Random Notes on the Occasion of Retirement"), *Kaizō*, 16 (April, 1934), 150–159.

MIYAKE SHŌTARO. "Chian Iji Hō" ("The Peace Preservation Law"), *Iwanami Hōritsugaku Jiten (Iwanami Dictionary of Jurisprudence*.) Tokyo: Iwanami, 1942. Vol. III, pp. 1834–1836.

MIYAKE SETSUREI. "Kempō Happu-go Tadashi ni San-ju Nen" ("On the Thirtieth Anniversary of the Promulgation of the Constitution"), *Chūō Kōron*, 34 (February, 1919), 77–80.

MIYAZAWA TOSHIYOSHI. "Kempō no Yukue" ("Whither the Constitution?"), *Jurisuto*, 100 (February 15, 1956), 190–193.

———. "Kikan Setsu Jiken to Minobe Tatsukichi Sensei" ("Professor Minobe Tatsukichi and the Organ Theory Affair"), *Hōritsu Jihō*, 20 (August, 1948), 42–44.

———. "Minobe Sensei no Gyōseki" ("Professor Minobe's Achievements"), *Kokka Gakkai Zasshi*, 62 (July, 1948), 7–16.

———. "Rippō Gyōsei Ryo Kikan no aida no Kengen Bumpai no Genri" ("The Principle of the Separation of Powers Between Administrative and Legislative Organs"), *Kokka Gakkai Zasshi*, 46 (October, November, December, 1932), 1–33, 35–60, 32–63.

MIYAZAWA TOSHIYOSHI, and others. "Kempō Kaisei Mondai to Kempō Chōsakai no Katsudō" ("Issues of Constitutional Revision and the Activities of the Constitutional Investigation Committee"), *Jurisuto*, 241 (January 1, 1962), 12–31.

———. "Shin Kempō no Ju Nen" ("Tenth Anniversary of the New Constitution"), *Jurisuto*, 129 (May 1, 1957), 2–19.

MOROHASHI NOBURO. "Sūmitsu-in ni okeru Nihonkoku Kempō Shingi" ("Deliberation on the Constitution of Japan in the Privy Council"), *Jichi Kenkyū*, 31 (May, June, July, August, 1955), 17–33, 31–52, 53–67, 65–74.

MUROFUSA TAKANOBU. "Gendai no Seinen wo Ugokashizutsuaru Seironka Shisōka" ("Political Writers and Thinkers Who Are Agitating Youth Today"), *Chūō Kōron*, 34 (January, 1919), 119–127.

NAKAJIMA SHIGE. "Tagenronteki Kokka Gakusetsu to Ronrigakujō no Jiga Jitsugen Setsu" ("Pluralistic State Theory and the Ethical Theory of Self-Realization"), *Dōshisha Ronsō*, 11 (May 25, 1923), 1–48.

NAKAMURA AKIRA. "Minobe Hakushi no Futatsu no Kempō Kaisetsu Sho" ("Two of Dr. Minobe's Interpretations of the Constitution"), *Hōritsu Jihō*, 19 (October, 1947), 51–54.

NAKASE JUICHI. Meiji " 'Demokurashii' no Nashiyonarizumu e no Tenkan—'Tennō Kikan Setsu' Ronsha Uesugi Shinkichi. Kita Ikki no 'Tenkai' Shisō" ("The Conversion of 'Meiji Democracy' to Nationalism—The Revolutionary Thought of the 'Emperor-Organ' Theorists Uesugi Shiukichi and Kita Ikki"), *Dōshisha Hōgaku*, 78 (March, 1963), 177–215.

———. "Meiji Kempō ni okeru Tennō Kikan Setsu no Keisei" ("The Formation of the Emperor Organ Theory Under the Meiji Constitution"), *Hōritsu Jihō*, 34 (April, 1962), 59–71.

———. "Minobe Tatsukichi no Shisō Keisei no Zentei—Ishin wo Meguru Takasago no Keizai to Shisō Jōkyō" ("The Premises to the Formation of the Thought of Minobe Tatsukichi—the Economic and Intellectual Conditions at Takasago About the Time of the Restoration"), *Keizaigaku Zasshi*, 45 (December, 1961), 11–17.

———. "Tennō Kikan Setsu Kakuritsu Katei ni okeru Minobe Riron no Tokushitsu" ("The Special Character of Minobe's Theory in the Establishment of the Emperor-Organ Theory"), *Dōshisha Hōgaku*, 72 (June, 1962), 155–195.

NOMURA JIICHI. "Gyōseihōgaku ni okeru Gyōsei Gainen" ("The Concept of Administrative Law"), *Hōgaku Ronsō*, 38 (July, 1932), 99–124.

————. "Nakamura Misanji Kihanteki Gyōseihōgaku Joron wo Yomu" ("Review of Nakamura Misanji's Introduction to Comparative Administrative Law"), Hōgaku Ronsō, 37 (February, 1932), 177–182.

ōMORI YOSHITARO. "Gendai ni okeru Jiyūshugi no Kōyō to Genkai" ("The Utility and Limitations of Liberalism in the Present Era"), Kaizō, 17 (May, 1935), 2–19.

SAKOMIZU HISATSUNE. "Kōfukuji no Shinsō" ("True Account of the Time of Surrender"), Asahi Shimbun (Tokyo), January 13–20, 1946.

SASA HIROO. "Minobe Tatsukichi Ron" ("On Minobe Tatsukichi"), Chūō Kōron, 50 (March, 1935), 287–296.

SATŌ ISAO. "Gendai Nihon Seijishi in kansuru Kinpan San" ("Three Recent Publications on Contemporary Japanese Political History"), Kokka Gakkai Zasshi, 55 (April, 1941), 417–529.

————. "Kempō Chōsa Kai no Hōkoku Sho—Gaiyō to Mondai Ten" ("Published Reports of the Constitution Investigation Committee—Highlights and Issues"), Jurisuto, 227 (June 1, 1961), 12 parts.

————, and others. "Kempō Chōsa Kai no Saishū Kōkoku wo Owarite" ("Completing the Final Report of the Constitution Investigation Committee"), Jurisuto, 303 (August 1, 1964), 10–26.

SATŌ TATSUO. "Kanri Hō—Ippan Seisaku" ("The Control Law—General Policy"), Jurisuto, 100 (February 15, 1956), 167–170.

————. "Nihonkoku Kempō Seiritsu Shi" ("History of the Establishment of the Constitution of Japan"), Jurisuto, 81 (May 1, 1955) to 148 (February 15, 1958).

SUEHIRO IWATARO, and others. "Nihon Hōgaku no Kaiko to Tembō—Zadankai" ("Japanese Legal Science: Its Past and Its Prospects—a Round Table"), Hōritsu Jihō, 20 (December, 1948), 3–59.

SUGIMURA SHOSABURO. "Hyōgi-in Hōgaku Hakushi Uesugi Shinkichi Shi no Kōryo" ("On the Passing of Councillor Dr. Uesugi Shinkichi"), Kokka Gakkai Zasshi, 43 (May, 1929), 155–157.

SUGIYAMA HIROSUKE. "Ichiki Kitokuro" ("Ichiki Kitokuro"), Kaizō, 17 (June, 1935), 243–250.

————. "Jiyūshugi Kyōju Ron" ("On the Liberal Professors"), Kaizō, 17 (April, 1935), 213–233.

SUZUKI BUNSHIRO. "Gikai to sono Zento" ("The Diet and its Future"), Chūō Kōron, 50 (May, 1935), 350–357.

SUZUKI YASUZŌ. "Tennō Kikan Setsu Ronsō no Kei-i" ("The Course of the Emperor-Organ Theory Debate"), Kaizō, 17 (April, 1935), 260–269.

TABATA SHINOBU. "Kempō Kaisei Ron ni Okeru Sasaki Setsu to Minobe Setsu" ("Sasaki's Theory and Minobe's Theory on Revision of the Constitution"), Dōshisha Hōgaku, 64 (March, 1961), 27–43.

————. "Meiji Kempō Sōan Kisōsha to Sono Kokka Shisō" ("The Drafters of the Meiji Constitution and Their Ideas of the State"), Dōshisha Hōgaku, 5–7 (July, November, 1950, January, 1951), 1–33, 45–73, 63–90.

————. "Sasaki Sōichi Hakushi no Teikoku Kempō Kaisei An ni tsuite" ("Concerning Dr. Sasaki Sōichi's Draft Revision of the Imperial Constitution"), Dōshisha Hōgaku, 81 (January, 1963), 1–33.

TAKAYANAGI KENZŌ. "Kempō Kaishaku no Kihon Mondai" ("Basic Issues in Constitutional Interpretation"), Hōritsu Taimusu, 21 (July, 1949), 2–11.

TANAKA JIRO. "Minobe Sensei no Gyōsei Sōshō Ron" ("Professor Minobe's Theory of Administrative Suits"), *Kokka Gakkai Zasshi*, 62 (July, 1948), 50–64.

———. "Nihon Kempō ni Kansuru Saikin Ni-San no Chosho" ("Some Recent Works on the Japanese Constitution"), *Kokka Gakkai Zasshi*, 46 (April, 1932), 112–131.

TANAKA SŌGORO. "Jiyūshugi no Shitotachi" ("The Apostles of Liberalism"), *Chūō Kōron*, 50 (May, 1935), 101–110.

TSUNETŌ YASUSHI. "Kaiken Mūdo no Genjitsusa" ("The Truth About the Revision Mood"), *Sekai*, 198 (June, 1962), pp. 67–71.

UESUGI SHINKICHI. "Kokutai no Seika wo Hakki suru no Aki" ("Time for Manifesting the Glory of National Polity"), *Chūō Kōron*, 34 (January, 1918), 9–104.

———. "Waga Kensei no Kompongi" ("Basic Principles of Japanese Constitutional Government"), *Chūō Kōron*, 32 (March, 1916), 19–46.

UKAI NOBUSHIGE. "Minobe Hakushi no Shisō to Gakusetsu—sono Rekishi no Igi" ("The Thought and Theory of Dr. Minobe—Its Historical Meaning"), *Hōritsu Jihō*, 20 (August, 1948), 45–49.

———. "Minobe Sensei no Hikakuhōteki Kenkyū" ("Professor Minobe's Studies in Comparative Law"), *Kokka Gakkai Zasshi*, 62 (July, 1948), 34–49.

WAGATSUMA SAKAE. "Shirarezaru Kempō Tōgi" ("An Unknown Constitutional Discussion"), *Sekai*, 205 (August, 1962), 63–67.

YANASE YOSHIMIKI. "Minobe Sensei to Shin Kempō" ("Professor Minobe and the New Constitution"), *Kokka Gakkai Zasshi*, 62 (July, 1948), 17–33.

YOSHINO SAKUZŌ. "Mimponshugi no Igi wo Toite Futatabi Kensei Yūshū no Bi wo Motorasu no Michi wo Ronzu" ("An Explanation of the Meaning of *Mimponshugi* and a Rediscussion of the Way to Perfect the Virtues of Constitutional Government"), *Chūō Kōron*, 33 (June, 1918), 92–135.

———. "Ware no Kensei Ron no Hihyō wo Yomu" ("On Reading Criticisms of My Constitutional Theory"), *Chūō Kōron*, 31 (April, 1916), 103–123.

Articles in Western Languages

BABA, TSUNEGO. "Toward Parliamentary Revival," *Contemporary Japan*, 3 (June, 1934), 14–26.

COLEGROVE, KENNETH. "The Japanese Privy Council," *American Political Science Review*, 25 (October, 1931), 881–905.

COLTON, KENNETH E. "Pre-war Political Influences in Post-war Conservative Parties," *American Political Science Review*, 42 (October, 1948), 940–957.

CROWLEY, JAMES B. "Japanese Army Factionalism in the Early 1930's" *Journal of Asian Studies*, 21 (May, 1962), 309–326.

IRIYE, AKIRA. "Japanese Imperialism and Aggression: Reconsiderations, II," *Journal of Asian Studies*, 23 (November, 1963), pp. 103–113.

KANOKOGI, KAZANOBU. "Interpretation of the Constitution," *Contemporary Japan*, 4 (June, 1935), 109–111.

KAWAI, KAZUO. "Mokusatsu, Japan's Response to the Potsdam Declaration," *Pacific Historical Review*, 19 (November, 1950), 409–414.

LEVY, MARION J., JR. "Some Aspects of 'Individualism' and the Problem of Modernization in China and Japan," *Economic Development and Cultural Change*, 10 (April, 1962), 225–240.

MCNELLY, THEODORE. "The Japanese Constitution: Child of the Cold War," *Political Science Quarterly*, 74 (June, 1959), 176–195.

MARAYUMA, MASAO. "The Ideology and Movement of Japanese Fascism," *The Japan Annals of Law and Politics*, 1 (1952), 95–129.

OGUSHI, TOYO. "Die Entwicklung des japanischen Konstitutionalismus seit dem Weltgriege," *Jahrbuch des öffentlichen Rechte*, 19 (1931), 366–409.

"RETIRED NAVAL OFFICER." "On Japan's National Polity," *Contemporary Japan*, 4 (December, 1936), 336–341.

ROYAMA, MASAMICHI. "Political Science," *Japan Science Review: Law and Politics*, (1950), pp. 74–78.

SILBERMAN, BERNARD S. "The Political Theory and Program of Yoshino Sakuzo," *Journal of Modern History*, 31 (December, 1959), 310–324.

TAGAMI, JOJI. "Public Law," *Japan Science Review: Law and Politics*, Vol. IV (1953), pp. 35–36.

TANAKA, JIRO and NOBUSHIGE UKAI. "Kokuhō-gaku or Comparative Constitutional Law," *Japan Science Review: Law and Politics*, Vol. I (1950), pp. 39–41.

UKAI, NOBUSHIGE. "Constitutional Trends and Developments," *Annals of the American Academy of Political and Social Sciences*, 308 (November, 1956), 1–9.

WARD, ROBERT E. "The Constitution and Current Japanese Politics," *Far Eastern Survey*, 25 (April, 1956), 45–48.

————. "Origins of the Present Japanese Constitution," *American Political Science Review*, 50 (December, 1956), 980–1010.

————. "Political Modernization and Political Culture in Japan," *World Politics*, 15 (July, 1963), 569–596.

Japanese Newspapers, Magazines and Journals

Asahi Shimbun (Tokyo: daily newspaper).

Bungei Shunjū (Tokyo: monthly magazine of arts and letters).

Chūō Kōron (Tokyo: monthly, Central Review).

Dōshisha Hōgaku, successor to *Dōshisha Ronsō*, which see.

Dōshisha Ronsō (Kyoto: monthly journal of the Doshisha University Law Association).

Hō Gakkai Zasshi (Kyoto: monthly, Kyoto Law Association).

Hōgaku Kyōkai Zasshi (Tokyo: monthly, journal of the Jurisprudence Association).

Hōgaku Ronsō (Kyoto: monthly, Kyoto Imperial University, *Law Review*.)

Hōgaku Shimpō (Tokyo: monthly, Chuo University *Law Bulletin*).

Hōgaku Shirin (Tokyo: monthly, Hosei University, *Law Review*).

Hōritsu Jihō (Tokyo: monthly, *Law Bulletin*).

Hōritsu Shimpō (Tokyo: monthly, *Journal of Law and Politics*).

Hōritsu Taimusu (Tokyo: monthly, *Law Times*).

Japan Advertizer (Tokyo: daily)

Japan Science Review: Law and Politics (Tokyo: annual, Union of Japanese Societies of Law and Politics).

Japan Times and Mail (Tokyo, weekly)

Japan Weekly Chronicle (Kobe)

Jichi Kenkyū (Tokyo: monthly, Studies in Self-Government).

Journal of Social and Political Ideas in Japan (Tokyo: three times annually, by Center for Japanese Social and Political Studies).

Jurisuto (Tokyo: fortnightly, *The Jurist*. Also written *Jiyurisuto*).

Kaizō (Tokyo: monthly, *Reconstruction*).
Keizaigaku Zasshi (Osaka Municipal University Economics Society)
Kōhō Kenkyū (Tokyo: monthly, Japan Public Law Association).
Kokka Gakkai Zassshi (Tokyo: monthly, journal of the Association of Political and Social Sciences).
Nichi Nichi Shimbun (Tokyo: daily newspaper).
Nihon Rekishi (Tokyo: monthly, journal of the Japan Historical Society).
Seijigaku (Tokyo: annual of the Japan Political Science Association).
Sekai (Tokyo: monthly, Iwanami).
Shisō (Tokyo: monthly, Iwanami).